Lieutenant General Sir
RICHARD HAKING
XI Corps Commander
1915–18
A Dutiful Soldier

To Ann + Bev — Thanks
for all your help and
encouragement.

Mike

"All I care about is doing my duty."
Haking, September 1917.

HAKING
A DUTIFUL SOLDIER

Lieutenant General Sir Richard Haking

XI CORPS COMMANDER 1915–18

A Study in Corps Command

by

Michael Senior

Pen & Sword
MILITARY

First published in Great Britain in 2012 by
Pen & Sword Military
an imprint of
Pen & Sword Books Ltd
47 Church Street
Barnsley
South Yorkshire
S70 2AS

Copyright © Michael Senior 2012

ISBN 978 1 84884 643 2

Typeset in Sabon

Printed and bound in England by
CPI Group (UK) Ltd, Croydon, CR0 4YY

Pen & Sword Books Ltd incorporates the Imprints of Pen & Sword Aviation, Pen
& Sword Family History, Pen & Sword Maritime, Pen & Sword Military, Pen &
Sword Discovery, Wharncliffe Local History, Wharncliffe True Crime, Wharncliffe
Transport, Pen & Sword Select, Pen & Sword Military Classics, Leo Cooper, The
Praetorian Press, Remember When, Seaforth Publishing and Frontline Publishing

For a complete list of Pen & Sword titles please contact
PEN & SWORD BOOKS LIMITED
47 Church Street, Barnsley, South Yorkshire, S70 2AS, England
E-mail: enquiries@pen-and-sword.co.uk
Website: www.pen-and-sword.co.uk

Contents

Acknowledgements

I owe a deep debt of gratitude to Professor Ian Beckett without whose advice and encouragement this book could not have been written. I would particularly like to thank the Leslie Church Foundation of the University of Northampton for funding which enabled me to spend valuable time at the Australian War Memorial in Canberra. My thanks are also due to the staff of a number of archives, libraries and museums who have provided patient and courteous assistance. These include: The National Archives at Kew; The Royal Archives in Windsor by permission of Her Majesty Queen Elizabeth II; The Imperial War Museum; The National Army Museum; the Royal Military Academy, Sandhurst; The Royal Hampshire Museum in Winchester; the Liddell Hart Centre for Military Archives in King's College, London; the Army Personnel Centre in Glasgow; the Army and Navy Club; the British Library; the *Association pour le Souvenir de la Bataille de Fromelles*; the *Archivo Historico Militar* in Lisbon; the *Bayerisches Hauptstaatsarchiv* in Munich and the *Landsarchiv Baden-Wurttemberg* in Stuttgart. I am grateful to the Royal Hampshire Museum for enabling me to use photographs of Richard Haking. The portrait of Haking on the front cover is by Francis Dodd and is held at the Imperial War Museum.

I am also pleased to acknowledge the help I have received from Peter Barton, Maureen and Andrew Blakesley, Dr Tim Bowman, Andrew Burnett, Chris Carleton-Smith, Anne Crabbe, Mike Day, Martial Delbarre Professor David French, Margaret Hartnell, Carole Laignel, Captain Ian Page, Edward Perkin, Andrew Rice, Ann and Bev Risman, Lilo Seelos, Jim Spence, Colonel John Wooddisse, Lieutenant Colonel Ralph Wooddisse, and from Denzil Walker who prepared the maps.

It has been a pleasure to work with Jamie Wilson, Richard Doherty and Jon Wilkinson of Pen and Sword Books Limited and I would like to thank them for their encouragement and advice.

Finally, a sincere word of thanks, as ever, to my wife, Jenny, for her constant support and practical help.

All the above have made contributions that have significantly improved this book. Any errors are, of course, mine.

Abbreviations

AAG	Assistant Adjutant General
AG	Adjutant General
AHM	*Archivo Historico Militar* (Lisbon)
AIF	Australian Imperial Force
AWM	Australian War Museum (Canberra)
BEF	British Expeditionary Force
BGGS	Brigadier General General Staff
BGRA	Brigadier General Royal Artillery
BRD	*Bavarian Reserve Division*
CEP	*Corpo Expedicionario Portugues*
CGS	Chief of the General Staff
CIGS	Chief of the Imperial General Staff
C in C	Commander in Chief
CO	Commanding Officer
CRA	Commander Royal Artillery
DAAG	Deputy Assistant Adjutant General
DNB	Oxford Dictionary of National Biography
FM	Field Marshal
GBE	Knight Grand Cross of the Order of the British Empire
GHQ	General Headquarters
GOC	General Officer Commanding
GOCRA	General Officer Commanding, Royal Artillery
GSO	General Staff Officer
HE	High Explosives
HMSO	His Majesty's Stationery Office
HQ	Headquarters
IWM	Imperial War Museum
KCB	Knight Commander of the Bath
KCMG	Knight Commander of the Order of St Michael & St George
KOSB	King's Own Scottish Borderers
MiD	Mentioned in Despatches
MOD	Ministry of Defence
NCO	Non-Commissioned Officer
OP	Observation Post
OR	Other Ranks
QMG	Quarter Master General

RA	Royal Artillery
RAF	Royal Air Force
RFC	Royal Flying Corps
RNAS	Royal Naval Air Service
RIR	*Reserve Infanterie Regiment*
RUSI	Royal United Services Institute
SAA	Small Arms Ammunition
TM	Trench Mortars
TNA	The National Archives

Maps

1: War Plans 1914. The German High Command intended to carry out an enveloping movement, or sickle sweep, through neutral Belgium to outflank the bulk of the French armies and capture Paris.

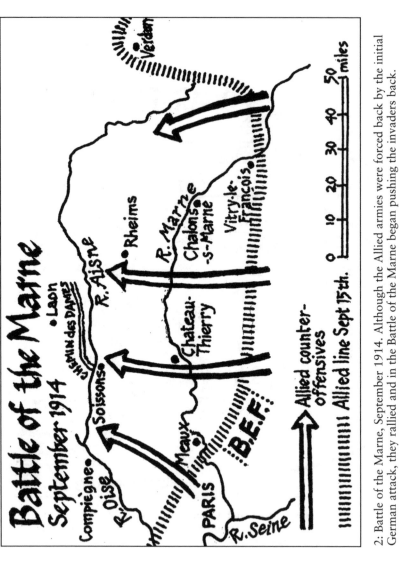

2: Battle of the Marne, September 1914. Although the Allied armies were forced back by the initial German attack, they rallied and in the Battle of the Marne began pushing the invaders back.

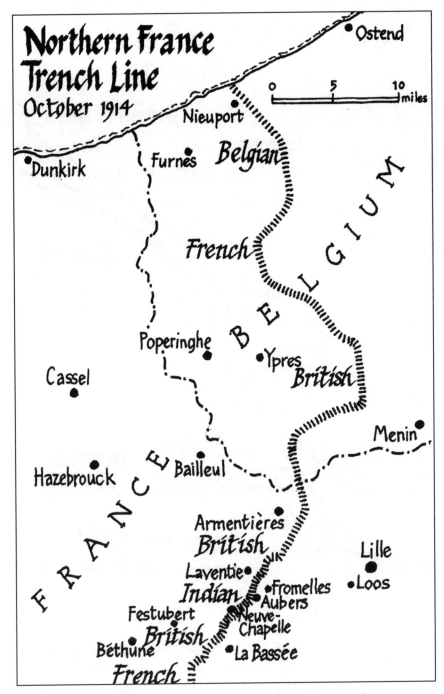

3: Northern France: Trench Line, October 1914. By October both sides were locked in a stalemate that resulted in opposing lines of trenches being created that eventually stretched as far south as the Swiss border and led to almost four years of attritional static warfare.

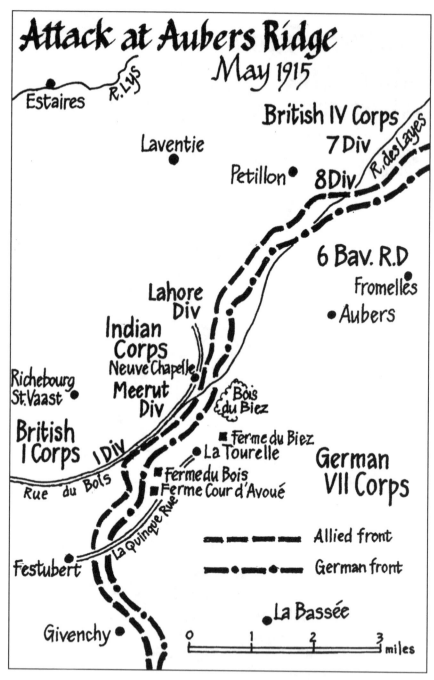

Attack at Aubers Ridge
May 1915

Estaires
R. Lys
Laventie
British IV Corps
7 Div
R. des Layes
Petillon
8 Div
6 Bav. R.D
Fromelles
Aubers
Lahore Div
Indian Corps
Neuve Chapelle
Richebourg St.Vaast
Meerut Div
Bois du Biez
British I Corps
1 Div
Ferme du Biez
La Tourelle
German VII Corps
Rue du Bois
Ferme du Bois
Ferme Cour d'Avoué
La Quinque Rue
Allied front
German front
Festubert
La Bassée
Givenchy
0   1   2   3 miles

4: Attack at Aubers Ridge, May 1915. This was the British element of a Franco-British offensive known as the Second Battle of Artois. Although intended to seize the high ground of the Aubers Ridge from the Germans, the offensive ended in failure.

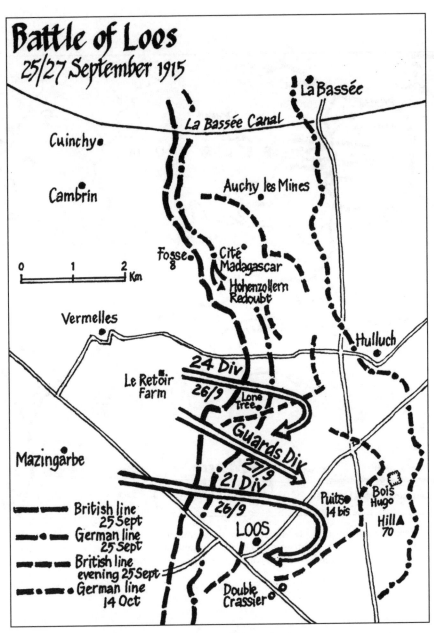

Battle of Loos
25/27 September 1915

La Bassée

La Bassée Canal

Cuinchy•

Cambrin•

Auchy les Mines

Fosse 8

Cité Madagascar

Hohenzollern Redoubt

Vermelles•

0   1   2 Km

Le Retoir Farm

24 Div

26/9

Lone Tree

Hulluch•

Guards Div

27/9

Mazingarbe•

21 Div

26/9

LOOS

Puits 14 bis

Bois Hugo

Hill 70

———— British line 25 Sept
—•—•— German line 25 Sept
– – – – British line evening 25 Sept
–•–•– German line 14 Oct

Double Crassier

5: Battle of Loos, 25/27 September 1915. This was another major British offensive but one that ended in partial success, although at a heavy cost in casualties.

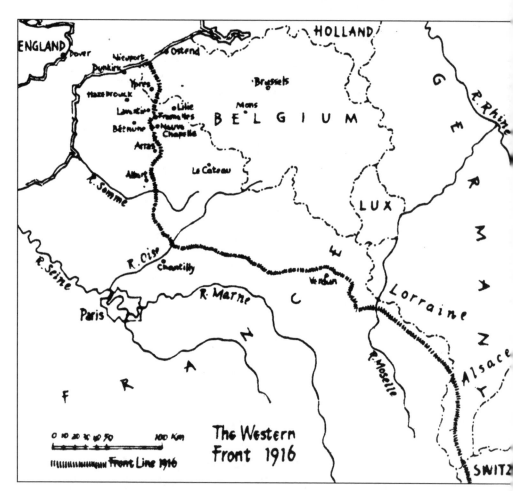

6: The Western Front 1916. Heavy casualties continued to be the main feature of fighting on the Western Front in 1916 with a major German offensive against the French along the Meuse and the Allied offensive in the Somme department.

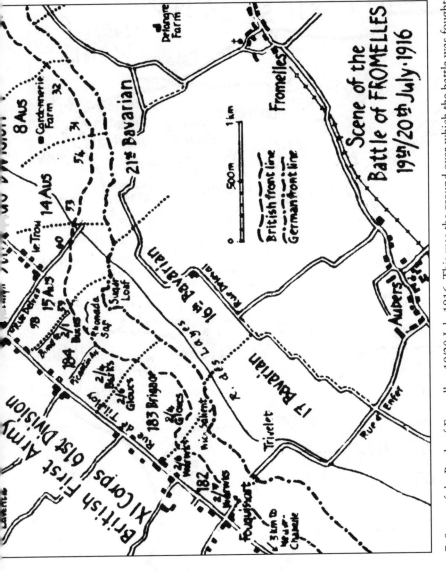

7: Scene of the Battle of Fromelles, 19/20 July 1916. This was the ground over which the battle was fought and which cost so many lives. Haking has received much criticism for the losses at Fromelles.

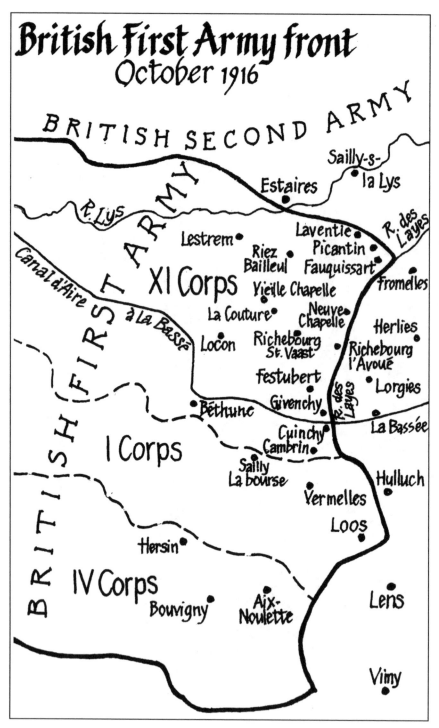

8: British First Army front, October 1916. Haking's XI Corps was part of First Army which held this section of the front in the autumn of 1916.

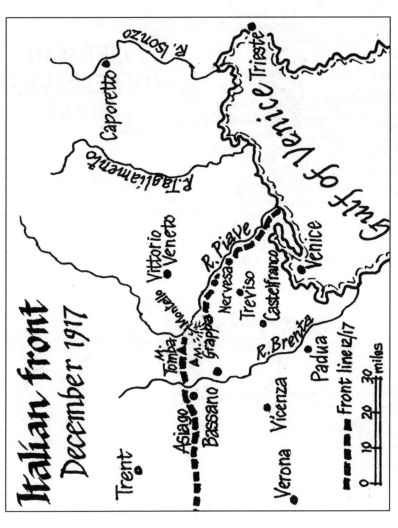

9: Italian front, December 1917. When it was deployed to assist the Italians in north-east Italy in late 1917, XI Corps saw service along the Piave river.

10: German Offensives, 1918. With the withdrawal of Russia from the war, the Germans were able to reinforce their Western Front for a final effort to force a decision in the west before large numbers of American troops arrived. This map shows the series of German attacks that began on 21 March.

11: Battle of the Lys, April 1918. Following the German spring offensive, this map shows how the Allied line was pushed back along the Lys. Portuguese troops were under British command in this clash.

12: British advances on the Western Front, 1918. The BEF led the Allied advance to victory in a series of attacks that began in the summer and ended with Germany suing for peace.

Foreword

The very title of Alan Clark's *The Donkeys* (1961) and John Laffin's *British Butchers and Bunglers of World War One* (1988) testify to the enduring popular image of the conduct of the war on the Western Front. The brilliantly scripted and acted television comedy series, *Blackadder Goes Forth*, first broadcast in 1989, equally caught every nuance of the clichéd critique of British generalship. In many ways, Richard Haking epitomises exactly the general impression of a blinkered 'blimp-like' attitude to warfare. Indeed, in Australia, he has attracted the epithet of 'Butcher' for his conduct of the attack at Fromelles in July 1916, as much part of the founding myth of the Australian military experience of the Great War as the landing at Anzac Cove in April 1915.

Yet, as with other British generals of the Great War, Mike Senior demonstrates that Haking was a soldier who thought deeply about his profession, and was sufficiently respected for his corps to be entrusted constantly with training new divisions (and the Portuguese expeditionary force) for the realities of the front line. Of course, Haking had his faults, not least in sharing the common belief in the 'offensive spirit'. Moreover, he owed much to Douglas Haig, who tried unsuccessfully to have him appointed to permanent command of First Army in August 1916. Equally, Haking was one of those who echoed Haig's critical views of Sir John French when King George V visited France in October 1915 shortly after the Battle of Loos, in which Haking had commanded some of the reserves whose precise location featured as a key factor in French's dismissal. Fromelles remains a disaster, and one for which Haking must take significant responsibility, but Mike Senior adds a new dimension to the analysis of what went wrong and why. Australians may not welcome a defence of 'Butcher' Haking, but will be compelled by Mike Senior's expert marshalling of the evidence at least to allow a degree of mitigation.

In tracing Haking's career, Mike Senior adds significantly to the historiography of the British army in the Great War, shedding new light not only on the controversies of Loos and Fromelles, but also on such key issues as trench raids and the army's 'learning curve'. His work also represents a major contribution to our understanding of the much-neglected level of corps command. Haking left no significant personal papers but Mike Senior has shown considerable ingenuity in piecing together an important story from archives in Australia, Britain, Germany and Portugal.

Professor Ian F. W. Beckett
University of Kent.

LIEUTENANT GENERAL SIR
RICHARD HAKING
XI Corps Commander
1915–18
A Dutiful Soldier

Introduction

The subject of this study is Lieutenant General Sir Richard Haking who commanded XI Corps 1915–18. During that time Haking served mainly in France, but also in Italy (December 1917-March 1918). There has been no previous study of Haking. This research takes the form of a review and analysis of Haking's career as a Corps Commander placing the activities of XI Corps in the context of events on the Western and Italian Fronts. It has three aims: first, to make a balanced assessment of Haking as a Corps Commander; second, to examine how Haking carried out his work as a Corps Commander; and third, to relate the experiences of Haking and XI Corps to a number of important topics connected with the conduct of the war – trench warfare on the Western Front, the British involvement in Italy, the Portuguese divisions in France, and the British victories of 1918. Each of these aims requires further comment and explanation.

The first aim, to assess Haking's generalship, must take account of his established reputation which can only be described as dire. British Generals of the First World War have frequently been criticized as incompetent and profligate with the lives of their men. They have been described as donkeys, boneheads, butchers and bunglers.[1] Haking is one of these much-criticized generals and the purpose here is to enquire whether his reputation, which places him firmly in the donkey category of commanders, is justified.

In examining Haking's unenviable notoriety it is relevant to distinguish between the criticisms of his contemporaries and those made subsequently by historians and other commentators. Certainly, a number of Haking's contemporaries did make derogatory remarks. Brigadier General Sir Philip Game of the 46th Division, for a time part of XI Corps, described Haking as "a madman", "a bully" and "a bad man".[2] General Sir Henry Horne, the First Army Commander from October 1916, had no great regard for Haking whom he considered dull and unimaginative – a "flat-catcher".[3] A number of officers provided negative comment about Haking during the compilation of the British official history.[4] Sir William Robertson, when CIGS, held Haking in sufficiently low esteem to object strongly to the possibility of him being appointed an Army Commander in 1916.[5] In April 1918 the Liberal War Committee wrote officially to the War Cabinet recommending that

1

Haking, along with General Sir Hubert Gough, should be dismissed on the grounds of incompetence.[6]

However, such criticisms can be said to be off-set by other, more complimentary, contemporary comment. Major General Sir Cecil Lowther who, as GOC the Guards Brigade reported to Haking in 1916, said: "He certainly takes everything in the best spirits and is an excellent man to work for."[7] Lieutenant General Adrian Carton de Wiart described Haking as having sound judgement and a great deal of moral courage.[8] A young officer who accompanied Haking on a tour of the trenches in 1917 commented: "met Gen Haking who was going to see the line . . . Haking is a jolly old boy and it was rather a good morning's excursion. He was very decent to me, listened to my views . . .".[9] The only communication between Haking and the compiler of the British official history arose from the complimentary remarks of General Sir Hugh Jeudwine concerning certain important defensive arrangements at Givenchy in 1918.[10] Also in connection with the events at Givenchy, Brigadier General A. F. V. Green commended Haking for his "strategic and tactical insight".[11] General Tamagnini, the GOC of the Portuguese troops on the Western Front in 1917 and 1918, was fulsome in his praise of Haking whom he saw as both an effective military leader and a friend.[12] Even Sir Philip Game, quoted above as criticising Haking on a personal basis, nevertheless described him as "a good soldier".[13] By and large, contemporary approval and disapproval tended to balance out.

Haking's seriously flawed reputation is more consistently in evidence in the writings of historians and other commentators. In general, historians have formed and promoted a poor opinion of Haking. Captain C. E. W. Bean, the Australian official historian, implied strong criticism of Haking in his chapters on the Battle of Fromelles (July 1916) – an operation commanded by Haking which failed and in which Australian troops suffered heavy losses.[14] The British official historian, Brigadier General Sir James Edmonds, while avoiding direct criticism of Haking in connection with the same attack, nevertheless made it clear that he "held no brief" for Haking.[15] The most damaging blows to Haking's reputation, however, have come from historians writing after his death which took place in 1945. Alan Clark regarded Haking as a "donkey"[16] and John Laffin described him as a "butcher" and a "bungler".[17] Philip Warner has remarked that: "Loyalty to and consideration for his troops did not appear to have been characteristics of Haking".[18] The involvement of Australian troops at Fromelles has caused Australian writers to be particularly damning of Haking, describing him as having "timeless faults",[19] and of being a "pernicious incompetent"[20] and "criminally inept".[21] What is particularly noticeable is that the level of adverse criticism by Australian writers has become increasingly strident over the past ten years or so. Authors such as Robin Corfield, Peter Pederson, Ross McMullin, Patrick Lyndsay and Les Carlyon have all roundly condemned Haking, often repeating the same terms of disapproval and blame.

While many historians critical of Haking have put forward firmly reasoned views, there are examples of criticism without supporting evidence. Christopher Wray, for example, in his book on the Australian General McCay, makes the comment: "After Fromelles, the epithet 'butcher' was added to Haking's name throughout the British Army."[22] This statement carried a footnote that cited Denis Winter's *Haig's Command*. In *Haig's Command*, however, there is only one brief biographical note on 'Butcher' Haking without any explanation or reference.[23] In fact there is no evidence that the epithet 'butcher' was applied to Haking during the war years. The earliest use of the word 'butcher' in connection with Haking came from an Englishman, Captain Philip Landon, a Staff officer at Fromelles, who commented to the British official historian that Haking became known as a 'butcher' after that attack. [24] Landon's remark, however, was made some twenty years after Fromelles at a time when criticism of Western Front Generals was becoming popular.[25] When Australian veterans of the 1916 Fromelles attack carried out a lengthy correspondence in the *Sydney Morning Herald* in 1919, they criticized the number of casualties, but there was no reference to a 'butcher'.

It is relevant here to note that Haking consistently refused to defend himself against criticism and this can be said to be a significant contributory factor in the development of his dreadful reputation. Edmonds wrote to Haking, as was the normal procedure of the official historian, asking for comment on Bean's chapters on Fromelles on no fewer than five occasions in 1927–28.[26] At that time Haking was in retirement and therefore readily available, but, on each occasion, he declined to comment. In addition, Haking left no personal papers, which might have provided insight into the important and controversial events in which he was involved. Nor did he leave any family to speak for him. Haking has been an easy target for historians.

In most general histories of the First World War, Haking's name is rarely mentioned – a passing reference, or one or two paragraphs at the most. Monographs on specific topics, for example the Battle of Loos or the action at Fromelles,[27] comment, usually negatively, on Haking, but their scope does not allow an overall evaluation of his military career. Haking was not without his serious faults, but, as this study will show, he also made some significant contributions to the conduct of the war. Historians and other commentators invariably ignore these positive contributions. In the chapters that follow both the negative and the positive aspects of Haking's generalship are identified and discussed to arrive at an objective assessment of his career as a Corps Commander.

The second aim of this study is to enquire how Haking carried out the role of Corps Commander. There was no formal job description. The *Field Service Regulations* of 1914 contained paragraphs relating to the function of the Commander in Chief, which was described (in bold print) as follows: "The Commander in Chief issues such orders on all matters connected with the efficiency and maintenance of the forces in the field as he considers necessary for the execution of his plan of operation, for the success or failure of which he is responsible."[28] The *Field Service Regulations* then described the role of "subordinate commanders" which would include Corps commanders. This was "to issue orders on all matters connected with the efficiency and maintenance of his command for the execution of the duties allotted to him."[29] The wording of these two paragraphs was ambiguous in the sense that there was no clear delineation of responsibility for "efficiency and maintenance" between the various levels of command. There seems, however, to have been little, if any, discussion among the senior BEF commanders on this issue. Much was clearly left to personal interpretation and the acceptance by all commanders of a practical working *modus operandi*.[30] This certainly seems to have been Haking's view of the matter.

The lack of precision regarding the managerial role of a Corps Commander was further complicated by an additional factor – the vast expansion of the BEF as thousands of recruits joined the army particularly in late 1914 and 1915. At the beginning of the war the BEF was made up of two Corps. I Corps was commanded by Sir Douglas Haig and II Corps by Sir Horace Smith-Dorrien,[31] and both corps reported to the Commander in Chief, Sir John French, at GHQ. Each corps consisted of two infantry divisions. As the army expanded the number of divisions increased and in December 1914 it became necessary to restructure the BEF. Two Armies were created, which reported to GHQ and each Army had two Corps. As additional divisions were raised they were allocated to Corps – usually between two and six divisions per Corps – and, as the number of Corps increased, then new Armies were formed. The BEF was numerically at its strongest in 1917, when 1.5 million men served on the Western Front in fifty-six divisions formed into seventeen corps and five armies.[32] Once formed, corps tended to remain for long periods in the same sector of the Front. They were, however, subject to transfer from one Army and one area to another as circumstances required. Similarly, the divisions that made up a corps were moved between corps – sometimes, as will be seen in XI Corps, with bewildering frequency. Divisions, composed of brigades and battalions, generally remained intact and were regarded as the basic operational formation of the BEF.

It was recognized in December 1914 that the re-structuring of the BEF into Armies and Corps presented a potential communications problem. A memorandum from GHQ stated that: "it is important to avoid turning Army HQs into post-offices pure and simple . . . No doubt with a few days experience things will right themselves . . . with common-sense there should be no difficulty in evolving a good working system."[33] The implication was that decisions would be made at GHQ and the consequent orders would be sent, via the Army HQ, to Corps who would in turn pass them to the divisions. In such a command system both the Army HQ and the Corps HQ would act as post-offices.

What exactly developed as the command system in the BEF is a matter of some debate.[34] The British official history emphasized the importance of the conferences held between the Commander in Chief and his Army Commanders and between the Army Commanders and the Corps Commanders together with their Staffs. Such conferences would communicate and discuss current important issues.[35] Tim Travers, however, has taken the view that Haig, who had followed French as Commander in Chief in December 1915, had such a rigid and aloof personality and such a fear that advice from subordinates would undermine his role that both he and his GHQ became isolated from the rest of the BEF. Travers considered that: "Added to the sense of isolation was the clear Staff College concept that the Commander in Chief should set strategy and let subordinates carry out the offensive, and so a very singular vacuum opened up between Haig and his GHQ and between Haig and his army commanders . . .". As a result of this vacuum "there existed, therefore, a strange laissez-faire system of command. Each Army worked largely independently. The Army Commanders, known at GHQ as the "Wicked Barons", were therefore left largely alone and there was deliberately not much direction from above."[36] These comments, however, did not reflect the full picture. As Peter Simkins has pointed out, Haig visited his Army commanders frequently when some major offensive was taking place. Hence: "Haig's numerous visits to Rawlinson in July and August, 1916, and his similar patterns of contact with other commanders during other battles . . . such frequent contacts could be construed as interference on Haig's part, but by no stretch of the imagination could they be taken to signify isolation."[37]

Travers, having described GHQ as "isolated" from the Army Commanders, then added: "the same kind of system seemed to work at Army and Corps level, although at a lesser degree of intensity."[38]

Referring particularly to senior officers' lack of knowledge of conditions at the Front, Travers commented: "It is clear that Corps, Army and some Divisional commanders did not normally visit the front, and that a wide gulf separated Corps HQ from Divisional HQ, and again that a rift sometimes existed between Divisional HQs and Brigade . . . a basic problem in command structure existed in the BEF, from GHQ downwards."[39]

Turning specifically to command issues at Corps level, Sir Aylmer Haldane wrote in his diary in August 1916 that Corps HQ "acted as a kind of post-office, with Divisions as mere tenants, so that Corps HQ did not seem to take responsibility for the front line or the rear lines and as Divisions moved there was no continuity". He later added: "What Corps Commanders do all day . . . I cannot imagine."[40] Haldane's comments are somewhat extreme and suggest a jaundiced view of the function of a Corps and of a Corps Commander. Andy Simpson, on the other hand, has argued that the role of a Corps: "expanded considerably . . . a Corps developed from being a relatively unimportant administrative link in the chain of command to playing a central role in the organization of operations and acting as the highest level of operational command."[41] According to Simpson, this development began in August 1915, just before the attack at Loos, when the I Corps artillery advisor (BGRA) was upgraded, given additional staff and placed in control of all the artillery in the Corps. This represented "a major increase in the importance of the Corps."[42] Following Loos, Sir William Robertson, then Chief of General Staff at GHQ, formalized the role of the artillery commander and the title of the BGRA was changed to GOCRA. Henceforth, the divisional artillery could be withdrawn from the command of the divisional GOC at the Corps commander's wish. In May 1916 the GOCRA was given command of the heavy artillery of the Corps and, in addition, an RFC Wing was assigned to Corps to act as spotter planes.[43]

Simpson has also related the growth in importance of the Corps to its increased role as a clearing house for information: "Crucially, it had been realised how important it was not only for them [Corps] to pass information back to Army, but forward to division, as a consequence of their access to contact aeroplanes."[44] Corps also became fully incorporated into the process of operations planning and Simpson refers to SS 135 *Instructions for the Training of Divisions for Offensive Action* issued in December 1916, which confirmed the Corps role in detailing the artillery plan for an attack. According to Simpson, the part played by the Corps in operational planning gradually increased and the nature of this planning responsibility only changed during the advances of

August-November 1918 when the fast-moving circumstances made it more appropriate for Corps to give divisions greater freedom in the planning and execution of attacks.

It can hardly be expected that the command system in the BEF developed in a uniform or consistent manner. Simpson contrasts the styles of the Army commanders Gough and Rawlinson during the Somme offensive. Gough tended to use Corps to transmit orders to Divisions whereas Rawlinson allowed Corps to act more independently.[45] Only by examining the actions and circumstances of individual commanders at various levels will a clearer picture emerge of BEF practice in this area.

This study provides a detailed description and analysis of the various command situations that faced Haking and XI Corps 1915–18 to show how Haking interpreted and carried out his role as a Corps Commander. It identifies the factors that motivated him and influenced his military thinking; the extent and nature of his authority and freedom to act; his influence on the divisions under his command; his relationships with his superiors and his subordinates; and his style of command. In discussing these issues, the command system in the BEF as it affected Haking and the XI Corps becomes apparent.

The third aim of this study is to explore a number of general aspects of the war in the light of the experiences of Haking and the XI Corps in France and in Italy. The first of these aspects is trench warfare with particular reference to the "offensive spirit", trench raids and casualties. During 1916 and 1917 Haking's XI Corps, part of the First Army, was positioned between Fauquissart to the north and Cuinchy in the south – a front of about ten miles. For XI Corps this was a period of concentrated trench warfare and, while the maintenance and strengthening of the trench system was of great importance to ensure adequate defensive arrangements, the main emphasis was on local aggressive action. The role of the First Army, as set out in late 1915 by French, was to carry out frequent minor operations to "wear out and exhaust the enemy's troops, to foster and enhance the offensive spirit of our own troops and to encourage them to feel superior to the enemy in every respect . . . Pressure on the enemy should be relentless."[46]

When Haig became Commander in Chief in December 1915 he continued this policy and issued instructions that trench raids, "wearing out fights" and various other acts of aggression should be carried out continuously and with vigour.[47] This general policy was followed by First Army and by XI Corps through 1916 and 1917. Its aims were to develop the fighting qualities of the divisions, to gather information about the German defences and their troops, to pin down the enemy and to support major offensives elsewhere on the Western Front – notably the Somme in 1916 and Arras-Vimy and Passchendaele in 1917. Despite Haking's frustration that he and his Corps were not involved in any of these major battles, he ensured, with marked enthusiasm, that XI Corps played its full part in harassing the enemy by encouraging gas attacks, mining, artillery bombardments and, in particular, trench raids.

After the war the Kirke Committee was, in general, critical of trench raids and concluded that while they were no doubt "wearying to the enemy", they were "probably more costly to ourselves in life and energy". The Kirke Committee also considered that raids had "no place in the conduct of the war when carried out merely as a sort of competition between formations . . .".[48]

Historians have put forward varied views on the benefits or otherwise of trench raids. Liddell Hart argued that raids were counter-productive. Not only did they cause casualties; they encouraged the Germans to strengthen their defences thus causing even more casualties when large offences took place.[49] To Lord Moran, raiding "dissipated like a spendthrift not only the lives but the moral heritage of the youth of England . . . The Army was to be bloodied in a hundred raids, a hundred limited operations, as the only way to preserve, or was it create, the offensive spirit".[50] A different view has been taken by Paddy Griffith: "The tactical benefits of British raids have . . . been buried in the literature under a mountain of ill-feeling . . . However, it must be said that there is nothing in military history to suggest that it was not in any way unreasonable to 'blood' [new troops] in small operations before they were committed to a big one . . . Green formations have to be given their battle inoculation gradually, otherwise they will be too fragile when it comes to a really severe test."[51] This view was also shared by Mark Connelly who considered that raiding: "served to instruct men in new skills and hone those already acquired further while complementing and maintaining the BEF's wider strategic philosophy . . . Overall the balance sheet might just read in favour of raids for they undoubtedly forced officers and men to stretch themselves, consider their own actions, the reactions of the enemy and the nature of their own and others' weapons. In static positional warfare raiding was the only way to test and sharpen infantry skills short of major offensive operations."[52] Andy Simpson has described raiding and patrolling as "a vital task" which also provided a welcome diversion from the routines of trench life.[53]

Tony Ashworth's opinion is that there was considerable resentment by trench fighters towards "high command" who pressurized units under their control to carry out what the troops considered to be futile "stunts". This resentment was "translated into subtle collective action, which thwarted the high command trench war strategy." In certain circumstances, for example where less aggressive units faced one-another or in sectors where no major attacks had taken place or were planned, a "live and let live" system developed. Opposing troops devised strategies, such as firing wide or carrying out daily bombard-ments always at the same times, for their mutual protection. Such strategies, claimed Ashworth, became "endemic in trench warfare" and clearly conflicted with, and reduced the effects of, the aggressive poli-cies of higher authorities keen to foster and develop the offensive attitude. [54] From his analysis of the activities of the 19th (Western) Division during the months leading up to the Somme offensive, James Roberts has reached the same conclusion: "High command's grandilo-quent rattling of the chain of command had been partially absorbed by the infantry; seemingly because the majority of infantrymen, left to their own devices, preferred a 'quiet' time." [55]

Malcolm Brown has discussed the philosophy of the offensive including the practice of raiding as revealed in the letters, diaries and memoirs of soldiers who experienced trench warfare. He summarized both sides of the argument as follows: "It has been claimed that its losses outweigh its gains, that, because of the inevitable casualties, it drained good and energetic battalions of their most enterprising officers and men, that it inspired COs to launch acts of bravado to provide worthwhile entries for the battalion diary and evidence of keenness for their superiors. The defenders of the philosophy assert that it kept the British as well as the Germans on their toes, that as well as wearing down the enemy it trained and honed Britain's largely amateur army for the set-piece battles that were bound to come in the fullness of time. As for those who had to carry out the doctrine in practice, many loathed and feared the whole business, but others found in it a remarkable personal fulfilment." [56]

As the following chapters will show, there was no doubt as to where Haking placed his commitment concerning the doctrine of the offensive and this was demonstrated in his whole-hearted promotion of a variety of minor operations designed to dominate no man's land, wear down the Germans and provide battle experience for his troops. What will be discussed in this study are the factors that formed Haking's allegiance to the offensive spirit; how the related XI Corps policies were derived and implemented; the degree of success of XI Corps minor operations; how Haking's aggressive approach was viewed by subordinates; and how Haking endeavoured to follow the policies of his superiors and his own aggressive inclinations. In addition, an attempt is made to interpret the statistics relating to raids and casualties in the First Army in 1916 and 1917 to determine whether Haking, a recognized "thruster", was particularly more militant than his fellow Corps Commanders. All of these considerations will be examined to assess Haking's performance as a Corps Commander in those years dominated, as far as XI Corps was concerned, by trench warfare.

The second aspect of the war that is discussed in relation to Haking and XI Corps is the British involvement on the Italian Front. Haking spent only twelve weeks in Italy between December 1917 and early March 1918 – a period that was notable for its lack of military action. Caporetto (October 1917) had occurred before the British had arrived in Italy in any strength, and the action on the Asiago plateau (June 1918) and the advances in the Val d'Assa and across the Piave (October/November 1918) took place after Haking's return to France. It is therefore not surprising that in the literature covering the events in Italy Haking's name is mentioned only in passing or not at all.

The war in Italy has received little attention from historians and the work of Plumer, Cavan and Haking in stabilizing the Italian Front, and the contribution of the British forces to the victory over the Austro-Hungarians deserves greater discussion.[57] This study focuses on the experiences of Haking and XI Corps during the short period of their stay. What is apparent is Haking's professional approach to the circumstances that faced him in the winter of 1917–18. It demonstrates that Haking, never a "chateau-general", worked vigorously and methodically along the sectors of the Front assigned to him. He ensured that adequate defensive arrangements were in place and he was also involved in the preparations for a future offensive.

The third aspect of the war that is examined is the extra-ordinary relationship between the British and the Portuguese forces on the Western Front 1917–18. Haking was accustomed to receiving "green" troops into his Corps and when Portugal sent a small Expeditionary Force (CEP – *Corpo Expedicionario Portugues*) to France in February 1917 they were immediately placed under his command. As with the British involvement in Italy, the story of the British- Portuguese experience in the war is largely untold.[58] Most accounts of the Portuguese on the Western Front are confined to the collapse of the CEP during the German offensive on the Lys in April 1918. This failure was indeed dramatic and has provided many anecdotes designed to criticize the Portuguese and point to their inferiority as soldiers. The topics, however, that have hardly been covered are: the delicate relationship between the CEP and the British Mission set up to help the Portuguese settle into trench warfare; Haking's role as Corps Commander responsible for the training and conduct of the CEP; his dealings with General Tamagnini, the Portuguese Commander; and the political as well as the military implications of the Portuguese presence in France.

Haking's experiences in Italy and with the Portuguese, although of short duration in both cases, were testing in that the circumstances required a high level of military and personal skill. Just how Haking performed in these two quite different situations is assessed in this study.

The fourth aspect of the war to be examined through the experiences of Haking and XI Corps is the defeat of the German army on the Western Front in 1918 – the Hundred Days. It was once again the fate of Haking not to take part in a major offensive in the final year of the war. The role of XI Corps from April until August was primarily to strengthen and maintain a solid defensive line and be prepared for any sudden enemy attack towards Hazebrouck and the Channel Ports. It will be seen that XI Corps played an important part in these defensive measures.

Following the British Fourth Army's crucial victory at Amiens in August, the nature of the war changed. The emphasis moved from defence to attack and the Fifth Army, to which the XI Corps had been transferred in July, adopted a more aggressive approach. XI Corps was to harass the enemy at every opportunity and, as Haking wrote, "hasten their withdrawal."[59] By 2 October XI Corps had taken Aubers and Aubers Ridge and on 18 October Haking entered Lille. When the Armistice was signed on 11 November XI Corps had reached the line Roubaix-Tournai.

Much has been written about the "learning curve" of the BEF.[60] This concept has been used to describe the significant change in tactics and technology, mainly from 1916, leading to the victories of the last few months of the war. The techniques used, particularly from August 1918 onwards, are seen by the proponents of the "learning curve" as the outcome of the lessons learnt during and after the Somme. Infantry, artillery, tanks and aircraft not only devised improved operating methods, they combined together more effectively than in any previous period of the war. It was this flexible, "all-arms" approach by the BEF that made a major contribution to the defeat of the German army on the Western Front. Gary Sheffield has written that: "The British army had by July 1918 tamed the new technology and worked out effective ways of harnessing it."[61] Paddy Griffith has endorsed this view: "In the Hundred Days [the BEF] would finally and decisively appear in its full stature and sweep all before it."[62] Prior and Wilson have identified a number of developments during 1916 and 1917 that together provided a "formula for success" in 1918. This "formula" served to "produce a strike force against which the enemy ultimately could provide no effective resistance". Nonetheless, Prior and Wilson have also cast some doubts on the evenness of the "learning curve". As they have commented: "Nineteen Seventeen is remembered as a bleak and barren year for the British Army on the Western Front." [63] Wilson, writing without Prior, has put forward the view that:

> the Western Allies entered 1917 with no clear vision of how, in the light of their 1916 experience, to proceed better . . . So in mid-1917 the British Army . . . proved to have no more decisive way of proceeding than had been evident in the year before . . . And the manner of conducting battle advantageously . . . would not be comprehensively to hand until 1918.[64]

Not all historians have supported the concept of a "learning curve". Tim Travers has argued that the "doctrine and tactics of the BEF in 1918 did not develop toward a real combination of all arms" and that "GHQ emphasized an infantry centred army." To Travers, the cause of the British successes during the Hundred Days was the cumulative effect of the attritional battles of 1914–17 together with the self-inflicted German failures in the first half of 1918.[65] In terms of a "learning curve" in defensive tactics and the introduction of a defence in depth, historians have argued that both learning and application were uneven in the BEF – a situation that caused G. C. Wynne to describe it as "the tangled muddle of the British defence doctrine."[66] This study, taking account of these varied views, therefore examines the extent to which the "learning curve" showed itself in the operations of Haking and the XI Corps.

The structure of this book is essentially chronological. Haking's early years, the factors that influenced the development of his military thought, and his military experience leading to his appointment as a Corps Commander in August 1915, including the Battle of Aubers Ridge, are covered in Chapter I. A chronology of Haking's life is attached as Appendix I. Chapter II deals with his involvement in the Battle of Loos (September 1915) – his first inauspicious action as a Corps Commander. Chapters III and V discuss Haking's role as a Corps Commander during the years of trench warfare 1916–17. These chapters, together with Appendices II and III, describe and analyze Haking's propensity for the offensive particularly in terms of trench raids and the casualties incurred by XI Corps. The major event in 1916 was the combined British-Australian attack at Fromelles, the largest operation conducted by Haking and the action from which most of his notoriety has been derived. Chapter IV describes the circumstances and course of that attack and seeks to show, contrary to accepted opinion, that Haking was not the chief culprit of that disaster and that the operation was far from being unsuccessful. Towards the end of 1917 Haking and the XI Corps staff and troops were transferred to Italy and Chapter VI discusses Haking's contribution on that Front. Chapter VII is devoted to Haking's relationship with the Portuguese Expeditionary Force, which he commanded in 1917 and also during the opening phases of the Battle of the Lys in April 1918. Haking's contribution during the final months of the war, leading to the Armistice, is covered in Chapter VIII. The final chapter, the Conclusion, summarizes the findings of this study. It reviews the experiences of Haking and XI Corps in relation to a number of general war issues; it discusses his personal characteristics; and, finally, taking account of the vicissitudes of his career and his acquired reputation, it makes a considered assessment of him as a Corps Commander.

The chapters that follow are therefore concerned with a description and analysis of the ways in which one Corps Commander, immersed in the military traditions of his time and not without his weaknesses, dealt with the difficult problems that he and his Corps encountered during the course of the war. The Corps level of command, together with the individual generals who carried out the role of Corps Commander, has not been sufficiently researched. This study contributes to an understanding of Haking as a Corps Commander and to the way in which the war was conducted in those sectors covered by XI Corps.

Notes

1. Criticism of British military leadership in the First World War began in earnest towards the end of the 1920s and continues to this day. An article in the *Daily Telegraph* of 30 July 2009, for example, complains of the "terrible and fruitless sacrifice" of the war and of "incompetent generalship". Useful comment on the vast amount of literature condemning British generals can be found in: Danchev, "Bunking and Debunking. The Controversies of the 1960s", in Bond (ed), *The First World War and British Military History*, pp. 263–288; Terraine "Understanding", *Stand To!* No 34, 1992, pp.7–12.; Sheffield. *Forgotten Victory*; Beckett, *The Great War 1914–1918*, pp.462–65.
2. IWM, Letters of Sir Philip Game to his wife, PWG 9 and 11, 1915 and 1916.
3. IWM, Letters of Gen Lord Horne to his wife, 5.2.1916.
4. TNA, CAB 45/134,136 and 138.
5. King's College London, Liddell Hart Collection, Papers of FM Sir William Robertson, 7/6/67.

6. TNA CAB 23/14 WC389A. 11.4.1918. See Bristow, *A Serious Disappointment*, p.177.
7. IWM, 97/10/1, Diary of Maj Gen Sir Cecil Lowther.
8. Carton de Wiart, *Happy Odyssey*, p.118.
9. IWM, 66/300/1, Diary of Capt RCG Dartford.
10. TNA, CAB 45/123F.
11. TNA, CAB 45/123F
12. AHM, 51/7/857/4. Personal diary of Gen Tamagnini.
13. IWM, Letter of Sir Philip Game to his wife 20.12 15. PWG 9 and 11, 1915 and 1916.
14. *AOH*, Bean, *The AIF in France 1916*, Vol. III Chs 12 and 13.
15. AWM, 3DRL/7935/34, Letter from Edmonds to Bean, 3.11.27.
16. Clark, *The Donkeys*, Chapters 7 (Aubers) and 12 (Loos).
17. Laffin, *British Butchers and Bunglers of World War One*, p.8.
18. Warner, *The Battle of Loos*, p.23.
19. Carlyon, *The Great War* , p.97.
20. McMullin, "The Forgotten Fallen", in *Sydney Morning Herald*, 19 July 2002.
21. Hutchinson, *Pilgrimage. A Travellers Guide to Australia's Battlefields*, p.109
22. Wray, *Sir James Whiteside McCay. A Turbulent Life*, p. 202.
23. Winter, *Haig's Command. A Reassessment*, p. 279.
24. TNA, CAB 45/135. 2.4.1937.
25. For example: Lloyd George, *War Memoirs*; Churchill, *World Crisis 1911–1918*; Liddell Hart, *History of the First World War* (First published as *The Real War 1914–1918*).
26. 10.10.27; 8.12.27; 18.1.28; 11.6.28; 2.7.28.
27. Examples are: Lloyd, *Loos 1915*; Pederson, *Fromelles*.
28. IWM, *Field Service Regulations, 1914*, Section 8.
29. Ibid., Section 9,
30. Palazzo in his *Seeking Victory on the Western Front*, p.9 describes this *modus operandi* as an "ethos" that "provided an equivalent structure for the decision-making process and was the basis for all operations".
31. Sir James Grierson commanded II Corps until his sudden death on 17 August 1914.
32. Beckett, *Great War,* p.162.
33. TNA, WO95/589.
34. "Command system" is used here to describe the command, communications and control (C3) arrangements in the BEF. Essentially this covers the management functions of decision-making, the transmission of those decisions and the control and monitoring of the resulting operations.
35. Edmonds, *History of the Great War: Military Operations France and Belgium,1916*, Vol I), p.25n. Henceforth *BOH* with date and volume.
36. Travers, "A Particular Style of Command: Haig and GHQ 1916–18", *Journal of Strategic Studies*, Vol 10, 1987, pp. 363–376.
37. Simkins, "Haig and the Army Commanders", in Brian Bond and Nigel Cave, eds, *Haig: A Re-appraisal 80 Years On*, p.96.

38. Travers, *The Killing Ground. The British Army, The Western Front & the Emergence of Modern War 1900–1918*, pp.101–118.
39. Ibid., p.109.
40. National Library of Scotland, Haldane Papers, Diary 11 August 1916 and 26 October 1916.
41. Simpson, "British Corps Command on the Western front 1914–1918", in Sheffield and Todman (eds),*Command and Control on the Western Front. The British Army's Experience 1914–18*, p97.
42. Ibid., p.101.
43. Ibid., pp.102–106.
44. Ibid., p.107.
45. Simpson, *Directing Operations: British Corps Command on the Western Front 1914–1918*, pp. 25–59.
46. TNA WO 95/159. OAM 97. French to Army Commanders 28.10.15.
47. Duff Cooper, *Haig* vol I, p.298.
48. Kirke Committee, *Report on Lessons of the Great War* (War Office, 1932), p.23.
49. Liddell Hart, *A History of the Great War*, p.308.
50. Moran, *The Anatomy of Courage*, pp.67–71.
51. Griffith, *Battle Tactics of the Western Front. The British Army's Art of Attack 1916–1918*, pp. 60–61.
52. Connelly, *Steady the Buffs!* pp. 77–92.
53. Simpson, *Hot Blood and Cold Steel, Life and Death in the Trenches of the First World War*, p.76.
54. Ashworth, *Trench Warfare 1914–1918. The Live and Let Live System*, pp.13–23.
55. Roberts, "Making the Butterflies Kill", *Stand To! No. 68, Western Front Association*, September 2003, pp.38–44
56. Brown, *Tommy Goes To War*, pp. 64–65.
57. Other than the *BOH* (*Italy 1915–1919*, I Vol., Edmonds and Davies) , the most comprehensive account in English of the British presence in Italy is by John and Eileen Wilks, *The British Army in Italy 1917–1918*. Haking's name is not mentioned.
58. De Meneses, *Portugal 1914–1926. From the First World War to Military Dictatorship* (Dept. Of Hispanic, Portuguese and Latin American Studies, Univ. of Bristol, 2004), provides an overview of the war and particularly the problems of the Portuguese soldiers. Haking and XI Corps are mentioned briefly.
59. TNA. WO 95/884. S.S. No 24/7.
60. Among the growing amount of work on this subject is: Wilson, *The Myriad Faces of War*; Travers, *Killing Ground*; idem, *How the War was Won*; Griffith, *Battle Tactics of the Western Front*; Sheffield, *Forgotten Victory. The First World War: Myths and Realities*; Robbins, *British Generalship on the Western Front 1914–18*.
61. Sheffield, *Forgotten Victory*, p.237.
62. Griffith, *Battle Tactics of the Western Front*, p.200.
63. Prior and Wilson, *Command on the Western Front, The Military Career of Sir*

Henry Rawlinson 1914–1918, pp 289–300, 394. See also, on their view of the uneven nature of the "learning curve", their *Passchendaele, The Untold Story*, and *The Somme*.

64. Wilson, "The British Army on the Somme; July-November 1916", in Howard, *A Part of History*, pp.52–62.
65. Travers, *How the War was Won*, pp.175–182.
66. Wynne, *If Germany Attacks. The Battle in Depth in the West*, p.240.

CHAPTER I

The Making of a Corps Commander

Richard Haking's early years are something of a mystery. *The Dictionary of National Biography*[1] and his *Times* obituary[2] give his date of birth as 24 January 1862, as does Haking's entry in the Hampshire Regiment Record of Officers' Services.[3] However, no birth certificate seems to exist and there is no record of his birth being registered. While it was not unusual for births to be unregistered at that time, Richard's two elder sisters, Mary and Ethel, did have birth certificates and both of their births were registered. However, to complicate matters, a third daughter, Hilda, was born in 1865 and her birth was not registered, nor does she have a birth certificate. There is no satisfactory explanation for the lack of the birth certificates and registration for the two younger children. It might have been an oversight on behalf of the parents, but it is also possible that both children were adopted.

As far as Richard is concerned, there is a record of his baptism at St Paul's Church in the parish of King Cross, Halifax, on 20 April 1862. The baptismal service was conducted by his father, who was a curate at King Cross, and the given names on the register were Richard Cyril Byrne Hacking.[4] The father's name was also Richard Hacking and for the next eighteen years there is more information available about Richard the father than about Richard the son.

Shortly after the baptism, Richard the father moved with his wife, Mary, and his three children, to Rodbourne Cheney in Wiltshire where he became the vicar. It was about this time that he changed his name, for reasons that are not apparent, and henceforth the family became known as Haking.[5] This change of name is curious since, in 1862, Richard the father had received a large sum of money from the estate of his father, also a Richard Hacking, amounting to around £8,000[6] – the proceeds from the sale of the family machine-making business in Bury. The Reverend Richard Haking, therefore, while not wealthy, can be considered as well-to-do by the standards of his time. When the Reverend Richard Haking died in 1894, his estate was valued at £3,457,[7] all of which was bequeathed to the three daughters with the son, Richard, receiving nothing.[8] All this may be peripheral to the career of the soldier Richard Haking, but it is at least interesting that there is no record of Haking referring to his family or his early life at any time. The entry in *Who's Who*,[9] which Haking could have influenced, is silent on these matters.

Nothing is known about the young Richard's up-bringing or schooling and it is quite likely that he was taught at home either by his Oxford-educated father[10] or by a private tutor. Whatever education he did receive, however, was good enough for the eighteen-year-old Richard to gain entry into Sandhurst in 1880. There seem to have been mixed views at that time about the calibre of Sandhurst entrants. Dr Welldon of Harrow is alleged to have said, "No clever boy goes into the Army",[11] but Spiers has pointed out that there was certainly an element of competition and, in 1877, three years before Haking's entry, there were 900 applicants for 100 cadetships.[12] In any event, Haking passed through Sandhurst apparently without much difficulty. The only remaining record states that "his conduct was exemplary",[13] and Haking was duly commissioned into the 67th Foot – the last to be so appointed because, almost immediately, the 67th Foot, in line with the Caldwell-Childers reforms, became the 2nd Battalion of the Hampshire Regiment.

From 1880, we know quite a lot about Haking the soldier, but nothing about his personal life. For example, he made no mention of his wife, Rachel Violette Burford-Hancock, although they were married for forty-eight years.[14] They had no children. We know nothing about his interests other than military, and, despite Haking being a clergyman's son, we know nothing about his religious beliefs. There is no evidence that he had any civilian friends. Haking left no papers, diaries, letters or memoirs. He was a very private man. The 1881 census lists Haking as a Second Lieutenant on board the vessel *Jumna* on his way to join his regiment in India. Once there, the Hampshires' regimental *Chronicle* shows him settling down to a not unpleasant way of life. At Bangalore, for example, he attended the Maharaja's Fancy Dress Ball as a Courtier. The *Chronicle* lists a number of other Regimental social events and commented that: "The chief outdoor pastime amongst the majority of the Regiment appears to be fishing . . . dancing appears to be all the go . . . the 'light fantastic' was practised with the aid of the concertina and the fife."[15]

It was not until 1885 that Haking, then aged twenty-three, had his first experience of action. In that year, the 2nd Hampshires formed part of a punitive expedition against King Theebaw of Burma, who had been involved in some anti-British activities. When the expedition reached Mandalay, Theebaw surrendered and Haking, as the Regimental Chronicler wrote, "had the honour (!) of being put in charge of the

King".[16] However, many of Theebaw's followers – Dacoits – took to brigandage and the 2nd Hampshires spent most of their eighteen months in Burma tracking down these bandits. Haking played his part in this activity and, on one occasion, led a detachment of sixty men for six weeks in the Chindwin Valley, successfully dispersing a gang of brigands. As a result he gained his first Mention in Despatches.[17]

Haking was gradually making a name for himself. In April 1886, the regimental *Chronicle* noted: "Lt Haking has been called away to another and higher sphere – he is an attaché in the Intelligence Department". Two months later, at the age of twenty-four, he was appointed the Regimental Adjutant – a post he held for five years. He had become proficient in Hindustani and while at Bangalore he attained a First Class Extra in Musketry and became a reasonable horseman. The Battalion returned home in 1888.[18]

Perhaps the most significant pre-war event for Haking was his selection for Staff College, which he attended from 1896 to 1898. It was said that he made "a great impression"[19] there, and Staff College certainly made a great impression on him. The class of 1896–97 at Camberley included two future field marshals – Haig and Allenby – and fifteen future generals, three of whom were Capper, MacDonagh and Edmonds.[20] Edmonds was later to write: "At the close of our two years, a scheme for 3 days' work, mounted, was set by an outside examiner, Brevet Lt. Col. Herbert Plumer . . . In his report he said that Haking, Colomb and myself had done well throughout."[21] Haking's affection for Staff College and his performance there were such that, within three years, he returned – this time as a professor.

In the meantime, after a spell in Ireland as a DAAG in Cork, Haking went with his Regiment to South Africa. It was during that campaign that he was Mentioned in Despatches for the second time for good staff work and "meritorious service"[22] as DAAG in Pietermaritzburg and as Commandant at De Aar Junction. Haig, who was also in South Africa, noted in his Diary for 19 November 1899: "reached De Aar at 10.45pm. Met by Commandant (Major Haking who was at Staff College with me) who handed list of troops and explained situation in district generally . . . Haking had not been to bed for 2 nights owing to troops passing through."[23] For his work in South Africa, Haking also received the Queen's Medal with three Clasps.

* * * *

Haking clearly had a taste for the academic life. His *Times* obituary and his entry in the *DNB* both remark that Haking's contribution as a teacher at Staff College was considerable, especially in the field of Tactics and Strategy. The biographer of Sir Ian Hamilton wrote that Haking was "a gifted trainer of men".[24] These judgements were written well after Haking's tenure at the Staff College, but they are supported by an interesting piece of contemporary evidence.

Haking had been promoted to Brevet Lieutenant Colonel in January 1901 on taking up his post at Staff College and, in September 1903, was made up to full Lieutenant Colonel. When January 1904 arrived, it was Haking's opinion that he should be promoted to the rank of Brevet Colonel after the customary period of three years. This view was not supported by the War Office, which insisted that the promotion to Brevet Colonel could come only after three substantive years as a full Lieutenant Colonel, i.e. in September 1906.

The issue was not just about protocol – there were substantial retirement and pension benefits available once the rank of full Colonel was achieved.[25] Haking was nothing if not persistent in pressing his case. In 1904, when he applied for promotion to Brevet Colonel, he was supported by the then Commandant of the Staff College, Colonel Henry Rawlinson. The War Office turned this application down only for Haking to make a further appeal one month later. This time, the War Office found a way around the problem. Under Article 36, Royal Warrant of 1900, such a promotion could take place if the applicant had given "distinguished service of an exceptional nature other than in the Field". Haking now based his case on this Article, which was submitted to the King for his approval in June 1905. Haking attached the following statement from Rawlinson: "He has been rather more than four years a Professor at Staff College and, during that time, raised the whole tone of the teaching there, and has done immense good by the force of his example, by his strenuous efforts and by his exceptional ability." The War Office was concerned at the possible repercussions of this use of Article 36: "It is open to objection that those who act first, and urge their claims most persistently are likely to come off best." The War Office eventually conceded the point: "If the military authorities certify that Lt. Col. Haking's service is of a 'distinguished and exceptional nature' we cannot raise any financial objection, whatever we may think of the merits of the case."[26] Haking was duly made Brevet Colonel in June 1905 some fifteen months earlier than the War Office would have wanted.[27]

This episode is revealing not only as evidence of Haking's outstanding work at Staff College, but also as an example of his stubbornness and determined self-interest. It is worth noting that a similar situation arose at the end of Haking's career. He had been Colonel of the Hampshire Regiment from 1924 to 1944 and, in 1945, he applied for the 1939–45 War Medals. As with the issue of promotion to Brevet Colonel in 1904, the matter was considered to be pressing at the boundaries of official protocol and, on this occasion, Haking's claim was unsuccessful.[28] This wayward persistency was a trait that emerged not infrequently during Haking's career.

Haking's Staff College career ended in 1906 after which he held a series of Staff appointments at Aldershot including GSO 1 with both the 3rd and 4th Divisions and, in 1908, as BGGS Southern Command. It was in that role, representing Sir Ian Hamilton, the GOC Southern Command, that Haking attended several annual Conferences of Staff Officers at the Staff College. His contributions there, although not numerous, were sensible and constructive. At the 1908 Conference Haking supported the idea of "war schools" for regimental officers:

> They would enormously improve the efficiency of the Regimental officer . . . There were a great number of schools of other sorts such as Hythe and Shoeburyness, but there were no schools for the ordinary regimental tactics and regimental administration in war . . . A system of war schools could be established in the British Army.[29]

At the 1911 Conference, Haking took part in the discussion on the need for the infantry and the artillery to work more closely together making "the best of accurate firing and use of ground by the infantry", and inferred that infantry commanders were not taking proper account of the artillery when making their plans.[30]

In 1911 he became GOC 5 Brigade and it was that Brigade that he took to France in 1914. By 1914, Haking had become part of the military establishment. At Aldershot he came into frequent contact with Haig who had become GOC Aldershot in 1911. It was with Haig that Haking was invited to meet and dine with the King in May 1912 and May 1913.[31] The links with Haig and with the King were to prove important as Haking's career developed.

* * * *

Haking may not have left diaries, memoirs or letters, but during his pre-war days in Aldershot, he did produce two training manuals that further enhanced his reputation as a teacher and a military thinker.[32] He wrote *Staff Rides and Regimental Tours*[33] in 1908, and *Company Training*[34] in 1913. Both were widely read and acclaimed. The review in the RUSI *Journal* says of *Staff Rides*: "he writes as one who not only knows his subject by heart, but who really enjoys imparting to others the instruction he is so well qualified to give".[35] *The Army Review* says of *Company Training* : "We believe that this book will fully realize the hope expressed by its author of assisting company commanders in the training of their companies."[36]

These two books are particularly noteworthy since they reveal many

of Haking's views and aspects of his personality. Both books are very
much the result of his time at Staff College.[37] In *Staff Rides*, Haking
refers to the Staff College with evident enthusiasm: "Any credit that
might accrue to this book is due to the Staff College and to its many
distinguished officers both on the directing staff and amongst the
students, whom it has been the good fortune of the author to serve for
several years."[38] Haking also expresses what almost certainly reflected
his personal experience: "If we wish to train regimental officers to be
staff officers we had better send them to Staff College, where they can
be properly instructed."[39]

Haking considered that formal education and training were essential
requirements for an effective officer:

> There has been in the past, a great deal of prejudice against "book
> learning" and the reason for this is partly due to our past experi-
> ence in war, where the bold dashing leader, who may not have
> been highly educated, always came more prominently to notice
> than others who may have carefully studied their profession, but
> who did not possess those qualities to such a marked degree, or, if
> they did, had no opportunity of showing them . . . In our small
> wars no great education is required of our officers to do their duty
> and pass muster, but in a great campaign, education is almost as
> necessary as determination of character . . . if we hope to master
> our profession and become able commanders, we must have
> resource to books.[40]

Nevertheless, Haking's enthusiasm for "book learning" was qualified: "We find that though officers can learn the principles of war from
books, and can even write excellent books on the subject, they are not
always able to apply those principles when they find the enemy in front
of them." The link between theory and practice could be found, in
Haking's view, in practical exercises – hence Staff Rides which he
defined as: "Practical instruction on the ground without troops in
peace."[41] These manoeuvres generally involved two supervised groups
of officers who, opposing one another, played out a military exercise.

As might be expected of an ex-Staff College professor, Haking wrote
in a clear, well-structured style. His themes were developed with academic assurance and in both *Staff Rides* and *Company Training* his
inclination was to put great emphasis on intellectual argument using
considerable detail to support and illustrate his point. The original
edition of *Staff Rides* is made up of just over 500 pages providing
advice on how to organize successful training exercises. In keeping with
the Staff College method, there were numerous references to, and

examples of, past military campaigns. In one paragraph in a section on "Strategical and Tactical Reconnaissance", Haking illustrates his point by referring to the invasion of Afghanistan in 1878, Napoleon's retreat through Bohemia in 1805, the Boer invasion of Natal in 1899, and the Russian invasion of Turkey in 1877.[42] Similarly, in the chapter on "The Preparation of the Scheme", Haking cites the passage of the Douro by Wellington in 1809, an episode in the American Civil War at Chancellorsville in 1863, the Modder River campaign in the Boer War, the action at Belfort in the Franco-German War of 1870, the attack at Port Arthur in the 1904 Russo-Japanese War, the battle of Salamanca in the Peninsular War of 1812, and the advance on Kars in 1877 during the Russo-Turkish War.[43] This approach to the teaching of strategy and tactics had been developed at the Staff College by Colonel G. F. R. Henderson, who had been the Professor of Military Art and History during Haking's years there as a student. The lessons had been well learnt.

Staff Rides is a book of formidable and often pedantic detail. The following examples illustrate this feature. In the chapter on "Preliminary Arrangements for a Staff Ride", Haking stresses the need to find suitable accommodation for the participating officers. He therefore goes to the trouble of proposing a draft letter: "Hotel proprietors in England are now becoming accustomed to accommodate officers for a Staff Ride, and the exorbitant prices formerly charged can be greatly reduced if arrangements are made beforehand. The following letter will usually meet with their approval:

'Sir, It is proposed to bring a party of eight officers to ——, from the ——th to the ——th February. The terms proposed are as follows; a daily charge of 11s. per head, to include two private sitting-rooms, one small, and one large enough to accommodate the whole party; a separate bedroom for each officer, bath, lights, attendance, bicycle or motor accommodation; a good breakfast, afternoon tea, dinner, and after-dinner coffee. Extras: Luncheon 2s. 6d., full board and lodging for an officer's servant 6s. a day, wines and mineral waters at ordinary prices. Please state if you are prepared to accept these terms'." [44]

No detail was too small for Haking to address. He offers the following advice on the use of bicycles during a Staff Ride:

A bicycle is no doubt a very useful machine and it can usually be hidden behind a hedge with a fair chance of it being there when the owner returns. But as most staff rides take place in winter, the roads and weather are not usually very suitable for rapid and comfortable riding. If it is intended to rely on bicycles it should be ascertained beforehand whether all the officers taking part are in possession of these machines. Officers have been detailed on occasions who are unable to ride a bicycle and they have been considered a source of embarrassment. It is undesirable to make senior officers ride about on a bicycle.[45]

A third example of extreme detail can be found in the chapter on "Work Done By Officers During A Staff Ride". It concerns

the supply of a force which is about to operate several days' march distant from the advanced depot . . . The main questions at issue are the number of mules which must be despatched with the division in the first instance, how they should be organised, and how many should leave the advanced depot each day in order to keep the division supplied and to feed the mules on the line of communication.

There then followed seven pages of calculations on what Haking described as "one of the most complicated administrative problems of war". This immensely detailed arithmetic exercise eventually arrived at the conclusion that the correct number of mules required was 14,400.[46]

The ability to deal with such an overwhelming amount of detail is, no doubt, necessary in certain areas of staff work, and Haking was clearly at ease with the minutiae and precision required.

Haking's second book, *Company Training*, reveals the basis of the military thinking that he held throughout the war. Haking put forward the view that military training must aim to mould human nature and overcome natural fears so that what he calls "the little black devil in us all" – (made up of fear, surprise, disrespect, and dejection) – can be defeated". [47]

Each of these negative aspects of human nature is discussed and two of them can be taken to illustrate Haking's style. "Fear," wrote Haking, "acts more powerfully upon the feelings of the individual soldier in war than any other emotion, and appears to be very infectious." He then distinguishes between "reasonable fear", which can be dealt with by, for example, digging trenches or taking cover to avoid enemy fire, and "unreasonable fear" which is a "vague and nameless dread of the enemy". "Unreasonable fear", wrote Haking, can be converted to "reasonable fear" if "the soldier in war can realize that the enemy is just as much afraid of him as he is of the enemy . . . If, to this, the soldier can add the knowledge that he can shoot better, advance more skilfully, and attack more vigorously than the enemy, his state of mind will improve still further." In this example, Haking uses a not unreasonable argument, though there is an element of optimism and a disregard of the possibility that the enemy soldier might well be equally skilful and vigorous.

A second negative characteristic identified by Haking was surprise. Haking recognized that to the untrained soldier, "the whole atmosphere of battle can be a surprise . . . the air is full of bullets, and any advance towards the formidable-looking position which is held by the enemy appears to be suicidal." However,

> the soldier, if properly trained in peace, will not be greatly surprised by his novel surroundings; he will know that the enemy is not everywhere and that one bullet sounds much more dangerous than it really is, and that the sound of five or six bullets to his untrained ear are apt to make him think he is under very heavy fire.

The approach employed by Haking to overcome this particular "natural fear" was what might be described as "mechanistic logic". In this case, Haking sets out to prove his point diagrammatically:

> A bullet sounds quite near when it is fifty yards away, and if we take a black-board and make a rectangle a hundred yards long and fifty high (say 50 inches by 25) and put a man on the same scale in the centre at the foot of the board, the height of the man, when standing upright, will only be one inch and his breadth half an inch. If we then dot a few bullets inside the rectangle, all of which will be heard by the man, he will understand that he is not very easy to hit even when he is standing up, especially at long ranges, and still more difficult to hit when he is lying down firing at the enemy.

Just how convincing this argument would have been to the average 1914 officer, or even soldier, who would have been well aware of the rapid -firing Lee-Enfield rifle and the Vickers machine gun, is difficult to say, but it is likely that many would have remained somewhat sceptical. The optimistic and perhaps wishful thinking approach in relation to fear and the academic argument adopted to deal with surprise both illustrate Haking's apparent belief that a forcefully presented argument, based on what can be termed "mechanistic logic", was a persuasive and powerful means of affecting a soldier's behaviour in battle. Examples of this will be seen in future chapters.

The "Concluding Remarks" in *Company Training* state that: "The training of an infantry company for war . . . is one of constant struggle against human nature." It is by nurturing the positive characteristics of the human mind – which Haking lists as self-respect, cheerfulness, content, emulation, duty, and character – that "the little black devil" can be defeated. In this way, a soldier "will go forward into battle in exactly the mental condition that we wish to produce by our training in peace – namely, confident of success."[48]

Going "forward into battle" meant, for Haking, the attack and the offensive and the bulk of *Company Training* is concerned with these two issues. Certain sections have been frequently quoted: "The importance of the attack, as compared with any other form of military operation, is so vast that it practically swamps the remainder."[49] "There is only one rule that can never be departed from and which will always lead to success, and that is always to push forward, always to attack."[50] "The only weapon which can possibly lead to success is the spirit of the offensive from the highest to the lowest."[51]

Haking is markedly less enthusiastic about defence: "It has been proved beyond doubt that defence is more difficult to maintain than the attack . . . the attack is on the rising tide and the defence is on the ebb."[52] For Haking, defence is only a temporary situation – "the offensive spirit is for the moment resting . . . directly the situation changes . . . the initiative must be taken and the offensive spirit immediately aroused."[53] Haking sums up his view about defence and attack in what is probably the most frequently quoted passage from *Company Training*: "Put any army you like against the other, put what we think is the stronger on the defensive, and imbue it with the defensive spirit, and the weaker on the offensive, and the latter will win as sure as there is a sun in the heavens."[54]

* * * *

It is important to note that this emphasis on the attack and the offensive was by no means confined to Haking. It was part of the mainstream thinking of the time and had been the subject of considerable debate in military circles during the years leading up to the Great War. The discussion centred on the problem of how to carry out a successful attack against well-hidden and well-protected defenders who were armed with weapons that were more deadly and more accurate than in any previous time in history.

During the forty years before the First World War – a period that coincided with much of Haking's military career – a revolution had taken place in the development of weapons. In the 1880s, all the European armies began to use small-bore bolt-action rifles which fired multi-rounds from spring-loaded clips inserted into a magazine. The

French Lebel rifle was developed in 1886. It was followed in 1887 by the German Mauser-Gewehr, and the British introduced the Lee Metford in 1888 and the Lee-Enfield in 1907. All these rifles were able to fire 10 to 15 rounds per minute with a range of up to 1,000 yards. Never had the infantryman been so well armed.

The development of the rifle was accompanied by the invention of smokeless explosives. The Frenchman Paul Vineille made smokeless powder (Poudre B) from a gelatinized nitrocellulose mixture in 1886. Only one year later, Alfred Nobel developed cordite, which was easier to handle and more powerful than Poudre B. The manufacture of smokeless explosives spread quickly and, by the time of the Boer War (1899–1902), the rifleman could, for the first time, deliver devastating fire without giving away his position.

The design of the machine gun was improved in 1885 by Hiram Maxim, who made the first water-cooled portable automatic version – a design taken over by the British Company, Vickers, in 1889. Trials showed that the Maxim could fire at twice the speed of the old Gatling gun and with greater accuracy. Other European countries produced their own machine guns based on the Maxim principles – the Maschinengewehr in Germany (1908) and the Hotchkiss in France. By 1911 lighter machine guns were being manufactured. All these weapons were able to fire at about 500 rounds per minute. Such was the fire-power of a single machine gun that it was estimated to be equivalent to eighty riflemen.

The design of artillery pieces was also revolutionized. Field guns were developed with recoil systems that required only small adjustments before the next round could be fired. The principal German field gun was the 15-pounder with a range of 11,000 yards, while the British standard field gun was the Mark I 18-pounder with a range of 7,000 yards. In 1897 the French produced the most celebrated field gun of the war – their 75mm Model, which could fire 15 to 30 rounds per minute over a distance of up to 9,000 yards. Such was the superiority of these field guns over previous models that they became collectively known as 'Quick Firers'.

The Howitzer, designed to lob heavy shells using a high trajectory, was also improved in the 1890s with the French 155mm Schneider, the German 10.5cm Howber and the British 60-pounder. In addition, heavy, long-range guns were developed, notably the German 'Big Bertha' which could fire a 2,000lb shell 15,000 yards and the French 264-pounder that had a range of over eighty miles. All these artillery weapons were able to fire either high-explosive rounds that detonated on impact or shrapnel shells with a time fuse that caused an explosion in flight.

During the period 1880–1914, the military authorities were not only grappling with the problems associated with testing and commissioning these significantly improved weapons, they were also having to assess how battle tactics would be affected by them. Traditionally, the assumption was that the initiative and the advantage were always with the attacker and not the defender. In 1880, the year that Haking entered Sandhurst, a handbook on Tactics asserted that: "the great advantage that an assailant has is his power of choosing his own time and point of attack. It is this, and the knowledge the defenders have that the assailants are moving – doing something behind a mysterious curtain they know nothing of – which gives such a moral power to the offensive and is so demoralising to the defence."[55] In 1889, a pamphlet "for the use of officers and non-commissioned officers of the Auxiliary Forces" stated that: "when the second line (the assault line) has passed through the firing line the Commanding Officer will at once give the command 'Charge' when, with loud cheers, drums beating and bugles sounding, the position will be assaulted."[56] Such words described the standard mode of attack employed by the British Army in the colonial wars of the nineteenth century. They also reflect a mindset that was still unaware of the effects of the small-bore rifle, the Maxim gun and the advantages to the defenders of wire and trenches, all of which had been used extensively in the American Civil War.

But assumptions about the superiority of the attack over defence were starting to be questioned. Even in 1877, at the time of the Russo-Turkish war, the correspondent of the *Daily News* had commented after the Russians had suffered a heavy defeat at Plevna: "The whole system of attack upon even the simplest of trenches will have to be completely changed in future. Assault, properly speaking, will have to be abandoned."[57]

By the early 1890s, the impact of the new weaponry and its effect on battle tactics had been incorporated into the Sandhurst syllabus. The Tactics notebook of H. C. Potter, a cadet at Sandhurst in 1894, contained numerous references to the improvements in rifle firepower and the advantages of defence. Under the heading, "The Effect of More Recent Improvements in Firearms on Tactics", Potter wrote: "a purely frontal attack is futile . . . The position of defenders, lying motionless behind cover, would be very difficult to discover, while their view of the attacker is much improved by the absence of smoke."[58]

Professor G. F. R. Henderson, who had taught Haking at Staff College in 1896, and who was an accepted authority on strategy and tactics, had observed the Boer War, albeit for a brief period, from Lord Roberts's headquarters. He summed up the lessons of the campaign:

The flat trajectory of the magazine rifle, smokeless powder and the quick firing field guns have wrought a greater change in tactics than did the substitution of the breech-loader for the musket and the rifled canon for the smooth-bore . . . Nowadays, the ground in front of a strong line of infantry, provided that the rifles are held a few inches above the level, is so closely swept by the sheet of lead as to be practically impassable by men standing upright or even crouching. The long deadly zone of this horizontal fire, which every improvement in the firearm tends to increase is the most potent factor in modern battle. Of little less importance is smokeless powder . . . At the crisis of the conflict, the quick firing field piece is far more effective than the gun it superseded. On troops whose power of resistance is already strained to the utmost, on masses of men and horses, on crowds breaking to the rear, on a line suddenly assaulted in the flank, the constant hail of shells, even if less devastating than might be imagined, is terribly demoralising . . . Such are the conditions of modern battle.[59]

However, Henderson was at pains to point out that not all the advantages were with the defender:

the object of the assailants' manoeuvres will be to place portions of his force on the flank, or flanks, of the position he is attacking. If he can accomplish this, the effect, moral and physical, of the enfilade fire he brings to bear on the enemy's front will be far greater than that which attended a similar operation when fire was of less account.[60]

Moreover, "if the defence has gained, as has been asserted, by these inventions, the plunging fire of rifled howitzers will add more than proportional strength to the attack."[61]

The British Army *Field Service Regulations* of 1905 incorporated much of Henderson's thinking and reflected the lessons of the Boer War. Section 106 of the *Regulations* recognized the advantages inherent in defence: "It should generally be comparatively easy for the defender to hide his dispositions and to effect a surprise. Entrenchments, moreover, are more easily employed by the defence, and by their aid a position may sometimes be rendered practically impregnable." As regards the offence (Section 107): "The strength of the assailant has always lain in his moral advantage conferred by the initiative, in his power of manoeuvring, of hiding his movements, and of concentrating unexpectedly against some weak or ill-defended point."[62]

The general mood, immediately post-Boer War, was that the

offensive, although essential to victory, had become an extremely hazardous undertaking that should be carried out only with great caution. Haking, in a lecture delivered at Staff College in 1905, made a similar point: "Modern arms and modern fortifications have so greatly increased the resisting powers of a fortress, that a successful siege must always be a very lengthy and very costly undertaking, thus sapping the strength of the field army."[63] The prevailing view following the Boer War was, therefore, that success could come only from superior fire-power and by attacks carried out by large troop formations out-flanking the enemy and concentrating on weak points.

By 1909, however, this guarded approach to the offensive had under-gone a radical change. A significant factor in this change was the interpretation, by the majority of the European military observers, of the lessons of the Russo-Japanese War of 1904–05. The Russian army was at that time considered to be one of the most effective in Europe, while the Japanese had received training from both German and British experts. Both armies were equipped with the most modern weapons – small calibre magazine rifles, quick firing artillery pieces and machine guns – equipment that was, in fact, to change little before the beginning of the 1914 war. Military observers from the main European countries took considerable interest in the course of the conflict with their attention focused particularly on the key issues of the offensive and the defensive.

The Russians were defending their territories in southern Manchuria and the Japanese, using a series of major offensives, gradually drove them out. The cost was high. At Port Arthur, the Japanese had 50,000 casualties and at the battle of Mukden they lost 70,000. The campaign confirmed that rifle and artillery fire could destroy massed infantry and that light field guns had little effect on entrenchments. But it also showed that carefully prepared attacks by committed troops, using initiatives such as sapping methods and the cover of darkness, could inflict defeat on the enemy. The main lesson absorbed by the European powers was that, even against defenders possessing modern weapons, barbed wire and elaborate trench systems, a determined offensive could be successful. The military observers concluded that the Japanese had won their battles because they were infused by the offensive spirit and that well-trained infantry with courage and a willingness to incur terrible casualties could achieve victory.[64]

As a consequence of the lessons learnt from the Russo-Japanese War, the Boer War came to be regarded as unrepresentative and could not be taken as an example of modern warfare. It was argued that the Boers were simply badly organized farmers, while the British were only accus-tomed to dealing with the uprisings of poorly equipped natives. It was the Russo-Japanese War, not the Boer War, that showed how future wars would be fought. This view was expressed forcefully by Kiggell, later to be Haig's Chief of Staff, at the Conference for General Staff Officers held in 1910 at Camberley: "After the Boer War the general opinion was that the result of the battle would for the future depend on fire-arms alone, and that the sword and the bayonet were played out. But the idea is erroneous and was found to be so in the late war in Manchuria. Everyone admits that. Victory is won actually by the bayonet or by the fear of it, which amounts to the same thing so far as the conduct of the attack is concerned. The fact was proved beyond doubt in the last war."[65] The same point was made by a British commentator in 1914:

> There were those who deduced from the experience in South Africa that the assault, or at least the assault with the bayonet, was a thing of the past, a scrap heap manoeuvre . . . the Manchurian campaign showed over and over again that the bayonet was in no sense an obsolete weapon and that fire alone could not always suffice to move from a position a determined and well-dispositioned enemy . . . the assault is of even more importance than the attainment of fire mastery which antecedes it. It is the supreme moment of the fight. Upon it the final issue depends.[66]

The offensive was once more in the ascendancy. But the conclusion that victory in any future war was dependent on an all-out attack had serious implications. Those countries involved in a major conflict would have to accept unprecedented casualties and the eventual victor would only succeed as a result of the superior tenacity and morale of its forces. During any offensive, the time would arrive when it was necessary for the attacking soldiers to cross the fire zone and meet the enemy head on. No matter how well prepared, the final assault in the face of lethal weapons would mean heavy losses. It was this very understanding that convinced the military authorities that their only course of action was to emphasize the virtue of the assault which required individual courage, high morale and extreme determination. Colonel F. N. Maude put the point starkly:

> The chances of victory turn entirely on the spirit of self-sacrifice of those who have to be offered-up to gain opportunity for the remainder . . . in other words the true strength of an army lies essentially in the power of each, or any of its constituent fractions, to stand up to punishment, even to the verge of annihilation if necessary . . . With troops trained to judge their leaders merely by

the skill they show in economising their men's lives, what hope of adequate endurance can ever exist?[67]

Maude also claimed that: "Success in the assault is all a case of how you train beforehand – to know how to die or to avoid dying. If the latter, then nothing can help you, and it would be wiser not to go to war at all." [68]

This grim logic took hold of military thinking in the years leading up to the First World War. It was a philosophy that also appealed to the Social-Darwinists of the time who saw the acceptance of the spirit of the attack and the accompanying long casualty lists as indicators of national prowess – signs that a nation was fit to survive. Further, it was a philosophy that was attractive to those members of the military establishment who saw in the offensive a justification of their profession – an opportunity to be heroic, dashing, courageous, decisive and self-sacrificing. These virtues, they believed, were the true characteristics of the soldier; virtues that singled them out from ordinary men. They were also virtues that were rarely associated with the less glamorous role of defence or a simple reliance on the firepower of modern weapons.[69]

This shift in military thinking from the post-Boer War approach of firepower and caution to a belief in the supremacy of the attack based on individual courage and high morale was reflected in the British Army *Field Service Regulations* in the years immediately before the Great War. The 1909 *Regulations*, in stark contrast to those of 1905, stated that: "Decisive success in battle can be gained only by vigorous offensive . . . Half-hearted measures never attain success in war and lack of determination is the most fruitful source of defeat."[70] Section 100 of the *Regulations* confirmed the importance of the Offensive: "if victory is to be won, the defensive attitude must be assumed only in order to obtain or create a favourable opportunity for **decisive offensive action.**" Section 105 stated; "The advance of the firing line must be characterised by **the determination to press forward at all costs.**" [Bold type as in the *Regulations*.] Significantly, this was the first occasion that the phrase "at all costs" had appeared in the British *Field Service Regulations*. The offensive had become an established imperative.

As if to emphasize these points, Section 105 of the 1909 *Regulations* was amended in 1914 to include: "The paramount duty of all leaders in the firing line is to get their troops forward . . . he must be imbued with the determination to close with the enemy." The heading of Section 110 of the *Regulations*, which, in 1909, had read: "The Decisive Counter-Attack", was in 1914 changed to: "The Assumption of the Offensive".[71]

However, not all senior officers followed wholeheartedly the doctrine of the offensive. Major General May, for example, writing in the *Army Review* of 1913, gave his opinion that the emphasis on the attack "threatens to become a stereo-typed phrase . . . a tribute to the prevailing fashion".[72] J. F. C. Fuller placed more emphasis than was usual in 1914 on the importance of quick firing artillery and the machine gun as a prelude to an infantry attack. Some authorities, understandably, had apparent changes of heart as the debate on tactics evolved. General Sir Ian Hamilton, who was later to command the Gallipoli campaign, noted at one time that: "sheer numbers of infantrymen, regardless of the *élan* that might have infused them, could not break a resolute defence".[73] On another occasion, however, he argued that new technology would be overcome by higher standards of initiative and *esprit de corps*, "New weapons could be overcome by new men."[74]

Despite some dissenters, the doctrine of the offensive had, by 1914, become firmly accepted by the senior officers in the British Army. Haig's Staff College notes indicated a basic belief in the offensive: "Only the decisive offensive could influence war." It was a view that Haig was to hold throughout his career.[75] Similarly, Thompson Capper, who was greatly influenced by the events of the Russo-Japanese War, wrote in 1908: "Foster and nourish by all means in our power the offensive and go-ahead spirit of our officers and men . . . success can be achieved if the troops are possessed of this unconquerable and determined offensive spirit."[76] Kiggell, during a discussion on the offensive in 1910 remarked: "victory is actually won by the bayonet, that settles the point".[77]

It should also be noted that the doctrine of the offensive was not simply a British phenomenon. Through a similar process of discussion and reasoning, all the main contestants in the war followed the same general approach. The German military strategist, General Friederich von Bernhardi, wrote: "those troops will prove superior who can bear the greatest losses and advance more vigorously than the others".[78] Similarly, Marshal Joffre, who was appointed Chief of the General Staff of the French Army in 1911, spoke of: "the eternal principles underlying the necessity of the offensive . . . the necessity of an unflinching will, of the subordination of all secondary missions to the principle object in view".[79] Hence the rigidity of the German 'Schlieffen' Plan and the French Plan XVII in 1914.

Haking, both at Staff College and during his time at Aldershot, would have been fully aware of and involved in the on-going debate on battle tactics. The doctrine of the offensive had not been hastily adopted and nor was it adopted without a clear understanding of its implications in terms of suffering and casualties. Defenders in trenches, armed with lethal weapons, had certain advantages over the attacker, but only the attacker could overwhelm a strong point, regain lost territory or win a victory. Haking, as his *Company Training* clearly showed, had become a fervent disciple of the attack and the offensive. His views, as expressed in his book, were extreme, leaving no doubt as to the force of his conviction, but they were in no sense novel. They reflected the views held by the British military establishment and by most senior British officers in the First World War. The arguments surrounding the cult of the offensive had been absorbed fully by Haking and it was with that mind-set that Haking went to France in August 1914.

* * * *

When orders to mobilize reached Aldershot late in the afternoon of 4 August 1914, 5 Brigade (part of the 2nd Division in Haig's I Corps) had just returned from summer manoeuvres and was considered to be in "good fettle".[80] On 13 August the Brigade crossed from Southampton to Boulogne and ten days later it was deployed south of Mons, across the Mons-Maubeuge road. On 24 August, following the fall of Namur, the British Army, together with the French on their right, began their Retreat. Five Brigade fell back 150 miles in nine days and, in one rear-guard action, lost 250 men of the 2nd Connaught Rangers, who were cut off and taken prisoner.

The Retreat from Mons had gained vital time for the British and French forces to re-group on the Marne and when the German First Army apparently abandoned the original 'Schlieffen Plan' and turned left to the north of Paris, Joffre ordered a major counter-attack. By 5.00pm on 9 September, the Germans were retreating to the Aisne and Haking's 5 Brigade had crossed the Marne.

Haking now advanced north and, despite some considerable opposition, crossed the Vesle, the Aisne and the Oise and 5 Brigade established itself on the Chemin des Dames. However, the Brigade now found that its flanks were unsupported and on 14 September it was ordered to fall back on Vermeuil. Two days later, the 5 Brigade War Diary records: "Heavy shelling commenced at daybreak and continued unceasingly until 11.15am – mostly Howitzers (General Haking slightly wounded and obliged to go to Hospital . . .)."[81] This wound obliged Haking to return to England where he attended a Medical Board on 16 October. The findings of the Board were: "He was wounded by a fragment of high explosive shell on Sept 16, 1914. The wound was in the front of the left arm and a piece of shell was removed on Sept 27 at American Ambulance, Paris. The wound is now healed and the muscle flabby." The wound was described as "slight, not permanent" and Haking was granted forty-two days' leave. On 4 November the wound was declared "completely recovered".[82]

Haking had commanded 5 Brigade since 1911, but he remained with it for only five weeks after arriving in France. He had led the Brigade in the opening weeks of the war with commendable vigour and determination and, while he was convalescing in England, he was again Mentioned in Despatches and rewarded by being promoted to Major General "for distinguished conduct in the field". Haking took up his new command with the 1st Division on 21 December 1914 and soon gained further laurels. Early in February 1915 some important ground had been lost near Cuinchy. The report in the *London Gazette* read:

> At 10.05am acting under orders of the 1st Division all ground which had been lost was brilliantly retaken. GOC 1st Army [Haig] reported that, "Special credit is due to Maj. Gen. Haking commanding 1st Division for the prompt manner in which he arranged this counter-attack and for the general plan of action, which was crowned with success.[83]

The most important event of Haking's eight months' command of the 1st Division was the attack at Aubers on 9 May 1915. Only two months previously, at Neuve Chapelle, IV and the Indian Corps had attempted to gain ground on the strategically important Aubers Ridge, but after some initial success the attack failed. Since that time the German defences along that front had been considerably strengthened by additional barbed wire entanglements and by the construction of a second line. It did not help the 1st Division attack that the British artillery suffered from a severe shortage of shells.

Haking commanded the southern section of the Aubers attack towards the line Bois du Ferme – Ferme du Briez.[84] The first assault by 2 and 3 Brigades took place at 5.00am preceded by a forty-minute bombardment. It soon became apparent, however, that the artillery had failed to cut the enemy wire or destroy the German strong-points. By 6.00am the 1st Division had lost 2,135 men and gained no ground.

A second assault was ordered for 7.00am again preceded by a forty-minute bombardment. Again the attack failed, and many of the wounded from the first assault, lying in no man's land, were killed by their own shells. Haking noted in his report of the operation that at 7.10am he had

> ordered General Officers 2nd and 3rd Infantry Brigades to withdraw under cover of heavy bombardment and hold the front trenches. At 7.30am a report to Corps that attack failed and that I didn't propose to send the 1st Guards Brigade [in reserve] because I think it would be useless.[85]

Despite the failures of the 5.00am and 7.00am attacks, the First Army Commander, Haig, insisted on a further attack and Haking made arrangements, this time using two battalions of the Guard Brigade and two battalions of 3 Brigade. The assault took place at 4.00pm, but by 4.40pm, as Haking's report recorded: "Both Brigadiers reported that the attack had failed and so I ordered them to withdraw under cover of artillery fire and re-occupy our original line."

Haking was quite ready to re-group and attempt a fourth attack, but his Brigadiers, Lowther (Guards) and Davies (3 Brigade), insisted that yet another attack would only be a repetition of the previous three and Haking dropped his proposal. Haig was all for setting up another attack at 8.00pm, but was dissuaded by his Corps Commanders. By nightfall on 9 May no ground had been gained and the First Army had lost 11,500 men. Almost 4,000 of these were from Haking's 1st Division. The implications of the Aubers attack are discussed in the next section.

* * * *

The purpose of this chapter has been to examine Haking's career until August 1915. Haking had reached the age of fifty-two and had his career ended at that point – if the wound from the shell splinter had proved fatal – it could reasonably have been said that the British Army had lost one of its brightest stars.[86] At Sandhurst and at Staff College Haking had acquitted himself well. He had the distinction of being re-called to the Staff College as a Professor, a role that suited his academic bent and which he carried out with considerable diligence and acknowledged success. He further confirmed his reputation as a military teacher with the publication of his two well-received Instruction books that had become standard texts.

Haking's early career with the Hampshire Regiment had shown him to be a capable and promising officer and by the age of twenty-four he had received his first MiD and become Adjutant of his battalion. In South Africa he performed well and was awarded a second MiD. Following his period of teaching at Staff College, Haking's career had accelerated. He held a succession of senior staff appointments – AAG 4th Division, GSO I for the 4th and 3rd Divisions and BGGS Southern Command and it should be noted that by 1914 twenty-five of Haking's thirty-three years of service had been concerned with staff work of one kind or another. However, by the end of 1914 he had been GOC of both a brigade and a division. During his years at Aldershot he had developed useful social and professional contacts with the King and with the future Commander in Chief of the BEF, Haig. His energetic leadership of 5 Brigade in the first fluid and eventful weeks of the war had brought him his third MiD.

Simon Robbins has pointed out that senior officers in the British Army of that time were bound together by social class, based particularly on ancestry, wealth and land; by influential social connections; by sport, particularly hunting and polo; by a public school background; and by attendance at Staff College.[87] Of these, only one, Staff College, applied to Haking. He had made his way essentially on merit, hard work and determination.

In this outline of Haking's career to 1915 certain important aspects of his personality and his career stand out. He was clearly of high intelligence, energetic, persistent and personable. He was ambitious and capable of pursuing his aims with a distinct element of self-interest. He had a strong academic leaning and was adept in expressing himself both verbally and in writing. He had an affinity with detail – a skill, however, that, on occasions, he tended to use to the point of tedium. Allied to this, he had a habit of presenting his point in a somewhat over-bearing "mechanistic logic" manner. It was a style of argument that might appeal to the intellect, but could be less effective in engaging the emotions.

During his career, Haking had witnessed the revolutionary development of fire-power, particularly the machine gun and quick firing artillery, and was well aware of the effects of these weapons in terms of casualties and suffering. Nevertheless, his acceptance of the cult of the offensive was complete – as far as he was concerned, there were no doubts or shades of opinion on that well-debated issue. His writings on the subject were forcefully and clearly presented, but they were by no means original and followed well-established military thinking of the time. In that sense, Haking can be considered as being anchored in the same military tradition and mindset as the great majority of his contemporaries.

The significance of Haking's performance at Aubers Ridge is that it confirmed his single-minded commitment to the offensive and demonstrated a natural inclination to conform with the orders of his superior – both regardless of the near certainty of heavy casualties. The continued attacks at Aubers did not endear Haking to his soldiers. As Robert Graves later wrote:

> Haking commands this division. He's the author of our standard text-book, *Company Training*. The last shows have not been suitable ones for company commanders to profit by his directions. He came over this morning and shook hands with the survivors. There were tears in his eyes. Sgt Smith swore half aloud: 'Bloody lot of use that is . . . busts up his bloody division and then weeps over what is left'.[88]

Haking's role in the attack at Aubers did, however, have the effect of confirming him as a "thruster" – a reputation that did him no harm as far as Haig was concerned – and within three months Haking was promoted to Brevet Lieutenant General in command of the newly formed XI Corps.

Such was the man who, for the next three and a half years, 1915 to 1918, was involved as a Corps Commander in the conduct of the war. How Haking carried out this role is the subject of the following chapters.

A chronological summary of Haking's life is given in Appendix I.

Notes

1. *Oxford Dictionary of National Biography.* (Henceforth *DNB*.)
2. *The Times,* 11 June 1945.
3. TNA, WO 76/515, 516, 2nd Battalion The Hampshire Regiment Record of Services.
4. The maiden name of Haking's mother was Byrne.
5. In *Crockford's Directory of Clergy* for 1864 the name of the Vicar of Rodbourne Cheney is Hacking, while the name given in the 1865 edition is Haking.
6. R. C. B. Haking's grandfather died intestate and the estate was valued at £40,000 before duties. This is the equivalent of some £2.5 million in today's money. Since he had five children and was a widower, the assumption is made that the estate was shared equally between the children, i.e. about £500,000 each in today's terms.
7. Equivalent to about £240,000 today.
8. The three sisters, Mary, Ethel and Hilda, never married. The 1901 Census showed all three living "of independent means". Hilda died in 1933 and bequeathed a legacy of £1,000 to fund an annual prize in Clinical Obstetrics and Gynaecology at the London Hospitals. See TNA, Ed 39/1234.
9. *Who's Who 1918.*
10. *Crockford's Directory* of 1870 records that Richard Haking graduated in 1855 Mus.Bac. Worcester College, Oxford and became Mus. Doc. in 1864 while at Rodbourne Cheney. Marlborough was the nearest major school, but there is no record of a "Haking" being a pupil there. Nor is there any record of a "Haking" at Eton, Harrow,Giggleswick, Sedbergh,Wellington College, Shrewsbury, Sherbourne, Winchester or Rugby.
11. AWM, 3DRL 7953/34 Pt 2, Edmonds to Bean, 14 November 1932. Welldon spelt "Weldon".
12. Edward M. Spiers, *The Late Victorian Army 1868–1902*. p.93.
13. From the *Gentlemen Cadet Registers*, Royal Military Academy, Sandhurst.
14. Rachel Violette Burford-Hancock was the daughter of Sir Henry James Burford-Hancock, sometime Chief Justice of Gibraltar. The marriage took place in Beckenham, Kent, in September 1891 when Haking was a Captain, aged twenty-nine. The Regiment was at that time on Home duty based at Chatham. One of Haking's fellow officers in the 2nd Hampshires, and his

successor as Adjutant, was Henry di Stella Burford-Hancock, the brother of Rachel Violette.

15. Royal Hampshire Regiment Museum. Winchester. *The Chronicle of the 2nd Hampshire Regiment 1879–82*, p.8. (Henceforth – *Chronicle*.)
16. *Chronicle*, XIV, No 129, p.8.
17. See C. T. Atkinson. *The Regimental History of the Royal Hampshire Regiment.* 2 Vols., pp.381–82.
18. *Chronicle*, XIV.
19. *DNB*.
20. See Brian Bond, *The Victorian Army and the Staff College, 1854–1914*. p.160.
21. LHCMA, Liddell Hart Papers, 15/1/19, Extract from "The Staff College Fifty-Five Years Ago", published in "*Owl Pie*", 1949. Edmonds, however, did not have a particularly high opinion of his fellow-students. In the same article, he wrote: "In the '90's the competition for the Staff College . . . was not very stiff." He was to describe the 1896–97 students as "very medium company." See also ibid., Allenby Papers, 6/3, 28 August 1936.
22. *London Gazette*, 16 April 1901.
23. Douglas Scott, ed., *Douglas Haig: Diaries and Letters 1861–1914*, p.143.
24. John Lee, *A Soldier's Life*, p.90.
25. For example, the right to immediate retirement on £420 per year.
26. That this was considered as no small issue is witnessed by the necessity for the documentation on the matter to be circulated to CGS, AG, MGO, QMG, and FM by J. S. Ewart, the Military Secretary.
27. Army Personnel Centre, Glasgow, Haking's Personal Papers, Minute sheet, 790 30/14. (Henceforth, Haking's Personal Papers.)
28. Haking's Personal Papers.
29. TNA, WO 279/18, Staff Officers' Conference, 1908, p.37.
30. TNA, WO 279/42, Staff Officers' Conference, 1911, p.12.
31. Royal Archives, Windsor Castle, RA/ 976/3, George V's Diary, 19 May 1912 and 13 May 1913.
32. Haking did remark, however, at the Conference of General Staff Officers in January 1911: "There is no doubt about it that there is a feeling against officers writing books." See TNA, WO 279/42, p.7.
33. Col R. C. B. Haking, *Staff Rides and Regimental Tours.* (Henceforth *Staff Rides.*)
34. Brig Gen R. C. B. Haking, *Company Training.* Henceforth *Company Training.*
35. *Journal of the Royal United Services Institute*, 53, 1909, p.1110.
36. *The Army Review*, V, July-Oct 1913, p.295.
37. For example, Haking lectured at the Staff College on 4 January 1905 on *Staff Rides.*
38. *Staff Rides*, Preface.
39. *Staff Rides*, Ch. 1.
40. Ibid.
41. Ibid.
42. *Staff Rides*, Ch. XI.
43. *Staff Rides*, Ch. IV.

44. *Staff Rides*, Ch. II.
45. Ibid.
46. *Staff Rides*, Ch. XVI.
47. *Company Training*, Chs. I, VIII, and XXII.
48. *Company Training*, Ch. I.
49. *Company Training*, Ch. VI.
50. *Company Training*, Ch. II.
51. *Company Training*, Ch. VI.
52. *Company Training*, Ch. VIII.
53. *Company Training*, Ch. II.
54. *Company Training*, Ch. VI.
55. *British Infantry Tactics and the Attack Formation Explained by an Adjutant of Militia*, p.14.
56. J. Thomas, *The Attack for Company, Battalion and Brigade*, p.17. Even at the 1911 Staff Officers Conference a Col. Boileau had put forward the thought that more use should be made of bugles and drums to encourage an assault. See TNA, WO 279/42, p.12.
57. Forbes, Macgahan, et al., *The War Correspondent of the Daily News* 3rd edn. p.368. Quoted in Paddy Griffith, *Forward into Battle*, p.64
58. The notebooks of H. C. Potter, later to command a brigade in the First World War, are held at the RMA Sandhurst. The notes are essentially a summary of "*Minor Tactics*" by Col. Francis Clery, a Professor of Tactics at Sandhurst in the 1880s.
59. Col G. F. R. Henderson, *The Science of War*. p.73. This extract was included as part of the *Encyclopaedia Brittanica Supplement* 1902.
60. Ibid., p.74.
61. Ibid., p.159.
62. *Field Service Regulations, 1905.*
63. The lecture was published in a booklet, *Four Lectures Delivered at the Staff College during the Senior Staff Officers' Course, held in January 1905.* The booklet is held at the Staff College, Shrivenham.
64. The Russo-Japanese War took place while Haking was teaching at Staff College and it was the practice for students and Instructors to meet each Saturday morning to discuss the actions of the previous week.
65. TNA, WO 279/496, Report on a Conference of General Staff Officers at the Staff College 17–20 January 1910.
66. A. E. Altham, *The Principles of War Historically Illustrated*. p.195. Quoted in Michael Howard, "Men against Fire; the Doctrine of the Offensive in 1914", in Peter Paret, ed., *Makers of Modern Strategy*, p.510.
67. F. N. Maude, *The Evolution of Infantry Tactics*. Quoted in ibid., p.521.
68. Ibid., p.146.
69. This point is discussed by Tim Travers, 'Technology, Tactics and Morale: Jean de Bloch, the Boer War and British Military Theory, 1900–1914', *Journal of Modern History* 51, 1979, pp.264–86.
70. *Field Service Regulations* 1909, Section 99.
71. *Field Service Regulations* 1909, Part I, Operations 1914.

72. See Travers, 'Technology, Tactics and Morale', p.275.
73. Ian Hamilton, *A Staff Officer's Scrapbook* 2 vols, II, p.48. Quoted in H. C. Johnson, *Breakthrough.* p.12.
74. Quoted in Travers, 'Technology, Tactics and Morale', pp.264–286.
75. Ibid., p.275.
76. LHCMA, Capper Papers, II, I/2, 1908. See also Keith R. Simpson, 'Capper and the Offensive Spirit', *Journal of the Royal United Services Institute for Defence Studies*, 118, 1973, pp.51–56.
77. TNA, WO 279/496, *Report of a Conference of General Staff Officers at the Staff College 17–20 January 1910.* Among others attending this Conference were Haking's student contemporaries at Staff College – Robertson, Edmonds, Macdonough, Furse as well as Kiggell. Haking was not present.
78. Gen. F. Von Bernhardi, *On War Today* vol. II, p.53. See Howard in *Makers of Modern Strategy.*
79. *The Memoirs of Marshal Joffre.* p.32.
80. G. D. P. Young., *A Short History of the 5th Brigade.* p.19. The 5th Brigade was made up of the 2nd Battalions of the Worcesters, the Ox and Bucks L.I., the Highland L.I., and the Connaught Rangers.
81. TNA, WO 95/1343.
82. Haking's Personal Papers. The only other known occasion that Haking had appeared before a Medical Board was in January 1901 just before taking up his position as a Professor at the Staff College. It was noted that: "He had now recovered from dysentery caused by military duty and was fit for service home or abroad". In G.Sheffield and J.Bourne, *Douglas Haig, War Diaries and Letters 1914–1918*, p.61, footnote 5, it is stated, wrongly, that "Haking suffered a bad head wound on 14 September 1914." Sir James Edmonds, in a letter to Capt. Bean, the official Australian historian, wrote of Haking :"I don't think he was much use after he was wounded on the Aisne in October 1914." AWM, 3DRL 7953/34, 2 July 1928. Edmonds was prone to gossip.
83. *London Gazette*, 12 February 1915.
84. Alongside the 1st Division was the Meerut Division. The northern section of the attack, towards Fromelles, was spearheaded by Maj. Gen. F.J. Davies' 8th Division.
85. TNA, WO 95/1228. Dated 12 May 1915.
86. A comparison can be made with Maj. Gen. Sir Thompson Capper, Haking's Staff College contemporary, both as a student and as an Instructor, and a fellow disciple of the offensive. Capper was killed leading his men in attack at Loos in September 1915. Haig's wrote in his Diary for (26 September 1915), that Capper was "a great loss" as he "combined great pluck and straightforwardness with a thorough knowledge of war". Sheffield and Bourne, *Haig's Diaries and Letters*, p.157.
87. Simon Robbins, 'The Right Way To Play the Game – The Ethos of the British High Command in the First World War', *Imperial War Museum Review*, 6 (Undated), pp.39–50.
88. Robert Graves, *Goodbye to All That*, p. 114. This incident is dated 24 May and so presumably "the last shows" refer to both Aubers and Festubert.

CHAPTER II

Haking and the Battle of Loos

XI Corps was formed on 29 August 1915. Initially, the Corps was made up of the Guards, 23rd and 24th Divisions and was temporarily placed under the command of the GOC Guards Division, Lord Cavan. Within days, 21st Division replaced 23rd Division, and, on 4 September, XI Corps became part of Sir Douglas Haig's First Army. The following day, Major General Richard Haking was appointed commander of XI Corps with the temporary rank of Lieutenant General.[1]

Haking owed his appointment to the support of Douglas Haig. Haig's Diary entry for 1 September 1915 read: "The CGS [Lieutenant General Sir William Robertson] came to see me – most anxious to assist in every way. I urged him that Haking should be put in charge of XI Corps at once."[2] Robertson agreed with this proposal and promised to put the matter to the British Commander in Chief, Field Marshal Sir John French. This was not the first time that Haig had put Haking forward for promotion to Corps Commander. Two months earlier, on 8 July, Haig had received a visit from the Prime Minister, Herbert Asquith. Haig noted in his diary that he and Asquith had discussed a number of issues including, "the necessity for promoting young officers to high command . . . We went through the list of Major Generals, etc. on the Army List. I said it was important to go down low on the list and get young, capable officers. He agreed. I said in reply to urgent questions that the best to command Corps seemed to be as follows, in order of seniority – Major Generals Morland, Horne, Gough and Haking . . . Mr Asquith wrote the names down."[3] Within a year, all four of the named Generals had been placed in command of a Corps.

Haig's patronage of Haking was based on several factors. They had attended Staff College together in 1896; both had been staff officers in the Boer War; when Haig was in command at Aldershot from 1912 to 1914, Haking had served there as GOC 5 Brigade; and, in 1914, while serving in Haig's I Corps, Haking had been promoted to Major General for distinguished conduct in the field. In addition, Haig was well aware that Haking was committed to the "cult of the offensive" – a "thruster" who had shown a markedly aggressive spirit on the Aisne in 1914 and at Aubers in May 1915. These were characteristics that Haig valued and he saw them as essential in the role he was planning for XI Corps in the forthcoming offensive – the Battle of Loos.

The purpose of this chapter is to examine those aspects of the Battle of Loos which involved Haking and XI Corps – particularly the handling of XI Corps as GHQ Reserves and the part played by XI Corps during the battle. The chapter ends with an assessment of Haking's role in these events.

* * * *

In June 1915, the French Commander in Chief, General Joffre, proposed a two-pronged attack against the German line Arras-Rheims, known as the Noyon salient. The French were to strike in the south from Champagne, while, to the north of the salient, a joint Anglo-French attack would take place in the Loos-Vimy area. Neither French nor Haig, whose First Army was to carry out the proposed attack towards Loos, was enthusiastic. They both considered the ground to be unfavourable. On 20 June, Haig made a reconnaissance of the area:

> I got a very good view of the country towards Loos, and the two lines of defences. To the east of Aix-Noulette the country is covered with coal pits and houses. The towns of Lievan, Loos, etc. run into one another. This all renders the problem of an attack in this area very difficult.[4]

French suggested that, instead of an attack against Loos, the British should plan an offensive against Aubers and Messines, but Joffre would not agree. This deadlock continued through July and into August and was only broken through the intervention of Lord Kitchener.

Kitchener was gravely concerned about the recent setbacks in Italy and particularly Russia. An offensive in the west would take some pressure off those countries and at the same time support the efforts of the French. Consequently, at a meeting with Joffre on 16 August, Kitchener agreed to the proposed joint attack in the Loos-Vimy area. French was informed of this decision which Kitchener repeated to Haig on 19 August: "[Kitchener] had decided that we must act with all our energy, and do our utmost to help the French, even though by doing so, we suffered very heavy losses indeed."[5] This reluctant compliance with Joffre's plan was an inauspicious prelude to what became a costly military failure.

The Battle of Loos is significant in several ways. It was the largest battle fought by the British up to that point of the war; the British employed gas for the first time; and it was at Loos that men of

Kitchener's New Armies first took the field. There is a further significant aspect of Loos – it resulted in the resignation of French as Commander in Chief of the BEF and the appointment of Haig as his successor. Loos aimed at breaking through the German lines between Loos and Hulluch, but it ended by gaining only some six square miles of strategically useless ground at the cost of 60,000 casualties. The French, both at Vimy and in Champagne, also failed to make any significant gains.

In Haig's view, however, the British attack at Loos could have been successful and the hoped-for breakthrough achieved. On the first day of the offensive, 25 September, some notable gains had been made. The position at mid-morning was that, in the south, Lieutenant General Sir Henry Rawlinson's IV Corps had taken Loos and pressed on to gain a foothold on Hill 70. To the north, Hubert Gough's I Corps had made progress against the German strongpoints of Fosse 8, the Quarries and the Hohenzollern Redoubt. British troops had penetrated the enemy's first line of defence over a frontage of some 8,000 yards and there is some evidence that, at midday on 25 September, the German troops were in a considerable state of panic.

Haig, writing to French, claimed that Bavarian prisoners had reported that the [German] 117th Division had been practically wiped out. Similarly, a prisoner of 25th Regiment

> stated that by mid-day on 25th everything was in confusion. Men and guns were streaming back . . . a German officer described vividly how, on the afternoon of 25th, on the main road between Cuinchy and Dorignies there were endless convoys in double line . . . it was a terrible picture of defeat.

Several British Officers, writing to the compiler of the British Official History some ten years after the battle, were also of the opinion that Loos could have been a victory. Major General Richard Hilton, for example, believed that:

> The real tragedy of the battle was its nearness to complete success. Most of us who reached the crest of Hill 70 and survived were firmly convinced that we had broken through . . . there seemed to be nothing ahead of us but an unoccupied and incomplete trench system . . . All we needed was more artillery ammunition to blast those cleverly located machine guns and some fresh infantry to take over from the weary and depleted Jocks. But, alas, neither ammunition nor re-enforcements were immediately available and the great opportunity passed.[7]

By the afternoon of 25 September, the offensive had come to a stand-still. Exhaustion and heavy losses meant that the attacking troops could do little more than consolidate their positions. The "fresh infantry", referred to by Hilton, never materialized. There were support troops available, but they were held too far behind the battle zone to be of any use, and this gave rise to one of the major issue of Loos – the handling of the reserves.

As far as Haig was concerned, a breakthrough could have been made if the reserves had been available at the right time. Haig was of the opinion that the critical period on 25 September was between 9.00am and 11.00am and that, had a fresh division been close up at that point, it could have pushed through without opposition.

> What was required was the advance of a considerable force of infantry to carry the offensive forward to its objective . . . to prevent the enemy . . . from consolidating a third line and holding up our advance long enough for his reserves to arrive by train. This he succeeded in doing because there were no fresh troops on the spot to continue the offensive when the divisions which had carried out the assault were exhausted.

Rawlinson supported Haig's view: "the want of a fresh division was badly felt. The opportunity once lost was never recovered."[8]

To Haig, the crucial factor in the failure at Loos was the mishandling of the reserves and this issue became the centre of acrimonious recrim-inations between Haig and the man who had been in control of the reserves – the British Commander in Chief, Sir John French.

The main body of the reserves for Loos was the 21st and 24th Divisions of Haking's XI Corps. The two divisions had only recently arrived in France. The 24th Division disembarked at Boulogne and le Havre between 30 August and 1 September, while the 21st Division did not complete its arrival until 14 September. The Divisions undertook various training programmes in the St Omer area until 18 September when orders were received from GHQ for XI Corps to concentrate near Lillers behind the First Army.[9] XI Corps remained in the Lillers area until 23 September – two days before the planned attack at Loos.

* * * *

That the handling of the reserves was to become a major issue was apparent long before XI Corps had positioned itself near Lillers. The issue revolved around two key questions: firstly, who would command the reserves; and, secondly, how would they be used?

A letter dated 7 August from GHQ to Haig set out quite clearly the availability of troops for the forthcoming battle and also the command structure: "The troops available for the operations will be those of your own Army [i.e. I and IV Corps], plus the Cavalry Corps and two divisions held in the General Reserve under the orders of the Commander in Chief."[10] That Haig's understanding of the situation was not the same as that of his superior officer is apparent from a discussion that Haig held with his two Corps Commanders, Rawlinson and Gough, on 8 September. They were discussing "which of their two Corps should be allocated the task of taking Pont a Vedrin". It was agreed that I Corps (Gough) should have that responsibility, but Haig added: "In any case, I propose that a division of the General Reserve should be pushed in the rear of the point of juncture of I and IV Corps so that when required it can push forward on Pont a Vedrin."[11] Since Haig was not in command of the reserves, this proposal was misleading and inevitably led to some confusion among his subordinates. Rawlinson's IV Corps Operations Order No. 35, dated 20 September, stated: "The 3rd Cavalry Division and XI Corps will be held in Army Reserve."[12] Major General C. St L. Barter, one of Rawlinson's divisional commanders, repeated this confusion between GHQ and AHQ control on 20 September.[13] Haig, whose First Army was to carry out the attack, clearly believed that the Reserves should be under his control so that he could use them as he wished. He was no doubt encouraged in this view as a result of Sir John French's somewhat ambiguous statement on 26 August that eight divisions would be employed in the main attack "comprising six divisions for the assault and two divisions in general reserve",[14] and also by Joffre's remarks at a meeting with French and Haig on 12 September: "It is indispensable that these divisions [the Reserves] are put, before the attack, at the absolute disposal of General Haig."[15]

French, however, maintained his stance on the matter and a note from GHQ, dated 18 September, to "Commanders of Armies and G.H.Q. Reserves" read: "The Cavalry, Indian Cavalry and XI Corps will form the General Reserve at the disposal of the Field Marshal Commanding in Chief. Separate instructions will be issued for the concentration of these troops."[16] On 19 September, Haig attempted to resolve the issue by writing to GHQ expressing his grave concern about the control of the Reserves: "I wish again to draw your attention to the fact that the whole of the disposable troops of the First Army are being employed in the attack on 25 September from its commencement, that there are no Army Reserves and that . . . the only troops in General Reserve are those detailed by G.H.Q."[17] Haig's efforts were, however, in vain. French was determined to keep the reserves under his personal control and Haig was to record in his First Army Operations Report: "At dawn on 25 September, the 21st and 24th Divisions were in GHQ Reserve."[18]

It is worth noting that, subsequently, French was to justify his control of the reserves as follows:

In view of the great length of the line along which the British troops were operating it was necessary to keep a strong reserve in my own hand. The XI Corps . . . were detailed for that purpose. The reserve was the more necessary owing to the fact that the 10th French Army [on the immediate right of the British troops] had to postpone its attack until one o'clock in the day; and further that the Corps operating on the French left had to be directed in a more or less south-easterly direction, involving, in case of our success, a considerable gap in our line.[19]

Apart from wanting to have reserves in case of emergency, it is likely that French had doubts about the wisdom of using inexperienced troops such as those of the 21st and 24th Divisions. "I feel quite sure," French had written to the War Office in January 1915, "that to put an Army, Corps or even a division composed of these troops . . . straight into the field under commanders and staff who are inexperienced in up-to-date European warfare might easily become a positive danger."[20]

* * * *

Whatever French's rationale as regards the control of the reserves may have been, the command issue, even as the battle commenced, was unresolved. Consequently, a second major issue developed. Where should the reserves be positioned? A letter of 18 September from GHQ, copied to First Army, stated that, at daybreak on 25 September, XI Corps was to be assembled in the Lillers area.[21] This was some sixteen miles behind the First Army trenches and entirely contrary to Haig's requirements for close and immediate support on the day of the attack. Haig responded immediately:

The whole plan of operations of the First Army is based on the assumption that the troops of the General Reserve will be close at hand and I consider it essential that the heads of the two leading divisions of XI Corps [21st and 24th] should be on the line Nouex les Mines-Beuvry by daylight on 25 September. This will entail a night march by these troops on night 24/25 and for this reason I strongly recommend that these troops should assemble in the area [around Lillers] by the morning of 23 September at the latest with a view to getting a complete night's rest on night 23/24 September.[22]

French acceded to Haig's wishes. On 19 September, he wrote to Haig: "two divisions of XI Corps will be assembled [around Lillers] by daybreak on 23 September".[23] On 23 September, Haig was informed that: "By daybreak on September 25 the heads of the two divisions of XI Corps will be on Noeux le Mines-Beuvry". [24] On the morning of 25 September, the day of the attack, the 21st and 24th Divisions were, therefore, some four miles from the British trenches and they remained under the command of French.

The first two hours of fighting (6.30am–8.30am) was the period during which the British made their greatest gains and Haig contacted French repeating his request that the 21st and 24th Divisions should be placed at his disposal. The response from GHQ, sent at 9.30am, reached Haig at 10.02 am and read:

> 21 and 24 Divisions will move forward to first Army trenches as soon as situation requires and admits. On arrival there they will come under control of First Army . . . [The] Guards Division will move up to ground vacated by 21 Division. XI Corps, less 21 and 24 Divisions, will remain in General Reserve.[25]

This message had been sent to both the First Army and XI Corps and Haking made immediate arrangements for the two divisions to move towards the front line: "The 21st moved off at 10.45am, the 24th at 11.00am."[26] In the meantime, French had decided to make a personal visit to both Haig and Haking. Haig made a note of the visit: "11.30am Sir John French came to see me and then went to Noeux les Mines to see Haking. He said he would put Haking under my orders less the Guards Division."[27]

The 21st and 24th Divisions had to march just over four miles to reach the British trenches, but their progress was painfully slow. Haig telephoned Sir William Robertson, the Chief of Staff, at 1.15pm: "Enemy now counter-attacking Hill 70 from south in great strength . . . 21st Division is so distant cannot be employed yet to help."[28] Haking, in a later report, confirmed that: "progress was slow and the divisions did not reach the positions ordered until about 5.00pm".[29] In other words, the reserves played no effective part in the first day of the battle.

The tardy advance of the 21st and 24th Divisions on 25 September became a further point of friction between French and Haig. There was no doubt that Haig and Haking had the responsibility for organizing the movement of the two divisions. GHQ had stipulated, when confirming the move of XI Corps to Noeux les Mines-Beuvry on 24 September, that: "All details in connection with the necessary moves will be arranged between First Army and XI Corps direct."[30] Similarly, when French had agreed that the 21st and 24th Divisions should move up to the British lines on the morning of 25 September, he had placed the necessary arrangements in the hands of Haig's First Army: "Arrange move in communication with First Army accordingly."[31]

There was serious disagreement as to why the march of the 21st and 24th Divisions had taken so long. Haking reported on 10 October: "Owing to the fact that the [XI] Corps was advancing through the administrative area of IV and I Corps, who were heavily engaged, progress was slow."[32] Haking's statement implied that the First Army arrangements to ensure a quick advance to the front were inadequate and that the roads had not been kept clear. Haig, when taxed by French on the point, responded that the arrangements for road control in the area had been quite adequate. Haig added:

> there was therefore no avoidable delay on 25.9.15, to the move-ment of the XI Corps caused by their having to move through the administrative area of I and IV Corps . . . I am quite satisfied that such delay as occurred was due to the bad march discipline and inexperience of the two divisions.[33]

In support of this statement, Haig compiled a series of reports from various Transport Controllers who had been on duty in the areas of I and IV Corps.[34] Generally, these reports concluded that the delays caused by traffic were minimal and that the problem was the inexperi-ence of the two divisions.

Eyewitness accounts, however, suggest that there were significant road delays. Colonel C. G. Stewart, GSO I of the 24th Division, described the situation:

> On the 25th, the Division Headquarters, when summoned up in advance by XI C., had a great deal of difficulty getting through. In one place on the only main road up to Vermelles, we were blocked by a Cavalry division moving *across* the road, who also blocked all the ammunition supply of divisions fighting, the wounded, etc. – and created great confusion. It was hours before we could ascertain what had become of the 73rd Bde. The 71st and 72nd took hours to get up at all.[35]

Colonel Stewart also noted:

> On 25th about 10.00am the division was ordered to move east-wards as soon as possible . . . The road to Sailly Labourse was much congested and at least one unit crossed the column of route . . . the road via Vermelles to the cross-roads Corine de Rutoire was very congested . . . the road to La Rutoire was greatly

congested with ambulances and artillery, etc. and the advance was necessarily slow.[36]

The War Diary of 2 Guards Brigade, who were making their way forward behind the 21st and 24th Divisions, noted: "September 25. Great delay on the road as 21st and 24th were on the same road ahead of us and 9th Cavalry passed through just outside Marles les Mines".[37]

The progress of the 21st Division was also delayed because of poor road control. Some twelve years after Loos, Major General George Forestier-Walker, the GOC of the Division, recalled that:

the weary long march [24th September] and its effects on the troops was due more than anything else to the fact that no arrangements had been made with the French authorities with regard to Railway traffic control at the level crossings. Following on this fatiguing march, and with entirely inadequate period of rest, the Division was kept on its legs for the whole of 25th September, due in very large measure to the lack of any efficient traffic control at the level crossing.[38]

Haking, whose note of 10 October had implied that road control in the First Army area was less than adequate and whose own XI Corps War Diary for 25 September stated that the 21st and 24th Divisions "were much delayed by blocks on the road",[39] now had a change of mind. On 3 November, he wrote to Haig:

In my letter of 10.10.15 I stated that owing to the fact that the Corps was advancing through the administrative area of IV and I Corps . . . the progress was slow. I wrote this letter when I was very busy preparing an attack by 12th and 46th Divisions . . . and the above mentioned statement was based on my own memory of verbal statements made to me by the GOC 21st and 24th Divisions on the night of 25th [September] at Vermelles where I was . . . busy with future rather than past events. I may have been mistaken about this, because I know that the most careful arrangements were made by First Army to ensure that the two roads were kept clear. I am of the opinion now that the delay was caused chiefly by their [21st and 24th Divisions] own indifferent march discipline, especially as regards first line transport . . . March discipline of these new divisions though good when marching without transport was certainly not good when marching with it, and constant halts and checks occurred.[40]

Having received Haking's letter, Haig immediately wrote to GHQ: "I have made further investigations regarding the movement of 21 and 24 Divisions on September 25 . . . The staffs and control officers again report that such delays and blocking that did occur was due to in-experience and faulty march discipline of the divisions themselves."[41]

There are difficulties in reconciling these opposed and contradictory versions of road control and march delays. The British Official History refers to the critical comments of Haig and Haking and concludes that: "This condemnation, according to a consensus of opinion of partici-pants in, and spectators of, the march is too sweeping . . . some other cause must be found."[42]

* * * *

It is clear that French and Haig saw the issues relating to command and control of the reserves at Loos from completely different perspectives. The British Official History claims that "an understanding" had been arrived at between French and Haig "as to the employment of the general reserve".[43] But no proper understanding existed. On French's part there was misplaced obstinacy and, on Haig's, wishful thinking. The differences between the two men were evident in the days leading up to the battle and they became the cause of major conflict in the weeks that followed.

The two documents that brought matters to a head were Haig's First Army Report on Operations for the period 22-30 September, and French's Despatch to the War Office of 1 November.[44] Haig's Report emphasized that the First Army attack was unsupported by the reserves, which were kept under the control of the Commander in Chief, and which did not arrive in time to be of any use. French responded that the reserves were placed on the morning of 25th September exactly where Haig had stipulated – on the Noeux les Mines-Beuvry line; that they had been put at Haig's disposal as requested; and that the problems met by the reserves when moving up to the front on 25 September were within Haig's area of responsibility. French wrote to Haig asking him to attach "explanations" to his report before it was forwarded to the War Office, but Haig used his reply only to justify the comments that he had already made.[45]

The discord between French and Haig rapidly increased. On 8 November, French wrote to Haig insisting that the First Army plan of attack should have taken into account the General Reserve situation and that Haig should have retained reserves from within the First Army to give any required support. French ended his 8 November letter: "The Commander in Chief directs that there shall be no further argument or correspondence on this subject which is hereby finally closed."[46]

But the argument was far from over. Haig took exception to two

paragraphs in French's Despatch of 1 November. These were concerned
with the precise times at which the 21st and 24th Divisions (on 25
September) and the Guards Division (on 26 September) were transferred to First Army control. French's Despatch, which was printed in
The Times of 2 November, stated: "At 9.30am I placed the 21st and
24th Divisions at the disposal of the GOC First Army, who at once
ordered the GOC XI Corps to move them up in support of the attacking
troops . . . at 6.00am the Guards Division arrived at Noeux les Mines
and on the morning of 26th I placed them at the discretion of the GOC
First Army." Haig contested both of these statements because they
implied that the reserve divisions were under Haig's control and ready
for action much earlier than they actually were, and he quoted from
telegrams sent from GHQ to disprove the accuracy of French's two
paragraphs. It was now Haig's turn to ask for textual changes: "As
these facts seem to be of importance, I should be glad if the necessary
corrections could be made."[47] The Chief of Staff, Robertson, replied on
behalf of French that the extracts from his despatch appeared to be
essentially correct and there was therefore no necessity to amend
them.[48]

But Haig would not let the matter drop. He accused French of
having: "a total misconception of the fundamental principles of the use
of reserves in battle, with the consequent results".[49] Haig was determined to show that the lack of reserves at the right time had prevented
a certain victory and that the man responsible for the debacle was the
Commander in Chief himself. It is ironic that, on the evening of 25
September, Haig received the following message from French: "At the
sunset of the First Day of the great battle we have now commenced, I
desire to convey to you and the First Army my hearty congratulations
and warmest thanks for the splendid work you have accomplished and
I feel confident that the fine courage and magnificent spirit which
animates all ranks will ensure a speedy and decisive victory over the
enemy."[50] Even on 25 September it was clear that the "magnificent
spirit which animates all ranks" did not, in fact, cover the two principal
British Commanders. By early November, the fragile relationship
between French and Haig had broken down irretrievably.

* * * *

The British Official History, in its account of the handling of the
reserves at Loos, says of Haking: "His position was a most embar-
rassing one."[51] Certainly, Haking was a new Corps Commander with a
new and inexperienced Corps and his "position" was between the main
protagonists in the reserves issue – French and Haig. To the first,
Haking owed the loyalty of a subordinate to a superior officer who was
also the Commander in Chief. To the second he owed the loyalty of a

newly promoted Corps Commander to the man whose patronage was responsible for his promotion.

There was, however, little doubt in Haking's mind as to where his loyalty should be placed. Writing to Haig on 3 November, Haking commented:

> There is no doubt that these divisions [the 21st and 24th] had a most difficult task to perform, and I am convinced that they would have had a much better chance of success if they had been deployed in rear of Vermelles early on 25th ready to confirm any success gained by I and IV Corps as suggested by GOC First Army [i.e. Haig] at the Conference held GHQ on 18 September.[52]

The positioning of the two divisions had certainly been discussed at the 18 September Conference, but Haig, as we have seen, settled for the line Noeux les Mines-Beuvry.[53] Haking's comment on 18 September Conference may not, therefore, have been totally accurate, but the intention was clearly to show support for Haig. Quite separately, but also on 3 November, Haking sent a personal, handwritten note to Haig. The note refers to the acrimonious correspondence between Haig and French: "I think your reply completely flattens the attempt to incriminate other people. I have added a bit to my report of the same nature. There is none to blame but GHQ and they know it."[54]

Reference has been made to Haking's change of opinion as to the cause of the slow progress to the front of the 21st and 24th Divisions on 25 September. On 10 October the cause was roadblocks while, on 3 November, Haking had decided to support Haig's contention that the problem was poor march discipline. Haking's revised view was included in the draft of the British Official History when it was being compiled in the mid-1920s. It met with severe criticism from many officers who had served at Loos. Apart from the march discipline issue, several took the opportunity to comment on the poor food arrangements for the two divisions – particularly the separation of the cookers from the troops. Major J. Vaughan (24th Division), commented:

> the report by the Commander of XI Corps as to the reason for the delay . . . is exceedingly severe. The delay was caused by the amount of traffic on the road . . . Further, owing to the break-down in the feeding arrangements all the men were hungry and no points were reached after 6.00pm where water bottles could be filled.[55]

Lieutenant Colonel R. R. Gibson (24th Division) wrote that, "the men were tired and dinnerless before they reached Vermelles. Yet

General Haking reported to his chief that his troops were rested and well-fed."[56] Major J. Buckley (21st Division) also thought that Haking's criticism of his Division's march discipline was "very unjustifiable".[57] Colonel C. Stewart (24th Division) commented that the supply arrangements were altogether wanting; that the removal of cookers and water carts from Brigade charge was lamentable; that, on 26 September, the men were tired and hungry; and that staff officers or guides should have been arranged by XI Corps.[58] Similarly, Forestier-Walker (21st Division) wrote: "I object to General Haking's suggestion that the march discipline was indifferent . . . the march discipline of the Division was, as a matter of fact, extraordinarily good."[59] It can be reasonably assumed that the compilers of the official history would have attempted to contact Haking for his comments on the draft chapters covering Loos. There is, however, no correspondence from Haking in the relevant files.[60]

* * * *

Haig had supported Haking's promotion to Corps Commander and Haking had supported Haig in his dispute with French over the Loos reserves. But there was a further reason for Haking to give his loyalty to Haig rather than to French. Since mid-1915 it was becoming apparent that French was losing the support of his superiors. Haig's diary entry for 8 July 1915 read:

> Visit from FM Earl Kitchener. He said how he found it difficult to get Sir J. French to comply with any of his suggestions, whereas in bygone days F[rench] obeyed the smallest suggestion. However, he (K) was ready to do anything – to black French's boots if need be – in order to obtain agreement to win the war. He wanted me to assert myself more and to insist on French proceeding on sound principles.[61]

Just six days later, when Haig was on leave in England, he was summoned to a meeting with King George V:

> He [the King] referred to the friction between Sir John French and Lord K and hoped that I [Haig] would do all I could to make matters run smoothly . . . there would be no back-biting and unfriendly criticism of superiors if the officer at the head of the Army in the Field – a most splendid body of men – was fit for his position! He (the King) criticised French's dealings with the Press, The Times, Repington, Lord Northcliffe, etc. All most unsoldier-like and he (the King) had lost confidence in Field Marshal French. And he had told Kitchener that he (K) could depend on his (the

King's) support in whatever action he took in dealing with French
. . . The King hoped that I would write to Wigram [the King's
Assistant Secretary] and said that none but he and Wigram would
know what I had written.

Later the same day, Haig saw Kitchener who also asked Haig to
write: "on any subject affecting the Army and in which he thought he
could be of assistance. He would treat my letters as secret."[62]

The intrigue against French continued after the battle of Loos. On 17
October, Robertson, French's Chief of General Staff, visited Haig:

As regards Sir John French, Robertson told me that when he was
in London, Lord Stamfordham [the King's Principal Private
Secretary] called him up on the telephone from Sandringham and
asked him by the King's orders whether he did not consider the
time had come to replace Sir John French . . . He saw the King
afterwards in London, and now he had come to discuss the point
with me. I told him . . . in view of what had happened in the recent
battle over the reserves, and in view of the seriousness of the situation, I had come to the conclusion that it was not fair to the
Empire to retain French in command. Moreover, none of my officers commanding Corps had any opinion of Sir John's military
ability or military views – in fact they find no confidence in him.[63]

The final blow against French came on 24 October during a visit of
the King to France. Haig wrote in his Diary:

After dinner, the King asked me to come to his room, and asked
me about Sir John's leadership . . . I told him I had done my
utmost to stop criticisms and make matters run smoothly. But
French's handling of the reserves in the last battle, his obstinacy,
and conceit showed his incapacity . . . I therefore thought strongly
that for the sake of the Empire, French ought to be removed. The
King said that he had seen Generals Gough and Haking that afternoon, and they had told him startling truths of French's unfitness
for command.[64]

The diary of King George V also records the 24 October discussions:

After tea, Generals Gough and Haking came to see me and we had
a long talk. . . . They pointed out that there was great want of
initiative and fighting spirit and no proper plans made in high
quarters and that everyone had lost confidence in the C-in-C . . .

They had no axe to grind but only wanted to win the war . . .
Douglas Haig came to dinner and I had a long talk with him afterwards. He entirely corroborated what the other two had said, but
went much further and said the C in C was a source of great weakness to the Army and no-one had any confidence in him any more
. . . All these things add to my worries and anxieties.[65]

Writing to Stamfordham the following day, the King repeated these
conversations:

The troops here are all right, but I find that several of the most
important Generals have entirely lost confidence in the C. in C.
And they assured me it was universal & that he must go, otherwise we shall never win this war. This has been my opinion for
some time.[66]

On 6 November, Haig noted in his diary:

Sir John French has returned from England and is in bed with a
heart attack. We wonder whether it is the result of my letter to
GHQ asking that his last Despatch [that of 1 November] may be
corrected.[67]

It can be seen, therefore, that the period during which Haig,
supported by Haking, was intriguing against French, was also the
period when Haig, again supported by Haking, was exchanging acrimonious notes with French on the reserves at Loos. It is little wonder
that both Haig and Haking, following their various conversations with
the King, Kitchener and Robertson, felt quite secure in their attacks
on their superior officer, the Commander in Chief. On 3 December,
Kitchener wrote to the Prime Minister, Asquith, recommending that
Haig should be appointed to succeed French. Sir John French was
persuaded to resign his position and Sir Douglas Haig took command
of the BEF on 19 December 1915.

* * * *

Despite the lack of reserves, the first day of the Battle of Loos was not
without its successes. In the north of the attack area, I Corps had
reached the Lens-la Bassée road and had captured the Hohenzollern
Redoubt, Fosse 8 and the Dump. To the south, IV Corps had over-run
Loos and Hill 70. Haig considered that the day had been a very satisfactory one with 8,000 yards of German front captured and, at certain
points, an advance of two miles.[68] However, although the main objectives of the day had been achieved, the cost had been heavy – some

15,000 casualties – and the British attack had come to a standstill.

On the immediate right of IV Corps, the French Tenth Army had suffered losses even greater than the British and had failed to make significant progress towards Vimy. Nevertheless, the British and French Commanders, French and Foch, took an optimistic view of the situation and when they met on the evening of 25 September, they agreed that the battle should be renewed the following day.

Haig was still hoping to make a breakthrough. However, since the troops of I and IV Corps were by now either casualties or exhausted, Haig's attack divisions were to be Haking's XI Corps – the reserves. Haking had received orders from Haig at 2.35pm on 25 September: "XI Corps to push forward at once between Hulluch and Cite Auguste and occupy high ground between Harnes and Pont a Vedrin both inclusive and secure passages over canal at these places."[69] But it was impossible to comply with this order since, at the time it was given, the 21st and 24th Divisions were still making their painfully slow way towards the battle area which they did not reach until early evening. Haig wrote in his Diary: "The two new Divisions were so slow in coming forward. It was 6pm before they began to cross our old trenches."[70] The First Army Report noted: "in view of the lateness of the hour and to give time to reconnaissances, the divisions were ordered to halt on reaching our advanced trenches and to prepare for carrying out the attack on the next morning."[71] Reaching the "advanced trenches" was, however, no easy matter. As they moved towards the Lens-Hulluch road in heavy rain, the troops of the 21st and 24th Divisions had to cross shell-torn, muddy ground inter-laced with old trench systems and littered with barbed wire. Most distressing of all, the ground was covered with dead and wounded soldiers. Already tired out, the men of the 21st and 24th Divisions had little prospect of rest on the night of 25/26 September.

In the meantime, the Germans had strengthened their second line defences and brought up reinforcements. They had also mounted a series of counter-attacks and by the morning of 26 September had recaptured the Quarries and tightened their hold on the crest of Hill 70, Bois Hugo and Hulluch. The open ground between Hill 70 and Hulluch, the direction of the attack of the 21st and 24th Divisions, therefore, was completely overlooked by the enemy. At 9.00am an effort was made by IV Corps to take Hill 70 and reduce the threat on the right flank. Similarly, I Corps attempted to take Hulluch on the left. Both of these attacks failed and, at 11.00am, the two reserve divisions began their advance over open and exposed ground towards the heavily defended German second line.

Despite this generally unfavourable situation, Haking's attitude was optimistic: "The tactical situation at the moment was that the enemy had been defeated."[72] He considered that he had an adequate number of troops to achieve success: "The 21st and 24th Divisions with a total of 16 battalions were attacking a front of 1,200 yards which gives at least ten men to the yard."[73] But Haking's optimism was unfounded. The 14,000 men of the 21st and 24th Divisions were fired on from both flanks as they moved forward in extended line towards enemy trenches defended by barbed wire that was waist high and some five yards deep. They were unprotected by either gas or smoke cover and the preliminary bombardment, which had lasted only one hour, had failed to cut the German wire. The verdict of the British Official History was that the men had: "passed the limit of their endurance".[74] The outcome was a disaster.

At 12.20pm, 63 and 64 Brigades of the 21st Division, fired on from Bois Hugo and Chalet Wood, broke and retreated back across the Loos-Hulluch road to the original British lines. Seventy-one and 72 Brigades of the 24th Division made encouraging initial progress in the northern section of the attack area. Despite the heavy machine-gun fire from Hulluch and Bois Hugo, groups of men from both brigades reached the unbroken wire of the German second defence line. The losses, however, had been extremely heavy – the area became known as "the corpse field" – and there were no more reserves to send forward in support. At about 1.00pm, the survivors of the 24th Division, lying helpless in front of the enemy barbed wire, saw men of the 21st Division retiring on their right and, "by common accord",[75] began to fall back across the Lens-Hulluch road. There is no evidence that the retreat of either the 21st or the 24th Divisions was a rout. The British Official History describes the retirement as "orderly" and "without panic".[76]

These were men who had been in France for only three weeks and who, until two days earlier, had not heard a shot fired in anger. They were thoroughly exhausted; they had done what they could; and their attack had failed. The general opinion of officers who had witnessed the events of 26 September was that the men had been asked to do too much. Lieutenant General Sir C. J. Briggs, the GOC of the 3rd Cavalry Division, noted later: "The 21st Division, being a new Division and for the first time in action, were called upon to carry out a task no new division could have adequately performed."[77] The opinion of Stewart of the 24th Division was that the most experienced troops would have failed.[78] Forestier-Walker, GOC of the 21st Division, considered that the use of "two divisions which literally never had had a bullet or shell fired at them was nothing short of criminal".[79] Colonel Stewart also recalled a conversation with Haking:

I had it from the XI Corps Commander himself . . . that these two divisions would be in reserve in a big operation at Loos on the idea that not having previously been engaged in this way, they would go into action for the first time full of esprit and elan, and being ignorant of the effects of fire and the intensity of it, would go forward irresistibly and do great things.[80]

When Haking spoke to men of the two Divisions, following their retirement, he was told: "We did not understand what it was like; we will do better next time."[81] For most of the troops who had gone into action on 26 September, however, there would not be a "next time". The 21st Division had lost 4,051 men and the 24th Division some 4,178 – over 50 per cent of the original force. Both Divisions were withdrawn from the line at nightfall on 26 September. Haking's XI Corps was then reconstituted as the Guards Division, and the 12th and 46th Divisions.

With the failure of the attacks on 26 September, the immediate problem was how to secure the gap created by the withdrawal of the 21st and 24th Divisions. Haig ordered the 3rd Cavalry Division to occupy the old German line west of Hulluch. He also made arrangements to bring up the Guards Division, which was now transferred from GHQ Reserve to Haking's XI Corps.[82] The Guards were immediately ordered by Haking to take Hill 70, the Chalk Pit and Puits No. 14 bis. Despite heavy losses, they were unable to do so, and withdrew to positions a hundred yards below the crest of Hill 70. Commenting on this action, the historian of the Guards Division, Lieutenant Colonel Cuthbert Headlam, wrote:

> Whether or not it was wise policy at this stage of the battle and when there were so few available reserves, to attempt the capture of these extremely strong positions with so comparatively little artillery preparation is open to doubt. It is tolerably clear at any rate that had Sir Douglas Haig known a little earlier of the loss of Fosse 8 and the Dump he would have counter-manded altogether this attack by the Guards Division.[83]

＊ ＊ ＊ ＊

The failure of the attacks on 26 and 27 September – on Hulluch, on Hill 70 and in the centre between Hulluch and Loos – effectively finished the Battle of Loos. However, fierce attacks and counter-attacks by both the British and the Germans continued for the next three weeks on the key points of the front – Fosse 8, the Hohenzollern Redoubt, the Dump, the Quarries, Puits 14 bis and Hill 70. When the battle came to a halt on 13 October, all these critical points remained in the hands of the Germans.

The attacks made on the final day, 13 October, are worthy of note in relation to Haking and his XI Corps. The objective of XI Corps was to capture Fosse 8 and the Quarries and the assaults were to be made by the 12th Division and the 46th Division. Considerable attention was given to the preparations for this attack. The 12th Division made a mock-up of the Quarries area using sandbags and the 46th Division built a dummy trench system. Advice was sought from officers who had previously been involved in fighting in the Quarries and Fosse 8 areas. XI Corps was to use gas and smoke and "every available gun would be at their disposal".[84]

Rawlinson's IV Corps was to attack simultaneously towards the Lens-la Bassée road. Rawlinson considered that the IV Corps and the XI Corps attacks should be staged quite separately, but at the First Army Conference of 8 October, his views were not supported. For his part, Haking was optimistic and in his "Scheme for the Attack for XI Corps", he wrote:

> In spite of the little time available, there is little doubt that with the assistance of smoke and of such gas cylinders as we can get into the trenches in the time, and with the very powerful artillery support placed at our disposal . . . we have a better chance of gaining our limited objective . . . than the troops who made the original attack on 25 Sept., partly because the enemy is more shaken and disorganised and partly because we are in a position to produce a tremendous artillery bombardment against a very small portion of the enemy's front.[85]

Haking placed great emphasis on the use of artillery prior to the 13 October attacks. For three days, 10 to 12 October, divisional artillery was devoted to wire cutting while the heavy artillery concentrated on the enemy trenches and the strongpoints housing machine guns. This programme continued until noon on 13 October when for one hour there was a particularly heavy bombardment on the enemy trenches. At 1.00pm gas and smoke were released; the heavy guns lifted to targets behind the German front line; and the divisional artillery continued to fire shrapnel shells into the enemy trenches. However, as the attacking troops were to discover, the three-and-a-half-day bombardment had little effect on the German defences.

The 46th Division, recently transferred from Ypres, arrived in the trenches opposite the Hohenzollern Redoubt during the night 12/13 October. The GOC of the Division, Major General the Honourable Edward Montagu-Stuart-Wortley, later wrote:

I was asked to send in my appreciation of the situation; and after consulting with Major General Lord Cavan, Commander of the Guards Division, I came to the conclusion that Fosse 8 could not be taken in one operation, but that the trenches defending it should be attacked separately. At a Conference held at 1st Army Head Quarters, I was informed that my views were not accepted, and that as the attack would be covered by the fire of nearly 400 guns, my Division would be able to occupy Fosse 8 without firing a shot, as the German Trenches would be absolutely flattened.

The Division relieved the Guards Division the night before the attack. The trenches were of a most intricate and confused description; no assembly trenches were available; the officers and men were ignorant of the ground.[86]

The GOC of the 46th Division clearly did not share the optimism of his Corps Commander.

The 46th Division attacked at 2.00pm and 138 Brigade entered the Hohenzollern Redoubt. However, as they moved forward, they came under machine-gun fire from Fosse 8 and sustained heavy casualties. Montagu-Stuart-Wortley made the following comment:

the Division made a most gallant attack; the Artillery preparation had been quite ineffective; the German trenches were practically untouched . . . the German trenches were strongly held; their artillery and machine gun fire was very accurate; with the result, that my losses were very heavy.[87]

The 12th Division of XI Corps, on the right of the 46th Division, managed to break into the Quarries but could go no further. The XI Corps attacks had failed and the total casualties were high: the 46th Division lost 3,768 men and the 12th Division 3,354. Rawlinson's IV Corps made little progress in their efforts to secure the Lens-la Bassée road and the efforts of 13 October stalled against a strong and determined German defence. The British Official History summarized: "The fighting on the 13/14 October had not improved the general situation in any way and had brought nothing but useless slaughter of infantry . . . The battle front of XI Corps remained unchanged."[88] Further south, the French had met with little success in their assault on the Noyen Salient. Winter was approaching; casualties had been high; gains had been minimal and the British and French agreed to bring the offensive to a close.

* * * *

The above outline of the Battle of Loos gives a context in which to comment on the activities of Haking and his XI Corps. The role that Haking played as a Corps Commander at Loos was largely determined by the circumstances at the time of the battle. He was a new Corps Commander with a new and inexperienced Corps and, at least for the initial stages of the battle, he was hardly in control of his Corps at all. Haking was nominally in charge of XI Corps, but, as GHQ Reserves, their orders came from French. It was French who gave the orders for XI Corps to move forward from Lillers to Nouex les Mines-Beuvry and thence to the British trenches. When French eventually released the 21st and 24th Divisions to Haig, he still maintained control of the Guards Division, which, as the XI Corps War Diary noted: "he personally desired the Corps Commander [Haking] to leave under him".[89]

During the morning of 25 September, the 21st and 24th Divisions were transferred to the First Army and again Haking was in nominal command of XI Corps. Haig, however, immediately began to re-allocate divisions and brigades to support I and IV Corps in a series of bewildering moves. At 11.25am he placed 73 Brigade of the 24th Division under the orders of the GOC I Corps. In turn, I Corps allocated the Brigade to his 9th Division near Fosse 8. At 1.25pm the whole of the 21st Division was placed under the control of IV Corps. That order, however, was cancelled at 2.55pm except that 63 Brigade of the 21st Division was transferred to the 15th Division of IV Corps in the Loos area. This hectic series of transfers came to a halt with the 2.55pm message at which time XI Corps was made up of the 21st Division (less 63 Brigade) and the 24th Division (less 73 Brigade). The Guards Division remained with GHQ throughout 25 September and did not rejoin XI Corps until 2.30pm on the following day. Apart from the allocation and re-allocation of divisions and brigades, it should also be remembered that XI Corps itself was moved piecemeal between GHQ and the First Army over a period of some thirty hours. While it was the nature of a Corps to see Divisions come and go, such rapidity of change was far from normal and reflected both the state of the battle and the dispute between French and Haig as to who should command the reserves. As far as Haking was concerned, it was a turbulent baptism as a Corps Commander.

During the early, critical stages of the Battle of Loos, Haking was, therefore, in command of XI Corps more in title than in fact. His main role was administrative – to make the proper arrangements to effect the orders received from French and then Haig. In this, Haking and his staff were far from successful. The March Tables[90] relating to the 21st and 24th Divisions on 25 and 26 September were clear enough on paper, but they did not work out in practice. The arrangements had been placed firmly in the hands of the First Army and XI Corps, but attention had not been given to proper road control and the result, for the 21st and 24th Divisions, was extreme confusion and delay.

The problem of providing hot food for the 21st and 24th Divisions was also handled poorly and arose from the separation of the cookers from the infantry units. Stewart of the 24th Division commented on the arrangements for 25 September:

> On moving off, the first line transport was formed up in accordance with 'Ammunition Supply and Transport Instructions' issued by A and QMG 24 Division on 24.9.15 in accordance with orders received from XI C[orps]. Thus all cooking vehicles became detached from their units and brigades.[91]

The same order applied to the 21st Division and a hand-written message, dated 25 September, from the 21st Division staff to 62, 63 and 64 Brigades stated: "When Division advances all train wagons will remain where they are in their respective areas until Division is clear of Noeux les Mines. Train will then advance."[92] Unfortunately for the troops of the 21st Division, the Transport, including the cookers, did not become available until after the fateful attack of 26 September. Haking's orders had provided for extra cheese rations for the two Divisions, but this hardly compensated for the lack of hot food. The Corps decision to separate the cookers from the troops was far from helpful to the tired men who made their way to the front on 25 September.

While the work of XI Corps HQ Staff can be criticized, the inexperience of many of the Divisional officers was also evident. Lieutenant Colonel Gibson of the 24th Division, commenting on the draft chapters of the British official history, expressed his views with some colour:

> Of ex-regular officers there was a paucity, and of these, the older ones had been dug out of the musty reading rooms of clubs in Cheltenham, Bath or Bournemouth. The younger ones were mostly the cast-offs from the Old Army owing to mental or physical disabilities. In one battalion, and it was typical of many, three ex-regular officers were given command of companies. The fourth was a militiaman. But of these three ex-regulars, one had to be left behind when the battalion embarked for France. He was too mad to be trusted with a company in the field. The second was gallant and sensible, but stone deaf. The third had the thickest head that ever grew on a man's shoulders.[93]

A further point must be raised in connection with the administrative competence of Haking and the XI Corps staff. At 2.35pm on 25 September, when Haig ordered the 21st and 24th Divisions to make an attack between Hulluch and Cite Auguste, the two Divisions were struggling to make headway towards the battle area. There was no possibility of the attack being made that afternoon, yet Haking simply complied with Haig's plan and issued a pointless order that could not be put into effect. It was a mindless error of judgement.

Haking must also be held responsible for a series of the unclear objectives and poor communication between himself, his staff and the two Divisions and there is no lack of eyewitness comment on this subject. Stewart complained on behalf of the 24th Division that:

> We had little real information of the situation all through; none of the actual locality . . . Nearly all the information which was supplied was altogether wrong and misleading, being quite unduly optimistic. The idea given was that the Germans had been heavily defeated and were retiring everywhere, and the reserve corps was to confirm success. There was no idea of meeting organised resist-ance . . . the situation was believed to be that the Germans had been driven from their entrenchments and open warfare was being resumed. Such an attack had been rehearsed under the eye of the Corps Commander by the division in the back area.[94]

Brigadier General R. M. Ovens made the same point: "the impression given to the 21 and 24 Divisions that the Germans were retiring every-where was a most regrettable travesty of the real facts of the case". [95] Lieutenant J. H. Alcock of the 21st Division also mentioned the lack of "real information": "On Monday, 12 September, officers of the brigade were addressed by the Corps Commander. We were told definitely that an attempt was to be made to break the line . . . there was throughout no idea of a definite or limited objective presented to us."[96] Similarly, Lieutenant Colonel Rainsford of 24th Division, commented:

> all COs from battalion commanders upwards were addressed by General Haking, commanding XI Corps, who gave a very hazy picture of what to expect . . . The idea gathered was that we were to advance indefinitely and that a line for the cavalry to advance by would be marked out by flags 'like the Grand National'.[97]

Haking's tendency to be over-optimistic is illustrated by his briefing of 2 Guards Brigade officers on 15 September at Lumbres. The War Diary recorded that Haking told them that an attack on the German lines was imminent; that the Germans had about 40,000 men to oppose our 200,000 in the locality where the attack was to take place; that behind their firing-line and supports they had only 6 divisions as a reserve to their whole western front. He then said that almost everything depended on the platoon leaders and he instructed them always to push on boldly whenever an opportunity offered, even at the expense of exposing and leaving unguarded their flanks.

This extract from the Diary ended with three exclamation marks indicating at least a degree of incredulity on the part of the writer.[98]

On 24 September Haking called a Corps Conference at Lillers, which was attended by all the Corps Commanding Officers and their Staffs: "Lieut Gen Haking commanding XI Corps, made an impressive address to all present. He said that we were on the eve of the biggest battle of the history of the world."[99] Later that day, the GOC of the Guards Division, Lord Cavan, repeated Haking's words that they were about to take part in "the biggest battle in the world's history" and said that "he had nothing to add to the stirring words spoken by the Corps Commander".[100] The Commanding Officer of the Welsh Guards, however, was less impressed: "General Haking made a fine speech, but spoke too low and too fast" and enigmatically added: "in view of later events [the speech] was worth remembering – as is much more which this general has written and said".[101]

Haking also failed to impress the men of 2 Guards Brigade when he spoke to them just before their attack on 27 September. He compared the German line to the crust of a pie saying that one thrust would break it and then there would be little resistance. When the Guardsmen appeared somewhat sceptical at this description, Haking added, "I don't tell you to cheer you up. I tell you because I really believe it."[102] This last sentence is revealing. Haking's mindset inclined him to believe in the best possible situation and it is typical that he should have written several weeks after the failure of 26 September:

> The tactical situation . . . was that the enemy had been defeated and driven from his main line of trenches and was holding on to a thin back line; if that could be carried the whole line would be broken.[103]

Following the transfer of XI Corps from GHQ to the First Army, Haking's role as Corps Commander took on a tactical dimension. The following examples of Haking's tactical decisions at Loos show both his strengths and his weaknesses. In implementing Haig's orders to take the

Bois Hugo-Huluch line on 26 September, Haking was immediately faced with a critical situation. The 21st and 24th Divisions were to advance between Hulluch and Hill 70 both of which were in the hands of the Germans. Haig's plan was that these positions, key in protecting the flanks of XI Corps, should be taken on the morning of 26 September by the 1st Division and the 15th Division respectively. However, their attempts to do this failed. Nevertheless, Haking, characteristically, took the decision to persist with the attack. He still had hopes that Hulluch would be taken by the 1st Division (described in the British Official History as a "reasonable expectation"[104]), and, with the advance of the 21st and 24th Divisions in the centre, Hill 70 could be outflanked. It was a gamble that did not pay off, but there was logic to it, and, given Haig's plan, Haking pursued his objective with vigour. Similarly, when Haking ordered the Guards Division to move forward on 27 September to capture the Chalk Pit and Hill 70, the outcome was unsuccessful. As has already been noted, the historian of the Guards Division considered this order to be far from wise. Nevertheless, the action was justified in that it served to consolidate an uncertain and potentially dangerous front.

A second example of Haking's tactical decision-making is the much-criticized artillery plan in support of the 46th Division on 13 October. The heavy guns were ordered by Haking to lift from the enemy emplacements one hour before the start of the attack, but the bombardment would continue using shrapnel shells. It is arguable that the heavy shells would have dispersed the smoke and gas that was being released, but the shrapnel shells certainly would not destroy the critical German strongpoints on and around the Hohenzollern Redoubt. Haking's decision to lift the heavy guns before zero hour was a repeat of a ploy he had used on 27 September when the Guards made their attack towards Hill 70. Haig had telephoned Haking on 28 September saying: "it was a mistake not keeping the heavy howitzers on longer, and that was the reason for the failure".[105] Haking's repeat of this tactic on 13 October was also a failure. When the 46th Division moved forward they found that the enemy strongpoints on the Redoubt and Fosse 8 remained intact. Whether a continuation of the heavy bombardment for an additional hour would have altered the outcome of the attack is unlikely, but the howitzers would certainly have done more damage to the German positions than the shrapnel shells.

An unattractive feature of Haking's conduct during and after Loos is his lack of empathy for the troops of his new and inexperienced Corps. It is striking that the senior officers of the 46th, 21st and 24th Divisions, despite their failures, took every opportunity to commend their men. Montagu-Stuart-Wortley considered that the 46th Division had made "a most gallant attack" on 13 October, despite the artillery programme being "quite ineffective".[106] Forestier-Walker defended the reputation of his men: "The 21st Division, as both its subsequent commanders have testified, was an exceptionally well-trained one. I doubt if a better ever crossed the Channel."[107] Similarly, Stewart wrote: "I was proud and cherished the 24th Division and its name was blackened in despatches, to my idea absolutely wrongly . . . I should do what I can to ensure justice being done to so many gallant officers and men who fell in their duty then and later."[108] Many senior officers who served with XI Corps at Loos made similar comments.

By contrast, Haking criticized his troops when, quite appropriately, he could have been their advocate. The prime example of this is the debate surrounding the slow progress of the 21st and 24th Divisions as they made their way to the front on 25 September. As we have seen, Haking first laid the blame on poor road and traffic conditions, but later changed his mind and accused the two Divisions of poor march discipline and inexperience. Given the amount of evidence confirming that the roads and railways were badly controlled, Haking's revised view can only be seen as political expediency to support Haig. It was more in Haking's interests to back his Army Commander against French than to maintain the reputation of his own Divisions.

A second example concerns the allegation that, on 25 September, the advancing 21st Division was fired on by its own artillery. Colonel Denny of that Division certainly believed that casualties had been caused by "friendly fire": "The shelling of our troops on Hill 70, at a critical time, by our own artillery was unfortunate."[109] Haking, however, would have nothing of this:

Troops that have failed in an attack are very apt to believe that they have suffered from their own shell fire, when really it was the enemy's, and many cases of this nature have been investigated and it was found that there was no real foundation for the allegation.[110]

Haking adopted a similar attitude when the troops of the 21st and 24th Divisions were accused of abandoning their rifles during their retreat of 26 September:

I think far more than 300 rifles were left on the ground. I asked several men what they had done with their rifles and they almost all told me the same story, viz., that they had helped to bring back a wounded man and had to leave their rifle behind. I am quite sure that a large number of unwounded men came back, many without their rifles and equipment, on the excuse of assisting a wounded soldier . . . I think that the most stringent orders should be issued to new formations that no wounded soldiers are to be taken to the rear by unwounded men.[111]

In the turmoil of 26 September, it is quite likely that some casualties were caused by "friendly fire" and that a number of retreating troops abandoned their rifles (though one eye-witness "saw no case of panic or fear. Men had their arms"[112]). Nevertheless, Haking's lack of identification with his men is apparent here as it was on other occasions; they lacked march discipline; they imagined they were being fired on by their own artillery; and they threw away their rifles. Even allowing for the general circumstances of failure, Haking was just too eager to find fault with his own rank-and-file.

An assessment of Haking at Loos must include some discussion on his involvement in the French-Haig controversy. As regards the handling of the Reserves, Haking was in a pivotal role. As one commentator later put it:

> . . . placing oneself in the position of the Corps Commander, as far as this is possible, one could scarcely fail to realize that there was a very serious misunderstanding between GHQ and AHQ as to the role of XI Corps at the commencement of the operation; and that the duties that the two supreme commanders were likely to demand of oneself, as the Corps Commander, were very liable to conflict. In that case, as Corps Commander, I should have felt it my duty not to rest content . . . until I felt no misunderstanding, and I could act wholeheartedly in absolute loyalty to both.[113]

But Haking had no particular wish to act "in loyalty to both". He was well aware that the demise of French was imminent and his main consideration was to back Haig, the architect of his recent promotion and the man likely to become the next Commander in Chief.

A revealing incident took place at the time of the visit of King George V to France shortly after the Battle of Loos. It was the King's practice to ask senior officers to write to him and he had requested Montagu-Stuart-Wortley to keep him informed about the progress of 46th Division. Montagu-Stuart-Wortley had cleared this with Sir John French, but had ceased his correspondence with the King following the transfer of the 46th Division to Haig's First Army.[114] On the day following the King's visit, Stuart-Wortley was approached by Haking who: "came to ask me whether I was in the habit of writing to the King – I told him exactly what I had done, but he informed me that by my writing to His Majesty I had incurred the displeasure of the Army Commander, then Sir Douglas Haig."[115] Since Haking had had no qualms about criticizing French, his Commander in Chief, during his meeting with the King on 25 October, and since Haig had been corresponding regularly with both the King and Kitchener on French's "unfitness for command", such an action, without discussion, can only be regarded as petty-minded and hypocritical.[116]

* * * *

Haking's conduct at Loos – the devious part he played in the reserves dispute and the fall of French; his ill-founded optimism; his lack of empathy with his men; and his mixed tactical and administrative performance – was not up to the standards that might reasonably be expected of a professional and high ranking soldier. He was a new Corps Commander, his divisions were inexperienced, and he was placed uncomfortably between French and Haig. These factors, however, cannot be said to excuse Haking's deficiencies at Loos. Colonel Stewart wrote to the Official Historian: "there was a tendency among certain commanders when an operation for which they were responsible did not succeed to attribute blame direct to units or officers under their command, when the true circumstances did not justify this being done".[117] These words were not directed specifically at Haking, but they might well have been.

Notes

1. A Corps HQ was originally made up of nineteen officers including a BGGS, a DA and QMG, an Artillery Adviser (BGRA), a Commander of Royal Engineers (CRE), and a Deputy Director of Medical Services (DDMS). In late 1915 the number of officers was increased to twenty-four as a result of Corps HQ assuming greater control of artillery and a GOCRA was appointed. Corps troops included a Cavalry Regiment, a Cyclist battalion, a Motor Machine Gun battery, a Signals Company, the Corps Ammunition Park, three Supply Columns, an ASC Company, two Mobile Ordnance workshops, two or more Heavy Artillery groups, two or more RE Companies, a Tunnelling Company, and a detachment of the RFC. A Corps commanded two or more infantry divisions. See *BOH, 1916*, I, p.58
2. Sheffield and Bourne, *Haig Diaries and Letters*, p.141.
3. TNA, WO 256/4, Douglas Haig Diary (Hereafter Haig Diary).
4. Sheffield and Bourne, *Haig Diaries and Letters*, p.128.
5. Ibid., p.137. For the background to Loos, see Rhodri Williams, 'Lord Kitchener and the Battle of Loos: French Politics and British Strategy in the Summer of 1915', in Lawrence Freedman, Paul Hayes, and Robert O'Neill, eds., *Strategy and International Politics*. pp.117–32; and David French, 'The Meaning of Attrition, 1914–16', *English Historical Review* 103, 1988, pp.385–405.

6. TNA, WO 95/158. These statements were part of a reply made by Haig (21 October) to certain queries from French in OAM 77, dated 16 October 1915. See also the NOTE in the *BOH 1915*,Vol.2, p.304.

7. Quoted in Philip Warner, *Field Marshal Haig*, p.174.

8. TNA, WO95/158. In replies to French's queries in OAM 77.

9. XI Corps was made up of the Guards Division under Lord Cavan; the 21st Division, commanded by Maj Gen G. T. Forestier-Walker; and the 24th Division under Maj Gen Sir J. G. Ramsay.

10. TNA, WO 95/158, GHQ letter, OAM 670.

11. Sheffield and Bourne, *Haig Diaries and Letters*, p.144.

12. *BOH 1915*, Vol. II, Appendix 17, p.452.

13. Ibid., Appendix 19, p.457.

14. Ibid., p.272.

15. Ibid.

16. TNA, WO 95/158, OAM 670.

17. Ibid., G.S. 164/21. In this connection, it is of interest to note Haig's memorandum to his Army Commanders on the eve of the Battle of the Somme: "G.H.Q. Reserve remains at the disposal of the Commander-in-Chief . . . and is not to be moved without his authority . . . The Commander-in-Chief hopes that forces already allotted . . . will prove sufficient to carry out the operations . . .". TNA, WO 95/164, OAD 17, Kiggell to Army Commanders, 21 June 1916. See also Haig's words to his Army Commanders at a Conference on 15 June 1916: "Reserves must not be wasted on impossible frontal assaults against strong places". TNA, WO 95/881.

18. TNA, WO 95/158, First Army Operations Report, 22–30 September 1915.

19. Sir John French, *The Complete Despatches of Lord French 1914–1916*. p 396. The despatch is dated 15 October 1915.

20. *BOH 1915*, II, p.274, Footnote 1.

21. TNA, WO95/158, OA 858.

22. TNA, WO 95/158, GS 164/21 to GHQ, 19 September 1915.

23. Ibid., OAM 875.

24. Ibid., OA 910.

25. Ibid.

26. Ibid., OAM 77.

27. TNA, WO 95/158, Note recorded as part of OAM 77.

28. TNA, WO 95/158, OAM 77.

29. Ibid.

30. TNA, WO 95/158, OA 910, 23 September 1915.

31. TNA, WO 95/158, OA 924. Letter timed 9.30am on 25 September.

32. Ibid., OAM 77. Haking's report (No 149) is dated 10 October 1915.

33. Ibid.

34. Ibid., GS 193, Haig to GHQ, 4 November 1915. Based on Haking's note to Haig dated 3 November 1915, RHS 283.

35. TNA, WO 95/2189, Part of Col Stewart's comments to Maj. A. F. Becke (Historical Section, British Official History), August 1925.

36. TNA, WO 95/2189, Col Stewart's Diary attached to the comments to Maj. Becke.
37. TNA, WO 95/1217.
38. TNA, CAB 45/120, Forestier-Walker, 24 January 1927.
39. TNA, WO 95/880.
40. TNA, WO 95/158, RHS 283.
41. Ibid., GS 193.
42. *BOH 1915*, II, p.278.
43. Ibid., p.273.
44. The points at issue are covered in TNA, WO 95/158, First Army War Diary, File on Loos. See also Peter Bryant, 'The Recall of Sir John French', *Stand To* 22/23/24, 1988, pp.25–29, 32–38, 22–26.
45. TNA, WO 95/158, OAM 77, GHQ to First Army, 16 October 1915; Haig to GHQ, 21 October 1915.
46. TNA, WO 95/158, OAM 77, 8 November 1915.
47. Ibid., GS 206, Haig to GHQ, 4 November 1915.
48. Ibid., Robertson to GOC First Army, 8 November 1915.
49. Ibid., "Notes on Certain Statements published in Sir John French's Dispatch of 1 November".
50. Ibid., 7 152, French to Haig, 25 September 1915.
51. *BOH 1915*, II, p.275, Footnote 2.
52. TNA, WO 95/158, RHS 283, Haking to Haig, 3 November 1915.
53. Ibid., GS 194/15(a), 21 Sept. 1915. See also Haig's Diary entry for 25 September 1915. TNA, WO 256/5.
54. TNA, WO 95/158, Copy of manuscript letter, Haking to Haig, 3 November 1915.
55. TNA, CAB 45/121, Vaughan, 16 June 1926.
56. TNA, CAB 45/120, Gibson, 10 August 1926.
57. Ibid., Buckley, 1 January 1927.
58. TNA, WO 95/2189, Stewart, 3 August 1925.
59. TNA, CAB 45/120, Forestier-Walker, 24 January 1927.
60. See TNA, CAB 45/120 and /121. Most of the correspondence in those files took place 1926–27.
61. Sheffield and Bourne, *Haig Diaries and Letters*, p.218.
62. Ibid., p.223.
63. Ibid., pp.165–66.
64. Ibid., p.167.
65. Royal Archives, RA/ 976/3, Diary of King George V, 24 October 1915.
66. Quoted in Harold Nicolson, *King George V* 4th imp. (London: Constable and Co Ltd, 1953), p.267. Haig noted in his Diary (14 April 1916): "[The King] told me how he had insisted on the Prime Minister removing Sir John French from command in France as a result of what he had learnt during his visit to the Army in France." (TNA, WO 256/4).
67. Sheffield and Bourne, *Haig Diaries and Letters*, p.167.
68. Ibid., p.155.
69. TNA, WO 95/880, 25 September 1915.

70. Sheffield and Bourne, *Haig Diaries and Letters*, pp.154–55.
71. TNA, WO 95/158, Operations Report, 22–30 September 1915.
72. Ibid., Haking to Advanced First Army, 3 November 1915, para. 4.
73. Ibid., para. 5. It should be noted that two brigades, the 73rd and 62nd of the 21st and 24th Divisions respectively, had been detached to help I and IV Corps.
74. *BOH 1915*, II, p.329. The *BOH* was referring to the 21st Division, but the description applied equally to the 24th Division.
75. Ibid., p.322.
76. Ibid., pp.329, 332.
77. TNA, CAB 45/120, Briggs, 28 August 1926.
78. TNA, WO 95/2189, Stewart to Becke, 3 August 1925.
79. TNA, CAB 45/120, Forestier-Walker, 24 January 1927.
80. Quoted in Bryant, 'Recall of Sir John French', *Stand To 23*, p.32.
81. *BOH 1915*, II p.335.
82. The transfer of the Guards Division from GHQ to the First Army was the subject of further dispute between French and Haig. French's Despatch stated that the Guards were at the disposal of Haig on the morning of 26 September. However, the message confirming the transfer did not reach Haig until 4.02pm.
83. Lt Col C. Headlam, *The Guards Division in the Great War* 2 vols. I, p.52.
84. TNA, WO 95/159, First Army Conference at Hinges, 6 October 1915.
85. TNA, WO 95/159.
86. Royal Archives, Windsor, RA/PS/GV/Q 976/3.
87. Ibid. Stuart-Wortley was removed from his command of 46th Division in controversial circumstances in 1916. See Travers, *Killing Ground*, pp.156–57.
88. *BOH 1915*, II, p.338.
89. TNA, WO 95/880, 25 September 1915.
90. TNA, WO 95/880, Appendix A to XI Corps Order No 2, 24 September 1915. Repeated in WO 95/2128, 21st Division War Diary.
91. TNA, WO 95/2189, Diary of Col C. Stewart sent to Becke, 3 August 1925.
92. TNA, WO 2128, Sender identification, QX102.
93. TNA, CAB 45/120, Gibson to Edmonds, 23 August 1926.
94. TNA, WO 95/2189, Stewart to Becke, 3 August 1925.
95. TNA, CAB 45/121, Ovens, 3 February 1926.
96. TNA, CAB 45/120, Alcock, date unknown.
97. TNA, CAB 45/121, Rainsford, 2 February 1927.
98. TNA, WO 95/1220. See also Rudyard Kipling, *The Irish Guards in the Great War* 2 vols. II, p.6.
99. TNA, WO 95/1220, 2nd Guards Brigade War Diary.
100. F. Petrie, W. Ewart, and Maj. Gen Cecil Lowther *The Scots Guards in the Great War*. p.108.
101. C. H. Dudley-Ward, *The History of the Welsh Guards*, pp.22–23.
102. Rowland Feilding, *War Letters to a Wife* ed. J. Walker. p.19. Quoted in Nick Lloyd, *Loos 1915*. p.181.
103. TNA, WO 95/158, RHS 283, Haking to Haig, 3 November 1915.

104. *BOH 1915*, II p.315.
105. TNA, WO 95/712, Telephone conversations of Lt Gen Sir Henry Rawlinson, 28 September 1915. See also Lloyd, *Loos,* p.206.
106. Royal Archives, RA/PS/GV/ 976/3.
107. TNA, CAB 45/120, Forestier-Walker, 24 January 1927.
108. TNA, WO 95/2189, Stewart, 3 August 1925.
109. TNA, CAB 45/120, Denny, 20 February 1926.
110. TNA, WO 95/158, RHS/259, Haking to Haig, 27 October 1915.
111. Ibid.
112. TNA, WO 95/2189, Stewart, 3 August 1925.
113. TNA, CAB 42/120, Stewart, 30 November 1927.
114. King George V's practice of soliciting reports from various officers is discussed in Ian Beckett, 'King George V and his Generals', in Matthew Hughes and Matthew Seligmann, eds., *Leadership in Conflict 1914–1918*, pp.247–64.
115. Royal Archives, RA/PS/GV/Q 976/3.
116. Simon Robbins has pointed out that Rawlinson, Robertson and Smith-Dorrien had also corresponded with the King. See Simon Robbins, 'The Right Way to Play the Game; the Ethos of the British High Command in the First World War', *IWM* 6, pp.39–50.
117. TNA, CAB 45/120, 3 August 1925.

CHAPTER III

Haking and Trench Warfare – 1916 (–1917)

Following the fighting at Loos, Haking was presented with a quite different challenge – a period of unrelenting trench warfare. XI Corps was, from 30 October 1915, reconstituted with the Guards, the 19th and the 46th Divisions and formed part of the First Army. The Corps HQ was established at Merville and it was allocated a front, previously held by the Indian Corps, that extended some eight miles from Picantin to Quinque Rue thus covering the ground already fought over in 1915 – Neuve Chapelle, Aubers and Festubert. With some adjustments from time to time, XI Corps was destined to serve in that area for most of the war.[1] The purpose of this chapter is to review Haking's actions in late 1915 and through 1916 and examine how he interpreted the role of Corps commander during that period.

From a military point of view, the ground to the front of XI Corps was far from attractive. It was a low-lying area, dotted by small villages and isolated farms, the ruins of which had become German strong-points. Concrete bunkers, built by the Germans as part of their front defence system after the Neuve Chapelle attack, housed machine guns. By mid-1916, the 1,500 yard sector held by the 16th Bavarian Reserve Regiment, for example, contained seventy-five such emplacements.[2] Water was generally only inches below the ground, and, in that part of France, rain invariably meant mud. The landscape was criss-crossed by drainage ditches, which, in peacetime, controlled the amount of surface water. However, a year of shelling and mine explosions had destroyed the drainage system and, in most parts of the front, flooding was a constant threat. Since it was impossible to dig trenches without them becoming water-logged, protective shelter was provided by piling up sandbags into parapets and parados. Unit records and personal memoirs frequently refer to the inhospitable conditions.[3] The historian of the 56th Division, serving with XI Corps in the Laventie-Richebourg sector in late 1916, commented with some feeling: "It was one of those bits of country where trenches are an impossibility – soil and water seem to combine in equal proportion. Naturally, war conditions did not improve the drainage, and at times large tracts of the country were flooded."[4] George Coppard, who served with the Machine Gun Corps, wrote of the Festubert area:

> I always think of my time there as one of the worst of my experiences, not so much because of enemy action but because of the miserable conditions. To start with, the front-line area was flooded and the communication trenches had vanished under water. There was no front-line trench. Instead, earthworks, constructed of sandbags piled on top of the original parapet, had been made. These earthworks or breastworks were like islands jutting out of the water, about twenty yards long, and spaced out every three or four hundred yards . . . Before we took over one of these islands, our gun team was issued with thigh-length rubber boots which were excellent provided the water did not reach over the tops.[5]

Edmund Blunden, in his poem *La Quinque Rue*, described the area as a "cemeterial fen".[6] Only during the dry periods of summer was the situation reasonably tolerable. In winter, it was miserable. The London Rifle Brigade spent Christmas 1916 in the Lestrem area where

> the enemy moved back to higher ground round Aubers in consequence of his trenches being flooded. Digging and consolidation were almost impossible at that time, owing to the very severe frost. The ground in front of the trenches and posts were a sheet of ice, and the ditches and flooded communication trenches were frozen hard.[7]

This difficult terrain gave severe operational problems. Haig noted in his First Army Operations Report of 15 November 1915: "After the heavy rainfall of the past week, the country has become water-logged, and the energy of the troops has been absorbed in coping with the water."[8] When, in March 1916, Haking was asked by his Army Commander, General Sir Charles Monro, to release the 33rd Division for service elsewhere, he pointed out that: "the difficulty of withdrawing a Division is not of a defensive nature, it is entirely a matter of construction work on the line".[9] In the same month, Haking wrote: "The greater part of the front held by my Corps is in a bog, and every shower of rain or period of frost or wet, causes great damage throughout the defences with the result that work is endless and that there is always a greater demand for labour than can be supplied."[10] In November1916, when XI Corps was depleted to two divisions, Haking wrote to his Army Commander: "I wish to make it quite clear that I am not anxious as regards the defence of the line . . . It is the maintenance of the line in this swampy ground which causes the chief difficulty."[11]

It would have been of little comfort to the British troops to know that the front-line German soldier faced the same grim conditions. Hindenburg described the area in his memoirs:

> there were the low-lying meadows of the Lys, several miles broad
> . . . in winter this low-lying area was to a large extent flooded, and
> in spring it was often nothing but a marsh for weeks on end – a
> real horror for the troops holding the trenches at this point . . . we
> could only expect the ground to be dry enough [for an attack] by
> the middle of April.[12]

A note in the First Army war diary for November 1915 commented on the condition of the German trenches: "Trenches, dug-outs, etc. – the first line trenches are fairly well built, but have suffered much through the recent bad weather and a great deal of work has been necessary. Communication trenches have been rendered almost useless." Against these comments, Haig wrote in red pencil: "By methodical use of Artillery, we must add to the enemy's discomfort and lack of sleep".[13] No doubt the German commanders had similar intentions.

Two geographical features extended virtually the length of XI Corps front. One was a large drainage channel, the River Laies.[14] The Laies was some six-feet wide, and, according to the weather, varied between three to six feet in depth. The Laies ran just behind the German lines for most of its length, but crossed into no man's land to the north of the XI Corps sector near Fromelles. It thus acted as an important land-mark and also as a German defensive feature. The second area of geographical significance was Aubers Ridge. Although only a hundred feet above the surrounding countryside, it enabled the Germans, dug in along the ridge, to overlook the British front line and communication trenches. German guns, with the advantage of over a year's registration, were able to shell the British positions with great accuracy. Aubers Ridge was a key feature both for the Germans, who valued its defensive significance, and the British, who sought its capture as a route to the vital German communication system around Lille.

The only significant high ground occupied by XI Corps during its time on the Western Front was in the area of Givenchy. It was noted by Lieutenant Colonel Gardner in a letter to the compiler of the British Official History:

> the Fromelles-Aubers Ridge terminated in a knoll on the southern
> and western slopes of which lay the scattered and almost invisible

ruins of the village of Givenchy, a position of great strategic importance overlooking the flats which stretch northwards from Bethune to the Lys.[15]

A note in the First Army war diary details the German troops facing XI Corps in March 1916.[16] The 6th Bavarian Reserve Division, made up of the 20th, 21st, 16th, and 17th Bavarian Reserve Regiments – some 12,000 men – held the line from Bois Grenier to Fauquissart. The line Fauquissart-Auchy was held by the German VII Corps with the 13th Division (9,000 men) positioned Fauquissart-Richebourg l'Avoue; the 2nd Guards Reserve Division (6,000 men) held the line Richebourg-Festubert; and the 14th Division (7,000 men) positioned Festubert-Auchy. While German divisions were transferred to other parts of the front from time to time, it was common practice for divisions to remain in the same sector for long periods. The 6th Bavarian Reserve Division, for example, maintained its position in the Fauquissart sector for some eighteen months. This enabled the Germans to become extremely familiar with the ground facing them – unlike many of the British divisions assigned to XI Corps whose tenure was often of short-term duration. In March 1916, XI Corps was made up of about 120,000 men,[17] which gave them a significant numerical superiority, but the German forces were well dug-in, had strong defensive systems and had the advantage of the high ground. The trench system facing XI Corps had been in German hands since autumn 1914 and was to remain so for the next four years.

* * * *

On 28 October 1915, two days before Haking had set up his new Headquarters at Merville, French, the then Commander in Chief of the BEF, had circulated to his Army Commanders a paper outlining the general policy to be followed during the winter months of 1915–16.[18] The document covered seven pages of foolscap and contained a number of key policy statements. The main objective, during the winter period when major offensive operations could not take place, was to "wear out and exhaust the enemy's troops, to foster and enhance the offensive spirit of our own troops, and to encourage them to feel superior to the enemy in every respect . . . Pressure on the enemy should be relentless . . .". This policy should be carried out by "the constant harassing of the enemy by minor enterprises", which could include local attacks and the use of smoke, gas, mining and bombing from the air. The use of artillery was emphasized both to support the minor operations and to check the offensive actions of the enemy. There should be coordination between the artillery and other formations and the "development of telephonic communications" was regarded of importance. The defensive system should be maintained "to deal effectively with any attack". Emphasis was placed on the training of all ranks, particularly the new formations, "in trench warfare and for offensive operations on a large scale". Finally, "in order to preserve the health of the troops, to provide as large reserves as possible and to facilitate training", the number of men in the trenches should be reduced "to what was absolutely necessary for the security of the front".

During November, Haig, the commander of the First Army, took up French's policy and elaborated it. In his *Instructions for Divisional Training*,[19] Haig wrote:

> Although we are disposing our forces with a view to holding our present positions for the time being, our action on all positions of the front must be imbued with the offensive and not the defensive spirit. Commanders must consider all the time what can be done to effect this. Small offensive operations, carefully planned, should be carried out with determination . . . Patrolling and sniping should be active and no battalion or company commander should be content unless he has absolutely the upper hand of the hostile troops in front of him.[20]

In these same instructions, Haig insisted that: "Special attention should be paid to the execution of the attack and the development of the offensive spirit". On 25 November, Haig again referred his Corps Commanders to French's policy document, this time in connection with artillery bombardments, which should be carried out "with a view to harassing the enemy and causing him losses".[21]

The agenda for the winter months had therefore been set by French and Haig and, as far as Haking was concerned, it was an agenda that suited his aggressive inclinations admirably. On 4 November, Haking published his XI Corps policy document, *Winter Campaign of 1915–16*.[22] This paper began by commending the "fine offensive spirit apparent in all units . . . every effort should be made from the highest to the lowest to foster and increase this spirit". At the same time, Haking recognized "a natural desire of the troops to have a quiet time in the trenches" and this was to be "discouraged in every possible way". An important method of fostering an offensive attitude among the troops was to "maintain the initiative throughout – whenever the enemy attempts the initiative, we must immediately reduce him to silence by a great outburst of fire far superior to anything he has produced".

The offensive action required by Haking was to take the form of small, local attacks, particularly over the ground towards Aubers Ridge; rifle and machine-gun fire, especially at night, against enemy positions; patrolling and reconnaissance to gain mastery in no man's land; and an emphasis on improving the co-ordination between the infantry and the artillery. Haking was therefore faithfully following the lead of his two immediate superiors and the XI Corps *Winter Campaign* document reiterated the policies set out by French and Haig.

As Appendix II shows, a common vocabulary had evolved in the BEF that was adopted within the senior command structure and repeated down the line by battalion and company officers. It was a vocabulary made up of key words and phrases that expressed and reinforced the prevailing mind-set and policies of the BEF. For example, the words "offensive spirit", "moral superiority", "wearing out" and "harassing" the enemy, avoiding "quiet times" in the trenches, etc were used with great regularity. Their constant use served as a form of bonding and as evidence of a unity of purpose. It is also possible that they might have served, on occasions, to avoid further thought on behalf of the user.

Certainly, Haking would have identified himself with this emphasis on constant aggression and the offensive spirit. Indeed, in his book, *Company Training*, published in 1913, Haking had advocated at length the virtues of the attack "on every possible occasion and without hesitation", and of the offensive spirit – "the only weapon which can possibly lead us to success is the spirit of the offensive".[23] Haking, therefore needed little prompting as regards the role of XI Corps and the instructions of his superiors were faithfully followed. The XI Corps operations report for 25 December, for example, noted:

> Bursts of rifle fire and machine gun fire were directed from time to time during the night on the enemy's trenches and on gaps in his wire. Two German patrols and two working parties were broken up . . . 19 Division patrols found the German trenches strongly held.[24]

In addition, the Artillery of both 19th Division and the Guards Division shelled a series of targets behind the German lines. Haking was not a man for Christmas Day fraternization.

* * * *

Haig became Commander in Chief of the BEF on 19 December 1915 and, on 14 January 1916, he set out his views as to the future conduct of the war:

> There is no doubt in my mind that the war must be won by the Forces of the British Empire. At the present time I think our

actions should take the form of (1) 'Winter Sports' or raids continued into spring , i.e. capturing lengths of enemy trenches at favourable points. (2) Wearing out fight similar to (1), but on a larger scale at many points along the whole Front. Will last about three weeks to draw in the enemy's reserves. (3) Decisive attacks on several points, object to break through.[25]

In particular, Haig confirmed his support of "minor enterprises" and in a letter to the First Army dated 27 January, he referred to some recent local raids: "the success achieved reflects credit on all concerned. The effect of such enterprises lowers the enemy's moral and raises the moral not only of the troops engaged in the particular operation, but also of the Division and the Corps."[26] Rawlinson, standing in for Monro as Commander of the First Army,[27] added his voice in support of the prevailing policy:

the various raids which have taken place and which are in prospect are, I am quite certain, a very good thing. It is most desirable to give every Division in the line some objective against which it can carry out an offensive raid . . . Those we have carried out have been excellent and the more we do the better.[28]

When Haking held a XI Corps Conference on 13 January1916, he presented a most optimistic picture of recent events. He compared the Corps' offensive operations with the "supine attitude" adopted by the enemy: "The importance of this comparison cannot be exaggerated, and all ranks are to be instructed as to what it means – our own moral[e] improved and that of the enemy lowered." Haking then went on:

Our patrols go out as they please and the enemy's rarely come out. We break down the enemy's defences and he makes little attempt to do the same to ours. If he does, we swamp him with our fire. Having broken his defences, we prevent him from repairing them; we enter his trenches and he never attempts to come into ours.

In conclusion, Haking asked his Division Commanders

to consider schemes for capturing and holding short lines of the enemy's trenches . . . By the delivery of such assaults and the capture of short lengths of the enemy's trench we shall be carrying out progressively the scheme of offensive operations which was initiated when the Corps first took over the line.[29]

It was in this spirit that a number of minor enterprises were planned to take place along the First Army front during the spring of 1916. As ever, Haking was keen for XI Corps to make a significant contribution. In a note to Monro dated 17 March, Haking made reference to the First Army Conference of 29 February, when Corps Commanders were encouraged to continue their offensive operations. At this point, XI Corps was made up of 19th, 33rd, 35th, and 38th Divisions and Haking was advising his Army Commander of a series of major attacks, involving all his divisions, that he had planned for 21 March. Haking was concerned about the amount of ammunition that would be made available to him to support these attacks and argued that all his divisions, except the 33rd, "are new formations and have never been into German trenches. I have saved up ammunition for weeks for this operation . . . and I am most anxious to improve the fighting spirit of these new Divisions and therefore I hope that the necessary ammunition will be forthcoming."[30] XI Corps did make a number of raids in March 1916, but on a scale much smaller than Haking's original plan, presumably because the preparations for the Somme offensive had prevented Monro from providing the additional ammunition required by Haking.

It was Haking's continuing aim to "improve the fighting spirit" of his divisions and he took the opportunity to do so on every possible occasion. At the XI Corps Conference of 13 February 1916, Haking addressed his Divisional Commanders using the, by now, well-used phrases: "You must use every endeavour to inculcate the offensive spirit in all subordinate commanders, down to Company and platoon leaders . . . killing Germans, lowering the enemy's moral[e] and raising that of our troops is the object to keep in view." Haking emphasized the necessity for all divisions to carry out minor enterprises:

> If activity is confined to one locality only, the enemy's reserves are drawn to this place and further small enterprises become difficult or impossible. If, on the other hand, activity is general along the line, the enemy is prevented from concentrating his reserves and the arrangement of further raids is facilitated.[31]

Haking's efforts to promote and execute an aggressive policy seem to have been appreciated. A handwritten note on the GHQ copy of the XI Corps Conference minutes of 13 February read: "The moral[e] of the [XI] Corps seems good. Gen. R. Haking continuously inculcates his

policy of cumulative aggression."[32] Similarly, at a First Army
Conference on 18 April, "the GOC said that he wished to say how
pleased he had been with the way in which minor raids into enemy
trenches had been carried out".[33]

However, the pressure from both GHQ and Army levels for
continued aggression was persistent. Monro, at his Conference on 29
February, raised the subject of minor enterprises:

> Stress was laid on the value of minor enterprises. Ruses and
> schemes by infantry should always be combined with artillery
> bombardment in order to induce the enemy to man his parapets
> and thus inflict loss on him by shell-fire. All minor enterprises of
> the kind referred to were useful not only in bringing infantry and
> artillery into closer touch, but also in encouraging the offensive
> spirit and initiative in all ranks. The GOC hoped that Corps
> Commanders would continue and even increase their efforts to
> arrange for the carrying out of such enterprises.[34]

* * * *

Haig had been pressed by both Joffre and Castelnau on several
occasions to take over the front held by the French Tenth Army, positioned between the British First and Third Armies. Haig had resisted
these proposals on the grounds that the BEF would be stretched too
thinly. However, on 21 February 1916, the Germans opened their
major offensive at Verdun. The French were now in desperate need of
troops to reinforce the Verdun sector and Haig, on 27 February, telephoned Joffre to say that arrangements would be made to relieve the
French Tenth Army. Consequently, the British Third Army lengthened
its line north to meet the right of the First Army, which was itself
extended south. A new Fourth Army, commanded by Rawlinson, was
positioned on the right of the Third Army. The British line, therefore,
by early March, was continuous from the Yser to the Somme – a total
of some eighty miles. The process of redistribution involved the transfer
of fifteen divisions. The First Army was now made up of I, III, IV, and
XI Corps. XI Corps, in lengthening its front to Auchy, received 33rd
Division from I Corps.[35]

A second consequence of the Verdun offensive was the firming up of
the plans for the battle of the Somme and for the supporting operations.
The tone and content of communications from GHQ and from First
Army now changed their character. It was no longer "Winter Sports".
Discussions and orders took on a new urgency. At the First Army
Conference on 24 March, Monro relayed to his Corps Commanders the
gist of a recent conversation with the Chief of the General Staff: "Sir
Douglas Haig wishes a general activity all along our front in reference

to entrenchments, to push forward saps, to join them up, to construct assembly and jumping off places and generally to convey to the enemy the impression all along the line occupied by the British that we intend a considerable offensive action." Monro ordered all the Corps Commanders to begin these activities immediately: "We want to hold over the enemy a menace of possible offensive action all along our part of the line by all artifices we possess." These "artifices" were to include night patrols, searching for wire, aerial reconnaissance, the construction of bogus observation stations, the construction of assembly trenches, the assembly of saps closer to the German lines, and obvious work to indicate the opening of gaps in the wire: "In short, all those preparations which will keep the Germans under constant expectation of an attack by us."[36]

Over the following weeks, a stream of communications from GHQ reinforced the message that all Armies were to be ready to carry out significant actions at short notice. On 3 April, Army Commanders were warned that they must be ready to mount an attack on a considerable scale on their fronts and they must have their schemes prepared for this purpose.[37] Similarly, on 22 May, a GHQ note to Army Commanders required that plans were to be prepared "with a view to engaging the enemy along the whole front during the period of offensive operations".[38] Five days later, a further note from GHQ ordered Army Commanders to submit their plans and schemes

> as early as possible . . . the Commander in Chief directed that these preparations should be carried out with all speed . . . raids by night of a strength of a Company and upwards on an extensive scale into the enemy's front system of defences. These to be prepared by intense artillery and trench mortar bombardment.[39]

While the main interest of the Army and Corps Commanders was the forthcoming Somme offensive, day to day operations continued, even though on a modified scale. The availability of ammunition, for example, was limited. At a XI Corps Conference on 19 March, Haking announced:

> The policy of the Corps is therefore to continue the offensive projects we have prepared, even if we have to carry them out on a smaller scale owing to the limited gun ammunition available. We must get at least small parties of one or more platoons into the German trenches opposite the front of each Division in the line. This is absolutely essential if we are to maintain the offensive spirit that we have created and nourished during the last few months in the Corps.

Haking concluded:

> We must make our men realize that they have the power of getting
> into the enemy's trenches and driving him out; nothing short of
> that will render us fit for greater operations later on, when we
> shall end the war with one or two great battles.[40]

It should also be noted that the British preparations for the Somme
did not prevent the Germans from carrying out their own minor enterprises. The First Army war diary for May 1916 reported a series of
German raids along the length of its front. I Corps suffered attacks on
11, 14, 20 and 27 May. On the XI Corps front, Haking reported that
a party of Germans had bombed and entered the trenches of 39th
Division on 29 May. Two British soldiers had been killed and a number
of troops had abandoned their rifles. Thirty-ninth Division had also
been raided on the Festubert sector on 26 May. On 30 May, a German
attack on the trenches near Neuve Chapelle provoked a British counter-
attack which resulted in 151 casualties. On occasions, enemy attacks
were large scale and on 11 May, I Corps trenches near the
Hohenzollern Redoubt were assaulted by an estimated German force of
two battalions resulting in 552 British casualties. A German raid in the
Vimy area on 21 May prompted a counter-attack by the British 99 and
142 Brigades which led to 695 casualties.

Despite these serious diversions, the work to deceive the Germans as
to the location of the main offensive went ahead. On 23 May Monro
asked his Corps Commanders for a progress report. Haking was able to
say that: "On the XI Corps front they had already doubled the number
of gun emplacements that were required, and also [reconstructed] all
last year's assembly trenches." Haking added that he did not consider
the construction of additional trenches would give any further advantage. Haking was supported in this by General Kavanagh (Cavalry
Corps) who thought that if assembly trenches were built too early then
the enemy would know that they were only a ruse. However, Monro
disagreed and both Haking and Kavanagh were instructed to continue
building dummy trenches.[41]

The following day, as though to redeem himself, Haking wrote to
Monro:

> As regards dummy trenches for joining up, there are already a
> large number in rear of our lines from Givenchy to Picantin and
> these are being cleared up and new sandbags placed on top so that
> they will show up to hostile aeroplane observation. We are also
> making a few more, and some dummy batteries. We are going to

put guns into the dummy batteries and fire from them, otherwise they do not seem much use.

Haking also added that night patrolling in the Corps was excellent – "better even than it was in my old Division" – that thirty raids had been carried out over the past six months; that wire-cutting had taken place using bangalore torpedoes and trench mortars; and that sapping work was underway.[42]

During the lead-up to the Somme, Army and Corps Commanders were often involved in time-consuming projects that eventually came to nothing. A prime example of this began when Kiggell, on behalf of Haig, wrote to Army Commanders on 18 May:

> It is considered that useful results may be obtained, in the direction of mystifying the enemy and disorganising his plans, by arranging for the simultaneous delivery of several raids, accompanied by concentrated bombardments. Armies will accordingly make arrangements to deliver on the night of June 3/4 as many organised raids along their front as their resources and time for preparation permit.[43]

Kiggell added that the intention to carry out these raids should be kept as secret as possible: "As a rule, there should be no need to make it known, even to Divisional Commanders, that there will be several simultaneous raids; nor should the exact date and hour of each raid be communicated prematurely to anyone to whom the knowledge is not really necessary." Army Commanders were asked to report back to GHQ by 27 May outlining their plans for 3/4 June.

The First Army copy of this "Very Secret" communication has pencilled on it, "Pressing", which indeed it was, since only nine days had been allowed to carry out the necessary planning. Nevertheless, Monro was able to respond on 26 May giving the locations selected for twelve raids and identifying which Divisions were to carry them out. Haking had clearly entered into the spirit of this mysterious project and, of the twelve projected First Army raids, XI Corps were to carry out eight – two each for 33rd, 35th, 38th, and 39th Divisions. Each raid was to involve two companies and the preferred timing was to be between 9.00 and 9.15pm. The highly confidential nature of the raids also appealed to Haking who took the opportunity to elaborate on Kiggell's wish for secrecy and introduce an even greater element of mystery. On 21 May Haking sent a handwritten note to each Divisional Commander:

The situation as to the enemy in front of XI Corps is not quite clear, especially as to his Reserves; that is to say, whether he has strong reserves of men and guns in rear, or whether they have been moved elsewhere . . . The result of this operation will be disclosed by secret agents specially prepared, by aeroplane observation, and by the subsequent action of the enemy.[44]

The Divisional Commanders were to prepare not one, but two raids "so that if at the last moment one raid fails, the other can go in at once". Haking, now fully immersed in the project, stressed that the raids must take place on the night of 3/4 June because "that is the date the Corps Commander has arranged for his information, and he cannot change it".

The Divisional Commanders were charged with maintaining absolute secrecy: "If the Corps Commander's intentions get out, the main object of the raid may be spoilt." Haking identified several "fruitful sources of leakage" and these included the CRA of the Division who might discuss the supply of ammunition with other artillery commanders; administrative staff such as those involved with ordnance supply "who do not appear to recognise any great responsibility as regards secrecy"; and conversations on the telephone, picked up by other signallers or the enemy. In a second handwritten note dated 21 May, this time addressed to Monro, Haking elaborated on his "sources of leakage":

I shall tell them [XI Corps Divisional Commanders] that we have had frequent examples of our plans being conveyed to the enemy owing to injudicious conversations on the telephone amongst officers and that one of the chief dangers is for another Division to know that a raid is going to take place. The officers of the other Division do not feel the same responsibility about other people's operations and are more likely to talk about them than they are of their own schemes.[45]

Haking was thoroughly caught up in the spirit of these arrangements and his efforts at subterfuge gathered pace. He directed his Divisional Commanders to

treat the operation in your orders to subordinates as an ordinary raid, which you are particularly anxious to be a success, because you have been specially ordered to carry it out by the Corps Commander. You will use every means in your power and every misleading device, to prevent any idea getting about that anything of extra importance is taking place . . . no-one in the Corps knows of these orders to you except the Corps Commander and the Brig Gen Gen Staff . . . the Corps Commander will inform divisional commanders on your flanks that owing to the recent activity of the enemy's artillery along our front . . . he intends to give the enemy a lesson on 3 June along the whole front of the Corps, and this will be sufficient reason for them about the raid you are carrying out.

The Divisional Commanders were to forward their schemes by 10.0am on 25 May and Haking ended his handwritten note with a touch of tidy bureaucracy: "Please acknowledge these instructions on the attached form."[46]

Having devised the above elaborate subterfuges, and having set the Divisional Commanders and their subordinates considerable extra work, Haking received a message from Monro on 29 May calling off the whole enterprise: "With reference to the Secret Letter from G.H.Q, the Commander in Chief has decided that, in view of the proximity of offensive operations . . . the simultaneous raids which were to have been carried out on the night of 3/4 June are not to take place."[47] Haking's frustration and disappointment can only be imagined, though it is likely that the news was received in the Divisions with considerable relief.

* * * *

The Battle of the Somme, led by Rawlinson's Fourth Army, was to take place some thirty miles south of the First Army positions. Haig wrote to Monro on 27 May instructing him to make preparations for deceiving the Germans as to the true place and timing of the main attack.[48] On 1 June Monro wrote to his Corps Commanders setting out the role of First Army in relation to the main offensive: "When the offensive takes place, the role of the First Army will be to deceive the enemy as to the real point of the attack, to wear him out and to reduce his fighting efficiency, both during the three days prior to the assault and during the bombardment operations."[49] Haking, in turn, communicated with XI Corps: "All we know is that a great offensive movement is being made or is to be made somewhere. That is enough for us. The role of XI Corps for the time being is a holding attack."[50]

Characteristically, Haking was not slow in putting forward his proposals to Monro. On 5 June he wrote: "I forward herewith a programme of the operations I am prepared to carry out from any date desired after 7 June, along XI Corps front." Haking added that numerous saps had been pushed into no man's land and old assembly trenches had been restored to give the Germans the impression that an offensive was to take place over the 1915 battlefields. He continued:

"As regards actual raids into the enemy's trenches, I have already eight prepared, which I shall carry out at the rate of about one a week, or perhaps two a fortnight."[51]

The "programme" referred to was a series of raids, involving gas, wire-cutting bombardments and smoke, which would begin on 26 June, five days before the start of the Somme battle (the original date for the Somme offensive was 28 June), and continue each day until 10 July.[52] At a meeting of XI Corps Divisional Commanders on 14 June, Haking confirmed the dates of the raids and stressed the importance of "the great battle which is to be fought to win the war . . . I would ask you to impress upon all ranks in your Divisions the immense importance of this attack and how we must all strain every nerve to ensure success and help our comrades who are bearing the brunt of the fighting elsewhere."[53] Haking's enthusiastic preparations were noted by Monro who commended XI Corps on two separate occasions. On 8 June

> the GOC First Army called attention to the fact that in XI Corps a model of the German trenches on a portion of the Corps' front had been laid out on a reduced scale in the vicinity of each Divisional HQ. The model was of considerable use in arranging raids or any other operation as it was possible to get the officers concerned to come to the Division HQ and show them exactly what had to be done.[54]

Similarly, on 22 June:

> The GOC referred to a scheme of operations which had been prepared by XI Corps for an attack on a wide front. All Divisions and Corps should be prepared with a scheme for an attack straight to their fronts with a view to holding the enemy in case it became necessary to make such an attack in order to assist in the main operations.[55]

A further general commendation was received from GHQ on 2 July,[56] the second day of the Somme offensive:

> The numerous successful raids carried out along our front during the last few days have undoubtedly been of considerable assistance to the main operations besides having added appreciably to the enemy's casualties. The Commander in Chief desires that his appreciation of the good work done may be conveyed to all who have planned and carried out the raids.

In all, thirty-two raids were carried out on the First Army front during the three week period 23 June-14 July and, of these, fourteen were raids by units of XI Corps. Despite the various accolades, it was clear that not all the raids could be described as successful. XI Corps had their share of failures. On 19/20 June, two officers and thirty other ranks of 2/5th Glosters raided the enemy lines with the aim of making identifications. The *Regimental History* of the Gloucestershire Regiment records: "After the raiding party had gone over the top, it was held up by the wire which was found to have been insufficiently cut. The party was thus exposed to a ruthless machine gun fire from the enemy and was eventually compelled to return to its own trenches after having suffered heavy casualties."[57]

On 13 June, a party from A Company, 2/4th Royal Berkshires, was detailed to raid an enemy trench in the Ferme du Bois sector. A practice raid had been carried out during the afternoon of 13 June and the men were equipped with bombs, battle clippers, butchers' cleavers and electric torches. There was a pre-raid bombardment of artillery and trench mortars and at 11.15pm the raid began. It was found, however, that the enemy wire had not been cut and although a small group entered the German lines, the raid was aborted. There were thirty-eight casualties – over a third of the total raiding party.[58]

The least successful of the XI Corps raids during the period around 1 July, in terms of casualties and failure to achieve its objectives, was that carried out by 12th and 13th Battalions, Royal Sussex Regiment of 116 Brigade, part of 39th Division. This raid took place on the night of 30 June with the aim of capturing and holding the German trenches on the Boar's Head. The raid was preceded by a three-hour artillery bombardment and an extensive use of smoke, but the German wire remained intact in many places and the enemy machine guns were not put out of action. The 116 Brigade war diary noted that:

> the enemy was undoubtedly well prepared for the attack. During the night he appeared to have brought up fresh troops and had a large number of MGs in action . . . Both battalions lost heavily during the advance to the enemy front line and also between front line and support line from machine gun fire . . . Large numbers of dead were seen lying in the trenches and the first troops to enter engaged in hand to hand fighting . . . [59]

The 13th Battalion entered the enemy trenches and support lines for a short time, but were then forced to withdraw. The 12th Battalion was held up by uncut wire, but managed to gain a foothold in the first-line trenches before having to retire. As the Brigade war diary summarized:

"The objective was gained, but could not be held and our troops had to be withdrawn to their original front line." The casualties in both battalions amounted to some 850.

Despite this obvious failure, Haking, in his report on the attack, stated that: "the attack must have impressed the enemy as regards our strength in this part of the line and our offensive power, and will make him hesitate to withdraw reserves, which is the objective of the instructions I have received". Haking went on to say that the Division had only been in France for three months and "until recently, has not shown much offensive spirit. I consider that this operation has greatly improved the fighting value of the Division and has produced the opposite effect on the enemy".[60] These self-congratulatory sentiments were to be repeated by Haking in connection with an even greater failure which took place some two weeks later – the attack at Fromelles on 19/20 July. Fromelles will be dealt with at length in the next chapter.

* * * *

During the first week of August 1916, it was confirmed that Monro, the First Army Commander, was to become Commander in Chief, India. It was Monro himself who recommended Haking as his successor.[61] However, Haig's appointment of Haking as First Army Commander resulted in a heated correspondence with Robertson, the CIGS. Both Robertson and the War Committee were opposed to Haking becoming an Army Commander. In a caustic letter to Haig dated 10 August, Robertson wrote:

> I did not agree with your selection . . . Even if I had agreed I doubt if either the [Secretary of State] or the PM would have approved judging from what they said when the matter was discussed at the War Committee today . . . I am influenced by nothing except the necessity to select the best man, and I do not consider Haking is the best.[62]

Haig then claimed that he had always intended Haking's appointment to be temporary until a more acceptable candidate became available. Eventually, Lieutenant General Sir Henry Horne, who had been in command of XV Corps on the Somme, was appointed GOC First Army on 1 October 1916. The exact reason why Haking was turned down by the War Committee for this position is not recorded, but it can be assumed that, in London, Haking's passion for the offensive was also linked with a reputation as a profligate user of manpower. However, it was characteristic of Haking that, when Horne took over command of the First Army, he resumed his role with XI Corps without demur.

Haking was, therefore, First Army Commander from 7 August until 30 September – a period of only fifty-four days and for most of that time he was well aware that his tenure of office was to be short-lived. Nevertheless, he took up his new duties with typical enthusiasm. One week before his appointment, Haking had received a note from First Army GHQ: "The enemy has shown a considerable amount of activity all along our front during the past few days. The Army Commander hopes that you will continue your measures of annoyance and carry out as many raids as you can."[63] Haking no doubt had this message in mind when he addressed his first Army Conference at Choques on 15 August. Referring to a recent conversation with Haig, Haking informed his Corps Commanders that the Commander in Chief

> is pressing the attack on the Somme and he does not want any more Troops brought against our comrades there, if we can possibly prevent it by our actions elsewhere. At the present moment, therefore, the policy of the First Army is to hold the enemy to his ground in front of us . . . we can only do this effectively by attacking, and, therefore, the Commander in Chief wishes us to be prepared, along all parts of our front, to attack and capture part of the enemy's system of trenches.[64]

Haking then outlined three types of operation that might be required of the First Army:

> I will tell you the type of order one might receive, so that you will all be able to work on sound lines and be ready to execute it at short notice. (a) . . . you are required to carry out a number of attacks at carefully selected spots along the whole front of the First Army . . . (b) . . . you are required to carry out an attack by at least one Division to compel the enemy to recall troops and prevent him from sending away any more . . . (c) The enemy's line has been broken on the Somme, and you are required to attack and carry the enemy's line in front of you.

The style of Haking's address to his Corps Commanders is revealing. It covers nine pages of foolscap paper and gives a far-reaching summary of the general war situation; the variety of attacks that the First Army might undertake; the importance of raids and how they might be carried out; work on defences and the use of artillery. It was presented in the form of a lecture and includes a number of the much-repeated phrases listed in Appendix II:

. . . we must at all costs do our utmost to wear down the enemy, reduce his moral[e] and at the same time improve the moral[e] of our own troops . . . Patrolling engenders an offensive spirit amongst all ranks and it gives us possession of the ground between our trenches and the enemy's, quite wrongly called no man's land, but which ought to be called British land. It keeps the enemy constantly alert and nervous, and it wears out his men, which has a good moral[e] effect on our troops.

It was a tour de force of well-meaning clichés and was essentially a monologue delivered by an ex-Staff College professor who was now clearly relishing the power and importance of his new, if temporary, role.

Following the Conference at Choques, the Corps Commanders began work on the various scenarios presented to them by Haking and, on 2 September, Haking was able to write to Haig: "I have caused Schemes for attacks to be prepared on the IV, I, and XI Corps fronts. These complete the offensive operations which the First Army will carry out whenever required."[65] A summary sheet attached to this letter listed the proposed places of attack: Vimy Ridge (9th Division); Auchy (32nd Division); North of Fauquissart (61st Division); and Givenchy (30th Division). Interestingly, the proposed attack by the 61st Division was towards the Sugar Loaf salient and Fromelles – exactly the same ground fought over on 19/20 July by the same Division.

GHQ, however, was not entirely satisfied with the scope of the attacks being prepared by the First Army and Haking announced at his Army Conference on 9 September:

In addition, the Commander in Chief has two schemes of attack for the First Army which must be prepared for at once. (1) An attack by three Divisions, with possibly a fourth, with the object of capturing and holding the whole of the Vimy Ridge, and its Eastern slopes . . . on the assumption that the main operations on the Somme have been successful . . . (2) An attack by four Divisions or more with a view to gaining the Eastern slopes of Vimy Ridge, even if the attack on the Somme is unsuccessful.[66]

IV and XVII Corps were ordered to prepare for these attacks and, on a hand-written sheet headed, "Notes given to General officers Cmdg IV and XVII Corps, personally", Haking made the following points: "No previous experience of a big attack; comments of encouragement necessary; an absolute determination to overcome all difficulties; the most infinite care in all arrangements for the attack . . .". Haking also expressed his opinion that: "it is better for the actual fighting commander to use his own methods which he believes in rather than to force methods upon him which he does not believe. He must go into battle feeling that he is carrying out his own schemes and not feeling that he would do it quite differently if he had his own way." Having written that, Haking nevertheless went on to give his view on the issue of a three brigade attack compared with a two brigade attack with one brigade in reserve: "Personally I am strongly in favour of an attack by three brigades . . . It causes less confusion in the end, makes every Brigadier work up to the final objective without waiting for reinforcements which may not be available, and gives a definite command over each small portion of the battlefield."[67] A week later, Haking received a note from Kiggell which had the effect of complicating the preparations for the proposed attacks. Two strong divisions were to be transferred from the First Army for action on the Somme, and replaced by a Division (24th) weakened by its actions there. Haking was told: "The First Army will not carry out any redistribution of troops for the present for the purpose of preparing the offensive against the Vimy Ridge. Such moves of troops are of secondary importance as compared with the necessity for maintaining the battle on the Somme."[68] During the weeks of September, the Corps of the First Army were further reduced in size as divisions were placed in reserve and, by the end of the month, the two Corps charged with the carrying out the attacks in the Vimy area were made up of two divisions and one division respectively.[69] The Somme had drawn in all available troops and the activities of Haking's First Army were therefore confined, once more, to small-scale attacks and trench raids.

Sir Henry Horne's first Army Conference took place on 5 October 1916: "He did not propose to make any [policy] alterations, which was an offensive policy and was to be continued."[70] However, a significant change of attitude in relation to the policy on large scale raids was becoming apparent. Horne had referred during his 5 October meeting

> to the fact that many of our raids failed to meet their primary object, that is of obtaining identifications, and asked, as a matter of curiosity, how Corps Commanders accounted for that fact. General Haking said everything possible was done in the way of impressing on all concerned the necessity for getting identifications – the fact was that men got excited and forgot about it.

Towards the end of October, Horne again raised the subject of raids and commented that conditions had changed since the First Army raiding policy of May 1916 had been introduced:

Raids on a large scale no longer serve to hold the enemy's troops, the favourable points had been raided again and again and the enemy knows them. They are wearying to the Divisions and expensive in officers, and carried out to orders, as at present, they are extremely unpopular. In short, they do not carry much weight. On the other hand, an active offensive is necessary in order to keep up the spirit of initiative, give the Germans no rest, to obtain identifications, and to maintain the position of 'top dog'. Under the circumstances, therefore, it seems preferable at present to discontinue the larger raids, but keep to keep up a constant aggressive action by means of strong patrols and unceasing mortar activity.[71]

Horne then asked his Corps Commanders: "Were the troops getting stale and the raids perfunctory? Has the time arrived to alter the system or to slacken off raids?" The Commanders of I Corps and the Canadian Corps, both considered that large, organized raids were now not "a good thing" and that strong fighting patrols "of a dozen men and a Lewis gun", initiated at battalion level, would be more productive. It is not difficult to predict Haking's feelings as he listened to this discussion, and he took the opportunity to give his view in no uncertain terms: "The GOC XI Corps was of the opinion that the number of raids ought to be increased. He deprecated any reduction in their number. He thought our raiding parties were too small, and that they stayed too short a time in the enemy's trenches."

Faced with these conflicting views, Horne came up with a compromise policy:

> It was a very difficult question to deal with . . . The policy must remain that the actual carrying out of the raids be left to Corps Commanders . . . Raids in strength should not be discontinued altogether . . . on the other hand, strong fighting patrols should be employed to a great extent to enter the enemy's trenches whenever possible . . . If patrols did not succeed in securing identifications then we would have to send in a raid on a larger scale to fight them.

Each of the Corps Commanders must have thought that their view had prevailed and that they were free to carry out raids as they wished. Certainly, Haking continued to encourage his divisions to be aggressive, though generally in terms of limited raids and patrols. Writing about the period October-December 1916, the historian of the 56th Division noted that: "The policy of the XI Corps (Gen Haking) was to annoy the enemy on all occasions and keep him always uneasy. The month of December was therefore devoted to most active patrolling, and the enemy lines were entered again and again."[72]

By mid-November 1916, the Army Commanders, directed by GHQ, were considering their policies for the coming winter and the following spring. The Fourth and Fifth Armies on the Somme were to continue a limited offensive, as far as the weather allowed. Meanwhile, the policy of the First Army was: "(a) To harass the enemy. (b) To prepare for the Spring Offensive. (c) To be ready for the unforeseen."[73] This policy would be carried out by active patrolling and raids, by concentrated bombardments, especially against trench mortars and gas attacks, and by improving defences and preparing for offensive operations against Vimy Ridge and Aubers Ridge. A comparison of the 1916–17 winter policy with that of 1915–16 shows that little had changed. In pursuing the policy of attrition and limited offensive, the First Army had in 1916 suffered some 50,000 casualties. The number of casualties in XI Corps amounted to 22,000.[74]

* * * *

While thoughts of the offensive and trench raids were generally uppermost in the minds of the First Army senior officers, the subject of defence was not neglected. However, given the prevailing aggressive mindset, "the defensive" was considered as something to be tolerated rather than glorified. The 1914 *Field Service Regulations* stated that: "The defensive implies loss of initiative, at least for the time being, and is usually the consequence of inferiority of some description."[75] Trench warfare was described as: "only one phase of operations" before an advance could take place.[76] Trenches themselves were considered as temporary shelters where there was "an insidious tendency to lapse into a passive or lethargic attitude".[77] French had expressed the view that: "Nothing would be more pernicious and render ultimate victory more difficult than . . . a purely passive defence frame of mind."[78] Indicatively, too, the opening words of a 1918 pamphlet devoted to *The Defence* stated: "Victory can only be achieved as a result of offensive action."[79]

Nevertheless, it was clear that considerable attention needed to be given to matters of defence. In his policy statement of October 1915, French had stressed: "the importance of constructing and keeping in repair adequate defences so that we may, without anxiety, be fully prepared to deal effectively with any attack that the enemy may be capable of making". French had also emphasized: "the importance of constant revision of schemes of defence, and [he] wished Army Commanders to satisfy themselves that all ranks know how to act in case of an attack on any part of their front".[80]

The particular front occupied by Haking's XI Corps was especially difficult to maintain because of the high water table. As Haking wrote in his 1915 *Winter Campaign* document:

> The work on the line will be very great, because the present trenches will, in many cases, prove quite unfit for occupation during winter. These trenches must be converted into breastworks as rapidly as possible, first by the construction of grouse butts with no parados and with machine guns trained on them from the rear. These will be held by day and night, by small parties, and a strong line will be occupied in the rear where the ground is better. Secondly, the grouse butts will be extended as rapidly as possible, and parados will be built and communication breastwork will be constructed to lead up to each group of butts when they are joined together.[81]

Haking instructed that all troops were to be involved in this arduous work: "The companies holding the firing line must work on it and do nothing else in the way of fatigues; the companies holding the support line must work on that line and the communications breastworks leading from it to the firing line." Even the troops in reserve and resting were to be involved in trench construction.

In January 1916, the Chief Engineer, First Army, made an inspection of the lines of defence and his report called attention to various weaknesses. His comments on XI Corps read: "Lestrem area. Many of the works here are in bad order, but are being taken in hand, and the defensive systems are, I understand, to be revised . . . System for Rue L'Epinette to Rouge Croix, poor. From Rouge Croix to Picantin reported good. Bad works are being taken in hand, I believe."[82] The maintenance of the line was a constant problem for XI Corps throughout 1916. Prompted by a note from Haig, Haking's Corps Conference of 13 January dealt with several matters of defence. Haig's memorandum had specified that: "in case of heavy hostile attack the defensive battle is to be fought in depth", and Haking considered that the XI Corps arrangements for this through reserves held at brigade, division and corps levels were adequate. Haking referred to the system of defence adopted in the French army, "which consists of holding the front trenches lightly during heavy bombardments and relying upon a counter-stroke to regain them if they fell into the hands of the enemy". Haking was strongly against this approach:

> Although this system may be suitable for the French army . . . it does not agree with the system of defence which is in accordance

with our national characteristics, i.e. the defence of the front line at all costs, which has been laid down in previous instructions received from First Army . . . Our experience has been that counter-strokes to regain lost trenches are more costly in casualties than the stubborn defence of the front line system.[83]

Despite these strongly expressed views, Haking was obliged to follow the instructions of Haig and of Monro. In February, a memorandum from Monro made it clear that:

The front line trenches are to be held as lightly as possible, consistent with safety . . . It is incumbent, therefore, on all Corps Commanders to arrange for the defensive system being so organised that if the enemy succeed in penetrating our front line he will be held by a series of 'pockets' formed by defended localities and communication trenches built for use as fire trenches. It is recognised that it is not possible to do this in all cases, but it is the principle to be aimed at and the GOC First Army desires that Corps Commanders will take particular care to see that, wherever possible, the defences are sited so as to attain that object.[84]

A further note from Monro dated 17 April served to emphasize the point: "There is a constant tendency to hold the front trenches too thickly . . . In the front trench will be only sentries and machine guns, and the support trench will be men destined to resist the actual attack."[85]

It seems that Haking had little enthusiasm for the concept of defence in depth. When he temporarily assumed command of the First Army in August 1916, he set out his views on defence:

We now come to the defence of our line. The best defence is offence, and we have so far been very successful in repelling any raids or attacks . . . by an immediate counter-attack delivered across the open . . . I want you all to thoroughly understand the Army policy as regards defence. If the enemy attacks and captures part of our line, I will not stop until we have got it back again . . . whatever the cost I am quite determined to regain any trenches we lose.

As regards work on defences, Haking charged every Commander:

Having first satisfied himself that everything is prepared for immediately driving back the enemy in the event of his trenches being rushed, he should then arrange the organization of the work to be done on the defences – wire, machine gun emplacements, dug-outs, drainage, train lines, OPs.

German raids or attacks on British lines, particularly if they were successful, were taken very seriously and were the subject of detailed reports. On 21 August, for example, a German raid in the area known as the "Kink", resulted in two men being killed and eight reported missing. The following day, Haking received a letter from GHQ [86] making the point that the same battalion, 1st Royal Irish Rifles, had been raided some eight weeks earlier near Carnoy and the enquiry had held that the defensive arrangements at that time were inadequate. Details of the raid on 21 August had reached GHQ and Haig himself now wanted to receive some explanation. Haking investigated the matter and reported back that the success of the German raid was due to a poor defence system and panic: "there is of course no satisfactory excuse for either of these causes, and the only thing that can be said is that the occurrence will be brought home to the Corps and the Division and that exceptional efforts will be made in the future."[87]

The defensive systems of both the British and the Germans in the First Army sector held out during 1916 against the numerous attacks and trench raids that were thrown against them. Both sides, and particularly the Germans with their lines of concrete pillboxes, were well-organized to repel even the most determined assaults and, as a consequence, the trench lines at the end of 1916 were essentially the same as those at the end of 1915.

* * * *

The above outline of events involving XI Corps in late 1915 and through 1916 make it possible to assess Haking as a Corps Commander during that period. At the time of the battle of Loos, when Haking first assumed command of XI Corps, his role was very much determined by the circumstances of the battle and the relationship between French and Haig at that time. From the beginning of November 1915, however, Haking was operating as an established Corps Commander firmly placed in the hierarchy of the First Army and the BEF. In the Introduction, it was noted that the role of a Corps Commander had no formal definition and that the *Field Service Regulations* made no clear distinction, other than that implied by the size of the formation involved, between the responsibilities held at the various levels of command. Decision-making in respect of the "efficiency and the maintenance of the forces" was the main common duty of all commanders from Commander in Chief down. The evidence in this chapter, however, suggests that the Commander in Chief made the key decisions and his subordinate commanders were simply expected to act on them. Certainly, Haking as XI Corps Commander, acted essentially as an executor whose role was concerned with implementation rather than with policy. His scope and freedom of action was severely limited. The hierarchical structure of the BEF was strictly top-down.

An examination of Haking's experience as XI Corps Commander supports this description. When, in October 1915, French outlined the policy to be followed during the winter months of 1915–16, it was directed to the Army Commanders. In their turn, the Army Commanders communicated French's instructions to their subordinates and so on down the line. Haig, as First Army Commander, elaborated on the Commander in Chief's document in his *Instructions for Divisional Training* (10 November 1915), and referred to parts of French's policy again on 25 November in connection with the use of artillery. Haking's memorandum, *Winter Campaign 1915–16*, was addressed to his Divisional Commanders and mirrored faithfully the instructions of both French and Haig. Haking's document was put out as a policy statement for XI Corps, but it was French's policy, not his. This same hierarchical process continued when Haig became the Commander in Chief. It continued through 1916, and was particularly evident at the time of the Somme. Orders concerning raids and other offensive operations – their timing, frequency and their cancellation – and also methods of defence, were generally initiated at GHQ and followed by the subordinate commanders. The tone and wording of the following instruction from the Brigade Major of 184 Brigade in June 1916, illustrates how this style of control was adopted by junior commanders: "The Brigadier again impresses on all officers that in the case of all operations of any raiding nature, the final instructions and orders as approved by the Brigadier-General must be implicitly followed."[88]

As mentioned earlier in this chapter, this system of command was supported by a common and regular use of key words and phrases. The same language of "offensive", "moral[e]", and "harass", for example, was used at GHQ, Army and Corps levels and below. It was enshrined in training and instructional pamphlets and it helped to support and develop a common mind-set among the senior BEF officers. The top-down method of control was accepted by Haking with equanimity and without question. When situations arose that put Haking out of line with GHQ and Army policy – the inconvenient removal of divisions from XI Corps, the lack of artillery ammunition, the construction of additional trenches and the preferred method of defence – then he was immediately ready to conform – even if not always enthusiastically – with the wishes of his superiors.

If any sentence reveals Haking's attitude to these issues, it was the one that he used during an Army Conference in June 1916. The discussion had been concerned with XI Corps raids and whether certain parts of the enemy line should be held. Haking simply said that: "It depends on what the higher commanders desired." Consistent with this type of thinking, Monro's response to Haking's comment was that: "he would ascertain from the Commander in Chief what was to be the policy".[89] When, in March 1916, Haig and Monro were encouraging the accelerated promotion of suitable officers, Haking noted in a memorandum to his Divisional Commanders: "The Army Commander has given me very clear instructions on this subject". A copy of this memorandum was sent to Monro with a handwritten note to confirm Haking's compliance with his orders: "I think this letter meets the intentions of the Army Commander."[90]

Similarly, the episode during May, when the simultaneous "secret raids" were being planned, was symptomatic of a strictly hierarchical command structure that encouraged the retention of important information and the isolation of subordinates. When Haking instructed his Divisional Commanders: "to use every means in your power and every misleading device, to prevent any idea getting about that anything of extra importance is taking place", the aim, significantly, was not to keep information from the enemy, it was to keep it from their own colleagues. Again, when Haking, on the same occasion, concocted a fictitious artillery scenario – "this will be sufficient reason for them" – he was duping not the Germans, but his neighbouring divisional commanders.

Haking's role as a Corps Commander, then, was primarily to ensure that the orders of his superiors were transmitted to his subordinates and carried out. While his authority was derived from that of the Commander in Chief and his Army Commander, Haking's principal tool in carrying out his orders was exhortation. He used every opportunity to urge on his subordinates and, in so doing, he persuaded, encouraged and cajoled. Haking's *Winter Campaign* document of 4 November 1915, begins: "The Corps has been distinguished since its formation for the constant offensive action it has been called upon to carry out . . . It is of vital importance . . . that every effort should be made from the highest to the lowest to further and increase this spirit."[91] When, on 30 May 1916, Haking lectured the officers of 184 Brigade, newly arrived in France, his objective was to promote the offensive spirit. An officer of the 2/1st Bucks Battalion, present at that meeting, remembered the occasion well, mainly because of Haking's "blood-thirsty" message.[92]

Haking may have used blustering tactics to motivate XI Corps, but he was capable of more gentle encouragement. When, on 9 July 1916, a party of 2/5th Glosters had taken part in an unsuccessful raid, Haking sent a handwritten note:

> I was very sorry to see that your raid last night was unsuccessful, but I understand the difficulties you all have to contend with. The only solution is to keep at it and for everyone to be determined to succeed . . . I am most anxious that no-one should be discouraged by small failures . . . Whatever happens, we must never accept failure.[93]

The main obstacle to Haking in carrying out his command function with XI Corps – and the reason why it was necessary to employ constant directives and exhortation as means of control – was the fact that his immediate subordinates, the Divisional Commanders, were constantly changing. In this respect Haking's experience with XI Corps in 1916 was kaleidoscopic. During the year a total of fourteen different divisions served in the Corps. The number of divisions in the Corps at any one time varied from two to five. Eight divisions stayed for three months or less and four stayed for one month or less.[94] While Haig noted in his Diary on 23 June: "Haking has done well in training new divisions and putting spirit into them",[95] the ability to generate any Corps loyalty or to develop a common identity across the Corps was clearly severely limited. The division was the key battle formation in the BEF. Charles Carrington, who had served in the war as an infantry officer with the Royal Warwickshire Regiment, noted: "the divisional spirit was the strongest influence". He described Corps Headquarters as remote and anonymous.[96] The Printed Books Department at the IWM contains many unit histories at various levels – army, division, brigade and regiment – but there is not one history devoted to a British Infantry Corps. The phrase *esprit de corps* was, ironically, a misnomer.

Nevertheless, Haking endeavoured to foster good communications with his Divisional Commanders and spent considerable time discussing issues with them. For example, when the 35th Division, under Major General R. J. Pinney, was part of XI Corps from February to June 1916, Pinney and Haking met on no fewer than thirty-three occasions.[97] During these meetings Haking and Pinney discussed, among other things, the use of machine guns, trench mortars, the Verdun battle, defence lines and minor operations. These discussions were often accompanied by some mild socializing – tea or dinner. Pinney noted that on 20 February he and Haking dined together and afterwards "played spillikin billiards". Most of these meetings involved Haking travelling to Pinney's Headquarters and they demonstrate a continuing effort on Haking's part to develop ties between Corps and Division. With that same purpose in mind, it was Haking's practice to write to divisional commanders at the time they left XI Corps expressing the wish "to have the pleasure of serving with you again before the end of the war".[98]

The overriding focus of BEF policy during 1916 was on various forms of offensive. Since Haking was by temperament and conviction an advocate of the offensive, this policy suited him admirably. Haking's reputation as a "thruster" was not ill founded. If anything, his inclination was to demonstrate his commitment to the "offensive" by putting forward schemes that exceeded the requirements placed on him by his superiors. In March, when the spring attacks were being considered, Haking proposed a series of raids involving all four of his Divisions and argued for additional ammunition to support his plans. During the abortive "secret raids" episode in May, Haking made his Divisional Commanders prepare not one, but two raids for the occasion. When the First Army was preparing a series of raids in support of the Somme offensive, XI Corps were ready with a disproportionately high number. As noted earlier, Haking's enthusiastic response to any call for raids did not go unnoticed and he received praise from his superiors on several occasions.

Despite Haking's belief in the necessity and value of raids and the offensive in general, there is evidence to show that his subordinates down the line held less enthusiastic views. The author of the history of the Guards Division remarked that Haking's exhortations to acts of aggression, as set out in the *Winter Campaign 1915–16* document, did not always come to fruition.

> The contemplated 'step by step' capture and presumably retention of tactical localities on the lower slopes of the Aubers Ridge in mid-winter was happily not embarked upon . . . Regimental officers and men, like the troops in the line, were somewhat apt to consider that [the Corps Commander] exaggerated the moral value of an aggressive policy in trench warfare and to resent continuously being called upon to carry out raids and reconnaissances for apparently no other purpose than to satisfy the insatiable curiosity of the Intelligence Branch of the General Staff.[99]

Referring to the various "stunts" undertaken in XI Corps, the historian of the 2/5th Glosters noted:

> It was never ascertained that [they] produced the effect that was intended, but they were very unpopular with the men, as they

never failed to draw retaliation from the enemy, the full brunt of
which fell on the front line troops. Many casualties were suffered
in this way.[100]

A report from a COs' Course in September, noted:

[The COs] all thought that the men did not like raids because they
did not see that they got value for them . . . The COs said the men
preferred an attack when intended to take and hold part of the
enemy's line. The men would then feel that they had done a good
job and be able to take a pride in it . . . what they dislike most is
giving a place up after taking it in some force.[101]

James Roberts suggests, from the experiences of 19th Division, that:
"It was a reasonably straight-forward proposition for the infantry to
either charade or 'posture' their own part in aggression." Artillery fired
wide to avoid retaliation and the infantry conspired to abort raids. At
one point, a series of fourteen raids were planned, but only three took
place.[102] Despite Haking's exhortations, his subordinates were able to
exercise a marked constraint on the power of a Corps Commander.
Haking's record of raids and casualties in 1916 will be discussed in
Appendix III.

The emphasis placed by Haking on "the offensive" and the benefits
of raids and other minor operations was related to an important aspect
of his role as XI Corps Commander – that of a trainer of inexperienced
divisions. While no directive has been found to indicate that XI Corps
had been designated officially for this task there is certainly some
evidence to show that Haking played a significant part in receiving
"green" troops into his Corps and training them to become battle-
hardened soldiers capable of dealing with the rigours of trench warfare.
During 1916 the First Army was, in the main, composed of I, IV, and
XI Corps. The analysis in Appendix IV shows, in terms of
division/months, the proportion of inexperienced divisions making up
those Corps during the year. The figures show that while the proportion of inexperienced divisions in XI Corps was 60 per cent, the
equivalent figures for I Corps and IV Corps were 25 and 10 per cent
respectively. This relatively high proportion of "green" troops in XI
Corps explains a number of Haking's comments quoted earlier in this
chapter. For example, in his note to Monro of 17 March Haking justified his request for additional ammunition to support his programme of
raids by arguing that all his divisions, except the 33rd, were " new
formations and have never been into German trenches . . . I am most
anxious to improve the fighting spirit of these new Divisions." XI Corps

at that time was made up of the 19th, 35th and 38th Divisions as well as the 33rd. Also, after the disastrous raid by the 12th and 13th Battalions of the Royal Sussex Regiment (39th Division) against the Boar's Head on 30 June, Haking reported that the Division had only been in France for three months and "until recently had not shown much offensive spirit. I consider that this operation has greatly improved the fighting value of the Division". Haking made similar comments following the attack by the untried 61st Division at Fromelles on 19 July. Haking's background, experience and inclination all fitted him to take on a major role in breaking-in new troops. Whether this role was official policy is unclear, but this aspect of Haking's activity was in practice a key part of his job as XI Corps Commander in 1916.

The overall impression arising from this review of XI Corps' experience of trench warfare in 1916 is that Haking played the part of a "good soldier". He was generally committed to, and always conformed with, the policies of his superiors. He accepted the strict hierarchical structure of the BEF without difficulty – it suited his character and he was an intrinsic part of it. There is no evidence of originality and XI Corps functioned in a workmanlike fashion without particular flair. There were inherent constraints in Haking's role. Despite Haking's efforts, XI Corps was not an operating formation that generated its own character, identity or style. During 1916, the number of divisions in the First Army, at any one time, averaged eleven[103] – too many for the Army Commander to exercise proper control. XI Corps, therefore, was a necessary geographical grouping of divisions and it was the role of the Corps Commander to ensure that the orders from GHQ and Army HQ reached and were carried out by the divisions. It was essentially an administrative convenience, not concerned with strategy or direction, but with the detail of implementation. Andy Simpson has argued that there was a "learning curve", based on the control of artillery and an increased freedom in the planning of operations, which evolved at Corps level during the war.[104] As far as Haking's XI Corps is concerned, there is no evidence of such a learning curve in 1916. Whether any change took place in 1917 will be discussed in Chapter V.

Notes

1. In February 1916, the British First Army took over the ground held by the French Tenth Army. In this process, the British XI Corps front was extended south to Auchy.
2. *BOH, 1916* 2 vol. II., p.126, Ft 2.
3. Examples other that those quoted here are contained in: Maj. F. W. Bewsher,

The History of the 51st (Highland)Division 1914–1918, p.297; Brig. Gen. E. Riddell and Col M. C. Clayton, *The Cambridgeshires 1914–1919*, p.35.

4. Maj C. H. Dudley-Ward, *The Fifty Sixth Division 1914–1918*. p. 101.
5. George Coppard, *With a Machine Gun to Cambrai*, p.57.
6. Jon Silkin, ed., *The Penguin Book of First World War Poetry* 2nd edn p.111.
7. *The History of the London Rifle Brigade 1859–1919*, p.179..
8. TNA, WO 95/160.
9. TNA, WO 95/162, RHS 890/1.
10. TNA, WO 95/162.
11. TNA, WO 95/167, GS 470(a), 2 November 1916.
12. Field Marshal von Hindenburg. *The Great War* ed. Charles Messenger, p.177.
13. TNA, WO 95/160, Para 8 of an isolated sheet. However, Maj. B. T. Wilson in his *Studies of German Defences near Lille* records that some sections of the German front line had reasonable accommodation with dugouts some 15 feet. deep, having electricity for lighting and drainage. The electricity was taken from the Lille tram system. Quoted in a report on Fromelles carried out in 2007 by Peter Barton on behalf of the Australian Army History Unit (Unpublished).
14. Also spelt "Layes". On German maps it is called the *Leierbach*.
15. TNA, CAB 45/123, Gardner to Edmonds, 8 August 1931.
16. TNA, WO 95/162.
17. TNA, WO 95/885.
18. TNA, WO 95/159, OAM 97.
19. TNA, WO 95/160 (First Army No 431 G.), 10 November 1915.
20. At a First Army Conference on 16 October 1915, Haig had expressed this policy somewhat more cynically: "The idea was to give everyone something to do as it was bad to sit down on the defensive." See TNA, WO 95/159.
21. TNA, WO 95/160, GS. 215/1(a).
22. TNA, WO 95/160, RHS/298.
23. Haking, *Company Training*, p. 103.
24. TNA, WO 95/160, RHS 658.
25. Duff Cooper, *Haig* 2 vols. I, p. 298.
26. TNA, WO 95/161, O.A. 336, Kiggell to First Army.
27. Monro had been despatched to advise on the future of the Gallipoli campaign towards the end of 1915.
28. TNA, WO 95/161, 4 January 1916.
29. TNA, WO 95/881, RHS 726.
30. TNA, WO 95/162, 62(a).
31. TNA, WO 95/881, RHS 837.
32. TNA, WO 95/881.
33. TNA, WO 95/162.
34. TNA, WO 95/161.
35. TNA, WO 95/161. See also the memorandum GS 275/44(a), 29 February 1916, and the note from GHQ OB/A 1574, 27 February 1916.
36. TNA, WO 95/162.
37. TNA, WO 95/163, OAD 291/11.

38. TNA, WO 95/163, OAD 910.
39. TNA, WO 95/163, OAD 912.
40. TNA, WO 95/881.
41. TNA, WO 95/163.
42. TNA, WO 95/163, GS 853/1.
43. Ibid., OAD 885.
44. TNA, WO 95/163, GS 849/5/1.
45. TNA, WO 95/164.
46. TNA, WO 95/163, XI Corps SS 849/5/1.
47. TNA, WO 95/163, GS 360/24 (a).
48. Ibid., OAD 912.
49. TNA, WO 95/164.
50. Ibid., Undated memorandum in Haking's writing (Presumably early June1916).
51. TNA, WO 95/164, GS/849/S/15.
52. Although the Somme offensive was postponed for forty-eight hours (thus beginning on 1 July), the First Army programme of raids took place on the dates planned. See TNA, WO 95/164, GS 405(a), Kiggell to Monro.
53. TNA, WO 95/164.
54. Ibid.
55. TNA, WO 95/164
56. TNA, WO 95/165, GS 420 (a).
57. A. F. Barnes, *The Story of the 2/5 Gloucestershire Regiment 1914–18*, p.40.
58. TNA, WO 95/3065, 184 Brigade war diary.
59. TNA, WO 95/2581.
60. TNA, WO 95/164, XI Corps Report on Boar's Head (39 Div.), RHS/57/676 attached to First Army Weekly Report, 23–30 June 1916.
61. TNA, WO 256/12, Haig's Diary, 3 August 1916, p.48.
62. Ibid. p.60.
63. TNA, WO 95/165, 30 July 1916.
64. TNA, WO 95/166.
65. TNA, WO 95//166, GS 446/1(a).
66. TNA, WO 95/166.
67. TNA, WO 95/166, Attached to Conference Report, 9 September 1916.
68. TNA, WO 95/166, OAD 149, 16 September 1916.
69. TNA, WO 95/167, GS 455(a), 30 September 1916.
70. TNA, WO 95/167.
71. Ibid. From a paper prepared by the MGGS First Army, 31 October 1916. Quotations in the following two paragraphs come also from this source.
72. Dudley-Ward, *Fifty Sixth Division*, p.101.
73. TNA, WO 95/167, Conference of First Army Commanders, 21 November, 1916.
74. Casualty figures for the First Army and for XI Corps are taken from the First Army weekly operations reports in WO 95/161–167. Casualties in January and February 1916 are not recorded and have been included on a pro-rated basis.

75. War Office, *Field Service Regulations*, Section 100.
76. Gen. Staff, *Notes for Infantry Officers on Trench Warfare*, Section 1.
77. Ibid., Section 4.
78. TNA, WO 95/159, 26 October 1915.
79. War Office, *The Division in Defence*, SS210, May 1918.
80. TNA, WO 95/159, OAM 97.
81. TNA, WO 95/160.
82. TNA, WO 95/161, Document headed "Notes".
83. TNA, WO 95/881, RHS 726.
84. TNA, WO 95/161, 610(G), 21 February 1916.
85. TNA, WO 95/162, First Army Conference, 15 August 1916.
86. TNA WO 95/166, OA 522.
87. Ibid., 802/19(G).
88. TNA, WO 95/3066, 29 June 1916.
89. TNA, WO 95/164.
90. TNA, WO 95/162, 25 March 1916.
91. TNA, WO 95/160, RHS/298.
92. Centre for Buckinghamshire Studies, DX 780, Letters of Ivor Stewart-Liberty, 1914–16. May, 1916.
93. TNA, WO 95/3066, SS 1206, 10 July 1916.
94. TNA, WO 95/159–171. Also WO 95/28–33, QMG Branch
95. TNA, WO 256/11, p.66.
96. Charles Carrington, *Soldier from the War Returning*, pp.102, 104.
97. IWM, 66/257/1, Diaries of Maj Gen R. J. Pinney.
98. For example, TNA, WO 95/885, 1 November 1916 to GOC 61st Division. Andy Simpson has pointed out the various methods used by Corps Commanders to foster communications with divisional commanders. See his *Directing Operations: British Corps Command on the Western Front, 1914–18*. Ch. 8.
99. Lt Col C. Headlam, *The Guards Division in the Great War*, p.106.
100. Barnes, *Story of the 2/5th Gloucestershire Regiment* , p. 40.
101. TNA, WO 95/167, Report on Commanding Officers' Conference, 10–17 December 1916.
102. James Roberts, "Making the Butterflies Kill", *Stand To 68*, September 2003, pp.38–44.
103. TNA, WO 95/29–33. The divisions in the First Army are listed, month by month, in the QMG Branch GHQ War Diary.
104. Andy Simpson, "British Corps Command on the Western Front, 1914–1918", in Sheffield and Todman, eds., *Command and Control on the Western Front*, pp.97–118.

CHAPTER IV

Haking and the Attack at Fromelles
– July 1916

Much of Haking's reputation as a "Butcher" and a "Bungler" arises from his involvement in the attack at Fromelles (also referred to as Fleurbaix) in July 1916 and this chapter examines Haking's role in that action. The attack, carried out under Haking's command, by the British 61st Division and the Australian 5th Division, has generally been regarded as a disaster. The British lost 1,550 men while Australian casualties amounted to 5,500. German casualties were fewer than 2,000. When the attack was called off, the trench positions were exactly the same as they had been fourteen hours earlier.

Both the British and the Australian official histories were highly critical of the operation. The verdict of the British Official History was that: "To have delivered battle at all betrayed a great under-estimate of the enemy's power of resistance."[1] The Australian Official History concluded: "The reasons for the failure seem to have been loose thinking and somewhat reckless decisions on the part of the higher staff . . . it is difficult to conceive that the operation, as planned, was ever likely to succeed."[2] Lieutenant General Sir Henry Wilson's diary entry for 30 July 1916 commented on Fromelles: "nothing was done. We took a hundred prisoners but no trenches we could remain in – a botch job."[3] In 1937, when the British Official History was being compiled, a number of officers who had served at Fromelles were invited to comment on the draft chapter covering that attack. Their remarks were overwhelmingly negative. Captain Wilfred Greene, for example, a staff officer attached to the 61st Division HQ wrote: "The operation was bound to be a costly failure. Those responsible for planning it showed complete ignorance of the ground . . . no amount of preparation or training would have enabled a success to have been made of an attack which was (a) tactically misconceived and (b) made with inadequate forces, inadequately supported by artillery over ground where it was not possible to consolidate the position captured, dominated as it was."[4] Lieutenant Colonel M. M. Parry-Jones, of the British 183

Brigade, summarized his comments on the draft chapter: "What could be expected of such an attack but failure."[5]

Accounts by historians of the Fromelles operation have invariably been adverse. Liddell Hart described it as "an attack which was the final link of an almost incredibly muddled chain of causation";[6] to Denis Winter, it was "a bloody reverse".[7] Anthony Farrar-Hockley wrote that there was "a singular lack of co-ordination between either of the attacking infantry forces or their artillery".[8] Robin Neillands referred to "the ill-conceived attack on Fromelles".[9] Lyn Macdonald described it as "an attack that turned out to be a catastrophe";[10] while Simon Robbins called Fromelles a "disastrous attack".[11] Paul Cobb concluded that it was "an entire tragedy";[12] and Martin Gilbert, in his account of Fromelles, implied criticism of what he described as "a brief interlude, far from the Somme, during that vaster battle. Yet its casualties were high."[13]

Fromelles was a serious disappointment for the Australians. It was the first Australian offensive on the Western Front and the troops, many of whom had seen service in Gallipoli, were keen to record a success. Instead, they suffered defeat and a heavy casualty list. There were twice as many Australian casualties during the twelve hours of the Fromelles attack as on the first day of the Anzac landings in Gallipoli on 25 April 1915. As the Australian writer Ross McMullin has pointed out, the losses of the Australian 5th Division during the night of 19/20 July were "equivalent to the entire Australian casualties of the Boer, Korean and Vietnam Wars put together".[14]

The suspicion also grew among Australians that the British military authorities wished to conceal and play down the true story of Fromelles and that suspicion continues today. The official British communiqué, issued immediately after the attack, referred to Fromelles as just one of "some important raids" in the Armentières area.[15] The word "raid" to describe Fromelles was used in the London *Times* of 21 July 1916 and also, the following day, in the Melbourne *Argus*. The emphasis in both reports was on the "140 Germans captured" and there was no mention of the heavy losses. C. E. W. Bean, the official Australian war correspondent and later the writer of the Australian Official History, soon became aware of the scope of the operation and the casualty list and risked censorship by sending a despatch, published in both the *Times* and the *Argus* on 24 July, which described the operation as an "attack" and the losses as "severe".[16] Chaplain Green, a participant at Fromelles, wrote to the *Sydney Morning Herald* of 19 July 1919, the third anniversary of the attack, saying that: "Very little is known of the Battle of Fleurbaix. It was never fully reported." The letter was headed: "The Mystery Battle of the AIF". Another contributor to the *Sydney Morning*

Herald observed: "To many Australians the Fleurbaix battle is some-thing rarely spoken of."[17] Captain A. D. Ellis, the historian of the Australian 5th Division, referring to the British communiqué of 20 July 1916, commented: "this official distortion of the facts of the Battle of Fromelles has resulted in a general and profound misconception of its purpose and its gravity".[18] Even in 1996 Ross McMullin felt able to write of Fromelles: "Because of this cover-up and the tide of wartime events, what occurred . . . is not well known."[19] In 2002 McMullin further claimed that "most Australians have never heard of the battle".[20] In 1997 Brigadier O'Brien of the Australian War Graves Office said of Fromelles: "We have hidden it away. It has almost been a conspiracy to hide the absolutely shameful disaster."[21]

Fromelles soon became part of the developing Anzac legend.[22] Bean, in his despatch following the Fromelles attack, reported: "Our troops in this attack had to face shell fire heavier and more continuous than was ever known in Gallipoli. Many of the men were quite untried previously and the manner in which they carried through seems to have been worthy of all the traditions of Anzac."[23] Chaplain Green, in his letter to the *Sydney Morning Herald* of 19 July 1919, wrote: "For dogged, self-sacrificing courage and extent of casualties [Fleurbaix] ranks with our second French battle, Pozières, and our terrible battle of Bullecourt . . . Many AIF officers of experience declare that they never knew Australians to fight better – certainly they were never confronted with a more difficult problem, not even at Lone Pine . . . Our heroic dead who fell in this first French AIF battle are entitled to their little bit of history, their place in our Hall of Fame. [The 5th Division] has made history at Bapaume, Lagnicourt, Polygon Wood, Menin Road and many other places, but it should have "Fleurbaix" inscribed also upon its banners."[24] The German press also played a part in establishing the Anzac legend and the *Berliner Tageblat* of 30 July described the Australian soldiers as "unsophisticated sons of graziers and heirs to the land . . . What their fathers had brought to the wild colony lay in their bearing and eyes, and they were not to be taken lightly. Good shots, cruel fighters, steel-hard fellows."[25]

Such sentiments, extolling the self-sacrifice and heroism of the Australian soldier at Fromelles, were supported by a number of personal accounts of the attack. In April 1918 Captain Hugh Knyvett of the 15th Battalion, gave a sombre picture of the carnage involved, but added the exaggeration that the Australians "had smashed five divi-sions of Bavarian guards."[26] In 1920 W. H. Downing described the terrible losses and courage of the 60th and 59th Battalions:

Hundreds were mown down in the flicker of an eyelid, like great rows of teeth knocked down from a comb, but still the line went on, thinning and stretching. Wounded wriggled into shell holes or were hit again. Men were cut in two by streams of bullets. And still the line went on . . . It was the Charge of the Light Brigade once more, but more terrible, more hopeless.[27]

In 1998 a bronze sculpture, "Cobbers", was unveiled in the Australian Memorial Park at Fromelles commemorating the courage of the Australian soldiers who had brought in the wounded from no man's land and a copy was erected in Melbourne in 2008.[28] There are no such dramatic memorials to the British. Fromelles, or Fleurbaix, has become an important feature of Anzac history and it is significant that, in terms of coverage in official histories, the Australian history devotes 119 pages to the attack while the British account is limited to sixteen pages. The German history deals with Fromelles in five lines.[29]

For many Australian soldiers the heavy casualties and the failure of Fromelles carried with them two further negative connotations – a growing lack of faith, following on events in Gallipoli, in the abilities of British senior commanders, and, regrettably, some considerable ill-feeling among Australian troops towards the British rank and file. Bean made the comment:

> The Australian troops came to the Western Front in the confident expectation of meeting with military direction that should embody both the quality of British arms and the experience of two years of warfare. But in this first major operation which they undertook it was obvious to every officer and man, that not only had the work of the staff of the Corps been muddled, but that the defects were those of character as well as intellect.[30]

When the history of the Australian Medical Corps was being compiled a contributor wrote of Fromelles: "The bitterness of the feelings against higher command was intense . . . and unequalled in the history of the AIF."[31] The Australian Official History noted:

> A particularly unfortunate, but almost inevitable result [of Fromelles] was that, having been unwisely combined with a British Division whose value for offence, in spite of the devoted gallantry of many of its members, was recognized as doubtful, the Australian soldier tended to accept the judgement – often unjust, but already deeply impressed by the occurrences of the Suvla

landing – that the 'Tommies' could not be relied upon to uphold a flank in a stiff fight.[32]

On 3 July 1920 a highly controversial play, *Advance Australia*, by a veteran of Fromelles, Father J. J. Kennedy, was performed in Bendigo, Victoria. One of the scenes was "near the trenches in the battle of Fromelles" and a main character was given the lines: "How we have been gulled! Australia's bravest and best abused and annihilated in order to save the dastards of the new English army who let us down every time." There was much opposition to this "disloyal" play, but there was also significant support.[33]

Taking account of the above perceptions of Fromelles, and placing them in the context of Anzac mythology, the writings of Australian commentators can be expected to be highly critical. In 1919 Lieutenant Colonel C. MacLauren, who was with the Australian Medical Corps at Fromelles, described the attack as an "orgy of blunders and of calamity".[34] Major General Brudenell White wrote in 1926 that both he and Gen Birdwood considered the attack to be a "most undesirable operation".[35] In 1930 Brigadier General H. E. "Pompey" Elliott, the commander of the Australian 15 Brigade at Fromelles, was particularly scathing in his comments:

> The whole operation was so incredibly blundered from beginning to end that it is almost incomprehensible how the British Staff, who were responsible for it, could have consisted of trained professional soldiers of considerable reputation and experience, and why, in view of the outcome of this extraordinary adventure, any of them were retained in active command.[36]

In more recent times, Australian writers have continued the condemnation of Fromelles. To John Laffin the attack was a "tragedy . . . the result of muddled thinking".[37] Peter Pederson considered that the "courage and endurance of the men who went over the top" was the only redeeming feature of Fromelles.[38] Matt McLachlan commented that: "the losses at Fromelles were obscene . . . the whole event was a folly".[39] Ross McMullin wrote, "the enterprise was pointless, a monstrous fiasco"[40] and, in an account of the attack, he concluded: "The battle of Fromelles remains perhaps the most tragic 24 hours ever experienced by Australians."[41] An article in the Melbourne *The Age*, dated 1 August 2009, summed up the general Australian view of Fromelles: "Even in a conflict defined by terrible and fruitless sacrifice, the Battle of Fromelles stands out as an exercise in bloody futility."[42]

Along with this catalogue of negative comment came the apportion-
ment of blame. Fromelles had been a costly failure and Haking was
identified as being "the operation's main architect"[43] and the "main
culprit"[44] of the debacle. According to "Pompey" Elliott "Haking must
take the chief blame."[45] In connection with Fromelles, Haking has been
described as a "mug soldier",[46] "a butcher and a bungler",[47] a "General
of strong personality and little ability",[48] and both the British and the
Australian official histories have implied strong criticism of his role in
that operation. However, what is striking is the level of animosity
against Haking that has surfaced in the past ten years or so. Robin
Corfield (2000), in his enquiry into Fromelles, clearly had no time for
Haking.[49] Peter Pederson referred to Haking as a "butcher" (2004).[50]
Mat McLachlan (2000), referring to Fromelles, said of Haking that he
was "not a man to give up a plan simply because it didn't work".[51] Les
Carlyon (2000) has written that Haking "had a gift for humbug that
borders on the spectacular"; and that he had "timeless faults that
would have got him into trouble with Napoleon or Julius Caesar".
Carlyon added the apparently damning comment that Haking
possessed "a doleful moustache".[52] Ross McMullin (2002) described
Haking as a "pernicious incompetent".[53] Garrie Hutchinson (2006) has
accused Haking of being "criminally inept",[54] and Patrick Lindsay
(2007) has called Haking "the blunderer, the man they would forever
call the butcher".[55] These condemnations are somewhat repetitious and
certain words and phrases tend to recur much as though there is some
concerted vendetta against Haking.[56] Nevertheless, they at least demonstrate that, ninety years after the 1914–18 war, there is still an
underlying antagonism towards the British military establishment and,
because of Fromelles, towards Haking in particular.

The above survey of the criticisms of Fromelles has a common theme:
the attack was a disaster and the general responsible was Haking. The
remainder of this chapter discusses the attack at Fromelles in the light
of these criticisms and arrives at some conclusions about Haking's
generalship. Contrary to the mass of negative comment about
Fromelles, the chapter concludes that, in this instance, Haking has been
unreasonably maligned. Moreover, while the operation was a tactical
failure, there is evidence that it was a strategic success.

* * * *

The attack at Fromelles had its origin in the events of the early days of
the Battle of the Somme, which had begun on 1 July 1916. Despite the
terrible British losses on the first day of that battle – some 57,000 casualties – Haig remained optimistic. On 5 July Lieutenant General Kiggell,
Haig's Chief of Staff, wrote to the commanders of the First and Second
Armies, Generals Monro and Plumer:

Prospects . . . are encouraging and the next few days may very possibly place us in possession of the enemy's defences from the Ancre to the Somme . . . The First and Second Armies should each select a front on which to attempt to make a break in the enemy's lines, and to widen it subsequently, on the assumption that success in the main operation would result in the enemy being much weakened and shaken in their front and probably contemplating retreat . . . The fronts should be notified as soon as possible.[57]

As noted in the previous chapter, the possibility of carrying out a major attack "to deceive the enemy" on a section of the front covered by the First and Second Armies had been discussed for several months as part of the preparations for the forthcoming Somme offensive. On 3 April GHQ had warned that: "Army Commanders must be prepared to mount an attack of considerable scale on their fronts and they must have their schemes prepared for this purpose."[58] Again, on 27 May, GHQ wrote: "Preparations for deceiving the enemy should be made . . . Raids at night of a strength of a Company and upwards on an extensive scale into the enemy's front system of defences. These to be prepared by intense artillery and trench mortar bombardment."[59] In line with these orders, Monro informed his Corps Commanders on 1 June: "When the Somme offensive takes place the role of the First Army will be to deceive the enemy as to the real point of the attack, to wear him out and reduce his fighting efficiency."[60]

Haking was well advanced in his preparations for a major attack on the XI Corps front. At his Corps Conference on 9 May Haking advised his Divisional Commanders that he was proposing

a more powerful and extended offensive to be carried out by XI Corps in conjunction with the Australian Corps on our left, the ultimate object being to gain the Aubers and Fromelles Ridge . . . I am elaborating a scheme with the GOC Australian Corps in the Second Army [Lieutenant General Godley] with the permission of the GOs in C First and Second Armies.[61]

On 21 June Haking's proposal for a joint British-Australian operation was taken a stage further: "The [First] Army Commander gave me permission to consult direct with the GOC Second Army as regards offensive operations on my extreme left flank. I saw GOC Second Army today and he agreed to all I suggested, and asked me to put my scheme of attack in writing and send it to him. This I have now done."[62]

When Plumer received Kiggell's 5 July note ordering the First and Second Armies to "select a front on which to attempt to make a break", he immediately wrote to Monro: "The only place I can attempt 'to make a break' wd. be somewhere on my right – in conjunction with your left. If it shd. happen that your left was the place you choose – we might make a joint arrangement."[63] Plumer's response no doubt took into account his own plans for a possible attack further to the north in the Messines area and his knowledge of Haking's proposals for a joint British-Australian operation at the junction of the two Armies.

As a result of Plumer's note, Monro, at his First Army Conference of 8 July, instructed Haking to prepare the necessary plans. The following day, Haking reported:

> I have prepared . . . a scheme of attack to capture and hold Aubers Ridge, from Aubers to Fromelles, both included, and to connect up the flanks with our original line . . . I am to continue to hold my present front of about 18,000 yards with two Divisions and to use one of these Divisions in the attack. I am also to be given a Division of the Second Army to assist in the attack together with some field and heavy artillery.[64]

Monro, however, was less than certain that the far left of the First Army front was the best place to launch an attack. On 9 July he sent a memorandum to GHQ listing alternative sectors where an attack might be "most advantageous". Apart from the Aubers Ridge sector, the list also included the Vimy Ridge, Hill 70, and Violaines and Monro gave his opinion that "an attack on Hill 70 appears most favourable."[65]

It was at this point that Haig received Intelligence information that the Germans had transferred nine battalions from the Lille-Lens area to the Somme as reinforcements.[66] The idea of a diversionary operation of some substance in the direction of Lille, some forty miles north of the Somme, aimed at deterring future similar transfers now became an interesting proposition to GHQ. Consequently, Monro dropped the Hill 70 option and on 11 July wrote to his Corps Commanders confirming an attack towards Fromelles-Aubers. However, Haking's ambitious plan to attack and take the Aubers Ridge immediately became subject to various modifications. A hand-written note by Haking stated: "MGGS [Butler] saw GOC XI Corps [Haking] on 11 July and informed him that GOC First Army [Monro] did not propose to order an attack against Aubers Ridge."[67] It then became apparent that Monro, following discussions with GHQ, planned an even greater modification. The attack was to be an artillery demonstration. The

> combined effort by the First and Second Armies . . . could be undertaken partially to form a useful diversion to help our

southern operations. An artillery demonstration with the threat of attack towards Lille will keep the enemy on the ground . . . The demonstration which can for the present be purely one of artillery combined with a few patrol enterprises for the purpose of reconnaissance should last at least 3 days . . . An approx. date for Artillery demonstration should be fixed by G.H.Q., say, 15 July.[68]

When, on 13 July, Haig's Deputy Chief of Staff, Major General Butler, held a meeting with Monro the nature of the "demonstration" took a further dramatic turn. It was decided that an infantry attack should accompany the artillery demonstration with the First Army providing two divisions and the Second Army one. Haking's plan, now reinstated and extended by an extra division, was confirmed in a note from Butler:

The role of the First Army is to fully occupy the enemy on its front and prevent the detachment of hostile forces towards the south. This role has hitherto been fulfilled by constant raids, bombardments, wire-cutting, and gas attacks, along the whole front. Some more incisive operation, however, is required, in order to obtain the best results, and for this purpose the attack on the left of XI Corps assisted by troops from the Second Army, under General Haking, has been projected.[69]

Butler's note was followed by the official order from GHQ: "The First Army will carry out an offensive operation as early as possible on the front Fauquissart-Trivolet road to La Cordonnerie farm as already communicated personally by Deputy Chief of the General Staff."[70]

Having been promised the artillery support of three divisions – two from the Second Army and one from either I or IV Corps of the First Army – Haking proceeded to draw up the plans for a three division attack on a front of some 6,000 yards.[71] However, on 14 July these plans had to be amended since the Second Army withdrew one of its promised divisional artillery units. At the same time, Haking became aware that the 5th Australian Division had no trained Trench Mortar personnel and that the 5th Division artillery, who had only recently arrived in the sector, had little experience of their guns or the ground in front of them. Haking therefore decided that the attack should take place with two, not three, infantry divisions and reduced the attack frontage from 6,000 to 4,000 yards.[72]

At 1.00pm on 15 July the First Army Order No. 100 was issued instructing the attack to proceed and Haking followed this by his XI Corps Order No. 57 detailing the arrangements for an attack on the front Fauquissart-Trivolet Road to the south of la Cordonnerie Farm. The wire-cutting operations and the bombardment had already begun on 14 July and they were to be continued to the early hours of 17 July when the attack would be carried out. In order to confuse the Germans, the artillery of I Corps was to bombard Givenchy and Cuinchy some seven miles south of the attack area.

At a Conference on 16 July attended by the Divisional Commanders of XI Corps and the GOC 5th Australian Division, Haking announced that "good news" had been received from the Somme and that "the moment offered a splendid opportunity for a blow on the XI Corps front, where the enemy was known to be weak both in men and in guns". Haking went on to clarify that the objective of the attack was to be limited to the enemy's front and support line trenches and that it was to be carried out "by each division on a three-brigade front, but only one half of the effectives of each brigade was to be employed". As regards artillery support, Haking explained that "every round of artillery and trench mortar ammunition was to be used in order to help the infantry . . . The zone of the attack being narrow in depth, it should be possible, with the ammunition available, to reduce the defenders to a state of collapse before the infantry attack took place."[73] Following this Conference, Haking wrote a letter to be read to all the troops involved in the attack outlining the objectives of the operation. The letter put particular emphasis on the artillery arrangements, including a series of "lifts", that would precede the assault:

> When everything is ready, our guns, consisting of some 380 pieces of all descriptions, and our trench mortars, will commence an intense bombardment of the enemy's front system of trenches. After about half an hour's bombardment the guns will suddenly lengthen range, our Infantry will show their bayonets over the parapet, and the enemy, thinking we are about to assault will come out of his shelters and man his parapets. The guns will then shorten their range and drive the enemy back into his shelters again. This will be repeated several times. Finally, when we have cut all the wire, destroyed all the parapets, killed a large proportion of the enemy, and thoroughly frightened the remainder, our Infantry will assault, capture and hold the enemy's support line along the whole front.[74]

Haking's next meeting on 16 July was at the First Army Headquarters at Chocques where he met Monro, Plumer and Butler. Butler's opening remarks, as recorded in his Memorandum of the meeting, must have come as a considerable shock to Haking:

[Butler] pointed out that the C in C [Haig] did not wish the infantry attack to take place unless it was considered that the artillery preparation had been adequate and that the Commanders were satisfied that they had sufficient artillery and sufficient ammunition not only to make the success of the attack assured but to enable the troops to retain and consolidate the trenches gained, so far as was humanly possible to foresee.

Butler also stated that: "the main object of the operation was to prevent the Germans from withdrawing troops from this part of the line and our information at the present time did not impose the necessity for the attack to take place tomorrow, 17th, as originally considered desirable". Butler concluded: "it was not the C in C's intention to direct the attack to take place unless they (the Commanders) were satisfied that the resources at their disposal of all kinds, including troops, were adequate for the operation".

The tone of Butler's Memorandum is calm and measured, but his comment that "a discussion followed on all these points" almost certainly concealed a tense and highly charged exchange of views. Haking was "most emphatic that he was quite satisfied with the resources at his disposal, he was quite confident of the success of the operation and considered that the ammunition at his disposal was ample to put the infantry in and keep them there". After some discussion between Monro, Plumer and Haking, Butler noted that: "Sir Charles Monro assured me that he was satisfied that the operation could take place." Butler then suggested that the troops and guns could be kept ready to carry out the operation later "if there were better indications of Germans withdrawing troops". It was also possible, said Butler, for the attack to be cancelled and reinstated at a later date. A further discussion followed "but the Commanders present were unanimously against postponement, the troops were worked up to it, were ready and anxious to do it, and they considered that any cancellation or change of plan would have a bad effect on the troops now, and a loss of confidence in the future when operations were ordered". Butler added: "General Haking was particularly emphatic on this point."

It was at this stage of the meeting that Monro and Haking, showing some signs of exasperation, put their view firmly to Butler: "unless it was to the advantage of the main battle that this operation should not take place they considered that the orders should hold good". Butler, taken aback by this approach, noted: "On the question being put to me in this form I stated that there was nothing in the general situation to prevent the operation taking place." Having received assurances yet again that all the resources were sufficient and available Butler "agreed (and it was settled) that the operation should continue".

It was typical of Haking that he could not leave the matter there: "General Haking then asked whether, in the event of his attack being very successful and little opposition being encountered, he could push on and extend his attack to (say) the Aubers Ridge." For the second time in five days, Butler made it clear that "the intention was a strictly limited objective . . . it was not the intention to embark on any more extended operations however inviting". Butler's Memorandum then noted that this somewhat dramatic meeting "was terminated". Consequently, at 3.00pm, XI Corps Order No. 58 was issued fixing the start of the final bombardment at 4.00am on 17 July with the attack to take place at 11.00am on the same day.

During the afternoon of 16 July it began to rain heavily. The possible effects of bad weather had not been discussed and Butler, having left Chocques, decided, with commendable concern and persistency, to return. Neither Monro nor Haking were there, but Butler took the opportunity of reviewing the proposed attack with General Mercer and Colonel Wilson of the First Army Staff. Butler received "satisfactory assurances" from both Mercer and Wilson and finally left Chocques after emphasizing to Wilson "that if the weather or any other cause rendered a postponement desirable, then it was clearly understood that it was in the power of the Army Commander [Monro] to postpone or cancel the operation at his discretion". Kiggell, Butler's superior, received a copy of the Memorandum and showed it to Haig. In Kiggell's handwriting the Memorandum is marked: "Seen by C in C and approved."[75]

The bad weather of the afternoon of 16 July continued into the following day. Haking received a series of reports informing him that, because of the poor conditions, the registration of the heavy artillery was incomplete. In these circumstances, Haking had no option but to postpone zero hour, which he did on three occasions during 16 and 17 July. On the third occasion, at 08.25am on 17 July, the operation was postponed for the day.[76] Haking immediately contacted Monro:

> It is with extreme reluctance that I am impelled to advise the postponement of the attack . . . Some of the heavy artillery batteries that were sent to me have never fired out here before and I was relying on yesterday afternoon and this morning to get them accurately registered, and to have more practice before the main operation commenced at zero . . . The infantry and field artillery who are to carry out the attack are not fully trained, and GHQ from what was said at your Conference yesterday do not appear to be very anxious for the attack to be delivered . . . I am of the

opinion therefore that the attack should be postponed. I should be glad to know if you wish me to carry it out tomorrow [18 July].[77]

Monro replied to Haking that the attack was not to take place on 18 July. He then reported the situation to GHQ saying that, given the circumstances, he did not propose to carry out the operation at all and asked for Haig's approval of the cancellation.[78] Early in the evening of 18 July, Monro received the following message from GHQ: "The Commander in Chief wishes the special operation . . . to be carried out as soon as possible, weather permitting, provided always that General Sir Charles Monro is satisfied that the conditions are favourable, and that the resources at his disposal, including ammunition, are adequate both for the preparation and execution of the enterprise."[79]

The decision whether or not to carry out the attack was therefore left with Monro. Only two days earlier at the Conference with Butler, Monro had given the undertakings now demanded by Haig. Although it was Monro's inclination to cancel the operation, he could not bring himself, having received Haig's message, to do so and the order for the attack to proceed was given. At 7.15pm on 18 July Haking issued the XI Corps Order No. 60 to the effect that the attack would now be carried out on 19 July. The artillery bombardment would begin at 11.00am and the infantry assault would take place at 6.00pm. Haking again wrote to the troops of the British 61st Division and the Australian 5th Division:

> As you know, we were going to have a fight on Monday [17 July], but the weather was so thick that our artillery could not see well enough to produce the very accurate shooting we require for the success of our plan. So I had to put it off, and GHQ said do it as soon as you can. I then fixed "zero" for Wednesday [19 July] and I know you will do your best for the sake of our lads who are fighting hard down south.[80]

The message was read to all the troops about to take part in the attack.

* * * *

The success of the Fromelles operation rested squarely on the ability of the British and Australian artillery to destroy the German wire and strongpoints in the attack area. The regiments of the Bavarian 6th Reserve Division, facing the British 61st and Australian 5th Divisions, had held the same stretch of line since spring 1915 and they had used their time to develop a formidable defence system. The British Official History noted: "As little fighting had taken place in this region for the past fourteen months,[81] the Germans had had ample opportunity to strengthen their breastwork defences, which now included many machine gun emplacements constructed of concrete, well-sited and concealed."[82] In a report written in 1919, Major B.T. Wilson remarked: "The amount of work done by the German soldier in his defence works was colossal, and the organisation that directed it must have been excellent."[83] The 16th Bavarian Regiment, for example, in the centre of the proposed attack area, had constructed seventy-five concrete bunkers along their 2,000 yard front. The strongest of these emplacements were sited on their main fortification, the Sugar Loaf salient, opposite the junction of the attacking British and Australian Divisions. The Sugar Loaf protruded into no man's land and was so positioned that the fire from its machine guns covered the entire central section of the assault area. The Sugar Loaf was to become the key factor in the forthcoming attack.

The British and Australian artillery amassed for the attack was an impressive force – 296 field guns and howitzers and seventy-eight heavy pieces; 200,000 rounds were allocated to the field guns, 15,000 to the howitzers and a total of 4,350 rounds to the heavies. Proportionately, this was even greater in density than the artillery used at Loos or on the opening day of the Somme.[84] Although impeded by the poor weather and the inexperience of much of the artillery, the bombardment, begun on 14 July, continued intermittently through to 18 July. The final seven-hour bombardment, including the "lifts", promised by Haking in his letter to the troops of 16 July, began at 11.00am on 19 July.

To the soldiers on the front line, both British and German, the bombardment gave every appearance of being successful. Captain Stewart-Liberty in the trenches of the 2/1st Bucks Battalion, opposite the Sugar Loaf, wrote: "We had only to peer over the top to be filled with an unholy joy at the sight of the German trenches. Our 'stuff' was churning up the German lines into mere mounds of earth, and their losses must have been terrible."[85] The history of the List Regiment (16th Bavarian Reserve), who were facing the 2/1st Bucks, recorded: "Shortly after 5.00pm [19 July] all telephone communication ceased and the Battalion Commander sent out runners to find out what the situation was in the front line. They came back and reported that the dugout was under heavy and continuous fire, the losses were considerable and the positions were badly damaged."[86] In other parts of the German line, opposite the Australian 5th Division, it was observed that: "The wire was completely swept away, and the trenches for the most part demolished."[87] The 61st Division's Report on Fromelles noted that: "the infantry reported that the enemy's parapet was shattered all along the line and that the wire presented no obstacle".[88]

However, despite the appearance of destruction and havoc in the German lines, the true effect of the British and Australian bombardment was extremely uneven. After carrying out aerial reconnaissance on 19 July over the attack area a German pilot reported: "the English artillery fire gave the impression of disorganised scatter-gunnery and uncertain targeting, with great gaps left untouched and shells falling on areas where there was nothing worth shooting at".[89] The conclusion reached by the British Official History was that: "The British bombardment appeared to be dealing faithfully with the German parapet, but it was not in fact accomplishing the destruction essential to the success of the infantry assault."[90] The most critical failure of the bombardment was that it did not destroy the German strongpoints. Of the seventy-five concrete emplacements along the 16th Bavarian Reserve Regiment's front only eight were destroyed and seven damaged, leaving sixty completely intact. The 61st Division Report recorded that: "portions [of the German line] did not suffer much, particularly the Sugar Loaf and the Wick. The enemy machine guns were not destroyed by the bombardment."[91]

* * * *

At 6.00pm on 19 July, zero hour for the attack, the order of battle was, (facing the German lines left to right), the Australian 5th Division (8, 14, and 15 Brigades) and the British 61st Division (184, 183, and 182 Brigades). The junction of the two Divisions was the Bond Street communication trench, which was immediately opposite the Sugar Loaf salient. Opposite the Australian and British forces (facing the British lines right to left) were the 21st, 16th, and 17th Bavarian Reserve Regiments of the 6th Bavarian Reserve Division. Along the line of the attack, the opposing trenches were between 100 and 400 yards apart with the widest section in front of the Sugar Loaf. No man's land was flat, open and, because of the recent heavy rain, water-logged. The river Laies, a heavily damaged drainage ditch, ran the length of the attack area mainly behind the German front line in the south but crossing no man's land after the Sugar Loaf and continuing into the Australian sector. The German guns, which were positioned on the Aubers Ridge overlooking the British and Australian lines, began their bombardment at 1.00pm. Although British air superiority had largely prevented observation by German spotter planes,[92] the pre- registered enemy artillery caused many casualties in the packed British and Australian trenches. The enemy machine guns had opened up some thirty minutes before the start of the attack clearly anticipating the forthcoming action.[93] It was a forbidding prospect for the assault troops who were yet to learn that the key German defensive point, the Sugar Loaf, was barely damaged.

The attacking troops had been ordered to deploy into no man's land at 5.30pm and position themselves as near to the enemy's lines as possible before the 6.00pm assault. On the right of the British front the battalions of 182 Brigade, the 2/7th and 2/6th Royal Warwickshires, moved their Companies into no man's land with few casualties. At zero hour the 2/7th Warwicks rushed the German line from fifty yards and, finding the wire and breastworks completely destroyed, took possession of the German trenches. The 2/6th Warwicks were less fortunate. They lost heavily as they advanced across no man's land and were stopped in front of the German wire – which was completely intact – on Wick Salient. In a matter of seconds the 2/6th Warwicks lost nine officers and 220 men.

The 183 Brigade attack was launched from their lines in front of the hamlet of Tilleloy. The two assault battalions, the 2/4th and 2/6th Glosters, had been heavily shelled while still in their trenches, the 2/6th losing fifty men. Both battalions suffered heavy casualties from shrapnel as they deployed through sally ports – openings in their parapets. Once in no man's land the Gloucester battalions were strafed by machine-gun fire and those few who succeeded in reaching the German wire were soon killed or wounded.

On the left of the 61st Division front (184 Brigade) the 2/4th Royal Berkshires also suffered badly as they emerged into no man's land through their sally ports. Two platoons managed to reach the enemy wire, which they found uncut, and they were forced to retire. The battalion on the extreme left of the British line, the 2/1st Bucks, having found the sally ports to be death traps, moved into no man's land by way of Rhondda Sap, a shallow trench that had been dug some 200 yards towards the enemy lines. Immediately in front of the 2/1st Bucks was the Sugar Loaf and it became all too clear to the advancing troops that the German defences had suffered little damage. The distance between the opposing trenches was at its widest at this point, some 400 yards, and the 2/1st Bucks had to cover a further 200 yards from Rhondda Sap to reach the enemy trenches. It proved impossible and of the 300 men who made the assault, only 100 managed to return to their own lines.

By 6.30pm, only half an hour after the start of the attack, the situation on the British 61st Division front was extremely serious.[94] Some temporary progress had been made on the extreme right (2/7th Warwicks), but elsewhere the attack had been thrown back with heavy casualties. In particular, the Germans still held the Sugar Loaf and this was to have a critical effect on the Australian 5th Division.

The three Australian brigades deployed into no man's land at 5.45pm not through sally ports, but over their parapets using scaling ladders.[95] On the far left of the attack, the Australians exploded a mine containing

1,200 pounds of ammonal in no man's land at zero hour. The purpose was to create a barrier – the debris from the explosion – that would protect the flanks of the 31st and 32nd Battalions (8 Brigade) from enemy enfilade fire. The Germans were still able, however, to man their machine guns and fire into the advancing Australian troops. With considerable losses, the companies of the 31st and 32nd Battalions pushed forwards and captured the German trenches.

In the centre, the 54th and 53rd Battalions of 14 Brigade also managed to capture the enemy trenches and they advanced towards their objective – the German support line. What now became apparent, however, was that the enemy second line just did not exist. The trench maps provided by British Intelligence were inaccurate. Isolated groups of the 54th and 53rd Battalions dug in and consolidated their position as best they could.

On the left and in the centre the Australians had therefore largely achieved their objectives. On the right, where the Australian 15 Brigade were alongside the British 184 Brigade, the situation was quite different. Attacking next to the 2/1st Bucks, the Australian 59th Battalion advanced at zero hour but after fifty yards they were caught in the enfilade fire from the Sugar Loaf and were unable to reach the German lines. Next to the 59th Battalion, the 60th Battalion lost heavily as it advanced and reached the German wire only to be caught by machine-gun fire from the Sugar Loaf.

In the confusion of battle, the overall picture was far from clear. Major General Mackenzie of the 61st Division had, by 7.30pm, received reports that his troops on the right had achieved some success but that little progress had been made in the centre. He had also been informed, wrongly, that a foothold had been gained on the Sugar Loaf. To Mackenzie, the overall situation was sufficiently positive to order, as was within his authority, the three British brigades to make a further attack at 9.00pm.

Brigadier General Carter of 184 Brigade had a somewhat clearer idea of the dire situation in front of the Sugar loaf. If the 2/1st Bucks were to make a second attack they would require considerable support from the Australians on their left. Consequently, Carter sent a message, through the normal Divisional channels, to 15 Australian Brigade: "Am attacking at 9.00pm. Can your right battalion co-operate?" Elliott, commanding 15 Brigade, was aware that the remains of the 59th Battalion were in no man's land, unable to move. Nevertheless, he took the courageous decision to bring up a fresh battalion, the 58th, for the 9.00pm assault.[96]

Meanwhile, the true extent of the British 61st Division losses was gradually emerging. Most of the assault battalions had lost half their troops. An attack at 9.00pm was out of the question. Major Christie-Miller of the 2/1st Bucks later wrote: "it [was] next to impossible to persuade the authorities that there was nothing left to attack with – the Battalion or what was left of it being mostly in No man's land and our trenches under intense bombardment".[97] The survivors of the 2/7th Warwicks, who had captured the German trenches on the extreme right, had now fallen back to their own lines and the other battalions of the 61st Division were in no fit state to renew the offensive.

When Haking became aware of the overall situation, he immediately countermanded Mackenzie's order for the 9.00pm attack.[98] At 8.30pm, therefore, Mackenzie, mindful of the request for support from the Australian 15 Brigade, sent a second message to the Australian 5th Division Headquarters: "Under instructions from the Corps Commander am withdrawing from captured enemy line after dark." However, owing, as the Australian Official History records, "to failure of the Headquarters of the [Australian] 5th Division", this message did not reach Elliott of the Australian 15 Brigade until 9.25pm. This was too late to stop the Australian 58th Battalion, together with the remnants of the 59th Battalion, already in no man's land, from carrying out the 9.00pm attack on the left of the Sugar Loaf. They were entirely unsupported on either flank. The Australian Official History described the attack as "one of the bravest and most hopeless assaults ever undertaken by the Australian Imperial Force". Two-thirds of the way across no man's land the German machine guns on the Sugar Loaf opened up: "The line was shattered and the men dazed . . . the two Companies of the 58th that had made the attack were practically wiped out."[99]

On the left of the Australian line, the situation of 14 and 8 Brigades had become increasingly untenable as they were bombed and counterattacked by German reinforcements. By 3.15am on 20 July most of the Australians had been forced back to their own trenches. Haking still held the hope that a further attack during the night by 184 Brigade might capture the Sugar Loaf, but Brigadier General Carter reported at 3.00am that it was impossible to mount such an attack. At 5.00am the Divisional Commanders met with Monro and Haking at Sailly and orders were issued to withdraw all troops still in no man's land and abandon the attack.

The Bavarian History of the War summed up the situation:

The three regiments [17th, 16th and 21st], together with the 6th Bavarian R. Pioneer Company, succeeded up to the morning of the 20th in driving, step by step, the British out of their positions, cutting them off or overpowering them. 20 machine guns were captured, and 500 prisoners. The 6th Bavarian R. Division could boast of having stood fast without help, and having defeated the aim of the enemy, viz. the joining up of his forces.[100]

The euphoria of the German troops contrasted with the British and Australian sense of failure. Sapper W. H. Hollwey's diary entry for 20 July reads: "Now it seems all like a nightmare."[101] Sergeant Major S.W.D. Lockwood of the 2/6th Glosters noted in his memoirs: "Everyone knows the Battle of Fromelles . . . was a disastrous failure . . . it led to us being named the 'Sacrifice Division'."[102] A. J. Winter of the Australian 14 Brigade wrote in his diary for 21 July: "Many a good man went 'west' . . . the whole show was a failure."[103]

* * * *

The tactical objective of the attack at Fromelles was to capture and hold a 4,000-yard stretch of the German line. It completely failed to do this and, in the process, incurred some 7,000 British and Australian casualties.[104] It was a defeat and Haking himself, on a number of occasions, acknowledged it to be so.[105] The purpose of this section is to discuss the extent to which Haking was personally responsible for the debacle at Fromelles.

The numerous criticisms of the Fromelles operation that have been made over the past ninety years can be summarized under the following headings: "muddled" thinking; inadequate planning leading to a reckless and futile loss of life; and the unwarranted blame levelled by Haking at the British and Australian troops. As regards the strategic thinking, there is every indication that it was both confused and inconsistent and it is understandable that Elliott, of the shattered 15 Australian Brigade, should call it a "tactical abortion".[106] Bean, in the Australian Official History, summarized "the changes of form through which the plans of this ill-fated operation had successively passed"[107] and the uncertainties that accompanied these various "changes of form" were further compounded by indecision as to whether the operation should take place at all.

This "muddle" cannot be regarded as Haking's responsibility. As already seen, GHQ ordered, in both April and May, that "attacks on a considerable scale" should be prepared. By 9 May Haking, liaising with the Australian I Corps, had produced a plan for such an attack "towards the Fromelles-Aubers Ridge" and this scheme was approved in principle by both Monro and Plumer on 21 June. However, between 21 June and 16 July the plan underwent a series of bewildering variations: a breakthrough at the junction of the two Armies; an effort by Monro to move the attack area from Fromelles-Aubers to Hill 70; the reinstatement by GHQ of Haking's plan; the proposal by Monro for an artillery demonstration; the enlargement of Haking's plan by GHQ to involve three divisions; the reduction in scope of the attack to two divisions; and then, on 16 July, the announcement that GHQ considered the operation unnecessary. By that time, however, arrangements were already well advanced for the attack to take place on the following day. The assault troops had been moved to the front and the preliminary bombardment had begun. Under these circumstances, it is little wonder that Haking was "most emphatic" that the attack should take place and Monro and Plumer supported him. When bad weather hindered artillery registration on 17 July, Haking, probably bemused and discouraged by the changes and indecision of the previous two weeks, proposed that the action should be postponed. Haking's note to Monro of 18 July is somewhat ambiguous. It could be read as meaning a postponement simply until the following day, or it could have referred to one of Butler's proposals of 16 July that the operation should be postponed indefinitely. Haking had good reason to have preferred the second of these options. Support from GHQ had all but disappeared, Plumer was hardly involved, Monro was lukewarm and Haking had learnt, only three days earlier, that the artillery and troops from the Second Army, far from being the seasoned I ANZAC Corps as originally discussed, were to be those of the 5th Australian Division [II ANZAC] whose experience of the Western Front was no more than a few days. At his Conference at Sailly on 16 July, Haking made this point clearly to the Divisional Commanders:

> I am aware that the arrangements made for this attack have had to be done in a hurry, I only got the order myself in the afternoon of the 14th [July] and I did not get the exact details of the force available for the operations until 15th [July] . . . many of the troops to be employed have had to be moved rapidly from one place to another and are new to the ground and there is a great deal of work to be done.[108]

Major General McCay, GOC 5th Australian Division, confirmed this same point in his report on Fromelles: "At 11pm on 13 July . . . I was informed that the 5th Australian Division would be employed in an offensive operation under the GOC XI Army Corps. At that time, the 5th Australian Division . . . had just taken over from the 4th Australian Division on 12 July . . . the Divisional Artillery came to the front on the night of 12 July."[109] Haking has been criticized for using inexperienced troops at Fromelles but, as he wrote to Monro after the attack: "it was absolutely necessary to use the two new Divisions [61st and 5th] because it would not have been practicable to move any other Divisions into the position in the time available".[110] Having provided Haking with green infantry and inexperienced artillery there is, therefore, something ironic about Plumer's note to Monro of 15 July: "I think we have given Haking all we can for his job."[111]

The entire episode could have been honourably shelved at, and subsequent to, the Conference with Butler on 16 July and the decision was squarely with Monro. On 17 July Monro, who had full authority to call off the attack, showed further vacillation and quite unnecessarily put the problem back to Haig who simply repeated his decision, relayed by Butler, of 16 July. Consequently, when the attack at Fromelles took place it was the result not only of confused thinking but also of blatant indecision. Both of these unfortunate features stemmed from GHQ and Monro, not from Haking.

Haking's plan for the attack certainly had its weaknesses. The key point of the assault – against the heavily defended Sugar Loaf salient – was at the junction of the First and Second Armies and therefore of the two Divisions involved. It was a disposition that inevitably brought problems of command and communication and the tragic fate of the 58th Australian Battalion on the evening of 19 July resulted largely from these difficulties. In addition, the width of no man's land was at its greatest in front of the most critical point of the attack, the Sugar Loaf – a formidable 400 yards. It is noticeable that, when the assault took place, the greatest successes were achieved on the extreme flanks where no man's land was around 200 yards wide.

Other weaknesses of the plan, however, were not of Haking's making. It was stipulated within the 61st Division, for example, that entry into no man's land should be through sally ports, which became easy targets for the German machine guns and resulted in many British casualties. The 2/4th and 2/6th Glosters and the 2/4th Royal Berkshires suffered heavily as they left their trenches through sally ports and the 2/1st Bucks, who became quickly aware of the problem, managed to avoid major losses only by entering no man's land via Rhondda Sap. Fortunately, the 5th Australian Division chose to advance over their parapets. The sally ports, however, although causing losses in the British battalions, did not prevent the attacking troops from being in their assault positions in no man's land at the appointed time.

Brigadier General Elliott of the Australian 15 Brigade, in his article in *Duckboard* in 1930, made a number of criticisms of the Fromelles attack. He commented that the proposed three-day bombardment leading up to the attack "cast aside any intention of secrecy or surprise (the supreme element in war)". In fact, although Haking was generally well aware of the importance of secrecy, it was impossible to move artillery, ammunition and troops in that sector without the Germans observing all that was taking place from their positions on Aubers

Ridge. Elliott also criticized Haking's plan because "no reserves were provided". Elliott therefore seems to have been unaware of the instruction give by Haking on 16 July to both the attacking Divisions that, "only one-half of the effectives of each brigade was to be employed – fresh troops would be available either to relieve the assaulting troops, repel counter attacks, or to undertake offensive operations".[112]

A further criticism by Elliott concerned the number of gas cylinders that had been placed in the British front line "when it was certain that the line would be bombarded". These cylinders, some of which had been used by the 61st Division on 15 July, were part of the programme of minor operations designed to support the Somme offensive. When the Fromelles attack was authorized it was clear that these cylinders presented a potential hazard and needed to be removed. This strenuous work took place during the nights preceding the attack and caused considerable fatigue amongst the infantry. As a result, alleged Elliott, the troops were thoroughly exhausted before the attack took place. Haking was well aware that the removal of the gas cylinders was a considerable undertaking and consequently, taking advantage of the postponement on 17 July, ordered that the assault companies "should be rested as much as possible during the nights of 18/19 and on the morning of the 19th; also that good breakfasts and dinners should be given on the 19th".[113] There is also evidence that the assault companies of both the 61st and 5th Divisions were able to have adequate rest. An officer of the 2/1st Bucks, for example, wrote, referring to 18 July: "It was a fine night and everyone slept well. At 6 in the next morning we were at breakfast, a good meal with, I remember, an extra ration of tobacco and cigarettes."[114]

Had the attack been successful then the British front line would have moved forward between 200 and 400 yards. This has given rise to the comment that the plan was flawed since such a forward movement would serve only to place the British trenches nearer the enemy guns on the Aubers Ridge. However, even prior to the attack, German guns were able to shell the British lines with pinpoint accuracy and it is unlikely that a movement of up to 400 yards would have made them more vulnerable than they were already.

The reasons for the failure of Fromelles were not the issues of planning defects, lack of secrecy, infantry fatigue, the hazard of gas cylinders or the use of the sally ports. Nor were the regrettable "changes of form" of the attack responsible for the subsequent disaster. Fromelles did not succeed in its local objectives because of two major factors: the formidable German defence system and the inability of the British and Australian artillery to silence the machine guns on the Sugar Loaf and Wick salients. By 17 July Haking was well aware of the inexperience of his artillery and it can be argued that he should have used the opportunity provided by the delays of 16/17 July to convince Monro of the wisdom of an indefinite postponement. That he did not do so is an indication not only of his personal commitment to the operation, but also of his characteristic over-optimism and, to that extent, Haking is blameworthy. However, it can also be argued that, given all that had taken place, Haking would have reasoned that the decision to call off the attack rested solely with his superior, Monro. In Haking's mind, the response by Haig on 18 July finally authorising the operation would have confirmed his view that the plan should proceed.

One further aspect of Haking's generalship at Fromelles merits particular comment and that was his denigration of the troops taking part. In his Report to the First Army (24 July), Haking wrote: "I think the lessons to be learned from the attack apply more to the Divisions who took part in it than to ordinary trained Divisions . . . The Australian Infantry attacked in the most gallant manner and gained the enemy's position, but they were not sufficiently trained to consolidate the ground gained. They were eventually compelled to withdraw and lost heavily in doing so. The 61st Division were not sufficiently imbued with the offensive spirit to go in like one man at the appointed time. Some parts of the attack were late deploying beyond our parapet, some parts though deployed did not make the rush at the exact moment given, and other parts carried the enemy's line . . . From my experience in this attack I am quite convinced that with two good Divisions we can carry and hold the line whenever it is desirable . . . I think the attack, although it failed, has done both Divisions a great deal of good."[115] Although Haking, along with Monro and Plumer, had confirmed to GHQ at the 16 July Conference that the troops "were adequate for the operation", he now gave his opinion that one Division was "not sufficiently trained" and the other lacked the "offensive spirit". There is little evidence to suggest that the infantry held back in their attempts to take the German lines[116] and Haking's remarks did no justice to the considerable courage shown by the troops involved in the attack. As one regimental officer later wrote, Haking's words were a "gross slander".[117] Thus, Haking's tendency in failure to criticize his troops and his lack of empathy as to their circumstances was once more displayed as it had been at Loos in September 1915. It was a regrettable and unattractive characteristic of his generalship.

* * * *

The above sections have discussed the failure of the attack at Fromelles and the consequent repercussions as regards Haking's reputation. There is, however, a further important aspect of Fromelles that requires consideration and that is the overriding strategic objective of the attack which, as set out in the First Army Order No. 100 of 15 July, was: "to prevent the enemy from moving troops Southwards to take part in the main battle". The "main battle" was, at that point, about to enter its second critical phase – the assault on the important Pozières Ridge.

It was clearly of great importance that German reinforcements should be prevented, if at all possible, from reaching the Somme.[118] When Haking wrote to his Divisional Commanders on 16 July, he ordered that all the troops who were taking part in the Fromelles attack should be made aware that: "It has been ascertained that the enemy is moving his troops from our front to resist the attacks of our comrades in the South. The Commander in Chief [Haig] had directed XI Corps to attack the enemy in front of us, capture his front line system of trenches, and thus prevent him from reinforcing his troops to the South."[119]

Historians have generally taken the view that Fromelles did not have the effect of preventing German troops on the XI Corps front from moving to the Somme. The British Official History relegated discussion of this issue to a footnote and concluded that, following the 19 July attack, Falkenhayn had prevailed on his Sixth Army that both IX Reserve Corps and the Guard Reserve Corps should be sent to the Somme area.[120] Peter Pederson has written that the Germans were well aware that Fromelles was simply a feint and that: "they could now move troops from the Aubers/Fromelles area to the Somme or anywhere else, defeating the whole purpose of the operation".[121] Similarly, Patrick Lindsay has noted that a captured copy of the British orders: "confirmed what the Germans already believed: that the attack was a feint . . . They therefore released the reserves that they had held near Lille and sent them south to fight on the Somme."[122] The Australian Official History stated that the result of Fromelles: "was to inform the enemy that only a feint was intended. The normal inference was that he could now move his troops without fear."[123] The writer of the Foreword to Paul Cobb's account of Fromelles claimed that the attack failed in its aim "to 'fix' the German forces in their sector and dissuade them from sending reinforcements down to the Somme" and Cobb later states: "The Germans were not deterred from redeploying troops to their Somme front."[124]

Despite these negative conclusions about the effect of Fromelles, there is some more positive evidence to suggest that the transfer of German troops to the Somme was at least delayed, if not prevented. The Intelligence Officer of the 6th Bavarian Reserve Division, which had borne the brunt of the attack, reported on 20 July: "There are no signs of any immediate repetition of the enemy attack . . . However, judging by the general situation, a new push is not impossible."[125] This was confirmed in a Bavarian document found in 1923: "An order was captured declaring that the object of the attack was to keep German troops engaged in the sector so as to keep pressure from the Somme . . . a repetition of these attacks is therefore to be expected."[126] As the otherwise sceptical Australian official historian conceded: "it may have occurred to the Bavarians that the expenditure of 7,000 troops for only a feint was unlikely".[127] Brigadier General H. E. Elliott of the Australian 15 Brigade, wrote to his wife immediately after the attack: "We have received the most gracious thanks of all the British – Generals Haking, Plumer, Godley and others . . . They say we accomplished our object which was to keep the Germans from moving their reserves from in front of us down to the Somme."[128] Even in 1930, Elliott was able to write: "the feint to distract the attention of the German staff from Pozieres . . . cannot with certainty be judged to have been completely ineffective."[129]

Various Australian histories, produced in the period following the war, also recorded that the overall aim of Fromelles was achieved. The author of the history of the Australian 5th Division wrote: "It should not be forgotten that while the operation itself was an unqualified local failure, its main purpose in preventing a withdrawal of enemy troops was doubtless to some extent achieved."[130] Lieutenant the Honourable Staniforth Smith recorded in 1919: "the attack had the effect of holding up, and even turning back, forces that were moving south to Pozières".[131] Many of the letters published in the *Sydney Morning Herald* on the third anniversary of the attack touched on the subject of German troop movements. Chaplain James Green gave a sober account of the attack and concluded: "Possibly it prevented the Germans sending men and guns to the Somme."[132] Lieutenant Colonel G. MacLaurin, writing on 26 July, was equally tentative: "it was rumoured that the Boche had temporarily diverted 13 troop trains from the Somme".[133] A soldier of the Australian 14 Brigade – the "Herald Digger" – was, however, more definite: "A captured German, who spoke excellent English, told us that his battalion was preparing to entrain when news of our 'breakthrough' reached them. Immediately, the men were ordered to detrain and were turned back to help their severely pressed comrades . . . Probably [the Germans] thought a new offensive might have started and he determined to hold his troops there until things developed a little more. Anyhow, the couple of days delay meant that these two German Divisions were not on the Somme, where every man was wanted, and our feint to hold his troops and keep him jumpy was successful."[134]

Given the heavy Australian losses and the belief that the story of Fromelles had been kept hidden from the public, it is, of course, possible and understandable, that the above positive remarks were based entirely on hearsay and were written to make the casualty figures appear to some extent worthwhile. But other positive comment about German troop movements came from British sources. An official report on the Fromelles action stated: "The operation, as one for holding the enemy, may have been a success."[135] This was also the view of the historian of the 2/5th Glosters who had been at Fromelles with the 61st Division: "[the attack] probably had the effect of keeping the German Divisions there, at any rate, for the time being".[136] Haig's diary entry for 20 July is quite definite: ". . . the enterprise has certainly had the effect of obliging the Enemy to retain reserves in that area".[137] One person who claimed to have no doubts as to the success of Fromelles was Haking. In September 1916, when he was temporarily in command of the First Army, Haking wrote to GHQ advocating yet another advance towards Fromelles: "[It] will be delivered at the same point, and with the same object, as the attack that was carried out by the XI Corps on 19 July and so successfully detained two hostile divisions which would otherwise have been moved southwards."[138] Haking repeated this claim in November 1916 in a note to the GOC 61st Division: "I particularly wish the division to realise that although the attack they made on 19 July was not a complete tactical success . . . the result of the operation was that the enemy was compelled to cancel an order for the transference of two Divisions from this front to the Somme."[139]

It might be expected that Haking would make such claims, but he did have some serious supporting evidence. British Intelligence Summaries in the period 20 July-19 August 1916 contained enthusiastic reports that German troops were not being withdrawn from the XI Corps front. The Summary for the period 1-16 August included the statement: "It is fairly clear that there has been no withdrawal of troops from Loos northwards and that the II Bavarian Corps, the XXVII Reserve Corps and 6 Bavarian Reserve Division are still in their normal positions [i.e. facing the XI Corps front]." Summary No. 581 reported on 14 August: "It is, however, clear from prisoners statements that . . . they know nothing of any movement of troops from their front." Of particular relevance is the information in Summary No. 586, dated 19 August: "It is generally understood that the XXVII Reserve Corps was to have been withdrawn from the La Bassée area about the end of July or beginning of August and sent to the Somme region. This move was cancelled as a result of our attack on July 19 near Fauquissart, which caused the enemy to change his plans, owing to his fear of further attacks of a similar nature."[140]

The Australian (Anzac II) Intelligence Summaries made similar points. Summary No. 66 of 4/5 September quoted a deserter from the

German 46th Reserve Division: "The fear of an attack on this front . . . causes [us] to work to strengthen [our] defences." Summary No. 74 of 13 September confirmed that although other German divisions in the vicinity had been moved to the Somme, they had been subsequently replaced and the 6th Bavarian Reserve Division, the 50th Reserve Division and the XXVII Reserve Corps had been retained in their normal positions.[141]

These Intelligence Reports are almost certainly the source of the firm claims made by both Haig and Haking that enemy troops had not been transferred south from the XI Corps front. However, Intelligence reports often tended to be optimistic in their content and, in themselves, cannot be taken as absolute proof that the Germans did not move troops. For a more certain indication of whether Fromelles achieved its main strategic objective, it is necessary to investigate the official German records of troop placements. Information in the German Official History,[142] together with the history of the 251 German divisions,[143] provides useful data. The German Official History contains maps and a schedule (*Zur Schlacht an der Somme 1916*) which shows the positions of German Divisions serving in the Somme area, and the history of the 251 Divisions gives details of the movements and positions of these divisions. The Table below summarizes the relevant information from these two documents.

German Troop Movements

Corps	Division	Sector	Ref. Page In 251 Divs	Dates In Flanders	Date To Somme
	183	In Reserve	624	June 1916	2 July
	3 Guards	In Reserve	73	June 1916	1 July
	50 Res.	Armentières	494	April–Sept 1916	Sept 16
	6 Bav. Res.	Laventie	139	April 1915–Sept 1916	Sept 27
XXVII RES.	54 Res.	la Bassée	515	Mar-Aug 1916	End Aug
	53 Res.	la Bassée	508	Mar- Aug 1916	End Aug
II BAV.	3 Bav.	Auchy-Loos	81	Oct 1915–Aug 1916	Aug 25
	4 Bav.	Auchy-Loos	102	Oct 1915–Aug 1916	Aug 25

Two criteria have been assumed. First, that the geographical area being considered is the fifteen-miles stretch of line Loos north to Armentieres – i.e. mainly the XI Corps front and the area most affected by the Fromelles attack. It should be noted here that the German divisions detailed in the British Official History as being moved south (those of the IX Reserve Corps and the Guard Reserve Corps) were transferred from the Souchez-Vimy sector which was well outside the XI Corps area and some twenty miles away from Fromelles. The second criteria is one of timing – that German troops who stayed in the Loos-Armentières area for a month or more following the attack can reasonably be considered as being kept there to defend the line against possible future operations. However, given the gruelling situation on the Somme, it would be unrealistic to expect that German divisions placed between Loos and Armentières would not be transferred south at some time to take part in the Somme fighting.

From the information in the Table, it can be seen that eight German Divisions (including those in reserve) were in position between Loos and Armentières on 1 July – the first day of the Somme battle. These divisions were, south to north, the 3rd and 4th Bavarian Divisions (II Bavarian Corps); the 53rd and 54th Reserve Divisions (XXVII Reserve Corps); the 6th Bavarian Reserve Division; the 50th Reserve Division; and, in reserve (some thirty miles behind the German front line), the 183rd Division (near Tournai) and the 3rd Guards Division (near Valenciennes).

Of these divisions, the 3rd Guards Division and 183rd Division (both in reserve near Lille) were moved to the Somme area on 1 and 2 July respectively and therefore well before the Fromelles operation took place.[144] The remaining six divisions remained in their positions facing XI Corps for periods ranging from five to nine weeks after Fromelles before they were transferred to the Somme region. Had any of these divisions been moved to the Pozières sector in, say, late July, the course of that attack, in which the I Anzac Corps was heavily involved, might well have been quite different. As it was, I ANZAC lost 23,000 men during the fighting around Pozières. If the Germans had received additional reinforcements from the Fromelles sector, that number could have been much higher.[145]

There is sufficient information in the above discussion of German troop movements in relation to the Fromelles attack to suggest that the statements of Haig and Haking, the Intelligence summaries, the comments from the various Australian sources, and the information contained in the German Official History and the history of the 251 German divisions, between them constitute a case to conclude that German troops were retained opposite the XI Corps front. As Monro said to a gathering of the townspeople of Merville: "it has been impossible for the Germans to move one Regiment from our front to send south. Our objective has been achieved."[146] The much-criticized attack at Fromelles on 19 July 1916 can be considered, from a strategic point of view, a success after all.[147]

* * * *

Haking's reputation has, over the years, been associated mainly with the attack at Fromelles. His generalship in that operation was certainly not without its weaknesses and aspects of it merit adverse criticism. However, the level of invective directed at Haking through his involvement in Fromelles, especially from Australian sources, has been unnecessarily extreme. As indicated, much of the criticism has been unjustified. The discussion in this chapter provides a more balanced and objective appraisal of Haking's role at Fromelles.

Notes

1. *BOH 1916*, Vol. II, p.134.
2. C. E. W. Bean, *Official History of Australia in the War of 1914–18: Vol. III: The A.I.F. in France 1916*, p.444 (Henceforth *AOH*.) Original publication date 1929.
3. IWM, Wilson Papers, DS/MISC/80, Reel 6.
4. TNA, CAB 45/134.
5. TNA, CAB 45/136.
6. Basil Liddell Hart, *History of the First World War*, p.325.
7. Denis Winter, *Haig's Command*, p.279.
8. A. H. Farrar-Hockley, *The Somme*, p.200.
9. Robin Neillands, *The Great War Generals on the Western Front 1914–1918*, p.271.
10. Lyn Macdonald, *Somme*, p.161.
11. Simon Robbins, *British Generalship on the Western Front 1914–18*, p.20
12. Paul Cobb, *Fromelles 1916*, p.8.
13. Martin Gilbert, *First World War*, p.268.
14. Ross McMullin 'Pompey Elliott and the Butcher of Fromelles', *The Australian Magazine*, July 20–21, 1996, p.18.
15. Quoted in *AOH*, Vol. III p.446.
16. See John F. Williams, *Anzacs: The Media and the Great War*, Ch. 6.
17. A Herald "Digger", *Sydney Morning Herald*, 2 August 1919.
18. Capt A. D. Ellis, *The Story of the Fifth Division*, p.82.
19. McMullin, 'Pompey Elliott and the Butcher of Fromelles', p. 18.
20. Ross McMullin, 'The Forgotten Fallen', *Sydney Morning Herald*, 19 July 2002.
21. Quoted in Robin S. Corfield, *Don't Forget Me Cobber*, p.417.
22. The birth of the Anzac legend has been identified by the Australian writer L. A. Carlyon, in his *Gallipoli* (New York: Doubleday, 2002), p. 174), as being the article by the *Daily Telegraph* correspondent Ellis Ashmead-Bartlett, published in the Australian dailies on 8 May 1915. The article praised the outstanding courage of the Australian troops in the opening days of the Gallipoli campaign. John Laffin's claim in the *Australian Magazine* of 7 August 1993 must be considered as the most extreme contribution to the Anzac legend: "The soldiery reputation of the Diggers of the Australian

Imperial Force rivals that of any army in the entire 3,500 years' recorded history of warfare – which is the consensus among military historians and generals." At least one modern author has written about Fromelles as though it was an exclusively Australian attack: "In July the English facing the [Bavarian] List [Regiment] were relieved by an aggressive Australian Corps . . . the Australians were ordered to keep the pressure on the Bavarians . . . The Australians raised the ante by obtaining permission to take the German front line." See W. Van der Kloot, *The Lessons of War*, p.127.

23. London *Times* and Melbourne *Argus,* 24 July 1916.
24. No Battle Honours were awarded in connection with Fromelles, although efforts were made in Britain after the war on behalf of the 61st Division, and efforts are continuing today in Australia on behalf of the 5th Division.
25. Quoted in H. R. Williams, *The Gallant Company: An Australian Soldier's Story of 1915–1918*, p.68.
26. Hugh R. Knyvett, *Over There with the Australians*. Quoted in J. F. Williams. Words on 'a lively skirmish', *Journal of the Australian War Memorial*, Oct. 1993, p.25.
27. W. H. Downing, *To the Last Ridge*, pp.8–10.
28. The sculpture, by Peter Corlett of Melbourne, depicts Sergeant Fraser of the Australian 57th Battalion rescuing a comrade of the 60th Battalion.
29. *AOH*, Vol. III, pp.328–447; *BOH 1916*, Vol.II, pp.119–135; *Der Weltkrieg 1914–1918*. X, p.407.
30. AWM, 41/676, From Bean's notes on the Medical History of the War. The Australians were not the only Dominion troops to find fault with British Generals. A Canadian soldier, William Oliver, wrote in November 1915: "There is a feeling growing very strongly everywhere that British Generals one and all are the most incompetent lot of bloody fools." See S. Gwynne, ed., *The Anvil of War: Letters between F. S. Oliver and his Brother 1914–18,* p.124.
31. AWM, 41/674, Note from Dr Lind, 29 September 1933.
32. *AOH*, Vol. III p. 447.
33. Corfield, *Don't Forget Me Cobber*, pp.371–77.
34. *Sydney Morning Herald*, 26 July 1919.
35. AWM, 2 DRL 970, White to Bean, 27 May 1926.
36. AWM, 4–14934, Article in *Duckboard*, 1 Sept 1930.
37. John Laffin, *British Butchers and Bunglers of World War One*, p.85.
38. Peter Pederson, *Fromelles*, p.116.
39. Matt McLachlan, *Walking with the Anzacs*. p. 104.
40. McMullin, 'Pompey Elliott and the Butcher of Fromelles', p.18.
41. Ross McMullin, *Pompey Elliott*, p.235.
42. Neil Tweedie, *The Age*, Melbourne, 1 August 2009. The same newspaper, on 7 November 2009, spoke of "the bloody human waste of Fromelles".
43. Peter Pederson, 'Bringing the Past to Life at Fromelles', *Battlefields Review 25*, 2003, p. 46.
44. Ross McMullin, 'Forgotten Fallen', *Sydney Morning Herald*, 19 July 2002.
45. AWM, 4–14934, Article in *Duckboard*, op. cit.
46. AWM, 2DRL 712, Papers of S. K. Donnan

47. Haking was identified as among John Laffin's ten 'butchers and bunglers'. See Laffin, *Butchers and Bunglers*, p.8.

48. AWM, 4–14934, Article in *Duckboard*, op. cit.

49. Corfield, *Don't Forget Me Cobber*, pp.74–75.

50. Pederson, *Fromelles*, p.112.

51. McLachlan. *Walking with the Anzacs*, p.97.

52. Les Carlyon, *The Great War*, pp.29, 96–97.

53. McMullin, 'Forgotten Fallen', op. cit.

54. Garrie Hutchinson, *Pilgrimage: A Travellers Guide to Australia's Battlefields*. p.109.

55. Patrick Lindsay, *Fromelles*, p.100.

56. For example, Ross McMullin describes Fromelles as a "folly" as does Matt McLachlan. Corfield, Pederson, McMullin, Lyndsay and Hutchinson refer to Haking as a "butcher".

57. TNA, WO 95/165, Kiggell to Monro, Plumer and Allenby, 5 July 1916, OAD 48.

58. TNA, WO 95/163, OAD 291/11.

59. Ibid., OAD 912.

60. TNA, WO 95/164.

61. AWM, 252 A183, Extract from Notes by Corps Commander for Conference at XI Corps HQ, 9 May 1916.

62. TNA, WO 95/164, SS 849/5/28, Haking to Monro, 21 June 1916.

63. AWM, 252 A185, Plumer to Monro, 6 July 1916.

64. TNA, WO 95/165, SS/1205.

65. AWM 252, A185, Monro to GHQ, GS 420/10(a), 9 July 1916.

66. See *AOH*, Vol. III, p.332.

67. TNA, WO 95/165, SS/1205.

68. AWM, 252, A185, G.S. 417, Monro to I, IV and XI Corps Commanders, 11 July 1916.

69. TNA, WO 95/165, Secret Memorandum, Note on Operations on First Army Front, 16 July 1916. Haking was not present at the meeting between Butler and Monro.

70. TNA, WO 95/165, OAD 66, 14 July 1916.

71. The three divisions were to be the British 31st and 61st, and the Australian 5th.

72. AWM, 252, A184, First Army Report on Fromelles. As a result, the 31st Division was not used in the attack.

73. AWM, 252, A184, First Army Report on Fromelles.

74. TNA, WO 95/165, RHS 1146, 16 July 1916.

75. TNA, WO 95/165, Memorandum of Visit to First Army, 16 July 1916.

76. AWM, 252, A184, First Army Report on Fromelles.

77. TNA, WO 95/16, G.S. 420(a), 17 July 1916.

78. TNA, WO 95/165, G.S. 420/15 A.

79. Ibid. Haig was still concerned that the Germans were transferring troops from the Lille area to the Somme and the Diary entry for 17 July noted: "The enemy seems to have withdrawn troops from that part of his front." Haig Diary. TNA, WO 256/11.

80. TNA, WO 95/885, RHS 1148/6, 18 July 1916.
81. i.e. since the attack on Aubers Ridge in May 1915.
82. *BOH 1916*, Vol.II, p.121.
83. Maj. B. T. Wilson, *Studies of German Defences near Lille.* Quoted in a Report on Fromelles (p.44) carried out by Peter Barton in 2007 for the Australian Army History Unit (Unpublished).
84. Beckett, *Great War 1914–18*, pp.166–67.
85. Centre for Buckingham Studies, *The Lee Magazine*, September 1916.
86. Dr Fridolin Sollender, *Vier Jahr Westfront: Geschichte des Regiment List. RIR 16.* p.124. Cpl Adolf Hitler served in the List Regiment in the Fromelles area in 1916.
87. TNA, CAB 45/172, German Records Relating to Australian Operations on the Western Front, Capt. J J W Herbertson, 1923, p.1.
88. TNA, WO 95/3033.
89. Hauptstaatsarchiv Kriegsarchiv, Munich, Artillery Flight No. 201, 6 BRD, Bund 8, Doc. Register No 2502. Quoted in a Report on Fromelles carried out by Peter Barton in 2007 on behalf of the Australian Army History Unit (Unpublished). Henceforth referred to as the Barton Report.
90. *BOH 1916*,Vol. II. p.124.
91. TNA, WO 95/3033.
92. Hauptstaatsarchiv Kriegsarchiv, Munich, 6 BRD, Bund 8, Doc. Register No 2502, Report of Artillery Flight 201. From the Barton Report.
93. The history of the 16th Bavarian Reserve Regiment and a report by the 14th Bav. RIB both make the point that in the late afternoon of 19 July an attack was considered "imminent" i.e. the exact timing was not known. See Sollender, *Vier Jahre Westfront*, p.214; and Report 8287 of 14 Bav. RIB to 6 Bav.Res. Div.29.7.1916. Bayerische Hauptstaadtarchiv Bund 8.
94. The summary of events of 19/20 July is taken from the report of the 61st Division in TNA, WO 95/3033.
95. The summary of the 5th Division attack is taken from its report, dated 25 July. See TNA, WO 95/165.
96. *AOH*, Vol. III, p.392.
97. Centre for Buckinghamshire Studies, Lt. Col. G. Christie-Miller, *The Second Bucks Battalion 1914–18: An Unofficial Record*, 2 Vols. Typescript. Vol 1 p. 185.
98. TNA, WO 95/885, XI Corps message G.R.16. Haking telephoned the order at 8.20pm.
99. *AOH*, Vol. III, p. 394.
100. TNA, CAB 45/172. From *Die Bayern im Grossen Kriege, 1914–1918.* Quoted by Capt J. J. W. Herbertson, 'German Records Relative to Australian Operations on the Western Front', 1923
101. IWM, 98/17/1, Diary of Sapper Hollwey of 3/1st (South Midlands Field Company), Royal Engineers.
102. IWM, 90/21/1, Sgt Maj S. W. D. Lockwood, 'First World War Memoirs, 1914–1918', pp.30–34.

103. AWM, PR 89/163, Diary of A. J. Winter, 55th Battalion, 14 Brigade, 5th Australian Division.
104. Australian casualties at Fromelles were more than three times those of the British. The reason for this has never been clearly established. XI Corps Orders to both the Australian and the British Divisions were the same: that two battalions from each brigade, i.e. half the available troops, should carry out the attack. However, the Brigade orders of the British 61st Division stipulated not only that two battalions per brigade should make the assault, but that only two of the four platoons in each battalion should take part. The reason for this difference in orders is not apparent. Corfield has raised the issue, without settling it, that the British troops were purposely held back allowing the Australians to take the brunt of the attack. However, this sinister interpretation makes little sense in the context of the assault plan. The usual explanation for the difference in casualty numbers is that the battalions of the 61st Division were under strength, which they were, but not to the extent that would account for the difference. It is known that McCay, the 5th Division Commander, pushed in extra troops and this would have contributed to the high Australian casualty figure.
105. For example, in his letter to the 61st Division. See TNA, WO 95/885, RHS 1194/2, dated 1 November 1916; and in his note to First Army HQ dated 24 July 1916 in TNA, WO 95/166, RHS 1146/15.
106. AWM, 4–14934, Article in *Duckboard*.
107. *AOH*, Vol. III, p. 350. Bean's summary, although incomplete, is succinct and damning.
108. AWM, 252, A183, Bean Papers.
109. TNA, WO 95/165, Marked 859/G, 25 July 1916.
110. Ibid., RHS 1146/15, Haking to Advanced First Army, 24 July 1916.
111. AWM, 252, A185.
112. AWM, 252, A184, First Army Report on Fromelles. This order was given at Haking's Conference with Divisional Commanders on 16 July.
113. TNA, WO 95/165, Australian 5th Division Report. The point is also covered in the 61st Division War Diary: See TNA, WO 95/3033.
114. Centre for Buckinghamshire Studies, DX/780, *The Lee Magazine*, October 1916.
115. TNA, WO 95/165, XI Corps to First Army, RHS 1146/15, 24 July 1916.
116. Hauptstaatsarchiv Kriegsarchiv, Munich, 6BRD, Bund 21, A report by 11 (Kompagnie) RIR 16, however, stated: "Some of the Australians only left the trench hesitantly, and this is when their officers moved up with drawn revolvers and tried to move them forward." Quoted in the Barton Report.
117. TNA, CAB 45/134, Capt Wilfred Greene to Edmonds, 13 May 1937.
118. The Germans had the same concern. The historians of the 241st and 243rd Reserve Regiments (XXVII Res.Corps), near la Bassée, both made the point that their objective was to prevent the British from moving men and artillery to the Somme. See Knoppe, *241 RIR*, p.208 (IWM, 02(43)445, Acc No 16113); and Winzer, *243 RIR*, p. 116 (IWM, 029430445, Acc No 10372).

119. AWM, 4 1/22/4, Pt. 1, Letter (RHS 1146) contained in the *Report on Operations on front of XI Corps on July 17 and 19/20, 1916.*

120. *BOH 1916*, Vol. II, p.135.

121. Pederson, *Fromelles*, p.107.

122. Lindsay, *Fromelles*, p.157.

123. *AOH*, Vol. III, p.443.

124. Cobb, *Fromelles*, pp.9, 158.

125. AWM, 27, 111/13, Translation of *Angriff der Englander am 19 und 20 July 1916 bei Fromelles.*

126. TNA, CAB 45/172, *German Records Relating to Australian Operations on the Western Front. Collected by Capt J. J. W. Herbertson in Connection with the Official Historian's Questionnaire, 1923.* The particular question put by Bean was: "What inference did the Germans draw from this attack?"

127. *AOH*, Vol. III, p.443.

128. AWM, 2DRL/0513, 7/4, Elliott to his wife, 20 July 1916.

129. AWM, 4–14934, Article in *Duckboard.*

130. Ellis, *Story of the Fifth Division*, p. 112.

131. Lt the Hon Staniforth Smith, *The Australian Campaigns in The Great War.* p.73.

132. *Sydney Morning Herald*, 19 July 1919, 'Fleurbaix: The Mystery Battle'.

133. *Sydney Morning Herald*, 26 July 1919, 'Fleurbaix'.

134. *Sydney Morning Herald*, 2 August 1919, 'Fleurbaix'.

135. TNA, WO 95/165, First Army War Diary, July 1916.

136. Barnes, *Story of the 2/5 Gloucestershire Regiment*, p.43.

137. Sheffield and Bourne, *Haig Diaries and Letters*, p.208.

138. TNA, WO 95/885, XI Corps, RHS 1194/2, 2 September 1916

139. TNA, WO 95/166, First Army No. GS 446/1(a). An effort has been made by the writer to identify the two divisions said to have boarded a train and then detrained. The XXVII Reserve Corps was made up of two divisions, but the records of the 54th Division, held in the *Hauptstaatarchiv* in Stuttgart (M113, M114 and M411) give no indication that the Division planned to move to the south by train. However, the records do confirm that the Division remained in the la Bassée area until the end of August/beginning of September. The records of the second XXVII Reserve Corps Division, the 53rd, have not yet been found. The records of the 6th Bavarian Res Division, held in the *Bayerisches Hauptstaatsarchiv* in Munich, also give no indication of training or de-training, but confirm that the Division remained opposite Laventie until late September 1916. .

140. TNA, WO 157/66, First Army Intelligence Summary, August 1916.

141. TNA, CAB 157/579.

142. *Der Weltkrieg*, 10, Maps and Schedule in back cover pocket.

143. *Two Hundred and Fifty One Divisions of the German Army which Participated in the War (1914–1918).*

144. Patrick Lindsay, the Australian author, implies (wrongly) that these two divisions were moved south *after* the Fromelles attack. See Lindsay, *Fromelles*, p.157.

145. See Christopher Duffy, *Through German Eyes: the British and the Somme 1916*, pp.183–192.

146. Sir George Barrow, *The Life of Sir Charles Carmichael Monro*, p.110.

147. It should be noted that the present writer has previously and erroneously asserted that Fromelles: "failed in its main strategic objective – to prevent the Germans from transferring troops south to the main battle of the Somme." Only the *BOH 1916*, Vol. II had been consulted. See Michael Senior, *No Finer Courage: A Village in the Great War*, p.170.

CHAPTER V

Haking – Trench Warfare – 1917

It had been agreed at Chantilly, in November 1916, that the Allied strategy for 1917 would take the form of simultaneous attacks by the Italians against the Austrians on the Isonzo and by the French and British against the Germans on the Western Front. However, the French Commander in Chief, Joffre, was replaced in December by General Robert Nivelle and, as a result, the strategy for the Western Front took on a completely different shape. Joffre's schemes, which promised slow attrition, had lost favour with the French government who eagerly adopted Nivelle's more attractive plans for a grand offensive to win the war. Nivelle proposed that the French would attack along the Aisne towards the Chemin des Dames with twenty-seven divisions; the elan of the French troops would prevail and a great victory would be gained. The attack began on 16 April and, after four days, the French had penetrated four miles on a sixteen-mile front. By the standards of the time, this was something of an achievement. However, the casualties had been high, some 180,000, the advance had stalled, and there was no sign of a decisive breakthrough. Nivelle had failed the French government and, on 28 April, Pétain replaced him.

The role of the BEF in relation to Nivelle's proposed master-stroke, was outlined by Haig to his Army Commanders on 2 January: "The French will withdraw the maximum number of their troops into reserve with a view to the delivery of a decisive attack on a large scale. In order to give this attack the best chance of success, subsidiary attacks will be made north of the River Oise by French and British troops. The British attacks will be carried out in the Ancre Valley, opposite Arras, and against the Vimy Ridge, by the Fifth, Third and First Armies respectively."[1] In the First Army, preparations were immediately made for an assault on Vimy Ridge and Horne allocated this task to Currie's Canadian Corps. As in the period of the 1916 Somme offensive, therefore, Haking's XI Corps found itself in a supporting role to the main action. The exact nature of this supporting role was at first, at least in Haking's mind, uncertain. In a note to First Army HQ, Haking wrote:

143

the situation had changed to this extent, that the offensive operations which were the foundation of the Corps' policy have now
become subservient to a policy of pure defence . . . the Army
Commander laid it down at the Army Conference on 25 January,
that XI Corps was to concentrate its efforts on defence, and whatever labour, material and energy was available should be devoted
to putting the line in such a state that it could be held by the
smallest possible number of troops.[2]

Haking's description of the part to be played by XI Corps was,
however, a misunderstanding of Horne's wishes and, on 29 January,
Major General Barrow of First Army Staff wrote a somewhat terse
response:

As this statement shows that some misconception exists as to the
Army Commander's intentions regarding the role of XI Corps, he
[Horne] has directed me to point out that he never expressed a
desire for an attitude of pure defence. What he desires is an active
defence, arrangements to hold the line with the smallest possible
number of troops when required, and a continuation of such
preparations as labour and materials permit for an offensive opposite the Aubers Ridge, with a view to the possibility of operations
being undertaken on that front; and this is the policy he laid down
for XI Corps at the recent Corps Commanders' Conference.[3]

The prospect of a possible attack towards Aubers Ridge was, no
doubt, of great interest to Haking, but his immediate concern was the
problem of "holding the line with the smallest possible number of
troops". XI Corps had been steadily reduced in size as divisions were
transferred to take part in the Fifth and Third Army operations in front
of Arras. At the end of December 1916, XI Corps was made up of four
divisions (5th, 34th, 37th, and 56th). In January 34th Division were
moved out, and, in February, with the transfer of 37th Division, XI
Corps was reduced to two divisions (5th and 56th). Moreover, in
support of the French, the BEF had extended its line south and, in the
process, XI Corps had gained a further mile of front to a point just
south of the la Bassée Canal.

Haking was clearly preoccupied with the problem of holding a
frontage of 16,400 yards with only five brigades. In a document headed
"Scheme for Holding the Front of XI Corps, from Boyau 27 to Bond
Street North with Five Brigades",[4] Haking set out in detail his proposals
for the placement of his twelve battalions and the available artillery. The
two sectors most likely to be attacked were, in Haking's opinion:

(i) The high ground on the right of the Cuinchy-Gavinchy sub-section, and, (ii) Neuve Chapelle. As regards (i), should we be forced back from the high ground the enemy would have excellent positions for observing our front line on either flank . . . He would have gained a very material advantage over us. As regards (ii), our loss of Neuve Chapelle would not materially help the enemy or improve his tactical position, but from a moral and sentimental point of view our loss would be of consequence.

As Haking was aware, the Germans were in the process of with-drawing their troops in front of the sector Arras-Loan to the Hindenburg line and, as he pointed out to Horne on 18 March: "A study of the enemy's lines of communication makes it quite clear that if he can create a military desert in the centre of his line, he can concen-trate considerable forces and protect his Northern and Southern systems, and at the same time use those forces for offensive purposes."[5] Haking's concern was that this situation could lead to an attack in the XI Corps area, particularly the sector Cuinchy-Givenchy.

In the same memorandum to Horne, Haking expressed his deep concern:

I am of the opinion, that considering the general situation, we are running an unnecessary risk in holding such a wide front, with very little artillery support, and at the very worst time of the year as regards labour in the line, and consequently with the Infantry very hard worked . . . The Divisions at present holding the XI Corps front have all their Brigades in the line. Each of these Brigades can only give one Battalion six days rest out of 24, because, owing to the extreme repairs to the line and to its communications, it is necessary to adopt a system of two Battalions in the front line, one Battalion in support engaged in work on the front line and communications, and one Battalion resting . . . I think it is my duty to point out further that the Divisions now holding the line will, in my opinion, suffer in mili-tary efficiency, owing to want of rest, if they are kept many weeks in the circumstances existing at present . . . The front we are now holding was originally held by four Divisions, and if four Divisions could be allocated for the purpose until our great offen-sive develops, there is no doubt that they would improve rather than deteriorate as regards military efficiency . . . Failing this I think the line should not be held by less than three Divisions until it is necessary once more to withdraw every available Division for an offensive.

It is perhaps indicative of the pressure felt by Haking that he, unusually, pleaded on behalf of his officers. Haking concluded his memorandum to Horne:

> The Company and Battalion Commanders are only human beings and subject to the ordinary frailties of human nature, which in most cases have not been eliminated by many years of military training. They are subject to some anxiety as to the safety of their own small portion of the line, and feel that there are very few men at their disposal to hold it. My Divisional Commanders bring their troubles to me, and I can encourage and cheer them and their troops to exceptional exertions, so long as I can tell them that we are helping in a great battle and that we are doing just as good work here for the prosecution of the war as if we were taking part in the more honourable and glorious battle itself. If, however, I am unable to tell them this, or if I cannot produce sufficient arguments to carry much conviction the situation is not satisfactory.

That Horne had some sympathy for Haking's position is evident from a letter he had written to GHQ some five weeks earlier: "I wish to retain the 21 Division [required to support the Canadians] until at least Z–10 . . . I cannot thin out the I and XI Corps fronts early in March without reducing the efficiency of the Divisions and running some risk of attack before commencement of the offensive."[6] A hand-written note on Haking's 18 March memorandum read: "The Army Commander spoke to GOC XI Corps on this subject and explained to him (i) That the offensive was starting, the day has now been fixed. (ii) An Infantry Brigade will be kept at Bethune as a reserve behind Givenchy. (iii) Arrangements for the 5th D[ivision] A[rtillery] to stay for the present in XI Corps are being made."[7] In addition, Horne increased the size of XI Corps so that, by the end of March, it was made up of the 5th, 49th and 66th Divisions. That the newly arrived Portuguese Division was also assigned to XI Corps for instruction was, however, considered as something less than beneficial. The Portuguese involvement with XI Corps will be dealt with at some length in Chapter VII.

*   *   *   *

As a result of Horne's intervention, Haking was now able to concentrate on his preferred area of activity – aggressive action in support of the attack on Vimy Ridge. Horne, in a letter to his Corps Commanders dated 8 March, had set out the role of XI Corps: "The tasks of XI Corps are: (a) Prior to Z Day,[8] to make every effort to induce the enemy to believe that an attack from a portion of XI Corps front is intended. (b) As far as labour and material allow, to continue the preparations for an attack on Aubers Ridge, in case circumstances demand the execution of that operation."⁹ Haking transmitted this instruction to his Divisional Commanders at his Corps Conference on 16 March: "We are required to divert attention from the Vimy attack by making a great display of activity against the Aubers-Fromelles ridge. This display is really a feint."¹⁰

Haking immediately made plans to deceive the enemy on his front and, on 26 March, Major General Anderson of the First Army staff, referred to a secret memorandum from Haking to Horne: "I forward a copy of instructions issued by the GOC XI Corps for a demonstration to be carried out with a view to inducing the enemy to suspect the possibility of operations against Aubers Ridge."¹¹ The demonstration was duly carried out and took the form of an artillery bombardment by the 49th and 66th Divisions, who expended between them 21,640 rounds of 18-pounder shells and 4,820 rounds of 4.5-inch howitzer shells. In the same secret memorandum, Haking instructed his divisions: "During the period 1 April–10 April the 49th and 66th Divisions will carry out one or more raids, even if only with small parties." The Givenchy-Cuinchy sector was to receive special attention:

In previous attacks towards the Aubers Ridge we have always commenced by showing activity on the front opposite Givenchy and Cuinchy. If we repeat this it might make the enemy believe that the demonstration against Aubers Ridge is real and it will also strengthen the defence of the Givenchy front at a time when our intelligence reports indicate some increase of the garrisons there and consequently suitable targets . . . the GOC 66 Division will arrange for one barrage by day and one barrage by night to be put up opposite Givenchy and Cuinchy.

Various other deceptions were planned to confuse the enemy. On 17 March, Haking wrote to Horne: "If a tank could be attached to my Corps the news of its arrival might be spread to the enemy and we could also test it in this muddy ground with a view to future operations."¹² One thousand tents were to be pitched conspicuously; bogus dumps were created; and observation balloons sent up. Further, "If roads are dusty CE XI Corps will arrange with Corps Road Officer for all available road-sweepers to make continuous and extended tours through the area and raise dust." As regards Observation Posts: "The normal procedures of getting under cover when hostile aeroplanes are sighted will be reversed and troops will fall in in the open and move about as much as possible."¹³

* * * *

By early May, the Germans had withdrawn to their new defensive position on the Hindenburg Line and the attacks by the Canadians and the Third and Fifth Armies on Vimy Ridge and in front of Arras had met with considerable success. The French Army, following its costly assault on the Chemin des Dames, was demoralized and subject to a number of mutinies. During the abortive strategy discussions at Chantilly in November 1916, it had been agreed that the BEF should make their major 1917 offensive in Flanders and it was that area, following the events of April 1917, that became the focus of British attention for the remainder of the year.

The First Army was cast to play a subsidiary role. At his Conference on 8 May, Horne outlined his policy as it applied to I, XIII and the Canadian Corps:

> In view of the fact that no fresh troops are available to relieve Divisions in the First Army, after the departure of the 24th Division and a considerable proportion of the Heavy Artillery now on the First Army front, offensive operations . . . will be limited . . . The ruling principles in the conduct of these operations will be careful selection of important objectives of a limited nature, deliberate preparation of attack, concentration of artillery and economy of infantry, combined in each case with feint attacks and smoke and gas on other portions of the front. Corps Commanders will submit their proposals for the above operations, and of any other operations proposed, so that the offensive operations of the three Corps concerned may be coordinated.[14]

In a separate section of his 8 May policy statement, Horne referred to Haking's XI Corps: "XI Corps will continue to carry out such offensive operations as may be possible on the extended front now held."

The aggressive activities of I, XIII and the Canadian Corps were, therefore, to be "limited" and even less was expected from XI Corps, whose main task was to hold the line. Making the best of this instruction, Haking, apparently not content with this somewhat passive role, was determined to do whatever he could to promote aggression on his front. In his document, "XI Corps Policy", dated 11 May, Haking told his Divisional Commanders: "The Army Commander has informed me that continued pressure will be brought to bear against the enemy by other Corps in the Army, and has directed me to continue the offensive policy of XI Corps."[15]

The remainder of the 11 May policy document provides a clear example of Haking's style in his efforts to encourage his Divisional Commanders to act aggressively. Paragraph 2 of the statement reads:

The Corps front on 20th instant will extend from the Hohenzollern to the Lys, North of Armentières, an extent of 37,000 yards. It will be held by three Divisions [49th, 57th and 66th] with a total strength of some 28,000 men. In almost every case each Brigade has two battalions in the front line, one in support and one resting and training in reserve. In most cases each Battalion has two Companies in the front line and two in immediate support. This gives us approximately:

7,000 men holding the front trenches i.e. 1 man to 5½ yards
7,000 men supporting them closely i.e. 1 man to 5½ yards.
7,000 men in close reserve i.e. 1 man to 5½ yards.
7,000 men in mobile reserve.

Taking those all together, we have a total of 28,000 men available for offensive and defensive purposes, i.e. 1 man to 1½ yards.

Paragraph 3 continues:

According to our latest information, we are opposed by 5½ German Divisions and each of these divisions as compared to one of ours is approximately as follows:

British Div. Trench Infantry, 9,400. Lewis Guns 200. M.Gs 48, Field Art 60 guns.

German Div. Trench Infantry, 6,300. Light M. Gs – Nil, M. Gs 72, Field Art 48–36 guns.

The comparative situation as regards Heavy Artillery is:

British: 36 guns and hows of 5" calibre and over.

German: 48 guns and hows. Of 5" calibre and over.

Thus, multiplying the British Division by 3 and the German Division by 5½, our comparative strength is as follows;

Trench Infantry – 6450; Light M.Gs +600; M.Gs –132; Field art. +36; Heavy Art. – 12 guns.

Haking then applied the force of arithmetic to assess the relative morale and defensive strengths: "The moral[e] of the opposing forces after our continuous success last year and this, may be taken as at least 3 to 2 (British to German). The strength of our front system of defences . . . may be taken as at least 2 to 1 (British to German)." Haking then sums up his argument:

Taking all these factors together, it is quite clear that although the Corps is extended over a very wide front and is limited in resources, it possesses considerable power of offence, if this power is skilfully husbanded and applied. Our main object is to cause material and moral[e] loss to the enemy, and we cannot do this by sitting behind our parapets. The action of offensive patrols and raiding parties is very effective especially as regards moral[e]; they improve our own and reduce that of the enemy.

Finally, Haking introduced with some relish an additional method of aggression:

Something more, however, is required and has now been rendered possible by the long continued pressure of the Corps against the enemy's front, and by the drying up of the ground . . . The Corps will . . . endeavour to establish small posts, skilfully concealed in the enemy's front line, well-defended by rifles, machine gun, Trench Mortar and Artillery fire . . . These are to be looked upon as outposts which can be temporarily withdrawn whenever it is considered necessary. Their main object is two-fold: (i) To make the enemy attack them in the worst possible circumstances to himself. (ii) To be used as bases for raids into the enemy's second line.

Divisional and Brigade Commanders were asked to consider Haking's scheme and submit plans for approval.

Horne, however, was not impressed by Haking's plan to occupy posts in the German line. "There are", wrote Horne,

limitations. It is not to our advantage to occupy posts permanently in the German system unless we are going to gain some decided advantage, such as the capture of a tactical point, the improvement of our position, the shortening of our line, etc. A small advanced and comparatively isolated post connected with the German front system, is bound to be, to some extent, a "cockshy", and to offer to the German favourable conditions for bombardment attack and rounding up. The permanent occupation of such a post is a strain on the men of the garrison, and on commanders, which is not good for moral. I do not feel it is useful as training or good for moral if men are instructed to fall back from a permanent post as soon as exposed to artillery and Trench Mortar fire.

Horne added that he did not wish to interfere with "the encourage-ment of the offensive spirit . . . but I think the establishment of small and exposed permanent posts in the enemy's front line . . . is likely to lead to loss on our part without corresponding or greater losses to the Germans."[16]

Haking was obliged to reconsider his proposal and at his Corps Conference of 22 May, he explained to his Divisional Commanders that:

> the Army Commander did not wish to run the risk of increasing the casualties which might be caused by a policy of such active offence. In these circumstances, the Corps Commander directed that posts in the enemy's line should not be permanently held . . . It was necessary to push parties over into the enemy's line and these parties should remain in that line for considerable periods of up to 24 hours. During that period as much damage as possible must be done to the hostile lines.[17]

One week later, Haking made a further appeal to Horne on this matter saying that the situation had changed in the Fauquissart-Boutellerie sector:

> On this front I am nowhere in close touch with the enemy . . . The result of this is that I am unable to get my patrols in touch with any hostile forces worth considering, owing to the distances . . . The situation also prevents me from carrying out raids, because there is nothing to raid . . . If I am permitted to establish some posts in the enemy's front line I can use these posts as a base for patrolling forwards, and for raids . . . I will be as careful as possible to prevent the enemy from gaining any temporary technical advantage, even on a small scale, by the capture of one of my posts.[18]

Horne finally agreed to Haking's modified proposal and a First Army memorandum of 12 June stated that:

> the Army Commander is in favour of the operation suggested, as long as the principles of his instructions . . . are borne in mind; that is men should not be isolated in small posts connected with the German system but not with ours . . . He agrees with the Corps Commander that circumstances have changed considerably since the original instructions on the subject were issued in the Winter. The short nights, the possibility of digging communication trenches across no man's land and the withdrawal of the enemy

from the front line, all lessen the danger of isolating small parties of which he was afraid when the original proposal was submitted.[19]

The Flanders offensive was preceded, on 7 June, by a successful assault, carried out by Plumer's Second Army, on the Messines Ridge. On 31 July, after a delay of nearly six weeks, Gough's Fifth Army began the main attack towards the Passchendaele-Gheluvelt Ridge which was eventually reached at the end of November. By that time, the British and Germans had each lost some 250,000 men.

In order to support the main attack in Flanders, the First Army had been stripped of divisions and its troops were spread thinly. Nevertheless, Horne ordered his Corps Commanders to "continue to act offensively with the resources presently available". Horne went on: "The objective of all such offensive action is to inflict as much damage as possible on the German divisions opposed to us, and to reduce their fighting value; to prevent any attempt by the enemy to reduce the number of divisions opposed to us, and to compel him through fear of attack, to retain his artillery opposite us and to expend ammunition."[20] The Corps Commanders were instructed to prepare and carry out minor operations, raids, artillery operations and gas attacks, and their proposals were to reach Army HQ by 12 June.

As Haking expressed it to his Divisional Commanders: "The task of XI Corps is very much as it was before, namely to keep in front of us as many hostile troops as possible, to draw the enemy's attentions away from the main operations. Whilst doing this we are required to press forward our preparations for the six division attack on the Aubers-Fromelles Ridge."[21] For Haking it must all have had a familiar ring – a repeat of the circumstances and instructions of July 1916 during the Somme offensive and of April 1917 when the Vimy-Arras attack was taking place. The plan for a six-division attack on the Aubers-Fromelles Ridge, however, was shelved – a decision no doubt helped by the unfortunate loss of a copy of the plan by the Headquarters of the 57th Division.[22]

As was his usual practice, Haking was not slow in making his proposals for offensive operations and in a memorandum to First Army Headquarters dated 6 June, he listed eleven raids that were to be carried out by his three Divisions – the 49th, 57th and 66th – on the nights of 7, 8, 9, 10 and 12 June. In addition, elements of the 49th and 57th Divisions were to "establish posts in the enemy's front system of defences".[23] On 22 June, the 66th Division was to take part in an "extensive operation . . . with a view to capturing and holding for five hours the whole of the enemy's front system of trenches on Givenchy

Hill". For this operation, Haking wrote to Horne, "I and my GOC, R.A., have gone most carefully into the requirements of the GOC 66th Division as regards Artillery for bombardment, barrage and counter-barrage work, and after exhausting all available resources of the Corps I am of the opinion that it will greatly increase our chances of success if I can be given 4 Howitzer (4.5") Batteries and 4 18-pounder Batteries." Haking added what for him was an important supporting argument: "This division has not been long in France and it would greatly improve its fighting value if it can successfully carry out the task I have given it."

Haking's plans for eleven minor raids and two sizeable operations proved too ambitious – especially since Plumer's Second Army, on XI Corps' immediate left, had made urgent requests for counter-battery work in support of their attacks in the Messines area.[24] In Horne's summary of proposed First Army operations, addressed to GHQ on 15 June, the XI Corps' proposals involving the 49th and 57th Divisions were cancelled. The attack by the 66th Division on 22 June, however, was approved.[25] In the meantime, XI Corps had been able to carry out a number of raids and Haking, at his Corps Conference on 16 June, presented the situation as regards casualties to his Divisional Commanders. Haking's information was intended to encourage, but it was also somewhat confusing:

> Since 1 June we have carried out 9 raids . . . during these oper-
> ations we have taken 46 prisoners including 1 officer. On a
> modest computation we have killed 435 of the enemy . . . In these
> operations we have employed some 52 officers and 1350 men,
> and, considering the importance of the results obtained, our casu-
> alties have not been excessive amounting to 10 officers and 244
> other ranks. (Not including the raid by 1/4 York and Lancaster on
> June 11/12 which were 2 officers and 78 ORs). In addition to this
> in defence of the line we have lost some 28 officers and 837 ORs
> . . . In the above figures the 1st Portuguese Division were not
> included . . . they suffered casualties to the amount of 1 officer and
> 293 ORs.[26]

Whether or not these figures were found to be uplifting to the Divisional Commanders is not recorded.

In mid-July, the pressure on XI Corps to provide counter-battery work in support of the troops on its flanks had grown considerably. XI Corps was not involved in any immediate major project, but the Corps on either side were. Haking explained his difficulties to Horne in a letter of 14 July:

The situation on my Northern flank demands a concentration of such guns as I can spare in that direction. I am also compelled to support the Portuguese Division. The result of this is that I have very few guns available on my right flank to meet the requirements [of I Corps]. My main trouble is counter-battery work. My left flank is the point of junction of two Armies and two Corps and the enemy is paying great attention to the destruction of my front line. East of Armentières . . . I have also got five raids in hand during the period . . . and Heavy Artillery is required for them . . . Later on, when the Armentières situation has developed, I might be able to do a little to help I Corps, but at present, I think it is doubtful, except as regards guns I already have which are covering my right flank.

Haking added a handwritten note to Horne: "I am afraid I cannot move any more guns to my right flank at present, but perhaps the above will meet the requirements of I Corps."[27]

* * * *

In August, Haking became involved in an important debate on future British tactics. A "secret" paper was circulated from GHQ on the subject of apparent changes in the way the Germans would deal with a major attack.[28] The paper noted that: "there has been a modification in the enemy's system of tactics, and that his present tendency is to reserve his most serious counter-attacks until later stages of the fight . . . doubtless on the theory that our troops at that stage, tired by their previous efforts, weakened by losses, and in some disorder, would be more easily overcome than earlier in the fight." The paper then asked: "If we accept the enemy's system of 'major' tactics, the question arises whether our dispositions for attack do not require some modification to ensure the defeat of such counter-attacks."

The discussion then centred on the depth to which an attack might be pushed; the artillery barrage required to cover the infantry to their final objective; and the physical capacity of the troops. As regards the last point, the issue was raised whether it was better to detail one brigade for the first objectives and two brigades for the subsequent objectives – a reversal of the normal policy. The paper also raised questions on "mopping-up" arrangements and the use of machine guns in offence and defence, and the value of rifle fire.

A second "secret" paper, initialled by W. H. Anderson, Horne's Chief of Staff, and dated 8 August, summarized the development of tactics used by both the British and the Germans since 1915.[29] "The present situation", wrote Anderson, is that the enemy has fully realised that the fulcrum of the battle has moved further back behind the front trenches, and we have only partially realised it . . . We have corrected the want of artillery and our trench destruction . . . is now so absolute as to obliterate nearly all traces of a front system. But though our artillery tactics have entirely altered the situation, the infantry are frequently disposed for an attack in depth as if the crux of the situation was still the capture of the front trenches, i.e. 2 Brigades in front line and 1 to go through to the final objective.

Anderson considered the problems associated with passing two brigades through one brigade and then proposed that: "Divisions should normally attack on a front of one brigade . . . a Corps of four divisions would, therefore, attack either on a three brigade front with three divisions in the front line and one in reserve, or on a four brigade front with all four divisions in line. The relief of one brigade by another is far simpler than the relief of one division by another."

Each of the four Corps Commanders in the First Army (Haking, McCracken, Currie and Holland) responded at length with their views – often in conflict – on the two "Secret" papers. Haking's submission[30] began in the manner that might be expected from an ex-Staff College Professor: "It is undesirable to consider the details of the tactics of a battle, without a clear idea of the strategical and tactical principles which rule the battle as a whole." After one and a half foolscap pages of general discussion, Haking then wrote: "At this stage of the war we are eating into the enemy's resources, we are biting off a bit here and a bit there, but the framework is not yet sufficiently corroded to enable us to smash it completely and break through. It appears that we should apply this eating away process to each battle front and arrange our objectives accordingly." In his penultimate paragraph, Haking answered the specific points raised in Anderson's papers: "(a) Depending on the particular locality let the Divisions . . . attack [in some places] in great depth on a one Brigade front, and in other parts of the line attack on a two Brigade front." Haking added that his Divisional Commanders were "very strong on this point". He continued:

(b) . . . limit all objectives as much as possible. This will greatly embarrass the enemy's counter-strokes . . . (c) . . . adopt the eating away process and thus carry on the offensive with short intervals of a few days for preparation, instead of long intervals of two or three weeks (d) . . . avoid the exhaustion of men, and ammunition supply caused by distant objectives, and advance our whole battle-front including guns and ammunition from day to day. (e) . . . make sure that when the objective is gained . . . the counter-stroke will be repulsed by the strong force established by us on the position captured . . . our Artillery barrage should have full scope over the ground in front of our selected line of defence.

On 9 August, Horne called a meeting of his Corps Commanders with the aim of reaching some degree of consensus.[31] There was clearly some difficulty in doing this. On the question of whether one or two brigades should lead the attack, the report of the meeting records: "General Holland thinks 2 to go through 1. Generals Haking and McCracken do not agree to 2 going through 1." After much discussion, Horne made a somewhat bland summary: "There should be both air and artillery superiority; tactics should be adapted to the particular ground and task and to changes in the enemy's tactics; objectives should be limited ensuring both the taking of the enemy's front line of resistance and the 'disturbance' of his artillery arrangements." Horne's written response to GHQ was, however, much more precise:

To meet the changes of tactics on the part of the Germans – (i) The divisions should be employed on a frontage suitable for one brigade. (ii) Depth of objective should be limited by two consider-ations – within range of covering artillery fire, and infantry can reach it in sufficient strength and with energy remaining to allow of reasonable probability of holding it against strong counter-attacks. (iii) The final objective should be selected as suitable for defence by one brigade and for the continuation of the attack.[32]

GHQ received a similar response from the Second Army.[33]

Having promoted this lengthy debate on the changed German defence tactics in August, GHQ wrote to Army Commanders two months later suggesting that German tactics had changed yet again:

A captured order of the [German] 5th Guards Infantry Brigade dated September 29, indicates that the enemy's defensive tactics may be changed. Since July 31 he has held his front line lightly, relying on a garrison distributed in depth to break up the assault and then on rapid counter-attacks. It seems now that, having found that method of defence ineffectual and very costly, he may attempt again to hold his front in strength . . . The Field Marshal Commanding in Chief would be glad of the views of the Army Commanders on the above.[34]

Such were the on-going tactical changes and conditions on the Western Front that faced the Army and Corps Commanders. As in August, Horne discussed the matter at his Conference and replied:

[The change in German tactics] is a confession of failure in tactical methods which were themselves designed to counteract the disadvantages of the system of holding the front trenches, to which a return is now advocated . . . But our chances of inflicting casualties and taking prisoners in the early stages of the battle will be increased. For the present, therefore, I think that we must continue our plan of selecting as our final objective a good tactical position, and of arriving there in sufficient force to welcome counterattack.[35]

At the same Army Commander's Conference, which took place on 8 October, Horne outlined the First Army policy for the winter months. A major attack was to be prepared for the Lens area.

Consequent on the work of preparation for action on a large scale, our raiding activities have diminished. We must now revert to our former offensive attitude, and carry out raids at frequent intervals . . . The I, XI, and XIII Corps have already adopted a system of holding the front line by a series of defended localities. The object is to have, during the forthcoming winter, the barest minimum of men in the front line, defence being secured by machine guns, and wire sited so as to shepherd any enemy offensive efforts into machine gun swept approaches.

However, Haking's natural interest in this latest instruction to adopt an offensive attitude and prepare for raids was, on this occasion, short-lived. The critical situation in Italy, following the victory of the Germans and Austrians at Caporetto on 24 October, had obliged the Allies to send support in the form of artillery and troops. Britain's contribution was a force of five divisions under the command of Plumer. As part of Plumer's force, Haking and his XI Corps Staff were also despatched to Italy. The First Army Order 177 of 16 November read: "XI Corps HQ and Corps troops will, on relief, be accommodated in Bethune, pending entrainment."[36] Haking was to be absent from the Western Front for four months – until March 1918.

* * * *

There is nothing to suggest that Haking was a man to indulge in retrospection, but, during his train journey from Lillers to Mantua, he might well have looked back over 1917 and concluded with regret that the critical operations of the war were passing him by. It was Haking's ambition that his XI Corps might be selected to take a leading part in a major and decisive battle. In June 1916, during the preparations for the Somme, he had written; "I shall limit the extent of the operations remembering that I must keep my Corps fit for a great offensive and not wear it out too much in the holding attack."[37] Similarly, he addressed his Divisional Commanders during a Corps Conference: "I would also ask you to be prepared at all times to obey an order to withdraw the whole Corps and to go into battle at the decisive point wherever it may be."[38] In his note to Horne of 18 March 1917, Haking also indicated clearly the difference that existed in his mind between the slog of holding the line in a supportive role and "the more honourable and glorious battle itself". Following the successful attack on Vimy Ridge, Haking wrote to Horne on behalf of XI Corps: "We all wish we had been able to take part in it, and hope that before long you will be able to give us an opportunity of adding to the successes of the First Army and its Commander."[39]

The opportunity to take part in a "glorious battle" had not arisen for Haking in 1916 and nor did it in 1917. When the major offensives took place – the Somme, Arras-Vimy and Passchendaele – XI Corps was allocated a subsidiary role. Haking was acutely aware of this and, referring to the Arras-Vimy attack, he described the XI Corps task: "The policy laid down . . . is to do in a very small way for the Vimy enterprise what the Vimy enterprise is meant to do for the greater project."[40] Even Fromelles, Haking's largest attack, had the official description "subsidiary" and, at various stages, such as in the summer of 1917, XI Corps was given only a supporting part within the First Army which itself was operating in support of the main operation in Flanders. It was well known that Haig believed that sending troops to Italy was a mistake and that the Italians would be better served by employing all the available troops in the West.[41] In those circumstances, it must have passed through Haking's mind that the reason why he and his staff had been selected for service in Italy was because they were the ones who could be spared.[42]

It might also have occurred to Haking, during his journey to Mantua, that, as far as XI Corps was concerned, the pattern of events in 1917 differed little from that of 1916. The main emphasis in both years had been on the defence of the line together with spasmodic aggressive actions – mainly in the form of trench raids. As was to be expected, Haking's XI Corps played its full part in carrying out trench raids. In the ten months January-October, 183 raids took place on the First Army front and, of those, fifty-eight were carried out by XI Corps. The prospect of a repeat of the Fromelles attack towards the Aubers Ridge was discussed several times during 1917, but all the proposed plans came to nothing. Resources, artillery and men, were constantly "limited" and Haking was obliged to cover a much extended front with the minimum number of men and guns. Planned raids were often cancelled, as in the June flurry of activity in support of Messines, and memoranda from Horne frequently included words of constraint such as – "no fresh troops are available"; "offensive operations will be limited"; and "objectives of a limited nature".[43] As Horne had said at his Conference on 8 October, "Consequent on the work of preparations for actions on a large scale, our raiding activities have diminished."[44]

As in 1916, Haking played the part of "a good soldier" carrying out the instructions of his superiors, taking an active part in the discussions on tactics and encouraging his Divisional Commanders as best he could. The constraints arising from the system of rotating divisions through Corps, evident in 1916, continued in 1917. During the eleven months January-November, ten different divisions passed through XI Corps. The difficulties arising from this procedure were not helped by the proportion of "green" troops allocated to Haking. The majority of his troops from March to August were new to the Western Front (66th, 57th and Portuguese Divisions). The length of stay of divisions in XI Corps varied between two and five months. Under these circumstances, as was observed in Chapter III, the task of a Corps Commander in attempting to create a Corps identity or spirit was insuperable. The loyalty of troops was directed to the battalion or the division – their natural "home" – not to the Corps. Nevertheless, the problems set out in Haking's letter to Horne of 18 March, in which he pleaded for additional resources to help his hard- pressed and over-extended Divisional Commanders – "they are only human beings and subject to the ordinary frailties of human nature" – revealed an empathetic side of Haking that was rarely seen. It might also have been a *cri de coeur* expressing his feeling that it was not only his subordinates who were being neglected – so was he.

Haking was well aware that in carrying out his duties he relied heavily on his personal efforts to persuade and motivate his subordinates – "to encourage and cheer them" as Haking expressed it. He saw it as a main part of his job. As in 1916, Haking used various forms of exhortation, from the repetition of the well-used phrases and key words ("offensive spirit" and "improving moral") that were familiar among the senior BEF officers, to bombarding his subordinates with arithmetic and statistics. Maintaining the morale of the troops was always considered to be of great importance. Haking's XI Corps Policy document of 11 May, the aim of which was to encourage an offensive attitude among his Divisional Commanders, clearly stated Haking's view that his main objective was to destroy the enemy which could not be done "by sitting behind our parapets . . . patrols and raiding parties . . . improve our own [morale] and reduce that of the enemy".[45]

Haking's belief in the offensive and in the importance of raids led him to use a variety of other forms of exhortation including a warning of the dire consequences of inaction. At a Corps Conference in January, Haking told his Divisional Commanders:

> If we do not raid the Germans they will raid us. A great advantage rests with the side that carries out the raids. In a Division that has been raided there is apt to be a feeling of depression at the thought that men have been killed and a good many unwounded prisoners have been taken without anything that could be called a fight. On the other hand, the feeling of elation of all ranks in a Division which has carried out a raid is very marked.[46]

At the same Conference, Haking announced the results of a Raids Competition that he had organized: "During the past week, the Corps Commander has looked over 30 schemes for raids sent in by battalions . . . These schemes showed considerable knowledge and the requirements of the operation and many have all the essential features of success stamped upon them." First prize went to Captain White of 1/5th London Regiment with Major Higgins (13th London Regiment) and Captain Douglas (2nd King's Own Scottish Borderers) as runners-up.

Since the epithet "butcher" has been ascribed to Haking, it is appropriate to examine the two years of intense trench warfare, 1916 and 1917, in terms of frequency of trench raids and the number of casualties incurred by XI Corps during that period. Haking, as we have seen, certainly encouraged raids and promoted the "offensive spirit" on all possible occasions. He regarded both of these activities as a main part of his job as a Corps Commander. But did Haking's XI Corps carry out more raids and suffer more casualties than other Corps in the First Army as a result of the aggressive attitude of its commander? The answer to that question is inevitably complex and involves a number of important caveats in terms of available information, statistical interpretation and particularly of terminology. An extensive discussion of raids, patrols and casualties in the First Army takes place in Appendix III.

Despite the various problems mentioned above, it is possible to conclude that XI Corps was not particularly more belligerent or casualty prone than other Corps in the First Army. During 1916–17, XI Corps carried out an average of 2.0 raids per division per month with I Corps having the second highest frequency at 1.8. The average frequency over the whole of the First Army front 1916–17 was only 1.5 raids per division per month. Given that the strength of a division during that period was some 10,000 these frequencies, including those of XI Corps, cannot be regarded as a major manifestation of the "offensive spirit". As regards casualties 1916–17, XI Corps incurred an average of 554 per division per month, while both I Corps (741) and the Canadian Corps (1,057) suffered considerably more. Overall, the available information is inconclusive, but it does not support the allegation that Haking was more of a "butcher" than other Corps Commanders in the First Army.

In terms of moving along the "learning curve" Haking certainly promoted the idea of having outposts in the thinly-held German front line, despite some initial opposition from Horne. In March he requested the use of a tank to make the enemy believe that a major attack was imminent. However, such events can hardly be seen as a significant moves along the "curve" and, in general, the tactics, technology and command procedures were very much as they were in 1916. Since XI Corps' task in 1917 was essentially to hold the line, this is not a surprising conclusion. Haking's performance in this respect was unremarkable just as the XI Corps' role was undramatic. There was little scope for great initiatives.

However, the discussions in August 1917 concerning the changes in German defensive tactics and the 'Secret' paper from Anderson which outlined the changes in operating circumstances since 1915 are indicative of a continuing effort within the BEF to learn from past experience and to adopt new and relevant tactics. Haking indicated his support of 'limited objectives', a 'bite and hold' approach and the establishment of a strong defensive position to off-set any counter-attack. That these discussions involved GHQ, Army, Corps and Divisional staffs endorses the view of the British official historian, noted in the Introduction to this study, that a communication system operated between the Commander in Chief and his subordinate commanders. Contrary to the opinion of Travers, GHQ did, at least on occasions, solicit and receive advice from below.

Most XI Corps activities were planned and carried out as a result of instructions from above. The discussion in Chapter III on trench warfare in 1916 identified a strong top-down style of command and control and, as far as XI Corps was concerned, this continued into 1917. There are numerous examples of GHQ instructions being transmitted via the Army and Corps Commanders to the Divisions. When, in August, a GHQ paper initiated a discussion on German defensive tactics, there were implied instructions on matters of "mopping-up" and the use of machine guns. Haking referred to these instructions:

"Paras 3 and 4 of GHQ letter do not contain matter for discussion, but lay down facts, which require immediate attention as regards definite instruction to Divisions."[47] Earlier in 1917, a GHQ memorandum had instructed the First and Third Armies "to carry out at 24 hours notice minor operations".[48] In July, Horne read out to his Corps Commanders "a GHQ instruction, and pointed out that it was the task of the First Army to do all in its power, and without delay, to simulate preparations for an offensive against Lille".[49] Both of these instructions were duly passed on by Haking to his Divisional Commanders.

Not only were orders affecting the operation of the Divisions initiated from GHQ, they were accompanied by a checking procedure. When Haig wrote to his Army Commanders in January, regarding certain proposed minor operations, he noted that: "The schemes which have already been submitted by Armies will shortly be returned, together with any remarks which may be necessary regarding the scope, object and execution of each operation and any amendments or adjustments which may be required. Revised schemes will be submitted by each army on 31 January."[50] In early June, Horne wrote: "GOs C[ommanding] Corps will consider and submit proposals for action on their respective fronts . . . Proposals to reach Advanced Army HQ by 12 June 1917."[51] As far as XI Corps was concerned, this directive style of command and control clearly started at the top and was copied down the line. It is difficult to discern any evolution towards greater independence or increased scope of action.

* * * *

To a marked extent, 1917 had, for Haking, been an undistinguished year. The four volumes of the British official history dealing with 1917, totalling 1,560 pages, mentions XI Corps on only three occasions and then only to give its position in the line and to say it was moving to Italy.[52] Much of 1917 had mirrored the events and situations of 1916. XI Corps had not been called upon to carry out any major operation and the daily grind of trench warfare together with the preparation and, often, cancellation of numerous projects, had been the dominant theme. It might well have been Haking's hope, as he travelled towards the Italian front, that 1918 would prove to be a more exciting and, as he would wish it, a "more honourable and glorious" year.

Notes

1. TNA, WO 95/168, OAD 258, 2 January 1917.
2. Ibid., GS 503/21(a), 29 January 1917.
3. Ibid.
4. TNA, WO 95/168.Undated without indication of addressee.
5. Ibid., SS 1226/16, 18 March 1917.

6. TNA, WO 95/168, G.S. 516/15(a), 11 February 1917.

7. The handwriting is that of Maj. Gen. W. H. Anderson of First Army General Staff.

8. The opening date for the Vimy attack, 9 April.

9. TNA, WO 95/168, G.S. 529/11(a).

10. TNA, WO 95/168.

11. TNA, WO 95/168, G.S. 1226/22, 22 March 1917.

12. Ibid., SS 1226/14, 17 March 1917.

13. Ibid., SS 12226/26.

14. TNA, WO 95/170, GS 561.

15. TNA, WO 95/882, SS 1230.

16. TNA, WO 95/170, G.S. 572/16(a), 16 May 1917.

17. TNA, WO 95/882, SS/837/200, 22 May 1917

18. TNA, WO 95/170, SS 1230/2, 30 May 1917.

19. TNA, WO 95/171, G.S. 604/10(a).

20. TNA, WO 95/171, GS 604/6(a).

21. TNA, WO 95/882, 16 June 1917.

22. TNA, WO 95/882, 23 June 1917. Copy No. 3 had been received by the 57th Division on 25 May. The loss was discovered on 4 June and it was eventually found on 27 July.

23. TNA, WO 95/171, SS 1230/4.

24. TNA, WO 95/171, Second Army, G 168; First Army, GS 604/13(a).

25. TNA, WO 95/171, GS 604/15(a).

26. TNA, WO 95/882, SS 837/21.

27. TNA, WO 95/172, SS 1226/30/4.

28. TNA, WO 95/173, Document headed "SECRET". Undated and with no addressee or signature.

29. TNA, WO 95/173. Headed "Notes on O.B./2089".

30. TNA, WO 95/173, SS 1236, 8 August 1917.

31. TNA, WO 95/173.

32. TNA, WO 95/173, GS 714, 10 August 1917.

33. TNA, WO 95/275, G 566, 12 August 1917.

34. TNA, WO 95/173, OA 192, 9 October 1917.

35. Ibid., GS 174, 10 October 1917.

36. TNA, WO 95/174.

37. TNA, WO 95/881, Letter attached to XI Corps Conference Minutes, 23 June 1916.

38. Ibid., 14. June 1916.

39. TNA, WO 95/882, handwritten note dated 10 April.

40. TNA, WO 95/882, XI Corps Conference, 16 March 1917.

41. Duff Cooper, *Haig*, II, p.183.

42. However, it should be noted that the selection of the 23rd and 41st Divisions together with Cavan and Plumer indicated that Haig had no intention of sending an inferior force to Italy.

43. These examples are from Horne's Conference on 8 May 1917. See TNA, WO 95/170, GS 561.

44. TNA, WO 95/173, GS 561.
45. TNA, WO 95/170, SS 1230.
46. TNA, WO 95/168, RHS 837/16, 12 January 1917.
47. TNA, WO 95/173, SS 1236, 8 June 1917
48. TNA, WO 95/168, OAD 350, 23 March 1917.
49. TNA, WO 95/172, 10 July 1917.
50. TNA, WO 95/168, OAD 258, 2 January 1917.
51. TNA, WO 95/171, GS 604/1/(a).
52. *BOH 1917*, Vols I-IV.

CHAPTER VI

Haking in Italy:
December 1917 – March 1918

Haking's XI Corps was in Italy from 1 December 1917 until 11 March 1918. During that period Haking was on leave from 29 January until 22 February and was therefore in Italy for only twelve weeks. The purpose of this chapter is to discuss the role of XI Corps in stabilizing the Italian Front following the disaster of Caporetto in October 1917. It begins by placing the British involvement in Italy in the context of events from 1915 to 1918. In the final section, an assessment is made of Haking's contribution as a Corps Commander.

Italy's entry into the war resulted from a series of complicated negotiations. Originally an ally of Germany and Austria-Hungary through the 1882 Triple Alliance, Italy had announced its neutrality at the outbreak of the war. However, on 24 May 1915, it decided to declare war on Austria-Hungary and side with the Entente. The reasons for this change of allegiance were essentially associated with Italy's aspirations for territorial gain. Italy and Austria-Hungary had long-term differences over the territories of Trentino in the north and Istria on the Dalmatian coast, the so-called *Italia Irredenta*. Some 750,000 people of Italian descent were living in those areas, which included the important port of Trieste. In January 1915 Austria-Hungary suffered a severe defeat in Galicia at the hands of the Russians and, fearing that Italy might now drop its neutral role and enter the war against them, offered the Italians southern Trentino. This offer hardly satisfied Italian ambitions and negotiations were immediately opened with the Allies. On 25 April agreement was reached. The secret Pact of London stated that, if Italy joined the Entente, then Italy's territorial requirements would be realized following a successful conclusion of the war. After several weeks of internal political manoeuvring, Italy declared war on Austria-Hungary on 24 May and immediately mobilized her forces.[1] The Austro-Hungarians opened the fighting by a series of naval bombardments and Venice was attacked by Austro-Hungarian aircraft.

With the Austro-Hungarians heavily committed on the Eastern front, the Italians planned to operate in two areas: the Trentino salient and the Isonzo salient. The line would be held in Trentino and General Cadorna would attack across the Isonzo. Although the Austro-Hungarians attempted several breakthroughs in the Trentino area, the following two years were dominated by no fewer than eleven Italian attempts to destroy the Austro-Hungarian army on the Isonzo. However, apart from an Italian success at Gorizia in August 1916, every battle ended without a significant result. Both sides suffered heavy losses and, after the tenth and eleventh Isonzo battles in May and June 1917, the Austro-Hungarians in particular were on the point of collapse. Despairing that it could achieve a victory against Italy on its own, Austria-Hungary now appealed for help from Germany. An Austro-German Fourteenth Army was formed under General von Below and, supported by the Austro-Hungarian Fifth and Tenth Armies, it launched an attack across the Isonzo on 24 October. The battle took its name from the village of Caporetto and the Austro-Germans, who had numerical superiority in that particular sector, broke through the Italian defences, virtually destroying the Italian Second Army in the process. The Italians dropped back, first to the Tagliamento river and then to the Piave, a retreat of some sixty miles. It was a bitter defeat for the Italians who lost around 600,000 troops, many of whom had deserted or given themselves up and become prisoners.

The collapse of the Italian front was a matter of considerable concern in both London and Paris. Lloyd George, without calling a meeting of the War Cabinet and without consulting Haig, immediately instructed the CIGS, Robertson, to send two British divisions to Italy, saying that the French were sending four. Consequently, on 30 October, the 23rd and 41st Divisions began their journey from France to Italy. Haig was ordered to provide a "good man" to command them and selected Lord Cavan.[2] One week later, Haig was further instructed to release Plumer, then with the Second Army on the Western Front, to become the commander of all British troops in Italy. The arrangement suited neither Haig nor Plumer. The Passchendaele offensive was at a critical phase and Haig noted in his diary: "Was ever an Army Commander and his Staff sent off to another theatre of war in the middle of a battle?"[3] Plumer was equally unenthusiastic and on 7 November wrote to his wife: "I have just received a great shock. I have been ordered to go to Italy to assume command of the British forces there. I am very sick about it and do not want to go in the least."[4] Nevertheless, Plumer set off for Italy on 9 November. Five days later, following a meeting with General Diaz, who had replaced Cadorna as the Italian Commander in Chief, Plumer sent his first report to London, giving a cautious assessment of the situation and requesting additional troops. By mid-December five British divisions and six French divisions had arrived in Italy.

After some initial confusion as to the most appropriate sector for the French and British troops, Plumer and General Fayolle, who shared command of the Franco-British force, agreed, following consultation with Diaz, to organize their troops into two groups. Plumer would command the French XXXI Corps (47th and 65th Divisions) and Cavan's XIV Corps (the British 23rd and 41st Divisions), while the French General Duchesne, under Fayolle, would command the French XII Corps (23rd, 24th and 46th Divisions). Haking, who had been transferred from France with his XI Corps Staff on 1 December, was also placed under Duchesne and given command of the British 48th and French 64th Divisions. The British 5th Division would be held in reserve. Plumer and Fayolle arranged their troops on a defensive line running from Val d'Astico via Bassano to Pederobba, known as the *linea inglese*, with a second line four miles to the rear from Bassano to the Piave at Crocetta. A defensive buffer was therefore in place to prevent an enemy breakthrough in the key sectors of Asiago, Monte Grappa and the Piave.

Despite the disintegration of the Italian Second Army at Caporetto, the majority of the Italian units remained in good fighting order and held off Austro-German attacks on all parts of their front during November and December losing only Monte Tomba. Elements of the King Edward's Horse, who were part of Haking's Corps troops, began to arrive in Italy in early-December and their historian later recorded that, by that time, "the situation on the Italian front had mended. In fact, it had become tranquil".[5] Both the Asiago and the Piave sectors were now relatively stable and when the heavy snows in January removed the threat of enemy attacks from the north through the Dolomites, Plumer and Fayolle decided, with the agreement of Diaz, to abandon the grouping system and concentrate their troops on the Piave from the Montello to Nervese. They remained there for the rest of the winter.

The very presence of the French and British troops from November 1917 was a major positive influence on the morale of the Italians. General Gondrecourt commented that: "the presence of the Franco-English forces always exercise a happy and much needed influence",[6] and the historian, G. M. Trevelyan, who spent over two years with a Red Cross unit on the Italian front, noted: "The moral effect of the arrival of the British and French troops was great and did a good deal to rally the Italians."[7] On 14 December, with the onset of winter and the lack of progress, the German High Command decided that all their forces should be withdrawn from Italy and that development, together with the re-taking of Monte Tomba by the French on 31 December, raised Italian morale even higher. Thereafter, despite an Austrian attempt in June 1918 to make a breakthrough in the Asiago sector, there was no serious possibility of an Allied defeat in Italy. The British and French forces had played a significant part in stabilizing the Italian front and, in the second half of 1918, they were to play an equally impressive role in the final defeat of the Austro-Hungarians.

* * * *

The entry in the XI Corps war diary for 1 December 1917 recorded that the "Corps Headqtrs closed at Lillers and re-opened at Hotel Aquila Dora, Mantua."[8] Two days later the Corps HQ moved to Padua and then, on 6 December, to Camposfiero where it remained for the rest of the month. Using Camposfiero as his base, Haking spent the following four weeks familiarizing himself with the Italian front, and establishing contact with his superior, Duchesne, with his own Divisions and with neighbouring Corps. His schedule was, to say the least, energetic. The XI Corps war diary notes that on 5 December: "The Corps Commander visited front held by VIII Italian Corps on the Piave E. of Nervesa in view of possibility of XI Corps taking over that part of the front." The following day Haking called on the Italian XIV Corps HQ at Fanzola and dined with HM the King of Italy. On 14 December "the Corps Commander visited Gen. Duchesne commanding French X Army at HQ in Castelfranco. He discussed with him the instructions which General Duchesne was about to issue with reference to holding the enemy should he break through the Italian resistance across the Brenta valley." On successive days from 15–20 December Haking reconnoitred ground in the vicinity of Monte Baldo and Monte Caina; visited the HQ of the French 64th Division at Bassano; viewed the defences of the French XXXI Corps near Monte Tomba; made a reconnaissance of the area around Valrovina; called on the HQ of the British 48th Division at Pozzoleone; and, on 20 December, made a further reconnaissance of the sector Rubbio-Monte Caina. For three days (21-23 December) the XI Corps diary recorded that "heavy snow prevented useful reconnaissance work in the mountains", but on Christmas Eve Haking continued his tour of the front by visiting the Pondifaldo and Validorina areas. On 27 December Haking attended a practical exercise by the 5th Division on the River Brenta. During the final three days of the month, Haking presented medals to men of 13 Infantry Brigade at Balzonella; inspected two battalions of 143 Infantry Brigade near Pazzoleone; attended a medal parade of 95 Infantry Brigade; and called on Plumer at GHQ.

Following his meeting with Duchesne on 14 December at

Lieutenant Richard
Haking, 1886.

Officers of the 2nd Battalion Hampshire Regiment (formerly 67th (South
Hampshire) Regiment) in India, 1882. Lieutenant Haking is on the back row, fifth
from left.

Officers of the 2nd Battalion Hampshire Regiment in theatrical costume in Burma in 1886. Haking is in the middle row, third from right.

The officers of the 2nd Battalion Hampshire Regiment back in India in 1887 with Haking standing far right.

Brigadier General Richard
Haking, c. 1913.

Haking (centre) with the
Portuguese General
Tamagnini and one of the
latter's staff officers in
December 1917.

Lieutenant General Sir Richard Haking.

The ruins of a German Observation Tower on Aubers Ridge.

The River Laies. A drainage ditch that ran the length of XI Corps' front, 1916.

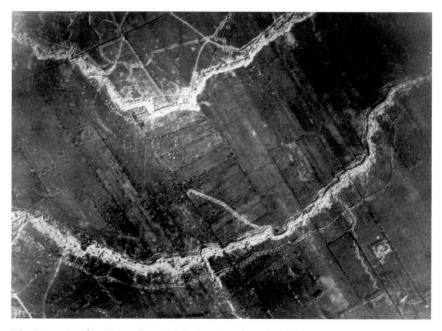

The Sugar Loaf at Fromelles, 1916, showing the Rhondda Sap.

Concrete bunkers of 16th Bavarian Reserve Infantry Regiment facing the XI Corps lines near Laventie.

VC Corner. This is the only all-Australian cemetery in France. On the walls behind the Cross of Sacrifice are the names of 1,298 Australians who died in the Fromelles attack and who have no known graves. In the garden are the remains of 410 unidentified Australians. The remains of 250 soldiers have been discovered near Fromelles and have been re-buried at the new Pheasant Wood Cemetery.

At Loos-en-Gohelle is the Loos Memorial, part of Dud Corner Cemetery. The memorial commemorates over 20,000 men who died in the area of the River Lys and who have no known graves.

The Sacrario Militare commemorating Italian and Austro-Hungarian dead in Asiago.

Mill Cottage, Bulford, Wiltshire where Haking retired in 1927.

Officers of 2nd Hampshires in the Isle of Wight on Gallipoli Day 1933. Haking, by then the Colonel of the Regiment, is seated front centre.

Haking as Colonel of the
Hampshire Regiment, 1938.

Aval Wood Cemetery
near the Nieppe Forest
contains the bodies of
men killed during the
BORDERLAND attack
of 28 June 1918.

The Portuguese Memorial at la Couture.

The Portuguese Memorial at la Bombe.

The Indian Memorial at la Bombe.

The 46th Division Memorial at Vermelles.

Poppies in no man's land near Lone Tree looking towards Loos.

The Quarries CWGC Cemetery near the Hohenzollern Redoubt, Loos.

Castelfranco, Haking took the opportunity to present his personal assessment of the situation on his immediate front:

> I think it is desirable for me to put down on paper what I understand is the situation at the moment, as the result of the interview granted to me this morning by the General Officer Commanding X French Army, and from studying the papers he gave to me to read . . . General Duchesne has decided, as far as XI Corps is concerned, that it is essential to maintain a position on the right bank of R. Brenta, extending from about Mt Caina on the right to Mt Busso on the left. This position could be held even if Monte Grappa was captured by the enemy . . . The 5th British Division, working under my instructions as regards the selection of the Infantry and Artillery positions, will carry out the detailed reconnaissance of the Monte Caina front, namely from Brenta to the valley running South of Rubbio. The 48th British Division will carry out the reconnaissance from the Rubbio valley to Monte Busso.

There was, however, one particular problem in making these arrangements which Haking pointed out to Duchesne: "There are considerable difficulties in carrying out the arrangements for the defence of this line because the whole area is full of Italian troops and our own troops (French and English) cannot therefore get close enough either to occupy the line or even to prepare it for defence . . . We are therefore called upon to get ready to hold a line and if necessary the offensive from it without having the power either of holding it or doing much to prepare it for any length of time beforehand." Some acceptable arrangement was apparently made with the Italians to overcome this problem since Haking was able to add: "The Italian authorities, however, appear to be willing to place Italian troops at our disposal who will construct the necessary defences according to our own designs. It will be necessary for arrangements to be made so that Italian troops can be placed at our disposal as soon as possible."

Haking ended his memorandum to Duchesne:

> I am sending you this so that I might be quite sure that I have interpreted the wishes of the GOC Xth Army correctly. If I have made any mistake, of course, I will at once change what is necessary. Perhaps I may be permitted to add that as a result of my own reconnaissance of the line, methods suggested to me this morning by the GOC Xth Army are absolutely in conformity with my own views on the subject. I am writing in English because I

don't want to use an interpreter and it takes some time to write a long letter in French. I will try and write in French in future.[9]

On 16 December Haking wrote to his Divisional Commanders (5th and 48th British and 64th French) outlining the general situation and specifying the role of XI Corps:

> The constant pressure of the enemy against the Italian troops on the Monte Grappa and Asiago positions, and the continued absence of snow, produced during the first weeks of December, a state of affairs which made it advisable, in the opinion of the Allied Commanders, to organize certain Groups of British and French formations, which would be so placed as to be able to meet the situation in the event of hostile success between the Rivers Piave and Astico . . . The role allotted to the Group under General Duchesne is to prevent the enemy debouching into the plain between the Brenta and Astico Rivers (both inclusive), to cover the withdrawal of the Italian troops, and to counter-attack.

The various units of the XI Corps were assigned sectors with the 48th British Division in front of Morostica, the 64th French Division north of Bassano and the 5th British Division in reserve near Tezze.[10] Haking also gave instructions to his Corps RFC squadrons who were charged with making a photographic reconnaissance of the area and liaising with the Artillery commanders.[11]

The nature of the country in which the British and French troops now found themselves was strikingly different from that of the Western Front and presented considerable problems. Difficulties arose with the placing of the Artillery because of the "peculiar nature of the ground on the mountains about the positions we are preparing for defence". Corps Heavy Artillery was to arrange counter-battery work on specific enemy positions: "As regards Field Artillery, there is not yet sufficient information to say what number of guns it is to bring into action to assist the defence of the position, but Divisional Commanders are now working out that problem which involves chiefly the matter of ammunition supply up the difficult tracks."[12]

The "peculiar nature of the ground" also presented the Infantry with special problems. Haking wrote:

> As a general principle of defence, the ground with its numerous spurs and deep valleys should be dealt with as follows: (a) The most advanced line protected by wire with gaps to permit the enemy to penetrate into ground well-covered by our fire and easy

for the delivery of a local counter-stroke. (b) Forward posts with machine guns and certainly Stokes Mortars pushed forwards on all spurs, the oak scrub being used extensively to hide the entanglements and provide posts for the wire. (c) The present Italian line to be retained as the main line of defence with 'T' heads run out wherever necessary, to provide the necessary flanking fire, command the valleys, sweep the sides of the spurs and cover dead ground in front of other parts of the line. (d) A second line to be constructed and wired throughout behind the crest of the position and out of view of all hostile posts of obser-vation . . . The line to form the locality for garrison of the main line in case of heavy hostile shelling, with carefully sited commu-nication trenches running up to the main line of defence.

Haking was also concerned about the welfare of the British and French troops in this new environment. He ordered that: "every effort should be made to improve the tracks running up the mountain from different parts of the valley"; that "a careful programme of transit prepared for troops, ammunition, food, and water, up those tracks with regular march tables and carefully selected halting places after each 30 or 40 minutes climb. The halting places being provided with aid posts and water"; and that "there should be fuel for the men in the trenches, and for the cook-houses, and means of providing hot meals as usual and hot coffee or tea at intervals during the night, especially to men in advanced posts". In the villages there should be "provision of hot water for baths and in any case the usual means for prevention of frost bite or trench feet".

Throughout December the main objective of the British and French Commanders was to position their troops so that, in the event of the Italians falling back from the front line, a solid defence could be presented. On 27 December Haking issued XI Corps Order No. 304:

As a result of reconnaissance carried out by the Corps Commander and Divisional Commanders, and in conformity with the instructions received from GOC Xth French Army, it is now possible to lay down definitely the probable action of XI Corps in the event of its employment on the southern borders of the moun-tain region . . . In the event of Italian troops being compelled to withdraw from their present position to the *Ligne Marginale*, the XI Corps will at once occupy the Blue Line La Rocca-La Gusella-Mt Campesana- Hill1057-Rubbio-M. Busso-Alto . . . In the event of the Italian troops being forced to withdraw from the *Ligne Marginale* the 48th Division will take the offensive against the Austrian (or German) troops following up the Italians, and will attack in direction of Mt. Trolla. In these circumstances, Advanced HQ XI Corps will be temporarily established at Rubbio, and the operations will be directed, according o the circumstances, by the Corps Commander.[13]

On 31 December the XI Corps HQ moved from Camposampiero to Lorregio. It was here that Haking took the opportunity to establish the principles and practice of his new HQ organization and, in so doing, he revealed his personal views concerning the nature of Staff work. At a Conference on 9 January 1918,[14] Haking addressed the HQ Staff:

I have assembled you together this morning because I want to discuss with you the important question of the organisation and working of the Staff. We have had one or two important changes on our Staff, we are dealing with a new higher Staff, and with new Staffs of lower formations. It is therefore our first duty to make certain that our own Staff is working in perfect harmony according to the policy that is laid down by me, which of course I receive from the Commander-in-Chief or his General Staff, and further that we at all times 'play up' to the higher Staff and do everything possible to assist the Staffs of lower formations.

The General Staff, especially in war, must always be the foundation upon which all other branches and departments base their considerations and their actions. The General Staff working under my directions lay down the military policy of the Corps. I will tell them when that policy changes and it is their responsibility to make quite sure that every other member of Staff, who may be only remotely concerned in the change is kept informed of the new situation . . . The General Staff must clearly understand that if anything goes wrong, they will be the first people I shall look to for their mistake. Their responsibility is greater than any other branch or department . . . If there is any trouble it is the duty of any member of my Staff to bring it to the notice of the Chief of his own branch or department, and if necessary, the latter should inform me. It is better to let me know too much than too little; I have had more experience of the Staff both in peace and war than any of you. I am always ready to help you in any of your difficulties, and you will always find me patient and sympathetic because I know so well what your difficulties are.

Having made it clear that the Corps Staff must work together "in absolute harmony", Haking turned to the subject of relations with "higher Staff":

There is one great axiom we can always apply with advantage. If anything goes wrong, let us all find out where we have made a mistake . . . Every good Commander and every good Staff will always act loyally towards their higher Commander and higher Staff . . . the letter and the spirit of the higher Commander's wishes and instructions as conveyed to us by his staff are willingly and energetically carried out . . . If the difficulties are so great that we cannot overcome them, then I can at all times go to the higher Staff or to the Commander-in-Chief and settle matters satisfactorily . . . Finally, I will remind you of a system which I have established in the Corps since its formation . . . If it is necessary to criticize the actions of a Divisional Commander or of a senior officer in a Division, or to bring to notice any glaring mistake or error, I will do it myself and write and sign the letter myself. If things are not going right let me know; I will soon put matters on a proper footing.

Attached to this memorandum, and headed "Rules for Guidance for Administrative Staff", was a twenty-foolscap-page document covering staff-related matters designed to "help the Troops in every way possible". It was a comprehensive document and the items ranged from the duties of the GOC Royal Artillery to the number of typewriter spaces that should follow a comma or a full stop. Haking's attention to detail in staff and administrative matters will be further discussed in the final section of this chapter.

* * * *

During January 1918 the French and British troops were transferred from the area south of Asiago to the Piave with the British XI Corps taking over from the Italian VIII Corps. On 17 January Haking set out his policy for XI Corps:

The line will be taken over by the 5th Division, with the 48th Division either in Corps or Army Reserve. The line is an easy one to hold, but I am anxious that all Commanders from the very first should thoroughly understand the policy I wish to adopt so that everyone in the Corps can be working on the same lines.

Haking went on to list his priorities: "first to put the line in a proper state of defence according to our own methods; secondly to find out by reconnaissance and observation what it is possible to do in the way of offensive action and, thirdly, do it".[15]

As regards defence, Haking considered that

with our machine guns, posts and our wire properly placed and defended we can make it practically impossible for the enemy to cross the Piave, even at night in small parties. During the period of preparation when we want to work without being interfered with the Artillery must co-operate closely with the Infantry – communications will also require careful inspection and probably extensive re-arrangement.

The role of the Artillery would be one of

retaliation which they can combine with good counter-battery work. That is to say if our Infantry are interfered with in their work, the Artillery can take on a destructive shoot against hostile batteries . . . The Artillery will not take on isolated offensive action, merely with the object of stirring up the enemy, until the Infantry are ready to profit by their action, when both arms will be working together to obtain definite results.

The task of the Royal Engineers was to "obtain a careful record of the various channels of the River Piave, the depth of water and rate of current". The Engineers would also "reconnoitre the river bed and discover and test the best means of passage by rapid bridging or ferrying". The RFC were also heavily involved and their role "will be to extend the work of the Infantry Observers to areas immediately behind the enemy's front on which observation cannot be brought to bear from the ground, also to confirm by photography, when possible, the reports of the ground observers."

Attached to this memorandum was a detailed description of the Piave river in the XI Corps sector. The description had some significance for a future XI Corps exercise, which will be described later in this chapter, and noted:

The current in some channels is very strong, even up to 10 miles an hour, and at present the depth of the channels varies generally from a few inches to a depth of 5 feet, with deeper holes in places. Although the river rises and falls frequently some one or two feet, the great rise takes place in the Spring when snow is melting in the mountains.

Between 24-27 January, despite poor weather and bad roads, the XI Corps moved its Headquarters from Lorregia to Merlengo. At the same time the 5th and 48th Division Headquarters moved to Visnadello and

Levada respectively. The relief of the Italian VIII Corps went well and the entry in the XI Corps war diary for 27 January read:

> It is worth recording that the relief of the VIII Italian Corps by the XI British Corps was carried out with a smoothness and easiness which could not have been bettered. The Italians gave our troops every facility and helped them in every way. They left numerous English-speaking officers both in the front line and with the head-quarters of formations to assist us after relief. They left steel helmets for the sentries to prevent the enemy from discovering that British troops were in the line and they left all the trenches and billets clean and in order.[16]

Haking was sufficiently impressed with the handover that he wrote to Plumer:

> [The] arrangements were so well thought-out, not only by the Italian Corps Commander [General Cavighia] and his Staff, but also by Divisional and Brigade Commanders and the Regiments concerned that that the whole relief was conducted with smooth-ness and rapidity . . . I would like to add that this letter is in no way dictated by any desire to pay a compliment to the soldiers of another nation, but is simply an expression of our gratitude to our comrades in the Italian Army for handing over to us a system of defence so well organized and so efficiently constructed.[17]

Both Fayolle and Plumer recognized the need to improve the fighting efficiency of the Italian troops. Plumer wrote to the War Office on 5 January:

> if we could help [the Italians] with their training and sound system of how to hold their line of defence it would certainly help them to be ready in Spring to regain lost ground and at any rate hold their lines with a better chance of security. It was decided to start our Schools and Ranges, etc. as soon as possible.[18]

A further memorandum from Plumer to the War Office, on 20 January, stressed "the vital importance of devoting the next two or three months to really strenuous practical training . . . The British and French are doing their best to aid all Branches of the Italian Army to raise their standards of efficiency."[19] However, as Fayolle noted: "The task is a delicate one . . . Their susceptibilities are very much on the alert and even in Gen. Diaz's entourage there is a strong feeling of resentment against any interference whatsoever on our part."[20]

Despite these "susceptibilities" various forms of training played an important part in improving Italian effectiveness. Plumer organized the British positions

> as a model with the object of showing the Italians how few men it is necessary to keep in the front line . . . Our Schools . . . Musketry School and Ranges, Physical and Bayonet Training Courses, Sniping School, Artillery School, Signalling School – are being formed close to GHQ and conveniently situated for visits of Italian officers . . . The Italians have also asked for any notes on training or notes compiled when visiting their lines and we think in this manner we should be able to furnish them with some useful information.[21]

The French also established Training Schools and an exchange of British, French and Italian officers between the various Schools was encouraged "to inculcate our methods into the Italian Armies".[22]

Haking supported the development of the Army and Corps Schools and on 18 January the XI Corps war diary recorded that: "C[orps] C[ommander] Inspected XI Corps School and gave opening address to the students."[23] However, the establishment of the Schools was not without incident. The GHQ and Corps Schools occupied the same training area and Haking wrote to Plumer on 24 January:

> The Commandant GHQ is at present exercising a control over XI Corps School which I do not understand . . . He orders my School to provide working parties and to detail men for sanitary duties and appears to consider that he is in command of the Corps School as well as the GHQ School . . . I can't provide any working parties or anything else *from my School* to assist the GHQ School.

The issue was presumably resolved without undue trouble since Haking provided the solution: "Of course, if this is the intention of GHQ, I can provide [working parties] from the Corps. I have already one Field Coy R. E., ½ Bn of Infantry and a few details of a Pioneer Bn provided by the Corps for the GHQ and of course more are available if necessary."[24] Haking's zeal to please his superior was, as ever, clearly evident.

* * * *

It was at this point (29 January) that Haking went on leave, thus missing the 15 Infantry Brigade Football League Competition eventually won by the 1st Norfolks. During Haking's absence, Major General

Fanshawe (48th Division) assumed command of XI Corps. The main activity during the three weeks of Haking's period of leave was the preparation for "an offensive on a small scale on XI Corps front on the Piave with a view to assisting operations elsewhere".[25]

The main attack was to be carried out by the Third Italian Army south of the XI Corps sector and the British 5th Division was to provide a diversionary operation. Fanshawe attended several meetings at the headquarters of both GHQ and the Italian Third Army to discuss the forthcoming attack and then handed over the project to Haking who returned from leave on 22 February.

Haking's next few days were hectic. His natural inclination was to be fully involved in the Piave attack, but, on the day of his return to Italy "a telegram was received from GHQ to the effect that XI Corps HQ, 7th and 41st Divisions and various other units and formations would return to France at an early date".[26] Despite the prospect of an early departure from the Italian front, Haking immersed himself in the preparations of the 5th Division attack. There is an interesting contrast in the approach of Fanshawe and Brind, the XI Corps BGGS, during Haking's absence, and that taken by Haking on his return. On 12 February Brind held a Conference for the Staff of XI Corps "to explain certain operations about to be undertaken by 5th Division . . . The operation is to be a divisional operation and it is not our business to butt in, but it is our business to do everything in our power to assist the Division."[27] By 28 February, however, a subtle change was evident in the tone of communications on the subject of the proposed attack. Haking's XI Corps Order No. 311 stated that: "In conjunction with operations which are taking place elsewhere, troops of XI Corps will, on day Z, . . . undertake certain operations . . . to force a passage of the Piave." It had now moved from being a Divisional to a Corps operation.[28]

Order 311 outlined the purpose and scope of the operation and, particularly, the role of the Artillery, the details of which covered twenty-five foolscap pages. An interesting feature of the Instructions issued by the 5th Division in relation to the attack was a summary, designed presumably to bolster British morale, of the abilities of the opposing enemy Divisions: "The 13th Schutzen Division has such a poor reputation as a fighting Division that it was withdrawn from the line before the offensive against the Italians last Autumn . . . the 17th Division also are not a notable fighting Division . . . , the 24th Division is reputed to have shown up indifferently as fighters." The Instructions also noted of the opposing troops that "their nationalities are, as usual, mixed" and listed Magyars, Rumanians, Serbs, Poles and Ruthenes.[29]

On 2 March Haking wrote a Memorandum to the troops of XI Corps:

I am anxious for all ranks to understand that the object of our attack is to assist the Italian troops on our right to gain some important ground on the right bank of the River Piave, and definitely drive back the enemy on the left bank along the whole of the lower course of the river. When this object is gained, there is no necessity for us to retain possession of the ground on the left bank of the river and our attacking troops will be withdrawn, after holding their position for 48 hours, by which time the Italians will have consolidated their position. The operation to be carried out by the 15th Brigade under Brigadier-General Oldman is a difficult one and will demand exceptionally good leading and initiative on the part of Company and Platoon Commanders and a thorough knowledge on the part of NCOs and men as to the task to be performed by each individual.

Haking's Memorandum then went on to describe the tasks, referred to later in this chapter, of each of the attacking Battalions – 1st Bedfords, 1st Cheshires, 1st Norfolks and the 16th Warwicks. The Royal Engineers "by skilful improvisation and by overcoming the difficulties of the work" were to construct "first a temporary and later a more permanent means of crossing the deep part of the channels". The Royal Artillery "can lead the Infantry with their barrage to their final objective" and the RFC were given the task of "driving back the enemy's fighting planes". Haking ended his Memorandum:

the Commander-in-Chief of the British forces in Italy has written to me to say that he knows that attention will be paid by all ranks to the smallest detail so as to ensure that the first attack of British troops in Italy, although made under exceptionally difficult conditions, will be successful. Both he and I wish you every success in your task . . . [We] assure you that every possible means, as regards previous reconnaissance, preparation of material, artillery action and work in the air, has been taken by Major-General Stephens in command of your Division, and by the Corps and the Army, to help you in your task.[30]

The aim of this carefully prepared attack was to "force a passage of the Piave at two points – about the Island of Lucca (1 mile E. Of Nervesa) and at the Ponte Priula railway Bridge". The attack, however, never took place. The XI Corps war diary for 1 March noted: "The weather which has been very good for the past month definitely broke and low clouds and some rain followed."[31] Norman Gladden, who was serving with the 15th Battalion, Northumberland Fusiliers, later wrote:

"During the night of 1 March the storm broke in earnest, swamping us out . . . on the following day the waters were still rising, the islands were shrinking fast and the Piave had become a mighty expanse of water dividing us absolutely from the enemy."[32] As a result of the poor weather prospects the attack was postponed by one day from 5 to 6 March. However, on 3 March the XI Corps diary read: "River Piave has risen considerably during the night and has washed away the piers of the temporary bridge it was proposed to pass the troops over." Similarly, the war diary of the attacking force, the British 15 Brigade, noted on 2 March:

> At 11pm two advanced posts of the Right Battalion had to be withdrawn from the Beach owing to the rise of the Piave. By 7pm on March 3 a rise of 43 centimetres in 24 hours was recorded. New channels in the river bed had filled and the main stream was running under arches of the bridges which were previously dry.[33]

It was inevitable, therefore, that the XI Corps Order 312 of 3 March should announce: "The operation of forcing the passage of the Piave which was to have been undertaken by the 5th Division early this month will not now be carried out and all Orders and Instructions issued from XI Corps HQ in this connection will be cancelled."[34] A letter from the Duke of Aosta, commanding the Italian Third Army, expressed regret at the cancellation of the operation: "This co-operation, so thoroughly and accurately arranged . . . would have constituted a new and brilliant episode in the comradeship in arms on the same battlefield."[35]

On the day that the attack was to have taken place, Haking received orders from GHQ: "The entrainment of XI Corps Troops and HQ for France . . . to commence as soon as possible."[36] Haking issued orders to that effect immediately. Plumer was also ordered back to France and Cavan took over as Commander in Chief of the British troops in Italy. Events moved quickly. On 9 March the XI Corps front on the Piave was taken over by the British XIV Corps and the 5th and 48th Divisions were transferred accordingly. On 11 March the XI Corps HQ at Merengo was closed and the XI Corps Staff and troops entrained for France. The first train arrived at Aire at 11.00pm on 13 March and by 16 March a new Corps HQ had opened in Hinges. XI Corps once again became part of the First Army. Haking and his Staff were on familiar territory and on 18 March orders were received that the 55th Division was to join XI Corps covering the Givenchy-Festubert sector. In early April the Portuguese Divisions also became part of XI Corps in the Festubert-Aubers sector.

* * * *

In Italy as in France, the opportunity to take part in a significant operation had once more eluded Haking. In his XI Corps document of 17 January 1918, Haking had referred to "four classes of operations which I want all commanders to bear in mind". The first of these classes was "the possibility that the Corps may be called upon to take part in a big offensive to force the passage of the Piave". As we have seen, XI Corps was not involved in a "big offensive" and was fated to miss even the opportunity of taking part in a relatively small operation on the Piave. Nevertheless, Haking's involvement in the preparations for the proposed attack on Lucca Island showed professionalism, attention to detail and an awareness of effective attack techniques. Included in the artillery arrangements were counter-battery work, trench mortar fire, creeping and protective barrages and a detailed plan of bombardments and harassing fire. The RFC was fully involved and was to play an important part in shielding the assault troops from enemy aircraft and in supplying photographic information. The Royal Engineers were given the difficult tasks of bridging the river and assisting in the ferrying of the troops.

Of particular note are Haking's instructions to the 1st Norfolks who had been given the important objective of taking the houses near the Ponte Priula railway bridge:

> The battalion may encounter difficulties from machine guns in these houses and every platoon and section must deal with the local situation without hesitation and push forward close to the artillery barrage, pass and surround any strong-points and press on to their objective leaving the actual capture of enemy's troops and machine guns to the mopping-up parties following in the rear.[37]

These planned arrangements constituted a good example of a joint-arms attack – tactics, which Haking was to use with success later in 1918. On 9 March Haking wrote to Major General Stephens, commander of the 5th Division: "It was unfortunate that we were unable to carry out the attack on the Piave . . . I know it was a great disappointment to you all."[38] It was no doubt a great disappointment to Haking also.

During his early weeks in Italy, throughout December, Haking made strenuous efforts to understand the geography of the front and the military situation. Over a four-week period he made over twenty visits to various sectors gathering information and making contact not only with his own commanders and troops, but also with his French and

Italian colleagues. Had snow not disrupted his programme, Haking's travels would have been even more extensive. It was an impressive sequence of meetings and conferences, often undertaken in poor weather conditions, and it no doubt contributed significantly, as did his support of the Corps training school, to the developing rapport between the British, French and Italian forces.

An aspect of Haking's character – his attitude to superior authority – was apparent on more than one occasion during his stay in Italy. It was typical that Haking apologized to Duchesne, his superior officer, for writing his "understanding" of the situation on the Italian front in English rather than in French, promising to write in French on future occasions. In the same memorandum, Haking was at pains to point out to Duchesne that "the methods suggested to me . . . by the GOC. Xth Army are absolutely in conformity with my own views on the subject". It was also in Haking's nature, when complaining to Plumer about the high-handed behaviour of the GHQ School Commander, to make it clear that, if Plumer wanted it that way, then Haking would accept the situation. To make doubly sure that he gave no offence to Plumer, Haking even offered additional XI Corps troops to act as working parties for GHQ.

Haking's facility with detail was once more apparent in the XI Corps administration policy. The policy also reveals his thinking on the relationship between his own staff and those of higher and lower units. One of Haking's comments, however, is particularly noteworthy: "Every good Commander and every good Staff will always act loyally towards their higher Commander and higher Staff." The sentiment is sound enough, but it has something of a hollow ring about it bearing in mind Haking's part in the events leading to the departure of Sir John French after Loos.

Overall, nothing of an exceptional nature took place during Haking's twelve weeks in Italy. By the time XI Corps had arrived from France the crisis following Caporetto was over and the front was stable. It was in that context that Haking carried out his role as a Corps Commander. He did what he was asked to do working with Plumer and Duchesne, and he carried out his duties competently ensuring that his Divisions acted appropriately in terms of administrative, defensive and, potentially, offensive measures. On the day of his departure from Italy, Haking received a farewell note from the Commander of the Italian First Army, Lieutenant General Pecori Giraldi: "The First Army would have been proud to go into action, side by side, with the fine troops we have so much admired, but although events have wished otherwise, we are certain that the XIth British Corps will, always and everywhere, fight valiantly against the common foe."[39] It can reasonably be assumed that Haking, like Plumer, was pleased to be returning to France with the anticipation that the opportunities for "fighting valiantly against the common foe" were more assured than they had been in Italy.

Notes

1. War was not declared against Germany until over a year later. For the background, see Beckett, *Great War*, pp.105-07; Richard Bosworth, *Italy and the Approach of the First World War*. pp.121–41; William A Renzi, *The Shadow of the Sword: Italy's Neutrality and Entrance into the Great War, 1914–15*, pp.137–61; John Thayer, *Italy and the Great War*. pp.307–70; and David French, *The Strategy of the Lloyd George Coalition, 1916–18*, pp.158–70.
2. *BOH, Military Operations, Italy, 1915–19*, p. 9. On Caporetto, see Mario Morselli, *Caporetto, 1917: Victory or Defeat?*; and Vanda Wilcox, 'Generalship and Mass Surrender during the Italian Defeat at Caporett', in Ian F W Beckett, ed., *1917: Beyond the Western Front*. pp.25–46. On the decision to go to Italy, see Matthew Hughes, 'Personalities in Conflict: Lloyd George, the Generals and the Italian Campaign, 1917–18', in Hughes and Seligmann, eds., *Leadership in Conflict*, pp.191–206.
3. Sheffield and Bourne, *Haig Diaries and Letters*, p.339.
4. Quoted in Geoffrey Powell, *Plumer: The Soldiers' General*, p.235.
5. Lt Col Lionel James, *The History of King Edward's Horse*, p.246.
6. TNA, WO 106/799, Report, 17 December 1917.
7. TNA, WO 106/808.
8. TNA, WO 95/4211.
9. TNA, WO 95/4211, Haking to Duchesne, 14 December 1917.
10. Ibid., XI Corps Instruction No. 1.
11. TNA, WO 95/4211, To 2nd Bde RFC, 18 December 1917.
12. Ibid., XI Corps, S.S. 4/15, 21 December 1917.
13. TNA, WO 95/4211.
14. Ibid., S.S.6.
15. TNA, WO 95/4211, S.S.7.
16. TNA, WO 95/4211.
17. Ibid., G.S. 1080/4, 29 January 1918.
18. TNA, WO 106/799.
19. TNA, WO 106/810.
20. TNA, WO 106/805, Report, 26 December 1917.
21. TNA, WO 106/799.
22. Ibid.
23. TNA, WO 95/4211.
24. TNA, WO 95/4211, G.T. 103.
25. TNA, WO 95/4211.
26. TNA, WO 95/4211.
27. Ibid., S.S. 11/2.
28. TNA, WO 95/4211.
29. TNA, WO 95/4214, 28 February 1918.
30. TNA, WO 95/4211, S.S. 11/45, Headed "Memorandum", 2 March 1918.

31. TNA WO 95/4211
32. Norman Gladden, *Across the Piave*, p.66.
33. TNA, WO 95/4217.
34. TNA, WO 95/4211.
35. Ibid., 4 March 1918.
36. TNA, WO 95/4211.
37. TNA, WO 95/4211, S.S. 11/45, Memorandum.
38. TNA, WO 95/4211, G.S. 1030/9.
39. TNA, WO 95/4211, Unsigned, 11 March 1918.

Chapter VII

Haking and the Portuguese
Expeditionary Force

Germany's strategy in the West for 1918 was decided at a conference held at Mons on 11 November 1917. To Ludendorff, the German Quarter-Master General, there appeared to be little or no choice. The Allied blockade was causing severe food and raw material shortages in Germany and a continuation of the long drawn-out struggle on the Western Front was no longer a tenable option. What was required was a major breakthrough and that had to be achieved before the Americans arrived in strength. The collapse of the Russian armies in the East and the subsequent transfer of German troops to the West had given Ludendorff a significant superiority in numbers – 192 divisions against 178 allied divisions. Since this advantage was only likely to be temporary – the Americans had promised a million men by July – then a 1918 spring offensive was essential.[1]

It was with these considerations in mind that Ludendorff planned Operation MICHAEL – a major attack in the St Quentin-Arras area over the old Somme battlefields. The aim was to separate the French and the British armies and advance along the river Somme. Once the front was broken, the German troops would move north and threaten the British flank and rear. At this stage, a second German operation, codenamed GEORGE, would attack between the la Bassée canal and the Ypres-Comines canal, cross the river Lys and head towards Hazebrouck and the Channel ports. In this way, the British troops would be encircled and defeated. Such a breakthrough, reckoned Ludendorff, would inevitably lead to the collapse of France and to Germany winning the war.

Ludendorff's plan almost succeeded. The Germans employed tactics that had already proved effective on the Eastern Front and at Caporetto and Cambrai. Artillery was brought up to the front, having been registered well behind the lines, thus providing an element of surprise, and storm troops were trained to infiltrate weak points leaving strong positions to be dealt with by supporting lines of attacking infantry.

Operation MICHAEL was launched on 21 March and by 4 April German troops had advanced twenty-eight miles on a front of fifty miles and were within sight of Amiens. After three and a half years of stalemate, mobile warfare had at last returned to the Western Front. But the Germans were unable to follow through their initial success. British and French reserves were rushed to the front. The German advance faltered as it crossed the old Somme battle area – a maze of abandoned trenches and shell craters – and progress was hindered as exhausted German troops delayed time and time again to plunder the captured British food-stores. On 4 April, a mixed Australian and British force successfully counter-attacked at Villers-Bretonneux and the German High Command finally recognized that Operation MICHAEL had been brought to a halt.

Nevertheless, Ludendorff was determined to carry through his planned strategy. On 9 April he launched Operation GEORGETTE – a scaled down version of the original GEORGE. The direction of the attack, which later became known as the Battle of the Lys, was over the 1915 battlefields of Neuve Chapelle, Festubert and Aubers. This sector was part of the British First Army front and the attack opened against the trenches occupied by the 2nd Portuguese Division, a major element of Haking's XI Corps.

The Portuguese troops had first been placed under Haking's command in February 1917. However, they were transferred one month later to First Army reserve, returning to XI Corps in June. Haking's direct command of the Portuguese troops was also broken in November 1917 when he was sent, along with Plumer and Cavan, to the Italian front. Haking returned to France in March 1918 just in time for the German Spring offensive and once again assumed control of the Portuguese 2nd Division on 5 April. In total, therefore, Haking had some six months' personal involvement with the Portuguese before the start of Operation GEORGETTE. Haking's dealings with the Portuguese during this period are well documented and they throw some interesting light on Haking as a Corps Commander.

* * * *

Portugal was the last European country to enter the war. Both Britain and Germany had recognized the neutrality of Portugal, but Britain had promised help to the Portuguese in defending their colonies in Africa – Angola and Mozambique – and when Portugal complied with a British request to seize German vessels in her ports then Germany responded, on 9 March 1916, by declaring war. The Allies invited Portugal to contribute a small Expeditionary Force, amounting to 55,000 men, to fight on the Western Front and the first contingent of 4,000 troops arrived in Brest on 3 February 1917.[2] The CEP (*Corpo Expedicionario*

Portugues) was commanded by General Fernando Tamagnini and, under a Convention agreed between the Portuguese and British Governments in January 1917, the CEP was to be integrated into the British Expeditionary Force. The Portuguese continued to arrive in France through the summer of 1917 and, after some initial training in the Aire-sur- Lys area, were eventually formed into two Divisions and assigned to the Ferme du Bois/Neuve Chapelle/Champigny/Fauquissart sectors – at that time considered a relatively quiet area where fresh troops could gradually become accustomed to the rigours of trench warfare.

In order to help the Portuguese settle as quickly as possible into the ways of the Western Front, the BEF set up a British Mission staffed by over sixty officers and a hundred other ranks, many fluent in Portuguese, under the command of Lieutenant Colonel C.A. Ker. These liaison officers acted as advisers, instructors and general consultants and they became the first to realize that the integration of the CEP was likely to be far from smooth. One of the first entries in the British Mission war diary, dated 7 February 1917, noted:

> Disembarkation proceeding smoothly in spite of the following difficulties – Captains of transport have no details of Bills of Lading. Personnel, vehicles, animals and blankets of a unit often arrive in different ships. Blankets arrive in bulk. The three ships not yet arrived contain portions of units already disembarked. Strongly recommend that two experienced Military Loading Officers be despatched to Lisbon.[3]

Entries in the war diary of the British Mission throughout February cover various other problems. A letter from Ker to the First Army General Staff, dated 18 February, painted a sorry picture: "What with mumps, venereal and glanders, we are kept pretty busy apart from training. They are terribly incapable people at this moment, but will get straight in time, I hope. In the meantime, they are a satisfaction to nobody." On 21 February, Brigadier General Graham Thomson of the First Army Staff had cause to tell the Portuguese Chief of Staff, Major Baptista, "that there had been a good deal of trouble at Étaples with the Portuguese personnel that had been there so far". When Ker visited the Portuguese 1 Brigade training area on 22 February, he found "little work being done".

Two weeks later, Ker felt obliged to report his first experiences of attempting to liaise with the Portuguese to their new Corps Commander, Haking. Ker prefaced his comments: "The following notes are an attempt to define the existing situation, as far as I find it, so that it may be possible to assess the real value of the Portuguese troops, and arrange for them a suitable training programme." There then followed ten lengthy paragraphs of criticism. Ker's first impressions were certainly not good and he began his comments:

The condition in which the troops arrive in the area of concentration is far from satisfactory. Fifty-one out of sixteen hundred horses and mules had to be destroyed in February for glanders. During the same month, there were 885 admissions to hospital out of 6,000 troops and of these 151 were cases of mumps and 117 were venereal. In addition, a number of animals had to be destroyed at Brest and on the voyage and there were a large number of admissions to hospital at Brest who have since been transferred to Étaples.

Ker then went on to comment on the "characteristics" of the Portuguese troops:

The discipline of all ranks appears to be very poor – orders, when given, are often discussed before being obeyed . . . The national characteristic – dilatoriness – is evident all the time. There are very few people who take hold and do things, there are many who talk about doing it . . . Nothing seems to happen without direct orders from Gen Tamagnini or his Chief of Staff. The result is that very little happens . . . The chain of responsibility as we understand it appears to be non-existent . . . Very few officers show any aptitude for handling men. The Staff show little aptitude for looking after their men or arranging administrative details . . . Neither officers nor men as a whole realise the conditions of modern warfare – their outlook is more like that of a bad British Territorial Division in, say, 1908.[4] To make matters worse, they are quite unaware of their own short-comings.

Ker then summed up his somewhat negative feelings: "When we have succeeded in equipping the Portuguese Expeditionary Force, and have taught it to feed itself and look after itself, it will be quite unfit to hold a portion of the line until it has been trained."

Such a catalogue of criticism illustrated the size of the task that faced the British Mission and XI Corps in trying to bring the Portuguese troops up to some sort of acceptable standard. However, towards the end of the report there are some positive remarks: "the rank and file appear to be willing to work, to be of average physique and intelligence, and to form not unpromising material out of which to make troops";

and "a number of officers and sous-officers seem possessed of a good deal of ability and to be keen on their work. They learn quickly and usually pay much attention to detail."

The message that Ker wished to get across to Haking was clearly that things were bad, but at least there was something to work on. Ker addressed the nub of the problem, as he saw it, in his concluding sentences: "the British Mission, and the Officer Interpreters attached thereto, have no defined status at present, nor will they have within a reasonable time if it is left to the Portuguese to give it to them . . . the assistance that the British Mission renders at present is therefore largely administrative". The Portuguese, said Ker, "had a limitless capacity for procrastination and prevarication and unless these unfortunate characteristics are overcome, progress will not be rapid".

Haking, who received Ker's report on 6 March, took the matter seriously and immediately arranged a Conference for 8 March at the British Mission headquarters at Aire. Present at the meeting were, from XI Corps, Haking with two of his senior staff officers; General Tamagnini and his Chief of Staff, Major Baptista, representing the Portuguese; and Ker and his seven British Mission section heads. The proceedings of the meeting are worth noting in some detail since they set the tone of the future relationship between Haking and the Portuguese.

Haking began by saying that the purpose of the Conference was to find out what the British Mission had done so far; what it should do in the future; and decide "what changes were necessary to ensure that the Portuguese Expeditionary Force should be prepared for the task in front of it". It was Haking's job, as the Corps Commander, to ensure that the Portuguese could take over a section of the front line effectively and in the shortest possible time. Taking account of the reports that he had so far received, Haking therefore saw the Conference as an opportunity to assess the situation and, where necessary, to knock heads together and get things moving in a more positive direction. When, therefore, Captain Glover, the British Mission officer in charge of Infantry Training, said that he had not been able to do much because he was "waiting for the Portuguese Brigade Major to put forward suggestions as to how he could help best", Haking reacted unsympathetically: "The Corps Commander said this was wrong, and that British Officers should make suggestions to the Portuguese Officers as to the best methods of training and point out mistakes that were being made." Haking went on: "It is the duty of the British Officers to teach the Portuguese Officers the details of trench warfare . . . the Portuguese Army knows all about ordinary warfare, but we had to teach them from our own experience of two and a half years the details of trench fighting."

What then followed was an interesting exchange between Tamagnini and Haking. Tamagnini claimed that the Portuguese officers had already been taught about trench warfare by being attached to British Army units and they could now teach their own troops. If that were so, responded Haking, would Tamagnini like these British officers returned to their own Army? Haking pressed the point further:

These British officers are highly skilled and would be most valu-able with their own units. They had been lent to the Portuguese to help to teach trench warfare and, if they were to do this, they must make suggestions and point out defects or mistakes direct to the Portuguese commanders. It would rest with the Portuguese commanders to take such action as they thought necessary.

In the light of these remarks, Tamagnini had little option but to say that he would like the British officers to remain and that he agreed with the Corps Commander's proposed procedure.

Having dealt with Infantry Training, Haking then questioned Major Gore-Brown, the head of the British Mission's Artillery section:

Do the Portuguese Artillery Officers realise the great necessity for accurate shooting to avoid hitting their own troops and make sure of hitting the enemy? Did they understand the importance of being able to open a rapid and accurate fire at the shortest notice, and were they sufficiently trained to know that this couldn't be done without good observation, good laying and fuze setting and good work generally in the battery?

Gore-Brown replied that some of the Portuguese Artillery Officers did know these things, but some did not, and that he had already put forward a clear artillery training proposal to the Portuguese Artillery Commander, but nothing had come of it. At this point, Haking inter-vened to support Gore-Brown's proposal and, the notes of the Conference record: "Tamagnini entirely agreed".

Gore-Brown next raised the question of the employment of his ten British officers who were, he said, at present doing nothing – largely because the Portuguese had not yet received their complement of guns. Tamagnini expressed his view that these officers were not wanted because the Portuguese Artillery was very well trained already. Haking again took over the conversation saying that, as the guns had not yet arrived he thought it would be better to keep six of the officers, one for each Portuguese Artillery Group. To this, Tamagnini agreed. Ker then suggested that the remaining four British Artillery officers would be required by the Portuguese "in the back areas". The artillery discussion ended with Haking deciding "to keep all ten officers in addition to Maj. Gore-Brown for the present".

By this stage of the Conference, Tamagnini and Baptista had come to realize how best to respond to their new Corps Commander. So, when Captain Cheetham, the Royal Engineers' section head, stated that at present he had not been able to do much because there was only one Portuguese Engineer officer in France, he was quickly supported by Tamagnini: "Capt. Cheetham is most useful in helping to instruct the infantry and I do not want to lose him." Similarly, when Major Gill of the Army Service Corps reported that he himself was doing work that would eventually be done by the Portuguese Supply officers, Tamagnini broke in saying that Gill was most useful and could not be spared. Tamagnini then expressed the same sentiments in relation to Captain Ormond, the British officer in charge of Ordnance.

Ker's position was also clarified:

He will act as a liaison officer between Gen. Tamagnini and his staff and the Corps Commander and his staff. He will bring to the notice of Gen. Tamagnini or his Chief of Staff anything he thinks requires special attention or alteration, and he will do everything in his power to ensure that he and the officers of the British Mission do their utmost to help the Portuguese officers and men, without in any way intervening with the responsible chain of the Portuguese command and control.

Haking's key message to Tamagnini, however, was contained at the end of the Notes of the Conference.

The Corps Commander wished Gen. Tamagnini to understand that he, the Corps Commander, was responsible for the defence of the line and that it was of great importance, when the Portuguese took over part of the Corps front, that the officers should have a thorough command of their men, and that the men should obey immediately and implicitly all orders given them.

Neither Haking nor Tamagnini realized at that Conference on 8 March 1917 just how severely those instructions would be tested one year and one month later.

* * * *

General Tamagnini may have felt somewhat browbeaten following the 8 March Conference, but at least there had been an attempt to clarify a number of important organizational and communication issues to help the Portuguese to settle into the war and become a reasonably efficient fighting force. Unfortunately, the problems that had surfaced in February 1917 did not go away. In his report to the XI Corps Commander dated 18 March, Ker was able to say that the Conference "had the effect of clearing the air, and our power for usefulness has been greatly increased". Nevertheless, he went on: "I am doubtful whether the discussions of the Conference have been communicated by the Portuguese staff to their subordinates." In Ker's view:

> The centralised system is the greatest stumbling block to progress. British Brigade Majors have had no difficulty in convincing Portuguese Brigade Majors of what is desirable. The Portuguese Brigade Majors have then to make proposals for Major Baptista's approval, instead of for their Brigade Commander's approval, and it is here that the difficulty arises. Major Baptista has more on his shoulders than any one man can possibly carry. His decisions are always so framed that they keep everything centralised, instead of giving subordinates power to help themselves. When discussing things with me, he falls back on the argument that he knows the limitations of his own people, and that is a very difficult argument to answer.

Ker was probably hoping that Haking would again give him support in his struggle with the Portuguese command system, but at that point the CEP was transferred from XI Corps to become a British First Army reserve unit. The British Mission, however, remained with the Portuguese and the entries in their war diary show a continuation of the difficulties and frustrations. On 4 April, there arose "a disciplinary action in breach of censorship". On 9 April, the First Army staff criticized the discipline of a Portuguese unit on the march. On 2 May, the British Mission sent a memo headed "Criticism of Portuguese Companies in the Line" to the Portuguese Chief of Staff and on 10 May this was followed by further complaints about the conduct of Portuguese troops attached to the 49th Division. One of the British Mission officers, Captain R.C.G. Dartford, kept a diary of his experiences with the Portuguese – or "the Geese" as he called them – and many of the entries record a significant level of frustration. The entry for 10 May, for example, read: "I get sick of explaining things to Capt. Pissaro", and on 26 June Dartford wrote: "Nobody works at deepening the trenches and then I find the 2 i/c spending all his energies building himself an extra dug-out at HQ – it's criminal."[5]

The Portuguese Expeditionary Force returned to XI Corps control on

15 June and, by now almost inevitably, the welter of complaints went on. The British Mission War Diary noted on 18 June that: "Brig. Gen. Studd, G.S. XI Corps, had a conference with Gen. da Costa to criticise the faulty system of holding the line". There seemed to be no real change in the problems relating to communications and lines of command. Captain Warner of the British Mission suggested, on 20 June, "a scheme for a small artillery and trench mortar attack to Gen. da Costa, in the presence of Major Freira, a senior Portuguese staff officer. The latter objected to Capt. Warner's method in proposing a scheme direct to the General." On this occasion, General da Costa supported Warner's plan and the scheme was carried out shortly afterwards. One week after the incident with Major Freira, da Costa raised objections of his own concerning British Staff Officers visiting the Portuguese line and the matter was only resolved by Studd again visiting da Costa and persuading him to give passes to any British Staff Officer that Studd wished to send.

The return of the Portuguese Division to XI Corps was accompanied by the removal of the experienced 49th Division to the Ypres sector. Haking was not happy about this exchange and lost no time in writing to his Army Commander, Horne:

I have been informed that the 1st Portuguese Division is to take over the line held by the 49th Division and that the latter is to go elsewhere . . . I am quite sure that the Portuguese troops are not as yet reliable. On the night of 11/12 [June] part of the line they are holding was heavily bombarded especially with gas shells, their total casualties being about 100 of which half were "gassed" cases. The front line was evacuated by the troops except for one or two gallant parties, notably Lewis gunners, who remained. The officers appeared to have but little command over their men and in one case a British officer attached to the Portuguese, finding a Company coming back in some confusion, reorganised it and took it back to the front line. The enemy never entered the front line. I am quite sure that at present if the enemy were to concentrate a number of trench mortars against our front line and at the same time put a medium barrage on the communication trenches and support line, that one hostile Division could easily drive back the Portuguese from any line they are holding, that considerable confusion would arise in the rear and that it is doubtful if the Regimental officers are sufficiently reliable to organise an effective counter-stroke . . . [The Portuguese troops] have always been leaning on British higher commanders and British supports close in rear of them, and they are not yet sufficiently tried and experienced to hold an extended Divisional front of 11,500 yards, which hitherto has been held by a very good British Division with all its Brigades in the line . . . Personally, I think it would be best to keep the 49th Division as the last to go in on the battlefront selected for it.

Haking added: "I have not shown General Tamagnini a copy of this letter because I think it would be undesirable to do so, and it would do more harm than good. I have told him, however, very clearly what is wanted."[6] Horne responded on 19 June saying that the 49th Division would remain as part of XI Corps until 11 July.[7]

Overall, the situation in terms of Portuguese discipline, control, and operating efficiency was, to say the least, unsatisfactory. The only positive item recorded in the British Mission war diary during the early summer of 1917 was the entry for 25 June: "First Army Horse Show, at which a Portuguese Officer won the Officers' jumping competition."

＊ ＊ ＊ ＊

Meanwhile, regardless of these problems, the war went on and the Portuguese had become part of it. After a period of familiarization with various British units, the Portuguese took over a sector of the front line near Neuve Chapelle. The British Mission war diary records the daily events of trench warfare in that sector in mid-1917:

2 June: 35 Battn. took over left Battn. sub-sector Neuve Chapelle relieving 23 Battn. Last night a Portuguese patrol of 1 N.C.O. and 2 men failed to return. The German wireless reports that they were captured.

4 June: Last night the Germans put up a heavy trench mortar barrage on 35 Battn. trenches near Duck's Bill. Under cover of the barrage they attacked the Duck's Bill Crater and Sap. Portuguese casualties were 1 killed, 5 wounded and 16 missing.

13 June: Another German raid. Portuguese losses severe. 14 killed and 95 wounded.

At his XI Corps Conference on 16 June, Haking made the following statement: "[The Portuguese] have only recently gone into the line and have arrived at a definitely active period and have, in consequence, been compelled to stand a good deal of hostile shelling – especially on the night 12/13 June when the enemy put an exceptionally heavy barrage on their line." Haking went on to say that the Portuguese had, to date, suffered casualties of one officer and 293 other ranks and added: "I am quite confident that they will shortly balance these losses by inflicting still heavier ones on the enemy."[8]

Despite these optimistic words, Haking was by no means happy about the general effectiveness of the Portuguese troops. The comments and reports from the British Mission and from XI Corps Staff continued to give him cause for concern. Moreover, Haking had recently toured the Portuguese trenches and questioned a number of Portuguese officers and men. What he had seen and heard had not impressed him and on 18 June he invited Tamagnini for a serious discussion covering a wide range of topics. The following day, Haking wrote to Tamagnini recording his concerns and giving his views as to how things could be improved.[9] The tone that Haking adopted in this memo – five pages of closely typed foolscap sheets – is interesting. It was almost as though he was the Staff College Professor again, quoting from the latest instruction manual. The content was highly critical, in fact there is not a single positive comment, but Haking gave no direct orders for remedial action, only advice.

The memo begins by highlighting three main areas for improvement:

(a) The organisation of the fighting and the work in the front system of defences.

(b) The relations between the commanders of Platoons, Companies, Battalions, Brigades, Division and Corps, and the assistance or hindrance these commanders receive from their staff.

(c) The training of the platoons and companies when they are actually in the front line and when they are at rest.

Each of these points was then dealt with in some detail. As regards (a) "there is no doubt whatever that the organisation of the fighting and the work in the trenches is not at present satisfactory. The two things are not worked in together and the result is that both are being neglected." To remedy the problem, Haking proposed that

the Battalion and Company commanders should prepare a comprehensive scheme for fighting and for the repair of the defences. They should decide each evening the exact number of men required for each during the next twenty-four hours and prepare the necessary instructions so that when the 24 hours commences everyone will know what he has got to do and where he is to obtain the material required for the work. The best way of dividing a fighting and working day is from an hour before dusk on one evening to an hour before dusk on the next. At this time of the year from 8 pm one day to 8 pm the next would be a suitable division of time.

The memo continued at length in this vein. Addressing the second area for improvement – the relationship between the various levels of command – Haking made the following comments:

From my conversation with all ranks I am convinced that a great deal I say to you never reaches the troops. My opinion is that 75% of what I say to you gets to the Division, 50% gets to the Brigades, 25% to the Battalions, 10% to the Companies and little more than 5% to the Platoons. In the British Army we should get over the difficulty by the Corps, Divisional and Brigade Commanders constantly going about among the troops and asking Platoon, Company and Battalion Commanders questions with reference to instructions that have been issued . . . Do your utmost to clear the channel of communication through various formations of your Corps, no-one obstructing the passage of orders downwards and no-one hiding instructions on the way up.

Dealing with his third concern – the training of troops in the line and in reserve – Haking wrote:

The instruction of NCOs and men in patrol and sentry work, in the construction of wire-entanglements, and parapets, is carried out far more efficiently in the front line than elsewhere, but it requires a regular programme and careful organisation to produce good results. My impression from visiting your trenches is that nobody is troubling much about any of these things.

Haking concluded the memo: "I am afraid I have written at great length, but I feel deeply interested in the success of your troops who have been with me almost all the time they have been in France . . . I have put down exactly what was in my mind."

So here we have a high-ranking British general writing to a high-ranking Portuguese general on topics and with advice that would have been common knowledge at that stage of the war to most subalterns and senior NCOs in the British Army. It can only be assumed that Haking viewed both the Portuguese troops and the Portuguese officers with some despair, and was thankful that the sector that they occupied was, at least for the time being, relatively quiet. In any event, such fundamental flaws in the Portuguese grasp of military organization were not allowed to interfere with the niceties of diplomatic relations and, on 11 July, King George V, during a visit to the Western Front, rewarded the contribution of the Portuguese by decorating their three Generals – Fernando Tamagnini (KCB); Samas Machado (KCMG); and Gomez da Costa (KCMG).

Bringing the Portuguese troops up to anything like a reasonable fighting standard was clearly proving to be an uphill struggle, but Haking persisted in his efforts. He held frequent Conferences – at least weekly – with the senior Portuguese officers and their staff and the British Mission war diary recorded the subjects discussed. The Conference on 24 August, for example, covered wiring, parapets, firesteps, sentries and bombs. On 14 September Haking listed fourteen recurring faults – weapons in poor condition, bombs and small arms ammunition not regularly checked, poor wiring, officers not taking an interest, parapets not repaired, inadequate training, and so on. The notes of the 14 September Conference ended: "The Corps Commander said he was continually having to speak of the same things over and over again. Faults were pointed out clearly, but they were not rectified."

The Portuguese no doubt thought that they were getting more than their fair share of negative criticism from their Corps Commander and their reaction probably explains the extraordinary handwritten letter sent by Haking on 18 September to General Machado, GOC the Portuguese 1st Division:

It has been brought to my notice that Officers of the Division under your command have been making statements to the effect that I am not going to trouble any more about the Portuguese troops, that I think they are no good, and that it is not worth making further efforts to make them good.

The statement is, of course, ridiculous and it is quite unnecessary for me to refute it, but it is a type of remark that would be readily seized upon by certain types of men and is likely to decrease rather than improve the morale of the Portuguese troops, which it has been my greatest care to build up.

As you know, I have on all occasions pointed out in the clearest manner, to you and to the commanders of the Brigades under you, every fault that I could find, with the object of turning the 1st Portuguese Division into a fine fighting force. Whenever I have seen anything well done I have also brought that to your notice. I shall of course continue in this manner as long as your division is under my command.[10]

It is desirable, however, in all military organisations, that the troops should have confidence in their leaders and such statements as the above, unless checked, are apt to reduce that confidence. Probably I am better aware of the defects in the Division under your command than any officer in it, but I am also aware of many good points which I am doubtful if some of your officers realise. It is, and will be, my endeavour to improve these good points.

I should be glad if you will inform your commanding officers that they will always find me ready to point out the faults of their officers and men, and that it is quite unnecessary for them or for any other officer under your command to invent ridiculous statements like the above. I am equally ready to acknowledge all good work that is done and all brave actions that are performed . . . and I am hopeful that I shall before long be called upon to appreciate the good work of the Portuguese troops far more frequently than to criticise any bad work.

The sting in the letter, which was read to all the officers of the Portuguese 1st Division, was in the last few words. Haking believed that there was still more to criticize than to praise and he was only "hopeful" that this might change. Less than a month later, Haking raised the issue of criticism once again:

Most of the work of criticism has been done by me, after that by General da Costa, after that by the Brigade Commanders, after that by the Battalion Commanders down to Platoon Commanders getting less and less on the way. What we want is for most of the criticism to be done by Company Commanders and so on, getting less and less as it goes up. The proper people must do their work. Everyone must do his own job and the seniors must trust the juniors to do their duty. If this is done, the Brigade Commander can then quietly go to sleep at night.[11]

Towards the end of November, Haking was transferred to the Italian front, but before his departure he took his leave of the Portuguese forces under his command. At his eighteenth Conference of CEP Commanders, held on 3 November, Haking announced that, as from 5 November, the 1st Division was to report directly to the GOC the Portuguese Expeditionary Force who, in turn, would report to First Army HQ. He then expressed "his thanks to them for the very soldier-like manner in which they had taken any remarks from him, however unpleasant they had been at times". He went on to say that "he had never tried to hide anything from them or make things out better than they were". It fell to General da Costa to thank the Corps Commander "for all that he had done for them".[12]

Two weeks later, a Secret and Confidential order was issued from XI Corps Headquarters to all the Divisions of the Corps excluding the Portuguese.[13] The order outlined the procedure that would take place

> in the event of a serious situation developing on the front held by the CEP . . . It must be clearly understood that no part of this memorandum is to be communicated to any officer belonging to or attached to the CEP, either Portuguese or British, because the arrangements suggested might weaken the resistance offered by the Portuguese troops in the front line and increase, instead of reduce, the confusion which is likely to occur in the event of a serious attack by the enemy.

The proposed arrangements, in the event of such an attack, were that the First Army HQ would immediately issue orders placing the CEP under the GOC XI Corps. The three British fighting units of the Corps (at that time, the 25th Division, the 38th Division and XI Corps Cyclists) would allocate one battalion each to safeguard the line of defence behind the CEP front and, in that way, contain any collapse of the Portuguese until reinforcements arrived.

Here, then, was official recognition that Haking, and indeed the hierarchy of the British Army, had finally given up on the Portuguese. While they were habitually referred to as Britain's "time honoured allies", the average Tommy simply and disparagingly called them the "the Pork and Beans" or "the Geese". A century earlier, Wellington had described his Portuguese troops in the Peninsula as the "Fighting Cocks" of his army, but in the First World War they were soldiers lacking spirit, discipline and leadership.

There were several reasons for this serious and potentially disastrous state of affairs. Despite the efforts of the British Mission and the Staff of XI Corps, the Portuguese officers and men were poorly trained. To make things worse, as the reports from the British Mission had frequently pointed out, many officers showed little concern for their troops and lacked the interest and ability to learn the skills necessary for success or even survival at the front. In addition, poor practices within the CEP undermined morale. For example, while Portuguese officers were allowed frequent periods of leave (from which a significant number failed to return), other ranks were rarely given the opportunity to go home. Bizarre practices had developed in some units when occupying the front line: "The best behaved men were kept in support, less satisfactory men held the front trench, and their worst villains were sent on patrols."[14] There were also unsettling political events back in Portugal. Pacifist agitators used the initial letters of the Portuguese Expeditionary Force (CEP) to read "*Carneiros de Exportaceo Portuguesa*" – meaning "Portuguese Exported Lambs for Slaughter" – and their pamphlets saw widespread circulation. It did not help that a number of Portuguese officers were actively against the war and against the British. Ker had cause on 16 July 1918 to write to Tamagnini:

> Officers returning from leave here . . . have been most indiscreet during the journey . . . and the Portuguese GHQ ought to issue very strict orders about this . . . I know there are some officers and men with the Portuguese forces in France who feel we are responsible for their being there and they do not see us through rose-coloured glasses.[15]

More directly damaging was the successful military coup of December 1917 that had brought Major Sidonia Pais to power. Pais, who had been the Portuguese ambassador in Berlin 1912–16, was sympathetic to the German cause and denied the CEP fresh troops to replace their mounting casualties. Consequently, by April 1918, the Portuguese 3, 4 and 5 Brigades were each some 1,200 men below their nominal strength of 4,660. The ramifications of Portuguese politics were even felt in France and Haig, the British Commander in Chief, was later to note that "General Tamagnini had a difficult time. His Chief of Staff had a private cipher with the War Minister in Lisbon unknown to Gen. Tamagnini!"[16]

All in all, the situation was not one that was likely to foster trust, discipline, loyalty or devotion to duty within the CEP and a Portuguese presence at the Western Front was regarded by the British as a political expedient rather than a serious contribution to the Allied war effort.[17] As Haig wrote in his Diary: "the Portuguese troops and their Portuguese officers are useless for this class of fighting."[18] It was likely that the Germans opposite the Portuguese in the Neuve Chapelle area had arrived at the same conclusion and it was by design rather than by chance that the sector held by the CEP was the focus of Operation GEORGETTE on 9 April 1918.

* * * *

Haking arrived back in France from Italy on 15 March 1918 and XI Corps took up its old position in the la Bassée-Armentières sector with its Headquarters at Hinges. By 8 April, following a series of Divisional transfers within the First Army, the Corps was made up of the 55th Division, the 51st Division, the 1st King Edward's Horse, the XI Corps Cyclist Battalion and the Portuguese 2nd Division. The 55th Division held the line Givenchy-Festubert with nine battalions covering 4,000 yards and by the Portuguese 2nd Division with sixteen battalions covered the remaining 10,000 yards of the line. The Portuguese 1st Division had been relieved on 5 April and the adjoining 2nd Division had been required to extend its line so that it now covered from Festubert-Neuve Chapelle-Laventie. The 51st Division, the King Edward's Horse and the Cyclist Battalion were in reserve.

On the morning of 8 April, however, some further divisional movements were agreed between XI Corps and XV Corps. The Conference to arrange these transfers was attended by the Commanders of the First and Second Armies and the Commanders of the XI and XV Corps and Haking took the opportunity to give his opinion about the Portuguese:

> General Haking brought forward the question of the complete relief of the Portuguese by the British. He stated he was convinced that if attacked they would withdraw at once . . . the condition of the ground was now suitable for an attack about Neuve Chapelle and that the position of the Portuguese troops in the line there was bait for the Germans.[19]

As a result of the Conference the right Brigade (5) of the Portuguese 2nd Division was to be relieved by a Brigade of 55th Division, while the two left Portuguese Brigades (6 and 4) were to be relieved by two Brigades of 50th Division, itself to be transferred from XV Corps to XI Corps on 9 April. The relief of the Portuguese Brigades was to take place on the night of 9/10 April. It was further arranged between XI and XV Corps, following the now usual practice of safeguarding the Portuguese front, that, until the Portuguese had been relieved, a line of defence, to be known as the Corps line, should run behind the Portuguese from le Touret, through Huits Maison and Bout Deville to Laventie. This line would be manned by such reserves as the two Corps could muster. XI Corps would be responsible for the section le Touret-Bout Deville and XV Corps for the line north of Bout Deville.

These arrangements were considered particularly necessary since, in March, there had been a number of Portuguese desertions to the enemy. Potentially more serious, the 7th Battalion of 2 Portuguese Infantry Brigade, then in reserve, had, on 4 April, staged a mutiny, refusing to return to the front line. Even though Tamagnini dealt with the mutiny quickly and effectively, Haking was not inclined to leave the Portuguese holding an important stretch of the front any longer than was necessary. A main aim of the proposed series of divisional moves was, therefore, to ensure that the entire XI Corps sector was held by British troops.

It can be seen from this summary of proposed transfers and reliefs that 8 April and the night of 8/9 April was a period of intense and complicated activity. In particular, the Portuguese had, during the night of 8/9 April, received the news that they were to be relieved on 9/10 April. It can be fairly assumed, therefore, that the minds of the men of the Portuguese 4, 5 and 6 Brigades were focused on the prospect of leaving their trenches rather than staying there. For the Germans, all these factors combined, fortuitously, to make the morning of 9 April the ideal time, and the Portuguese sector the ideal place, to launch Operation GEORGETTE.

A report,[20] dated 12 April, by Major G. C. de Glover of the British Mission attached to the 2nd Portuguese Division, outlines the events of 9 April:

> 4 am. At about this hour a heavy hostile bombardment was opened on all back areas with guns and HE shells . . . There was little doubt from the outset that the enemy proposed to attack the Portuguese, owing to the intensity of the bombardment and the fact that HQs were being shelled . . . XI Corps was informed by telephone that the situation looked serious and it appeared that it would be necessary to call up the British who were to garrison the Corps line.
>
> 4.20 am. Artillery reported that an SOS had been sent up from Ferme du Bois II, held by Inf. 17. This was the last heard of this battalion, and it appears probable that the entire battalion was taken or destroyed. Inf. 2 holding Neuve Chapelle I was also never heard of, and there appears to be very few stragglers of either of these two battalions. It is also probable that a number of both of these battalions were destroyed by our guns which were installed North and South of the main la Bassée Road.
>
> 4.45 am. A direct hit was obtained on the Divisional HQ which fell into the Chief of Staff's room, which was luckily empty at the time. General Gomez da Costa was very near the shell when it exploded. This somewhat disorganized the working of the Portuguese Staff.
>
> 4.50 am. General da Costa ordered various staff offices to go in motor cars to the various Brigades HQ and try to ascertain what was going on. These officers took a long time to start and Liaison Officers [British] with Brigades state that they did not reach the Brigade HQ's until about 8 am. The Portuguese Staff appeared to have no idea of how to organize a system of runners or despatch riders and it was a long time before any chauffeurs or motor cyclists at Div. HQ could be found. The wireless was useless

owing to the loss of the cipher book at Divisional HQ and also because, it was ascertained afterwards, wireless stations at Brigade HQ's had been destroyed.

8 am. As far as can be ascertained the enemy attack commenced shortly after 7 am. and, by 8 am., most of the front line [A line] was captured.

9 am. It is clear that B line [the second line] was taken at 9 am. At about this time [British] Liaison Officers from Divisional HQ were sent to get in touch with the British Brigades of the 50th and 51st Divisions who were moving up to occupy the Corps line . . . By this time all the [Portuguese] Brigade HQs in the line were on fire or destroyed and communication with them even by runner was difficult.

9.30 am. It is reported by Capt. Dartford that stragglers were commencing to retire through Laventie about this time.

9.45 am. There is little doubt that B line was taken along most of the front by 9 am.

10 am. About this time a copy of a pigeon message sent by the right Brigade of the 40th [British] Division was received stating that Portuguese were falling back and that the British flank would have to be drawn back soon.

11 am. It was estimated from reports of stragglers that enemy was on the line Laventie-Rouge Croix-Richebourg.

11.30 am. Preparations were made to move the [Portuguese] Divisional HQ from Lestrem to Calonne. There is little doubt that at about this time a more or less general rout had set in.

12.15 pm. A proportion of the remaining British Liaison Officers at la Gorgue were ordered to try and rally the Portuguese and make them fight. This was found to be quite impossible and all the men seen were thoroughly demoralised and quite out of hand.

1 pm. An order for the Portuguese Division from XI Corps to hold the River Lawe at all costs was received at Lestrem. It was impossible to obey the order, as by that time all the Portuguese Divisional HQ had moved from Lestrem and the greater part of the Division were in rear of it, and disorganised.

2 pm. The 2nd Portuguese Division had practically speaking ceased to take part in the battle except for a few isolated units and the defence was taken up by the 50th and 51st [British] Divisions.

Attached to Glover's Report is a "Very Secret" note from Ker, the Commander of the British Mission.[21] Ker was scathing about the Portuguese 2nd Division Officers:

Major Godhino, Chief of Staff, displayed plenty of courage, but was altogether at sea as to what to do next, and on one occasion forgot to carry out an important order, namely to order the Reserve Brigade forward. Captain Campos, the Chief Q Officer remained in a cellar throughout the proceedings, although his General and Chief of Staff were at their posts, and he displayed profound incompetence. The remaining G and Q staff officers appeared too bewildered to do anything useful.

As regards the Artillery and Brigade Staffs: "Their tendency was to do nothing and await orders." Ker commented about the Portuguese troops:

I am convinced that many units did well and killed Germans; but I am equally convinced that some units did practically nothing . . . If the Portuguese had moved into crater positions, as they had often been advised to do on such occasions, the defence would have been very much stronger, but these and many other instructions were apparently forgotten in the heat of action . . . After passing through the Corps line the retreat became a rout. The roads in the rear were crowded with Portuguese in all stages of demoralisation. Many of the infantry had thrown away rifles and equipment: officers, I think because they were afraid of their men, made no attempt to rally them, or even organise them into parties . . . General Gomez da Costa and Lt. Col. Serpa were the only two Portuguese officers who did anything to help the British at this period.

A particularly unfortunate event took place during the confusion that accompanied the retreat of the Portuguese. Private W. A. Tucker, in the reserve line with the XI Corps Cyclists at Lacouture, graphically recorded the following:

'Look, Jerries!', suddenly shouted one of our chaps. And, scrambling towards us, through barbed wire debris and swampy shell-holes, were troops right enough. Dimly through the mist and the smoke of bursting shrapnel (from our own guns) we made out the unfamiliar helmets and uniforms. 'Let them have it', shouted one of our Corporals, and six of our Lewis Guns did just that. We repeated the performance every time anything or anyone exposed itself for the next half hour or so; but we began to be puzzled. It seemed a funny kind of attack. Then in the middle of another sally, we heard our Corporal yell, 'Hold it lads, they're not Jerries.

They're bloody Portuguese'. No-one had told us anything about the Portuguese and we must have killed scores of the poor devils.[22]

The disintegration of the Portuguese 2nd Division had many eye-witnesses. The drafts of the British Official History were circulated, in the early 1930s, to officers who had taken part in the actions of 9 April 1918 for their comments. Lieutenant Colonel A. H. French wrote:

> The Portuguese sector offered obvious bait and we assumed that in the event of an attack the Portuguese Corps would vanish at a very early stage . . . I only saw our Oldest Ally on the run. By the way, I suppose that diplomatic relations would prevent you telling the story of the theft of XI Corps Cyclist Battn.'s cycles by the Portuguese from La Coutoure Strong Point.[23]

Colonel C. H. Hawkins commented: "As you know, the Portuguese Corps originally occupied the front that was attacked and according to reports from eye-witnesses they were in such a hurry to leave that they took off their boots and slung them around their necks, in order to run more quickly."[24] Lieutenant General Sir Hugh Jeudwine, who had commanded the 55th British Division, wrote: "I know of no case in 55th Div. area where the Portuguese did well. Those who fell back on 166 Brigade had no arms and were only kept to dig, both officers and men, by the threat of shooting if they did not obey."[25] For Brigadier General F. P. Crozier the threat of shooting became a reality: "The failure of our allies, the Portuguese, on April 9th 1918, came near to losing much ground for us, and because of that I ordered the shooting, by machine gun and rifle fire, of many Portuguese in order to stem the tide."[26] Lieutenant P. F. Leith, who was attached to the Portuguese 5 Infantry Brigade and taken prisoner at le Touret, wrote from Lille on 12 April: "We got very heavily bombarded on the morning of the 9th and when the German Infantry attacked the Portuguese put up a rotten show, or rather, no show at all, so the enemy came through quite easily."[27] Colonel H. J. Humphreys, attached to the 153 Brigade HQ on 9 April, recalled a lighter incident: "A young subaltern in charge of clerks, came to make a report to the General. He had encountered a battalion of Portuguese and given their rifles to his clerks. 'But', he said to the General, 'I gave them a receipt and I hope I did right, Sir'."[28]

German accounts of the morning of 9 April confirm that the defence made by the Portuguese was patchy and generally weak. The 1st Bavarian Reserve Division found that "the trench garrisons surrendered after feeble resistance". The 8th Bavarian Reserve Division account read: "It was not until the third system was reached at 9.30 am that in places slight resistance was offered and the first prisoners captured." The 35th Division took the first system "without resistance", and the 42nd Division summarized: "9.40 am 1st system captured; 10 am 2nd system captured".[29] In his memoirs, Hindenburg commented: "Most of the Portuguese left the battlefield in wild flight, and once and for all retired from the fighting."[30]

General Gomez da Costa, the Commander of the CEP 2nd Division, gave an account of the events of 9 April from a Portuguese point of view.[31] In particular, da Costa referred to the extended line that he had been obliged to defend:

> Portuguese Corps Order No. 23 ordered me to take over the defence of the whole sector. I replied in a note written on 4 April 1918 stating that I could not assume responsibility for the defence of the sector with four Infantry Brigades where there had previously been six, particularly when the four Brigades were short of 139 officers and 5972 OR. I likewise drew attention to the grave shortage of Artillery on my front . . . The state of affairs being that which I have attempted to explain above, I could not help but feel certain that the retention of the Division in the line would, in case of a strong enemy attack, lead to disaster. That is of course what actually happened, and it did not require great penetration of foresight to foresee it[32] . . . For 8 hours the Division resisted the attack of 8 highly trained [German] Divisions who were also highly experienced in war. Obviously, it could not win the day, it could only die; and that is what it did. It left 50% of its strength on the battlefield.

According to da Costa, the Portuguese 2nd Division started on 9 April with 721 Officers and 20,350 Other Ranks and ended the day with 394 Officers and 13,252 Other Ranks. Only one Brigade Commander survived and nearly all the Battalion and Company Commanders were lost. Da Costa's final comment was that "the 2nd Division fought on the whole with gallantry and left nearly half its strength on the field – it should not be ill thought of."

There is some evidence to suggest that certain Portuguese troops did indeed fight "with gallantry". Da Costa noted that a platoon of Inf. No. 8 held up the Germans on the B line "until they were decimated". The Commander of this Battalion, Major Xavier da Costa, collected together a few men and some stragglers and garrisoned some old trenches where they "put up a fight against the enemy, gradually retiring from trench to trench . . . Only 3 men reached Laventie. Major da Costa was killed during the retirement." Captain Roma, of the 13th

Battalion near La Couture, ordered his Company to make a bayonet charge: "The Company gallantly jumped the parapet and charged the Bosches, however such was the intensity of the fire that before they could reach them they were almost all knocked out." In the Neuve Chapelle sector two Companies (9 and 10) of the 1st Battalion "put up a fight and left nearly all their men behind". One observer, Major R. G. Johnston of the Royal Artillery, noted:[33]

> Although the battle of the Lys was a Portuguese defeat, it was an honourable one. Their position was sited on a low-lying water-logged area – no proper trenches. The German artillery superiority was in the proportion of at least 4:1. Yet on 9 April some of the Portuguese posts in the front line held out until 11.00 am; on the right the 10 Infantry Regiment held its ground until all the defenders had been killed. The Marais Saint post withstood repeated assaults until 4 pm. La Couture did not surrender until 11 am on 10 April. Even when the 2nd Division was smashed, small parties attached themselves to British units and continued the defence.

Despite these, and no doubt many other acts of individual courage, the overall picture, nevertheless, was one of Portuguese incompetence and lack of fighting spirit. The deficiencies listed in so many British Mission Reports and at so many XI Corps Conferences became disastrously evident during the events of April 9.

* * * *

When the Portuguese 2nd Division collapsed, they had, on their southern flank, the British 55th Division (XI Corps) and on their northern flank, the 40th Division (XV Corps). The plan, developed in the event of a Portuguese retreat, was hastily put into effect. The 55th Division brought up its reserve brigade and, with the 11th Cyclist Battalion and 1st King Edward's Horse, was able to stem the German advance in the south. The effect of this was to divert the Germans towards the north-west, placing great pressure on the 40th Division, which was forced to drop back. British reinforcements, the 51st Division from the Lillers direction, and the 50th Division from Merville, were delayed severely on their way to the battle area, mainly because the roads were blocked by the retreating Portuguese. The eight German divisions who launched GEORGETTE were now supported by a further seven divisions and, by the evening of 9 April, they had reached and crossed the Rivers Lawe and Lys – an advance of four miles on a front of some ten miles.

With the 51st and 50th Divisions now in place, 10 April saw little further movement in the southern and central areas, but the Germans continued their advance in a north-westerly direction towards the Ypres-Comines canal and succeeded in taking Armentières and part of the Second Army front including Messines, Ploegsteert and Hillebeke. By 11 April the Germans had extended their advance over a thirty-mile front and, two days later, they were less than five miles from their first major objective, the crucial rail-junction of Hazebrouck, itself only twenty-two miles from the Channel.

This was a crisis situation for the British Army and it caused Haig to issue his famous Order of the Day: "There is no other course open to us but to fight it out . . . Every position must be held to the last man . . . With our backs to the wall and believing in the justice of our cause, each of us must fight on to the end."[34] As though in response, the approach to Hazebrouck was successfully blocked by 4 Guards Brigade supported by the newly arrived 1st Australian Division.

The Germans were now obliged to press north towards Ypres. On 15 April they gained Bailleul and the Ravensberg Ridge, but were stopped at Meteren. The newly-appointed Allied Supreme Commander, Foch, belatedly introduced French troops to the battle to defend the Kemmel area. Although Mont Kemmel was taken by the Germans on 25 April, the impetus of GEORGETTE was now lost and, on 29 April, Ludendorff abandoned the offensive. Since the opening of Operation MICHAEL on 21 March, the Germans and the Allies had each lost 350,000 men. But the British Army, the destruction of which was the aim of MICHAEL and GEORGETTE, was still intact and time was running out for the German High Command.

* * * *

Any attempt to judge Haking's influence on the CEP must face the unfortunate fact that, when they were most needed, the Portuguese officers and troops failed to perform as an effective military force. In fact, with some exceptions, they retreated ingloriously from the field of battle. By collapsing so rapidly on the morning of 9 April, the CEP put the British Divisions on their flanks (the 55th and the 40th) in serious danger. They also opened the way for the Germans to threaten Hazebrouck and the Channel ports. In so doing, the Portuguese were directly responsible for at least a proportion of the British casualties incurred before Operation GEORGETTE finally stalled.

It should be said, however, that while the Portuguese fought poorly on 9 April, many divisions of General Gough's Fifth Army on the Somme had performed little better on 21 March when faced with the German attacks of Operation MICHAEL. On that occasion, the German storm troops easily penetrated the areas near la Fère, Ronssoy and St Quentin and the entire Fifth Army front crumbled in little over an hour. On both 21 March and 9 April German artillery, tactics and superior numbers had proved too much for British and Portuguese alike.

Haking had said on many occasions that it was his task to make the CEP "a fine fighting force" and, in this, he clearly failed. But could he have done more than he did? It is clear from the information in this chapter that Haking took his responsibility for the CEP very seriously. He went out of his way, for example, to accompany Tamagnini to a variety of British military events. On three successive days in June 1917, Haking invited Tamagnini to a tank display, a Canadian division exercise and a 1st Division training activity. Tamagnini was appreciative of these invitations and noted that "they were all for a purpose" and that he learnt much from them.[35] Haking spent what was probably a disproportionate amount of his time dealing with the numerous issues of Portuguese discipline and command. Between 10 August and 3 November 1917 he took part in eighteen Conferences with CEP officers. He supported the British Mission in their work and became personally involved in advising and cajoling the Portuguese at all levels – from lecturing Tamagnini on the basic principles of trench warfare to fact-finding tours in the Portuguese forward lines.

Haking's efforts in this respect were not entirely wasted. It can be seen from Tamagnini's personal diary that a good working relationship developed between the two men and at times Tamagnini was fulsome in his praise of Haking. On 20 June 1917 Tamagnini wrote in his diary: "from the beginning [Haking] has been very helpful to me with his support and his advice on trench warfare and organisation which he knows very well from his knowledge of 3 years of war."[36] Tamagnini also noted: "With General Haking as Commander of the British XI Corps . . . there was more and better communication."[37] When Haking was posted to Italy, Tamagnini wrote in his diary:

> I am going to miss him because he was my counsellor about trench warfare and other CEP matters . . . He was a person who had a way of acting and thinking that I understood well – that pleased me, and he has shown himself during the time we have had together as a good friend.[38]

The basic problem, however, remained. The Portuguese were poorly officered and this was something outside Haking's control. Poor discipline, poor training and poor morale prevailed among soldiers and officers alike. It did not help that political intrigue in Portugal meant that reinforcements were held back. Taken together, these factors resulted in such a marked lack of purpose and commitment within the

CEP that a military disaster was always a possibility. It was a situation that neither Haking nor anyone else in the British First Army was able to change. Horne had made the point to Tamagnini:

> The Army Commander has some reason to fear that [Portuguese] Battalion and Company officers do not sufficiently mix with their men. They must share their dangers, difficulties and privations. They must interest themselves not only in training, but also in the welfare of their men. Questions of good feeding, clothing, health must be their immediate concern. The men must feel that their officers are their comrades. It is by such means that officers gain the confidence of their men and inspire them as their leaders.[39]

There is no evidence to suggest that Horne's advice had any effect.

It was a political decision to bring the Portuguese to the Western Front and the Convention agreed between the British and Portuguese Governments specifically stated that "the CEP will . . . act always as a whole under the command of a Portuguese General Officer" and the rank of that officer "will correspond to that of a Lieutenant-General" – i.e. the same rank as that held by Haking.[40] This system of command was not unusual – the Australian and the American Forces, for example, had a similar relationship with the BEF, but with the poorly-officered Portuguese this arrangement only served to frustrate Anglo-Portuguese co-operation and maintain the unsatisfactory standards of the CEP.[41] The situation was aggravated, as frequently experienced by members of the British Mission, by the marked sensitivity of the Portuguese over matters of command. When Haking was planning some leave in March 1917, he felt obliged to write to Tamagnini:

> I forgot to tell you this morning that I want to go on leave from 24th March to 3rd April. Would you have any objection to my sending the enclosed suggestion to the 1st Army when asking for leave, because that appears to me to be the only way out of the difficulty as regards command.

The attached letter to the First Army requested leave and added: "I would suggest that during this period the Portuguese Expeditionary Force should be placed in Army Reserve, so as to avoid the difficulty of seniority, because there is no one in the XIth Corps except myself senior to General Tamagnini."[42]

Tamagnini was well aware that his close relationship with Haking did not meet with the approval of some of his senior commanders. One of these was the Commander of the 1st Division, General Machado, who considered that Tamagnini was a puppet of the English (*vendido aos ingleses*). Nevertheless, Tamagnini judged that Haking had the best interests of the Portuguese in mind and that he genuinely wanted the Portuguese soldiers to perform well.[43] When the Lisbon War Office commented to Tamagnini that some Portuguese officers had accused Haking of interfering in the command of the CEP, Tamagnini responded: "in my continuous contacts with this General in my or his HQ, I have found perfect companionship . . . his counsel was very useful for me . . . I always found him of good will and pleasant."[44] Similarly, Tamagnini, unlike some of his colleagues, came to appreciate Haking's somewhat brusque and direct manner. Tamagnini noted in his diary on 16 June 1917: "I have great admiration for Haking . . . [he] only says what is needed to be said . . . clearly and with method." [45]

The British–Portuguese Convention seems to have been a somewhat mysterious document and appears not to have been circulated even at Haking's level. During an XI Corps Conference in September 1917, Haking requested the "occasional" use of a Portuguese Brigade in the front line. The notes of the Conference record that: "the Corps Commander asked [Tamagnini] if there was anything in the 'Convention', of which he had heard but not seen, that would prevent Gen. Tamagnini from doing as was suggested."[46] On this occasion, Tamagnini agreed to the proposal, but ignorance of the contents of the Convention led only to an uncertain relationship between British and Portuguese senior officers and, as we have seen, the officers of the British Mission were frequently frustrated by this lack of clarity. It was not until late January 1918 that an order from the Portuguese Government re-organized the CEP: "One Division of four brigades to be in the line under a British Corps Commander. The Portuguese Corps Commander to exercise administrative control only over the Division in the line." This order was a major change from past practice and the British Mission war diary noted with ill-concealed satisfaction: "The receipt of this order caused many heart burnings in the Portuguese Corps."[47] At least the command structure had been clarified, possibly emanating from Lisbon for political reasons, but it was somewhat late in the day.

It could be argued that once the calibre of the CEP had become clear, they should have been removed from frontline duties. However, such a move would almost certainly have been considered as an insult by the Portuguese Government and therefore diplomatically unacceptable.[48] It also ignores the context of the Portuguese involvement. They had arrived in France to fight, not to act in some less direct role, and with the considerable losses sustained by the British on the Somme and at

Passchendaele there was a desperate need for frontline troops: hence the continued efforts of Haking and the Military Mission to make the CEP more effective.

By November 1917, however, Haking and the British Army hierarchy had at last given up any hope of raising the standards of the CEP to an acceptable level. On his return from Italy in March 1918 Haking quickly assessed the condition of the Portuguese troops and at the Conference of the First and Second Armies on 8 April Haking made his opinion clear: "The G.O.C. XI Corps stated that . . . the Portuguese troops were totally unfit to stand any attack and that they ought to be relieved and replaced by British troops at once. The GOC 1st Army decided that this should be done."[49] The chosen way of dealing with the problem was to develop the Corps Line and plan to cover any Portuguese collapse by bringing in British reserve troops. As a handwritten XI Corps report noted:

> Arrangements were made by the Army and details were worked out by XI and XV Corps to supply British troops to garrison a back line of defence . . . The object of this was to prevent the enemy from breaking right through in the event of the Portuguese being attacked and driven back.[50]

This approach, following the disastrous morning of 9 April, worked reasonably well as Haking's XI Corps and du Cane's XV Corps co-operated to provide back-up brigades.

Haking's main contribution to stemming the GEORGETTE offensive, however, was on the southern flank of XI Corps in the sector covered by the 55th Division. Current thinking within the BEF as to defence was based on a three-zone system – a thinly defended forward zone, a heavily defended battle zone and a rear zone. This meant a series of fortified positions, which would hold up an enemy attack with the main battle zone defence taking place on what was termed the Line of Resistance.[51] Haking's general attitude to this defence in depth has already been noted. Such a system, in Haking's view,

> does not agree with the system of defence which is in accordance with our national characteristics, i.e. the defence of the front line at all costs . . . our experience has been that counter-strikes to regain lost trenches are more costly in casualties than the stubborn defence of the front-line system.[52]

Haking was not alone among Corps Commanders in opting to hold the front line in strength rather than developing a defence in depth. The

III Corps Commander, Butler, for example, had also adopted the same view, even though he was positioned next to XVIII Corps who had organized an in-depth system of defence. The varied opinions in the BEF about the best method of defence caused Travers to comment about the three-tiered system that it was: "a defensive system that was not understood, did not work and did not properly exist at all." Jeudwine of the 55th Division later wrote: "To this day I don't clearly comprehend what this term [Battle Zone] implies – nor have I ever met anybody who did."[53]

One of Haking's first tasks, following his return from Italy, was to inspect the defence system along the key Givenchy sector held by the 55th Division and he formed the view that a three zone arrangement was not appropriate. In 1932, Brigadier General A. F.V. Green of XI Corps, wrote to Edmonds, the compiler of the British Official History, saying that insufficient attention had been given to two matters that were of "incalculable value" in saving the situation on 9 April. The first matter was the "self-sacrifice of XI Corps Cyclists and King Edward's Horse whose tenacity in spite of appalling casualties was the only bar to a collapse of the line behind the Portuguese". Green's second point was:

> The strategic and tactical insight of General Haking who, though newly returned from Italy, realised at once and took immediate steps to rectify the inherent weakness in the line from Bethune onwards. It was in conference with the GOC 55th Division (and subsequently with Brigade Commanders) that the defensive line measures were decided on, in place of the hitherto vague and uncertain policy, which resulted in a defence being put in an almost impossible situation.[54]

Jeudwine also remembered the conference referred to by Green. Jeudwine wrote to Haking in 1931 recalling how Haking had

> laid down, with our entire agreement, that in front of Givenchy, the Line of Resistance must coincide with the front line, because there it would be fatal both to us and to the Corps on our right to allow the enemy the complete observation over rear areas that possession of our front line would give . . . Our defence was modelled on these lines.[55]

Haking forwarded Jeudwine's letter to Edmonds so that it might be used in the Official History and added: "We would have no truck with the 'defence in depth' idea at Givenchy, and we should have lost the battle if we had."[56] An XI Corps report written soon after the April 1918 attack confirms Haking's role:

> In three instances it was pointed out by the [XI] Corps Commander at a conference held at 1st Army HQ that it was impossible to hold a position in depth unless troops were available to defend the various lines. It was decided therefore that the troops should stand and fight on one line only and all arrangements were made to that end.[57]

The 55th Division held firm and Givenchy remained in British hands.[58]

Haking's strategic contribution to the Battle of the Lys, particularly in the sector defended by the 55th Division and in deploying the Corps reserves to cover the Portuguese, was therefore considerable. As regards the CEP, Haking did what he could in what amounted to a hopeless cause.[59] Haking's attitude and approach to the Portuguese problem was summed up shortly after the CEP 1st Division officers had accused him of losing all interest in them. At a Conference in September 1917, Haking is reported to have said: "I do not mind what officers commanding battalions think of me, so long as I do my duty; all I care about is doing my duty."[60]

Notes

1. See, on the background to the German offensives in 1918: Martin Kitchen, *The German Offensives of 1918*; Gregory Blaxland, *Amiens 1918*; John Terraine, *To Win A War, 1918,. The Year Of Victory*.
2. As early as 10 October 1914 Sir Edward Grey, the British Foreign Minister, had invited the Portuguese to "depart from their attitude of neutrality and to range themselves on the side of Great Britain and her allies". See F.R. de Meneses, *Portugal 1914–1926, From the First World War to Military Dictatorship*, p.12.
3. TNA, WO 95/5488. References to British Mission memoranda etc. in this chapter are from this file.
4. The Territorial Force was established in 1908 as part of Haldane's reforms. Ker's assessment echoed that of Emile Daeschner, the French representative in Lisbon, who, in 1916 wrote: "the Portuguese army should certainly be able to supply 50,000 or 60,000 men, or maybe even more, but the main difficulties would result not so much from lack of armaments, which we should be able to supply, but rather for the almost complete lack of training, from the absolute lack of any notion of discipline at all levels". Quoted in F. R. De Meneses, *Portugal, 1914–1926: From the First World War to Military Dictatorship*, p.51.
5. IWM, 66/300/1, Capt R.C.G. Dartford Diaries.
6. TNA, WO 95/171, XI Corps, GS 1399/27.

7. Ibid., First Army, GS 623.
8. TNA, WO 95/882, SS 837/21.
9. TNA, WO 95/882.
10. TNA, WO 95/882, SS 996/2.
11. TNA, WO 158/871, From a Conference held at Lestrem, 12 October 1917.
12. TNA, WO 95/882, GS 1399/45/18.
13. TNA, WO 95/882, GS 1399/41.
14. Major R.T. Rees, *A Schoolmaster at War*, p.92.
15. Archivo Historico Militar, Lisbon, 51/3/858/5. Henceforth – AHM
16. See Robert Blake ed., *The Private Papers of Douglas Haig, 1914–19*, p.311–322, Extract dated 21 July 1918.
17. Emile Daeschner, the French representative in Lisbon wrote in Spring 1916 in relation to the Portuguese troops: that one of the main difficulties was: "the open opposition of part of the officer corps, two-thirds of which are notoriously opposed to the war". Quoted in De Meneses, p.51.
18. Sheffield and Bourne, *Haig Diaries and Letters*, p.400.
19. TNA, WO 95/176.
20. TNA, WO 95/5488, GL 755, App. 69.
21. TNA, WO 95/5488, GL755, App. 70. Ker had recently been promoted to Brigadier General.
22. IWM, 67/96/1. Notebook of W. A. Tucker, p.30.
23. TNA, CAB 45/125(F), French to Edmonds, 6 December 31.
24. Ibid., Hawkins to Edmonds, 28 December 1933. Col Hawkins's comments are supported by a report by Lt Col James of 1st King Edward's Horse written on 14 April 1918: "Portuguese continued to pass back many in panic having removed boots to run faster. As they had abandoned arms I did nothing to stay them being glad to have them clear of my front". See TNA, WO 95/883, K.E.H. 365/18.
25. TNA, CAB 43/123.
26. Brig. Gen. F. P. Crozier, *The Men I Killed*, p.48.
27. TNA, WO 95/5488, App. 78A.
28. TNA, CAB 4/123 (F), Humphreys to Edmonds, 6 July 1931.
29. *BOH 1918* Vol. II (1937), Footnote, p. 168.
30. Field Marshal von Hindenburg, *The Great War*, ed. Charles Messenger, p.178.
31. TNA, WO 95/5488. Written "In the Field, 3 May 1918".
32. Gen. da Costa stressed the serious effect of extending and therefore weakening his line. In one historian's opinion, "The Staff blunder which made one [Division] responsible for holding six important miles in an avowedly threatened area is one of the most gruesome of the war." See C.R.M.F. Cruttwell, *A History of the Great War 1914–1918*. p.516. Given the poor morale of the Portuguese, it is doubtful that two additional brigades would have altered the outcome of 9 April. As far as Haking was concerned, the decision to extend the Portuguese line was a *fait accompli* when he took over the Portuguese on 5 April.
33. Major G. R. Johnston, 'The Portuguese Army in the Great War', *The Army Quarterly*, XXXV, October 1937, p.68.

34. Brig Gen John Charteris, *Field Marshal Earl Haig*, p.333. Haig does not record this Order in his Diary.
35. AHM, 51/2/857/3.
36. AHM, 51/2/857/3.
37. AHM, 51/4/859/3/XVIII.
38. AHM, 51/7/857/4.
39. AHM, 52/3/858/6, First Army GS 965., 3 January 1918.
40. TNA, FO 371/2761, *Memorandum of the Arrangements for the Employment of Portuguese Forces in the British Zone of Operations in France.*
41. The Portuguese were particularly sensitive to the issue of subordination. The President of the Chamber of Deputies, Antonio Macieira refused to visit the CEP when it emerged that permission would be required from the British High Command. See De Meneses, p.57.
42. AHM, 52/3/858/5.
43. AHM, 51/2/857/3.
44. AHM, 51/4/859/3/XVIII.
45. AHM, 51/2/857/3.
46. TNA, WO 95/882, SS 837/36, Conference, 25 September 1917.
47. TNA, WO 95/5488.
48. When Lord Derby wrote to his Portuguese counterpart in September 1917 that the Portuguese troops could be attached to a British Corps under the command of a Corps Commander, Norton de Matos responded "with the rude frankness of a soldier" that Portugal's position could not deviate from that agreed in the Convention of 3 January 1917. See De Meneses, p.60.
49. TNA, WO 95/883, Hand-written, undated and unsigned report.
50. Ibid.
51. For a discussion on the "defence in depth" system see Travers, *How the War was Won*, pp.50–65. Also see G. C.Wynne, *If Germany Attacks, The Battle in Depth in the West*, pp.233–238 and Ian Beckett, "Gough, Malcolm and Command on the Western Front" in Brian Bond, ed., *Look To Your Front*, pp.1–12
52. TNA WO 95/881 RHS 726.
53. TNA, CAB 45/123F. Jeudwine to Edmonds, 21 August 1931.
54. TNA, CAB 45/123(F), Green to Edmonds, 7 January 1932.
55. TNA, CAB 45/123(F), Jeudwine to Haking (not dated, but presumably at the time of the Green/ Jeudwine correspondence).
56. TNA, CAB 45/123(F), Haking to Edmonds, 25 August 1931. This is the only known correspondence between Haking and the official historian.
57. TNA, WO 95/883. Handwritten report, undated and unsigned.
58. See Travers, *How the War was Won, Factors that Led to Victory in World War One*, pp.91–94.
59. The Minutes of the War Cabinet, 11 April 1918 (TNA, CAB 23/14, 398) note that the Portuguese Government had offered to send reinforcements following their losses in April 1918. The Minutes recorded that: "The Chief of the Imperial General Staff (Sir H. H. Wilson) pointed out that although the Portuguese troops might be considered fair, the officers were inefficient and

that, from the military point of view, it was not advisable to ask our men to lie alongside them in the line." It was agreed at the Cabinet meeting that: "The Secretary of State for Foreign Affairs (A. J. Balfour) should take the necessary diplomatic action with a view to preventing any further Portuguese reinforcements being sent". At the same meeting, the War Cabinet discussed whether it would be appropriate to "send a complimentary telegram to the Portuguese Government, congratulating them upon the valour of their troops during the present fighting". No such telegram was sent. (TNA, CAB 23/14, 389 and 390). The Portuguese were never again used in the war as combat troops.

60. TNA, WO95/882, Conference, 21 September 1917.

CHAPTER VIII

Haking in France: April – November 1918

Ludendorff's strategy to drive apart the French and British forces and to take the Channel ports was pursued with increasing desperation from March until mid-July 1918. By a series of carefully planned assaults – MICHAEL (21 March); MARS (28 March); GEORGETTE (9 April); BLÜCHER (27 May); GNEISENAU (9 June) and FRIEDEN-STURM (15 July) – German troops had threatened Amiens, Hazebrouck and Paris and had thrown the Allies into a state of considerable alarm. By mid-July the Germans had made major territorial gains. In so doing they had abandoned their strongly held positions from Rheims north to Ypres and had extended their front line by creating three major salients in front of Chateau Thierry, Montdidier and Merville. Moreover, Ludendorff's greatest fear, a dramatic and overwhelming increase in the number of American troops, was being realized. Some 80,000 Americans arrived in March; 118,000 in April, and 245,000 in May. All of Ludendorff's assaults had started as tactical successes, but one by one, they had lost momentum and had finally ground to a halt. Strategically they constituted a failure. The Germans had lost almost one million of their best troops and Ludendorff's depleted and near-exhausted army now occupied a front that was much more extended and weaker than it had been in March.

It was in these circumstances that Foch, recently appointed as overall co-ordinator of the Allied forces on the Western Front, launched, on 18 July, a counter-attack at Villers-Cotterets, north of the Marne. The French and Americans broke through the German defences and advanced six miles in two days taking 25,000 prisoners. This success was a major blow to Ludendorff, who was obliged to withdraw his troops to the Vesle.

The tide had now turned in favour of the Allies. On 8 August the British Fourth Army attacked east of Amiens and advanced four miles, virtually destroying the weak German Second Army. For Ludendorff, this was "the black day of the German army in the history of the war . . . our war machine was no longer efficient." Two days later, Ludendorff, who had now given up any hope of Germany winning the war, reported the grim situation to the Kaiser who despairingly responded: "We have reached the limits of our strength. The War must be brought to an end."[1] But serious peace negotiations were slow to develop and there was still much fighting to take place. In the following three months the British Army was to play a major part in a series of Allied victories that eventually resulted in the defeat of the German Army and the Armistice of 11 November. The purpose of this chapter is to examine the activities and contribution of Haking's XI Corps during the dramatic events of the summer and autumn of 1918.

* * * *

By 20 April the direction of the GEORGETTE offensive had moved north towards Ypres and the XI Corps front was on the line Arrewage-east of the Nieppe Forest-west of Merville-Festubert. The Corps was made up of the 5th, 50th, 51st, 55th and 61st Divisions, together with the remnants of King Edward's Horse and the Corps Cyclists. Between them, these units had lost 10,890 men during the period 8-20 April. The line had stabilized, but there were still fears of a possible renewal of the German offensive. On 15 April, for example, Major General Stephens of the 5th Division, wrote:

> From information received from Battalion Commanders in the line . . . it is evident that the enemy made very strong attacks against the left of this Divisional front yesterday morning and afternoon. In the morning a concentration of German Infantry in Vierhouck was broken up by MG fire – during the ensuing 5 hours the enemy made the most strenuous endeavours to assemble and launch attacks . . . The troops in the front line were firing almost continuously for a period of 5 hours with rifles, Lewis and machine guns and considerable difficulty was caused in keeping an adequate supply of SAA . . . . On one occasion an enemy attack in five lines was beaten back as soon as it started – and on another our artillery opened fire on hostile guns coming into action in the open and on mounted detachments. Battalion Commanders are confident that very heavy casualties have been inflicted on the enemy.[2]

The defensive positions along the XI Corps front had been constructed hastily and many were far from satisfactory. Measures were urgently taken to improve the situation. In his summary of operations for the week 19-26 April Haking noted:

> On the morning of 23 April the 2/5th Gloucesters of the 61st Division (in conjunction with the 51st Division on their right) carried out an operation to straighten the line between

Bacquerolles and la Pierre-au-Beure . . . as a result the line has been shortened and strengthened between the Clarence River and Bois de Bacault . . . On the night of the 25th, the 5th Division attacked Farms and enclosures about . . . le Vert Bois. The attack was quite successful . . . The territorial gains give us one or two good positions further forward and a greater depth in front of the forest.

During that same week four enemy machine guns and 296 prisoners were captured. The Germans attempted a counter-attack on Bacquerolles Farm, but this was repulsed and a further eighty-one prisoners were taken. Haking commented in his report: "This is the only occasion during this past week upon which an attack materialised. On several days reports of hostile assembly for attack have been received, but after our artillery had concentrated upon the indicated areas no hostile infantry action followed."[3] The perceived danger of a major German attack on the front of XI Corps gradually diminished towards the end of April and the XI Corps war diary noted: "Since [23 April] on the front of the Corps the enemy has attempted nothing more formidable than raids."[4]

Nevertheless, as a result of the constant threat of a German attack and the events of the previous three weeks there is evidence of some considerable tension within the First Army. In early May, Haking acting on the advice of his doctors, had taken a day's rest at the coast. Horne, the Commander of the First Army, who had recently refused a request from Haking for leave in England, was far from sympathetic and wrote to Haking on 6 May:

I understood that you wished to go to the sea on Sunday and return on Monday . . . I then sat down and wrote to you pointing out that the II Army were expecting a continuation of the attack on a very early date and that I considered it essential that you should be present in case of the attack, or the effects of it, spreading to your front . . . I had hoped that I had made it clear last week, when I was compelled to refuse your request for leave to England, that in my view the military situation did not justify me granting leave to a Corps Commander except for very exceptional reasons. That is certainly my opinion today.

Horne continued with a barbed proposal: "If, however, the medical people think that it is essential that you go away I might arrange for Congreve to take your place whilst you take a turn in charge of defence organization. You could probably be spared there for a few days change. I hope you are feeling better." This proposal might have been a sign of some concern on Horne's part or, more likely, it was a scarcely veiled threat. Haking seems to have assumed that the second of these possibilities applied and, chastened and displaying his usual inclination to conform with his superior's views, he immediately sent off two letters to Horne who, by this time, had learnt that Haking had in fact left for the sea on the Saturday rather that the Sunday. Haking's first letter read:

> I am extremely sorry there was a mistake about my going off on Saturday afternoon. I was coming back on Monday and unless I went on Saturday afternoon I would not get a day on the coast. As a matter of fact the arrangements for bringing me back worked very well. I got your letter in good time and was home before daylight ready for any hostile attack. I won't try any more trips to the sea until things get really quiet. I wouldn't have gone this time only the Doctor made such a point of it. I am quite all right now.

In his second letter Haking wrote:

> It was my fault entirely. I did not realise that it made any difference whether I went away on the Saturday night or Sunday morning and I wanted to get back on Monday morning. I am very sorry I ever listened to the doctors at all and still more sorry that I should have caused you any worry. I am quite all right now and I don't believe I was ever half as bad as the Doctors made out. I can only repeat that I am very sorry that I have given you so much trouble.[5]

Haking clearly had no wish to exchange jobs with Congreve. He was eventually granted seven days' home leave on 6 July.

The XI Corps weekly operations reports for May showed signs of a growing confidence that the immediate situation was under control and that the Germans were content to remain in their existing positions. Both sides carried out frequent patrols and raids. The XI Corps report for the week 10–17 May recorded that five small raids had been carried out along the Lys by the 5th and 61st Divisions, while the Germans had attacked a Lewis gun position on the extreme right of the 5th Division. On 20 May the 1st Battalion, East Surreys had carried out a small operation "in order to shorten and straighten our line" and the following day the Germans attempted a counter-attack.[6] In the week 24–31 May four raids were made again by the 5th and 61st Divisions and the Germans attacked a post on the right flank of XI Corps. These infantry raids were accompanied by continuous artillery fire with both sides targeting towns, prominent buildings and machine-gun posts along the front frequently using gas shells.

During this period the main task of XI Corps was to maintain a strong defensive position. At his Corps Conference on 27 May, Haking emphasized that

> with regard to defences, the fundamental principle is that the troops must fight to maintain their present positions and Divisional Commanders must realise that every man and every gun at their disposal is to be used to this end. As a result of the construction of numerous back lines of defence, there is a tendency for the men to fall back if heavily pressed; but it is of vital importance that present positions be maintained. If we are driven back further the enemy will be able to seriously threaten the Hazebrouck-Lillers Railway, and menace the position of the Corps on the right on the Hinges-Mt Dernenchon Ridge. The heavy Artillery should work on the same principle and it is their duty to support the infantry to the end. The stolid defence and maintenance of the Corps front must be their main consideration, and should be adhered to even at the risk of losing some guns.[7]

Haking had opened his Conference of 27 May with the dramatic announcement that the Germans had launched a thirty-division offensive on the Chemin des Dames: "The Corps Commander read out a wire from the First Army regarding the German attacks between Soissons and Rheims and between Locre and Voormizeele." Within a week, the Germans had advanced to the Marne with Paris only fifty miles away. These serious events served to confirm the continuing need to ensure that the First Army front was secure and well defended. With this in mind, Horne wrote to the GOC Second Army, Plumer, on 8 June suggesting that the defences at the junction of the two armies should be reviewed:

> The front system of defences are held by the Northern Corps of the First Army (XI Corps) as the first line of resistance, but there does not appear to be good co-ordination of the systems at the junction of the First and Second Armies. In view of the GHQ Instruction that any further advance on Hazebrouck by the enemy was to be stopped and that the line Nieppe Forest–Hinges was to be held, I consider it essential that the main line of resistance of the XI Corps should be clear of Forest, as a system close to or within the wood cannot be well-supported by artillery.

Horne went on to say that while the front of XI Corps, including the main line of resistance had been constructed east of the Nieppe Forest, the adjoining XV Corps (Second Army) had its main line of resistance some 2,000 yards within the Forest. This meant, wrote Horne, that:

> the XV Corps main line of resistance is echeloned a considerable distance in rear of that of XI Corps and does not connect with it. This constitutes a real danger to the left flank of the First Army which would be turned if the enemy secured possession if the Bois d'Aval.

Horne then proposed to Plumer that a joint operation, which had already been discussed between the Commanders of the XI and XV Corps, should take place "with the object of advancing our front, at the junction of the two Armies, to the general line Arrewage-Verte Rue-La Becque."[8]

Haig had already ordered that minor operations should be carried out on the British front to keep German forces in the north and so assist the French in their efforts against the enemy attacks on the Oise. Horne consequently instructed his Corps Commanders to

> submit proposals for such operations as soon as possible . . . In the case of XI Corps, the proposals discussed by the GOC XI Corps, with Lt Col Nicholson, GSO 1, First Army, yesterday, have been forwarded to Second Army, with a suggestion that operation referred to should be carried out as one of those to be executed under the instructions [from GHQ]. A scheme for the XI Corps portion of the operation will be submitted by XI Corps.[9]

Six days later, on 14 June, the XI Corps Order No. 359 outlined the proposed attack. It was to be code-named BORDERLAND and it was to take place under the command of Haking.[10] Two divisions were to be involved – the 5th Division from XI Corps (First Army) and the 29th Division from XV Corps (Second Army). The objective was to capture the German defences on the line Swing Bridge-le Cornet Perdu-la Becque. This would have the effect of moving the British front line eastwards from the Nieppe Forest in such a way that the lines of resistance of both the First and Second Armies would be effectively connected.

Each Division was to use two battalions from each of two brigades. Secrecy was to be a key feature. Detailed plans were drawn up for the artillery, but: "Nothing will be done prior to zero hour which may draw attention to the front of the attack . . . GOs C 5th and 61st Divisions will arrange for wire to be cut from now in such a way as to avoid special attention being drawn to the front of the attack." A diversionary demonstration using smoke was to be made by the 5th and 61st Divisions at zero hour across the Lys Canal and three RAF squadrons (the RAF was created on 1 April, absorbing both the RNAS and RFC) were to deal with the enemy aircraft, balloons, batteries and the movement of reinforcements.[11]

On 17 June these arrangements were discussed and confirmed at a Corps Conference. Emphasis was placed on gaining and circulating Intelligence information as to the German defences, positions and the nature of the front to be covered. In this connection, the RAF were to provide photographs "of certain houses in the enemy's lines to see whether they were prepared for defence". Artillery details were reviewed and the requirements of the two Divisions were agreed. At zero hour a gas shell bombardment lasting three minutes would be carried out on the German batteries. The plans concerning ammunition supply, the provision of water, arrangements for dealing with the wounded, pack transport and prisoners were all settled. Zero hour was fixed, but "the hour is not to be communicated until instructions are received from Corps HQ".[12]

Two days later a significant setback occurred. At a meeting involving Plumer, Horne, Lieutenant General de Lisle of XV Corps and Haking, de Lisle announced that "sickness had developed in the 29th Division and he considered that this, added to the troops being tired from long periods in the trenches, rendered them unfit to carry out more offensive movement than a limited objective. He was of the opinion that they could not take la Becque." Haking insisted that the operation could only take place with two divisions as planned and the attack, which was to have taken place the following day, 20 June, was postponed. Plumer immediately made arrangements for the 29th Division to be replaced by his 31st Division, which would be reinforced by three battalions of the 74th Division. This was to be done "as soon as possible with a view to the operation being carried out under the present arrangements as soon as the 31st Division was ready . . . 28 June was agreed as a date to work for."[13]

The operation was duly launched at 6.00am on 28 June and it was a considerable success. The day was fine and the ground was dry and hard. The attack went forward as planned under a creeping artillery and machine-gun barrage at

a pace of one hundred yards in four minutes. Both of these were accurate and intense and the troops have expressed great satisfaction with them. News began to come in almost immediately from both flanks and observers reported the attack progressing well in the centre also . . . at 9.30am confirmation was received from the infantry in the centre that all objectives had been captured up to time. The assault was pressed with great dash, and those enemy Machine Guns which came into action were engaged by the troops on either flank, with bombs and bullet, till they could be rushed.

At 10.37am Haking received a message from the 5th Division: "We have reached all objectives and have 'hit them up'. A bottle of whisky would help us hold on."[14]

German resistance was overcome in many cases with particular ferocity. One report noted that a British Support Company "encountered a party of Germans in the Orchard who were wearing Red Cross Brassards. These men were attacking the leading wave with bombs from the rear and therefore were bayoneted to a man." Similarly,

> a strong party from the right Company bombed southwards along the German front line as far as south of the River Bourre. A large number of enemy were found by this Company hiding in shelters and holes; they were successfully disposed of . . . Large numbers of Germans were killed in the captured positions with the bayonet and in one instance 37 Germans were found heaped together – all of whom had been bayoneted.[15]

The attack had advanced 2,000 yards on a front of some 6,000 yards and had succeeded in its main aim of joining up the resistance lines of the First and Second Armies and gaining "room for the XV Corps East of the Bois d'Aval". The XI Corps report of the action concluded: "It is estimated that the 32nd (German) Division has had a permanent loss of 1,000 – (450 prisoners and at least 550 killed) – and it is certainly not fit for offensive operations even if it was before. The moral[e] of the 5th and 31st Divisions is very high indeed."[16] Colonel F. J. Brakenridge of 31st Division later wrote: "I remember we were all very bucked over this 'Push', the success being a pleasant change following the long dull period after Hazebrouck, a very different affair."[17]

* * * *

On 23 May 1918 the Fifth Army, disbanded after the German offensive of March, was reconstituted with Lieutenant General Sir William Birdwood as its Commander. The Fifth Army Order No. 2, dated 29 June, read:

> The Fifth Army will, at 10.00am on July 1st, take over from First Army, the sectors held by XI and XIII Corps . . . The Fifth Army will consist of XI Corps (5th, 61st and 74th Divisions) and XIII

Corps (3rd, 4th and 46th Divisions) with the 19th Division in GHQ Reserve.

It added that the XI Corps front would continue to be from Arrewage to a point north of Festubert while the XIII Corps front would run from Festubert to Bruay on a line east of Bethune.[18] Haking's long association with the First Army, which had begun in August 1915, thus came to an end.

The summary of XI Corps operations for the first week of July noted that the attack of 28 June "disclosed no preparations for offensive action by the enemy . . . The general situation on the Corps front is that there are no indications of an attack in the immediate future."[19] The Fifth Army war diary for the same week commented that the XI Corps front "had been reasonably quiet" with only spasmodic shelling and machine-gun fire.[20] Nevertheless, despite the inactivity of the enemy, the importance of the Fifth Army front in protecting Hazebrouck and the Channel ports continued to make defence the prime consideration. The Fifth Army policy, as noted on 20 July, "remained unchanged, and all possible labour has been concentrated on improving existing defences."[21] Every effort was made by constant raids and patrols to harass the Germans, pinpoint their positions, secure identifications and, generally, avoid any possibility of being taken by surprise by a sudden enemy offensive.

The emphasis on the defence resulted in elaborate procedures and arrangements that were communicated throughout the Fifth Army. Instructions from the Fifth Army HQ stipulated that the XI and XIII Corps should

> select one line of trenches where we intend to fight, and to use all our available strength in maintaining that line . . . Within the Battle Zone, the existing defences will be organized into three systems . . . In the rear of the Battle Zone, arrangements will be made to orga-nize the defences, as they are prepared, in systems . . . A line known as the line of retention will be selected on each Corps front . . . the line of retention will be a line where the utmost endeavour will be made to stop the momentum of the enemy's advance, or alterna-tively, the line which will be regained by counter-attack should the enemy succeed in penetration . . . The maximum number of troops will be held within the defences of the system which contains the line of retention – the battle position.

As part of the various systems, a number of strongly-held positions, known as Nucleus Garrisons, were to be established: "The object of such garrisons is to provide a bulwark behind which respective supports and reserves can be formed and moved or, alternatively, to provide a framework for reinforcements in the event of a rapid advance of the enemy." [22]

Despite his strong reservations about the defence in depth system, as shown at Givenchy in April, Haking conformed with Plumer's orders. An XI Corps memorandum outlined the arrangements in the event of

> a hostile attack coming as a surprise . . . It is quite impossible to get orders to the front line, and the troops holding it must fight a rear-guard action back to the main line of resistance. All details of that rear-guard action will be carefully worked out beforehand and each Platoon Commander will be thoroughly conversant with the amount of resistance he is to offer, his best line of retreat if forced back and the particular part of the main line of defence he is to occupy and hold . . . It is absolutely essential that he should fight and delay the advance of the enemy's infantry as long as possible and only retire when he is perfectly certain that the enemy has broken through on both his flanks. [23]

The same memorandum detailed the arrangements to be followed by the artillery:

> We must prevent the enemy from dealing with our front trenches by TMs alone, and thus setting free his artillery to act against our communications, battery positions and our Headquarters, with HE and Gas. The action will then follow certain definite lines. We shall commence an intense bombardment on the front system with all types of guns, howitzers and TMs . . . The enemy will be compelled to show his hand . . . and will retaliate with counter-battery work. In order to maintain our bombardment of the enemy front system we shall then be compelled to direct the fire of a certain number of guns to deal with the enemy's artillery offensive otherwise our guns could hardly remain in action. What Heavy Artillery is to be diverted for this purpose must be decided by the Corps Commander . . . The Divisional Commander can call on the Corps to increase the fire of the Corps Heavy Artillery on any of the targets . . . and diminish their fire on the front trenches if he wishes. By this means we will gain the initiative at the start and shall materially weaken the enemy's power of attack.

An XI Corps document dated 11 July gave further instructions "for the Artillery Defence of the front in case of hostile attack" and divided artillery action into four phases – Harassing Fire, to be used when "the enemy are concentrating opposite the Corps front"; Counter-Battery Bombardment, which would "open when the enemy opens a heavy bombardment on our front"; Counter-Preparation which would depend "on the intensity of the [enemy] bombardment"; and SOS artillery action which was to be used "to destroy attacking infantry."[24]

The Corps RAF squadron was also fully involved in the defence programme. During the week ending 5 July "photographic machines were protected by a large number of scouts . . . By day, a large number of targets have been engaged by MG fire from the air, and numerous bombs dropped."[25] During the following week the Corps squadron successfully photographed Merville–Plate Becque area, and enemy positions were again harassed by machine guns and bombs. During July, therefore, infantry, artillery and the RAF worked together to ensure a sound defensive system that would avoid any repetition of the traumatic events of 9 April.

Throughout July there was still considerable nervousness within the British Army that a further German offensive might take place. Wilson, the CIGS, referred, in a memorandum dated 25 July, to "the present period of crisis".[26] On the XI Corps front during the period 15-20 July it was feared that an attack was imminent in the Kemmel area and that "a feint or at least a demonstration"[27] might take place. Appropriate defensive measures were taken, but no enemy attack occurred. XI Corps Order No. 376 noted on 17 July that: "On our own front there is still little indication in forward areas to show that the enemy means to undertake offensive action."[28] The XI Corps operations report dated 20 July commented that: "Although several small enemy patrols have been seen their action was the reverse of aggressive."[29] This view was repeated in the report of 26 July: "To sum up, there are no concrete indications that the enemy is preparing for an infantry operation on a large scale opposite the Corps front. From the statements of prisoners it appears the enemy is awaiting an attack by us."[30]

As the threat of a major German attack receded, XI Corps adopted a somewhat more confident and relaxed attitude. An XI Corps Horse Show was held at Rocquetoire on 27 July. There were forty-one events including wrestling on horseback and an inter-battalion tug-of-war and "the Corps Commander expressed his appreciation of the satisfactory turnout".[31] Lieutenant General Sir Ivor Maxse, the Inspector of Training, gave a lecture on 1 August at Linghem, which was attended by Haking, his Divisional Commanders and his training staff officer. Haking also promoted the Corps School, and Divisional Commanders were encouraged, with commendable anticipation, to send their officers on the "Training for Open Warfare" programme. On 10 August

Haking and his Divisional Commanders met HM the King at Bourecq Church.

For the past four months, since early April, attention had been focused on the defensive, but from the end of July a more aggressive approach was adopted. Foch wrote, during the last week of July: "The Allied Armies have . . . reached the turning of the road . . . The moment is come to abandon the generally defensive attitude hitherto imposed by numerical inferiority and to pass to the offensive."[32] A note from Birdwood dated 31 July illustrated the new mood: "the role of the Fifth Army will be to take such offensive action as is possible within the resources of the Army . . . Corps Commanders will, therefore, please submit proposals for action on their respective fronts."[33] Haking, as usual, responded immediately and at his Corps Conference of 31 July he announced to his Divisional Commanders that: "he had two operations he proposed to carry out if resources were available. One would require several divisions, and as he did not know whether these would be forthcoming, the best thing to do was to consider what we could do with our own resources."[34] Three days later, Haking circulated an XI Corps policy document headed: "Offensive Attitude to be Adopted by the Corps." It stated that any sign of an enemy withdrawal must be followed-up "with the greatest vigour. Raiding parties must kill or capture the garrisons of small posts with the triple object of obtaining information as to the enemy's dispositions, reducing his moral[e] and thus increasing his desire to withdraw, and causing him loss of personnel."[35]

The first indication of a German withdrawal came in early August. The Fifth Army operations report for the week 2–9 August read: "Withdrawal on the front of the Army was commenced by the enemy on 5th August. Our patrols are keeping in touch with the enemy and have made ground up to 2,000 yards from our original line."[36] The historian of the Black Watch noted that, on 31 July, the battalion had taken over the

> front line in the Robecq sector, XI Corps, Fifth Army. After six days in the line an officers' patrol reported that the enemy were evacuating their front line. Captain R. A. Andrews immediately ordered his Company (D) to advance, and to them fell the distinction of beginning the 'Advance to Victory' on the XI Corps front.[37]

On a number of occasions during July, XI Corps patrols had reported that there were "no signs yet apparent that the enemy is attempting to dig a defensive line on the East of the Plate Becque."[38] Consequently,

when the Fifth Army notified XI Corps that the Germans were withdrawing from their defensive positions between the Clarence River and
Locon, Haking on 9 August, ordered the 5th and the 61st Divisions to
prepare for an attack across the Plate Becque. However, the crossing of
the Plate Becque proved no easy matter: "In spite of the fact that we
have maintained close touch with the enemy, and that every endeavour
has been made to follow-up immediately any withdrawal on his part,
our line has not substantially altered during the week."[39] It was not
until 18 August that the Plate Becque was eventually crossed "and the
following days brought further advances along the whole of the Fifth
Army front". By the end of August, the XI Corps front had advanced
to a line Neuf Berquin-Estaires-Lestrem and Haking was able to report
to the Fifth Army HQ that "a further retirement to the Aubers line is
considered probable in the near future." [40]

* * * *

The success of the French counter-attack on the Marne on 18 July and
the devastating victory of the British Fourth Army in front of Amiens
on 8 August triggered a series of German withdrawals along the
Western Front. The salients created by the advances in the spring were
gradually reduced as the Germans pulled back and shortened their
front. On 22 August Haig wrote to Birdwood:

> The effect of the two very severe German defeats and the contin-
> uous attacks to which the enemy has been subjected during the
> past month has been to wear out his troops and disorganise his
> plans. Our Second and Fifth Armies have taken their share of
> this effort to destroy the enemy and already have gained consider-
> able ground from him on the Lys sector of the front . . . The
> methods which we have followed hitherto in our battles with
> limited objectives when the enemy were strong are no longer
> suited to his present condition . . . To turn the present situation to
> account the most resolute offensive is everywhere desirable. Risks
> which a month ago would have been criminal to incur ought now
> to be incurred as a duty. It is no longer necessary to advance in
> regular lines and step by step. On the contrary, each Division
> should be given distant objectives which must be reached inde-
> pendently of its neighbour.[41]

While the Fifth Army was not called upon to take part in any major
offensive, it was responsible for pushing the Germans eastwards as they
reduced the Merville salient – a continuing process as the First and
Second Armies on either side of the Fifth Army themselves pressed
forward.[42] In his XI Corps policy statement of 26 August, Haking wrote:

It is not the intention of the Corps Commander to force a withdrawal, but it is his intention to follow-up and hasten a withdrawal . . . It is therefore of the highest importance for troops in the front line, first to ascertain immediately any withdrawal, and secondly, to follow-up with the greatest vigour, acting on a pre-arranged plan, and without waiting for any further orders . . . In those parts of the line where patrols and raiding parties can find no properly constituted and garrisoned hostile posts our line must be advanced and permanently held.

In the spirit of Haig's message to Birdwood, Haking added:

It is essential that every Battalion and Company Commander should have a definite scheme of advance, with definite objective to gain without waiting for orders from anyone . . . They will not wait for orders but will act on their own initiative directly that they discover that the enemy is withdrawing.[43]

The nature of the XI Corps advance was not a series of major leaps, but continued harassment leading to limited German withdrawals. Birdwood described the process as "pursuing the enemy with minimum force."[44] These withdrawals were slow and, frequently, hotly contested. Haking's operations report for the first week of September noted that "considerable resistance had been encountered" in the Laventie area and "our advance was held up for some time by machine gun fire".[45] On 6 September, however, Haking reported: "the line on which the enemy is now standing runs roughly from Givenchy-lez-la-Bassée . . . to north of Neuve Chapelle and thence to Fleurbaix". In other words, the Germans, after almost five months, were once again back to the front line they had occupied prior to their offensive of 9 April.[46]

Progress on the XI Corps front, if not dramatic, was steady and news of significant victories elsewhere on the Western Front gave cause for great optimism. The XI Corps War Diary for 27 September recorded the successful attack at Cambrai by the First and Third Armies and on successive days the diary contained news of the advance of the Belgian and Second Armies to the north and south of Ypres and of the Fourth Army's success at St Quentin where it broke the Hindenburg Line. On 30 September the news arrived that an armistice had been signed with Bulgaria.

The XI Corps continued its policy of harassment as the Germans gradually withdrew. It was not until 30 September that the 19th Division of XI Corps crossed the River Laies – a feature that had played such an important part in the failed attack on Fromelles in July 1916.

On 2 October the 19th Division took the village of Aubers and the Aubers Ridge, the object of costly and unsuccessful attacks by Haking's 1st Division in May 1915. Two weeks later troops of XI Corps were approaching Lille and the XI Corps HQ was set up in Fromelles. These names – the Laies, Aubers, Aubers Ridge and Fromelles – were all important German defensive features, which Haking had striven so hard to overcome, unsuccessfully, during the past three years. That they were now in British hands must have given considerable satisfaction.

Haking's proudest day of the war, however, was probably 18 October 1918. By 5.30am XI Corps troops had completely encircled Lille and the Germans withdrew from the city. The XI Corps War Diary records: "the Corps Commander visited Lille with BGGS. He entered the Canteleux Gate and walked to the Mairie where he was received by the Maire of Lille . . . Lille was freely decorated with the flags of the Allies which had been kept concealed from the enemy when he left." On that same day Haking wrote to the Governor of Paris:

> The Corps under my Command occupied Lille last night. We should all be very proud if you will allow the Corps flag which I am sending with this letter, to be placed among the decorations on the Lille statue in the Place de la Concorde, Paris, as a small tribute of our affection and admiration for the French Nation, from XI Corps.

The Governor of Paris, General Moinier, responded: "I have received the Flag of the XI Army Corps, the Corps which was the first to enter Lille . . . the population of Paris will feel deeply touched by the beautifully worded tribute that you have attached to the flag in your handwriting."[47]

Elaborate orders were issued for the control and protection of Lille, the responsibility for which was allocated firstly to the 59th Division of XI Corps and then to troops of the Fifth Army. The entry in the diary of Major G. R. Codrington records the official entry of the British into Lille:

> The 47th Division marched through the town preceded by the Corps Commander – large crowds, flags, bands, police, sand on the road and the whole thing complete. On arrival at the Grand Place the Army Commander and Corps Commander and Staff dismounted, met the Maire and his entourage, made speeches to them, and then the Army Commander presented his flag to the city – much enthusiasm, Marseillaise and God Save the King, the tremendous Entente.[48]

XI Corps, now made up of the 47th, 57th and 59th Divisions, persisted in its role of harassing the enemy. As an operations report described it, "the advance was energetically continued".[49] Despite continuing German resistance, often fierce, the Scheldt was crossed on 22 October. By 27 October the Germans were positioned "firmly on the right bank of the Escaut" with his main defensive line "along the Tournai-Herrines railway line".[50]

The various units of XI Corps had shown great tenacity throughout the period of advance. An example of this was acknowledged by Haking in a note of 24 October:

> The Corps Commander wishes his appreciation conveyed to Lt Col Lembecke and all ranks of the 25th Battalion King's Liverpool Regt. on their determination and endurance displayed between October 18th and 21st. This Battalion advanced a distance of 30 miles, forced a crossing over the River Scheldt and engaged the enemy on the Eastern banks all within a space of 33 hours, a feat which could not have been surpassed. [51]

The 25th Battalion King's Liverpool was part of the 59th Division, which Haking praised for

> the work so cheerfully done by them, frequently under very trying circumstances, during the last two months . . . A Division that has shown such energy and determination cannot be described as a "B" Division, and the Corps Commander directs that henceforward, in the XI Corps, the 59th Division will never be referred to in that manner.[52]

The XI Corps advance continued up to 10 November: "By 18.00 both Divisions [47th and 59th] reported that they were on their objectives for the day; the line ran Toufflers (south of Roubaix) to Bourghelles (west of Tournai)."[53] As far as XI Corps was concerned, that was the end of their war. A note from Fifth Army HQ dated 10 November stated: "the XI Corps will be withdrawn from the line as early as possible and its front will be taken over by the III Corps".[54] The XI Corps war diary entry for 11 November simply read: "Wire received from Fifth Army stating that hostilities will cease at 11.00am today – troops to stand fast on positions reached at hour named."[55]

Haking's war ended somewhat earlier. On 4 November "the Corps Commander proceeded on leave to UK" and, on 13 November, the Corps war diary read: "A wire was received from GHQ and forwarded c/o AMLO Boulogne for Lt Gen Haking and ADC to report to Adv.

GHQ immediately for special duty. Lt Gen Haking and Gen Green proceeded following day to SPA."[56] Haking had been XI Corps Commander continuously since September 1915 – a period of thirty-eight months.[57] There is no evidence to suggest that his departure was marked in any particular way.

* * * *

It is likely that the final few days of the war were, for Haking, an anti-climax. The XI Corps war diary suggests that he was not at the front, nor with his Corps, when the ceasefire took place. Nevertheless, Haking could look back over the past seven months in France with some satis-faction. The XI Corps, pushed back by the Germans during the GEORGETTE offensive, did not break and fought with determination during the difficult days following 9 April. On 17 April Haking was able to write to Horne:

> since the beginning of the battle on the 9th inst. the enemy has suffered very heavy casualties. This is accentuated by the fact that the Divisions of the Corps have either stood their ground like 55th Division, have held on to localities for a very long time and retired very slowly like the 50th and 51st Divisions, or have occupied a definite position and held it so far in spite of several heavy attacks like 5th and 61st Divisions.[58]

From 19 April until 5 August, the emphasis in both the First and Fifth Armies was on defensive measures to counter any possible renewed German offensive. During this period Haking, despite the altercation with Horne over leave, carried out his duties with diligence. As seen, the front of XI Corps was systematically strengthened by attacks in both April and May to straighten out the line and Haking ensured that the Army instructions for defence in depth were closely followed. German counter-attacks and raiding parties were dealt with without particular difficulty.

An important XI Corps contribution to the defence of the First Army front was the successful BORDERLAND attack of 28 June and it is relevant to compare that operation with the unsuccessful attack on Fromelles some two years earlier. There were some significant similari-ties between the two operations. The aim of both attacks was to take and hold a section of the German front some three miles in length. On both occasions Haking was given command of two divisions, one of which was part of an adjoining Army. On both occasions the division lent to Haking came from Plumer's Second Army. Also, on both occasions, there was a late and disruptive change of the assault division provided by the Second Army. Both attacks were supported by British air superiority and also by diversionary bombardments some miles away. As at Fromelles the date of the BORDERLAND attack was postponed at the last minute.

However, there were also some significant differences between the two attacks. The preparation for Fromelles, subsequently accepted as hasty, lasted six days whereas for BORDERLAND it was fourteen. At Fromelles it was not possible and there was no effort to maintain secrecy, while secrecy was a key feature of BORDERLAND. The operation report confirmed that: "An attack can be prepared with secrecy against positions such as those now occupied by the enemy." Luck favoured BORDERLAND. The weather and the state of the ground – not insignificant factors – were considerably more favourable to the infantry and to the artillery during BORDERLAND than at Fromelles. In both operations the assault troops were massed in the front trenches, but whereas at Fromelles the enemy shells caused hundreds of casualties, the troops at BORDERLAND escaped any significant bombardment. As Captain L. F. Machin of the 2nd KOSB later wrote: "I shudder to think what would have happened to our attack if the enemy had discovered our assembly position before [zero hour]."[59]

While Fromelles had an overall tactical objective (later criticized as being inexact), BORDERLAND was planned with a series of clearly defined infantry objectives each carefully supported by the artillery. During the advance of the 1st Royal West Kents, for example, the "barrage was closely followed and each objective captured according to time-table."

The artillery arrangements in BORDERLAND were far superior to those of Fromelles. At Fromelles the firing of the inexperienced gun crews was far from accurate causing many casualties among their own troops. At BORDERLAND the artillery operation was planned with both a creeping barrage to cover the advancing troops and a standing barrage to deal with the enemy behind their front positions. Moreover, the BORDERLAND artillery had begun wire-cutting "on the whole Divisional front about June 15th and [it] was carried out gradually without drawing the enemy's attention to the front of the attack or leading [the enemy] to conclude that an attack was intended". The Heavy Artillery also performed well as it "paid special attention to houses, farms and all possible strong-points in and behind the enemy's lines and gradually demolished them". At Fromelles only a small proportion of the German strong points were destroyed. The infantry described the BORDERLAND barrages as "excellent" whereas a Regimental officer at Fromelles considered that: "The total effect of our artillery preparations on the Hun was nil."[60] The Fromelles attack lasted some fourteen hours and failed to gain a yard of ground while

BORDERLAND was completed in four hours with an advance of 2,000 yards. Casualties at Fromelles amounted to 7,000, while the BORDER-LAND report stated that the losses were "light" – later amended by hand to "moderate" – and noted in the British official history as fewer than 2,000.

There were two crucial differences between the two operations. First, the German defence system at Fromelles, manned by Bavarian Regiments familiar with the terrain and taking full advantage of their position on the Aubers Ridge, was made up of a series of steel-rein-forced concrete bunkers. At BORDERLAND the enemy defences were entirely different – hastily-constructed trenches without significant strongpoints. The British Official History described the German defences as "poor, shallow trenches and shell holes so that movement by day was impossible: the dug-outs were only rough weather-proof shelters, and the wire was salved British material, badly erected with none in the hedges or ditches."[61] The attacking British troops had neither a Sugarloaf nor a Wick Salient to contend with. The second key difference was the relative experience and performance of the artillery units. At Fromelles the artillery bombardment was largely ineffective. At BORDERLAND the wire cutting and the creeping and the standing barrages were all successful. The creeping barrage was particularly effective and the British Official History noted that it was "a principle of the 5th Division to be in the enemy's trenches before the barrage lifted [so] that they were among the Germans, with the bayonet, before the latter had time to bring their machine guns into action, or even to offer fire with their rifles."[62]

It was these two major differences – improved British artillery and weaker German defences – that enabled Haking to describe BORDER-LAND as a "complete success".[63] At BORDERLAND Haking was able to take advantage of opportunities that were not present two years earlier and thereby gain the tactical success that he had failed to achieve at Fromelles.

It could be argued that the two attacks illustrated clearly the change of operational approach taken in the War Office publication SS 109 (*Training Divisions for Offensive Action*) of May 1916 compared to that taken in SS 135 (*The Division in Attack*) dated November 1918.[64] The first was concerned only with infantry matters, while the second emphasized that: "Infantry must be practised in cooperation with the artillery, trench mortars, tanks, machine guns and contact patrol aeroplanes, which will accompany them into attack." However, both at Fromelles and at BORDERLAND, Haking had used all his available resources – infantry, artillery, trench mortars, machine guns and aeroplanes. It was not simply the factor of cooperation that caused

BORDERLAND to be a success; it was the relatively changed circumstances that made the difference.

The use by XI Corps of infantry, artillery and aircraft as a "combined arms" force was not confined to the BORDERLAND operation. A similar approach was used in the efforts to cross La Plate Becque when "the Corps squadron carried out successful contact work with the attacking infantry . . . Artillery machines materially assisted in keeping down hostile artillery fire" and "photographic machines" provided valuable information for use by the artillery. The weekly XI Corps operation reports invariably included a section on "Aviation" and co-operation between the artillery and the RAF was recorded as a normal procedure: "Anti-aircraft MGs, which have of late become particularly active against our machines, have, at the request of the RAF been severely dealt with."[65] The XI Corps operation reports were mainly concerned with infantry and artillery matters with Aviation covered in only three or four lines. However, while the RAF may have been considered as the junior partner in the XI Corps organization, the use of aircraft was now clearly seen as indispensible. Haking, even from his days as a Southern Command staff officer in 1911, had recognized the value of co-ordinated infantry and artillery action and the use of aircraft as an additional military tool was readily accepted.[66]

Haking's acceptance of the evolving military tactics was, to a large extent, based on his natural inclination to follow dutifully the orders and wishes of his superiors. Haking's successful wire-cutting tactic which preceded BORDERLAND, for example, followed Birdwood's instruction of 26 July: "Where belts of wire, both old and new, protect the enemy's positions, steps for destruction should be taken early. This must be done unostentatiously." Similarly, Haking's XI Corps policy statement of 2 August which called for raiding parties to gather information, reduce the enemy's morale and kill Germans followed Birdwood's memorandum, issued two days earlier, which ordered: "Constant raids . . . with the objects of (1) ascertaining the enemy's intentions and hindering any reduction of forces opposite us (2) inflicting loss on the enemy and improving our position."[67]

Haig's letter to Birdwood of 22 August brought about a significantly new approach to the conduct of operations on the Western Front. It encouraged a major change from previous "battles with limited objectives" to "distant objectives" which must be reached by Divisions acting "independently of [their] neighbours". Henceforth, a "vigorous offensive" should be waged with all ranks acting "with the utmost boldness and resolution".[68] Birdwood's Special Instruction No. 5, written in anticipation of German withdrawals in September, emphasized that: "All ranks must understand that it is neither necessary nor desirable to move in waves and lines. Independence of action will be encouraged". Birdwood also noted in early September that "a return to conditions as nearly as possible approximate to mobile warfare is necessary".[69]

Haking again adopted and echoed these directions with his usual enthusiasm. In his XI Corps policy of 26 August he wrote: "It is essential that every Battalion and Company Commander should have a definite scheme of advance, with a definite objective to gain, without waiting for orders from anyone . . . The artillery, also, must be on the alert to change their SOS line immediately to suit the new conditions." In the same document, by way of example, Haking announced that: "The first objective to be arrived at by XI Corps, in the event of hostile withdrawal, is the Lawe River–Chapelle Duvalle–Acton Cross." Battalions and Companies were given subsidiary objectives.[70] Haking repeated the new policy at his Corps Conference of 28 September: "the fact that Commanders of all units and formations must realise is the importance of initiative on their part, as it will help enormously in the whole operation if we can get Platoon and Company Commanders to use initiative and go on and take small localities one after the other".[71]

Prior and Wilson have commented, in connection with Rawlinson and his Fourth Army, that "expertise in technical aspects of conducting battles had become so widespread throughout the British Army [in 1918] . . . that the importance of [Army] command in accomplishing victory had diminished absolutely."[72] This may have been the situation in the Fourth Army, but in the Fifth Army the command system, while adapted to the dramatically changed operating circumstances, continued as before. Birdwood's policy, influenced by Haig, was transmitted to Haking for implementation. Hence Birdwood's orders of 31 July for offensive action and Haking's XI Corps policy "Offensive Attitude to be Adopted by the Corps". Haking repeated this policy on 28 September and encouraged his subordinates to use their "initiative" in the new conditions of mobile warfare. The onward transmission of orders and the use of exhortation to gain their acceptance was as much a part of Haking's role in the second half of 1918 as it had been in previous periods of his command.

April-November 1918 was a period of achievement for Haking's XI Corps and, while Haking followed the lead of his superiors, he did so with enthusiasm and efficiency. In defence it had stood firm ensuring that a repeat of 9 April could not take place. In attack it had shown commendable aggression and carried out its role of harassing the German withdrawals with persistence and tenacity. Haking's personal contribution was, as in previous years, executive in nature – ensuring that the policies and orders from the Army were effectively communicated and followed. There is no evidence to suggest that he originated matters of policy. It can be said, however, that during the last dramatic months of the war, Haking accepted and faithfully carried out the policies and tasks that were given to him with diligence and with success. When, in late October, Haking reviewed the performance of the 59th Division, he wrote: "The energy and power of 'sticking it' reflect the highest credit on all ranks."[73] Such an assessment could equally be made of the activities and contribution of Haking and the XI Corps during the summer and autumn months of 1918.

Notes

1. Erich Ludendorff, *My War Memoirs* 2 vols. II, pp.679, 684.
2. TNA, WO 95/883, G.A.287, XI Corps to First Army HQ, 17 April 1918.
3. TNA, WO 95/883, G.S. 43/3.
4. TNA, WO 95/883.
5. IWM, 62/54/6, File 46, Papers of Lord Horne. Horne was no admirer of Haking as the comments quoted in the Introduction show.
6. TNA, WO 95/883, XI Corps, 43/7.
7. TNA, WO 95/883, S.S. 6/4.
8. TNA, WO 95/883, First Army, G.S. 1257/1, 8 June 1918.
9. Ibid.
10. The attack was later officially named "La Beque". See *BOH 1918*, III, p.195.
11. TNA, WO 95/883, 14 June 1918.
12. Ibid., S.S. 6/7.
13. TNA WO 95/883, Notes of a Conference held at HQ XI Corps, 19 June 1918.
14. Ibid. *BOH 1918*, Vol. III, p.197, Footnote 1, records that the bottle of whisky was duly sent.
15. TNA, WO 95/883, "Borderland" operation report.
16. Ibid, XI Corps "Preliminary Report on Action N of Merville on June 28 1918". The 32nd (Saxon) Division was in fact immediately withdrawn and sent to a quiet sector near Verdun.
17. TNA, CAB 45/119, Brakenridge to Edmonds, 16 April 1933.
18. TNA, WO 95/521. At this point XI Corps was made up of some 70,000 men. See WO 95/887, Notes of Admin Conference, 17 July 1918.
19. TNA, WO 95/883.
20. TNA, WO 95/522.
21. Ibid.
22. TNA, WO 95/522, Fifth Army Instructions for Defence No. 7. This form of defence had long been employed by the Germans. In his memoirs, Hindenburg, referring to early 1917, noted: "In future our defensive positions were no longer to consist of single lines and strong points but a network of lines and groups of strong points. In the deep zones thus formed we did not intend to dispose our troops on a rigid and continuous front but in a complex system of nuclei and distributed in depth and breadth." See Hindenburg, *Great War*, p.140. See also the discussion on this subject in Chapter VII of this study.

23. TNA, WO 95/883, XI Corps S.S. 6/8, "The Organisation of the Corps Front for Artillery in Defence".

24. TNA, WO 95/883, XI Corps Artillery Instruction No. 15.

25. Ibid., XI Corps Summary of Operations, G. S. 43/22.

26. *BOH 1918*, Vol. IV, Appendix V, p.529.

27. TNA, WO 95/883, XI Corps Command No. 376.

28. Ibid.

29. Ibid., G.S.43/21.

30. TNA, WO 95/883, G.S.43/22.

31. Ibid., Proceedings of a Conference, 31 July 1918.

32. Quoted in Cyril Falls, *Marshal Foch*, p.153.

33. TNA, WO 95/522.

34. TNA, WO 95/883, XI Corps Conference.

35. TNA, WO 95/884, 3 August 1918

36. TNA, WO 95/522, S.G. 491/21.

37. Maj. Gen. A.G. Wauchope, *A History of the Black Watch (Royal Highlanders) in the Great War 1914–18* 3 vols. III, p.323.

38. TNA WO 95/883, G.S. 43/21, Corps operations report for 12–19 July. On the 'Hundred Days' generally, see J. Paul Harris and Niall Barr, *Amiens to the Armistice: The BEF in the Hundred Days' Campaign*; and Simon Robbins, 'Henry Horne', in Beckett and Corvi, eds., *Haig's Generals*, pp.97–121.

39. TNA, WO 95/522, S.G. 491/24.

40. TNA, WO 95/884, G.S.43/31, 31 August 1918.

41. TNA, WO 95/522, S.G. 436/23. Similarly, Haig at a meeting with Gen. Byng (Third Army) on 19 August said: "Now is the time to act with boldness and in full confidence." See Sheffield and Bourne,*Haig, Diaries and Letters*, p.447.

42. See, for example, John Terraine, *To Win A War: 1918, The Year of Victory*, p.204.

43. TNA, WO 95/884, S.S. No. 24/7.

44. TNA, WO 95/522, Corps Commanders' Meeting, 2 September 1918.

45. TNA, WO 95/884, S.S.43/33.

46. Ibid.

47. TNA, WO 95/884. The statues, representing the provincial cities of France, were draped in black as a sign of mourning until their liberation..

48. TNA WO 95/887, Excerpt from the Diary of Maj. Gen. G. R. Codrington, then a "Q" staff officer in XI Corps.

49. TNA, WO 95/884.

50. Ibid., V.S. 18/43.

51. TNA, WO 95/884, G.S.68/22.

52. TNA WO 95/884, 23 October 1918.

53. Ibid., G.S. 43/47. It should be noted that the 24-hour clock system had been introduced on 1 October.

54. TNA, WO 95/522, First Army Order No. 25.

55. TNA, WO 95/884

56. Ibid. Haking joined the International Armistice Commission. Green was

DAQMG of XI Corps. Haking's papers as Chief of the British Delegation are in TNA, WO 144.

57. Only Poulteney, Morland and Ferguson served longer as Corps Commanders.
58. TNA, WO 95/883, G.A.287.
59. TNA, CAB 45/119, Machin to Edmonds, 14 May 1933.
60. Centre for Buckinghamshire Studies, Christie-Miller typescript, *Second Bucks Battalion 1914–18: An Unofficial Record*, Vol. I, p.184.
61. *BOH 1918*, Vol.III, p.196,
62. *BOH 1918*, Vol.III, p. 197.
63. Quotations relating to the Fromelles-Borderland discussion are taken from the Preliminary and Final Reports on Borderland. See TNA, WO 95/883.
64. Both Pamphlets are held at the IWM.
65. TNA, WO 95/883, G.S. 43/24.
66. See Chapter I.
67. TNA, WO 95/522, 31 July 1918.
68. Ibid., 26 September 1918.
69. TNA, WO 95/522, S.G. 436/31.
70. TNA, WO 95/884, S.S. No. 24/7.
71. Ibid., V.S. 6/11.
72. Prior and Wilson, *Command on the Western Front, The Military Career of Sir Henry Rawlinson 1914–1918*, p.397.
73. TNA, WO 95/884, 24 October 1918.

Haking: An Assessment

The purpose of this study has been to assess Haking as a Corps Commander and determine whether the poor reputation that he has acquired is in fact justified. This final chapter summarizes the personal characteristics that shaped Haking's style of command; the main factors that influenced his actions; his interpretation of the role of a Corps Commander; and the degree of success or failure achieved by Haking in carrying out that role. The chapter concludes, contrary to the generally accepted view, that, on balance, Haking made a positive contribution to the conduct of the war and that his dismal reputation is largely unjustified.

Nothing substantial is known about Richard Haking until his entry into Sandhurst in 1880 at the age of eighteen. It is therefore not possible to examine his early years in the hope of discovering the key to his adult character, his acquired opinions or his personal values. Any speculation about the effects of an adolescence spent in remote Victorian country parsonages, as a vicar's only son, with three sisters as his main companions is bound to be inconclusive as is any discussion about his possible adoption at birth into the Hacking family. That Haking left no personal papers is also unhelpful when seeking an understanding of his military opinions and actions. Nevertheless, as this study has shown, Haking possessed distinct and identifiable personal characteristics and attitudes, whatever their origins, that were evident throughout his Army career and which impacted on the way he carried out his duties as a Corps Commander. These characteristics were by nature enigmatic – a curious mixture of strengths not infrequently offset by elements of weakness and less attractive features.

Haking was of high intelligence and academically inclined. He gained entry into both Sandhurst and the Staff College without apparent difficulty and was considered "exemplary"[1] at the first and as giving "a good impression"[2] at the second. That he was recalled to the Staff College as a Professor and was thought by the College Commandant to have "exceptional ability"[3] is testimony to his skill in presenting himself and his thoughts clearly and with vigour. His two books, *Staff Rides and Regimental Tours* and *Company Training*, together with his published Staff College lectures, established him as a leading military teacher and their contents demonstrated a formidable grasp of detail and strength in written presentation – facilities that became evident, along with his verbal skills, in his future military reports and conferences.

There was, however, a less appealing side to Haking's intellectual ability. He tended on occasions to adopt the manner of a somewhat pedantic Staff College professor. His address to the officers of the 1st Division before Loos ran to eighteen foolscap pages and his first Army Conference in August 1916 was essentially a monologue read from eight pages of text. His devotion to detail may have been useful as when drawing up *Rules and Guidance for Administrative Staff*, as he did in Italy in 1917, or when used to calculate the number of mules required to carry food for a marching division, but it could also be tedious. A feature of Haking's academic approach was his habit of employing "mechanistic logic" – when reasoning that was meant to persuade and convince failed through lack of emotional appeal. Hence the exclamation marks in the war diary of the 2nd Irish Guards just before their attack at Loos. On that occasion Haking had announced to sceptical listeners that the British had five times more troops than the Germans and that the Guards should advance even if it meant leaving their flanks exposed. Also before Loos, Haking stated that: "if a great line of determined men rush forward to carry a breastwork, protected in parts only by wire entanglements, with the nerves of the defenders greatly shaken by our previous bombardment, and with many of them put out of action, that the line will be carried". Haking introduced this remark with the words "It stands to reason" – a phrase not guaranteed to carry or impart conviction.[4] This same approach was also apparent in May 1917 when Haking used various arithmetic calculations in an attempt to convince his divisional commanders that aggressive action was possible despite a reduced number of troops on an extended front. His clinching point – that British morale was superior to German morale "by at least 3 to 2 (British to German)" – was difficult to substantiate and hardly obvious to his subordinates.[5]

There were, however, some more positive aspects of Haking's well-meaning efforts to encourage his troops. He was capable of giving praise and boosting morale. Haking's words to the 2/5th Glosters, who had taken part in an unsuccessful raid in July 1916, were aimed at encouraging further efforts: "I understand the difficulties you all have to contend with. The only solution is to keep at it and for everyone to be determined to succeed . . . I am most anxious that no-one should be dismayed by small failures."[6] It was also Haking's practice to send a complimentary farewell note to a division that was on the point of transferring from XI Corps and he frequently expressed the hope that the division would return to his command or fight alongside XI Corps at some time in the future. An enthusiastic example of such a note was written by Haking to the Guards Division in February 1916 on the occasion of their transfer to XIV Corps:

> Ever since the Division was formed and posted to this Corps, it has proved itself to possess the finest military spirit . . . The fine discipline and soldierly bearing of all ranks is also a matter for you all to be proud of; you have been an example to other Divisions with whom you have been associated and that example has produced the best results and has raised the fighting value and efficiency of the whole Corps. I am very sorry to say good-bye to you. . . . I can only hope that the XI Corps will find itself before long side by side with the XIV Corps with the Guards Division ready, as it always will be, to lead the way to victory.[7]

When the 38th Division left XI Corps in June 1916 Haking wrote: "On the departure of the 38th Division from the XIth Corps, I should be glad if you would convey to all ranks my appreciation of their work since they have been in France." Haking went on to commend all the Brigade Commanders, the Staff, the Engineers and the Artillery and particularly praised "those gallant officers, non-commissioned officers and men . . . who have successfully raided the German trenches, driven back the enemy in many hand-to-hand encounters, and proved themselves to be superior to the enemy in all respects."[8]

From time to time, Haking revealed a paternalistic and lighter side to his character. An officer of the 2nd Royal Welsh Fusiliers recorded an inspection of the battalion carried out by Haking in March 1916. Haking "chatted and chaffed, pinched their arms and ears, asked how many children they had, asked if they could be doing with leave to get another. As he passed from one 1914 man to another he dug his elbow into the CO's ribs and exclaimed: 'You are a lucky fellow.'."[9] When Haking ordered the IV and XVII Corps to prepare for an attack in September 1916 he wrote a note to himself: "Comments of encouragement necessary."[10] In March 1917 Haking wrote to Horne: "The Company and Battalion Commanders are only human beings and subject to the ordinary frailties of human nature."[11]

These worthy efforts to encourage and give confidence to his troops were sometimes diminished by less positive aspects. It was to be expected that a Corps Commander should present an optimistic outlook and when Haking visited the 20th Division HQ in June 1916 it was recorded that he was "most optimistic, as usual".[12] On numerous occasions, however, Haking crossed the line between worthwhile encouragement and implausible over-optimism. Both aimed to bolster morale, but the second tended to produce scepticism. When Haking compared the German line at Loos to the crust of a pie saying that one thrust would break it, his words were received with some disbelief. The main point of this incident, however, is that Haking felt it necessary to add: "I don't tell you to cheer you up. I tell you because I really believe it."[13] Haking's mindset was such that there is every reason to accept that he really did mean what he said.

One of Haking's more regrettable characteristics was his tendency to display a lack of empathy with his troops. This unfortunate trait was generally associated with failure and was apparent after both Loos and Fromelles and contrasted starkly with the praise he lavished on his troops after la Becque and the advance to Lille. Haking was a man of unusual determination and energy. When proposals for harassing the enemy were demanded by his superiors, Haking invariably responded swiftly and with more projects than had been called for. Haking could never be described as a "chateau general". Lowther, when in command of 1 Guards Brigade, commented: "I keep very busy all the time what with accompanying Haking on his inspections". He also noted how a Staff officer attempted to prevent Haking from visiting the front "as there were so many projectiles flying about in these parts. Not that Haking would mind that in the least."[14] His reconnaissance schedule during his early weeks in Italy in December 1917 was remarkable in its intensity. His efforts to bring the Portuguese troops to a reasonable standard of efficiency included many meetings and trench visits and showed a marked determination in difficult circumstances. On the other hand, however, Haking's determination and energy also showed in his efforts to forward his personal interests as in his pursuit of promotion while at Staff College and his self-interested support of Haig during the controversy with French over the reserves at Loos.

A further personal characteristic that was apparent through Haking's career was his extreme respect for authority. Time after time, Haking displayed an over-zealous tendency to conform with the wishes of his superiors. When Haking found that his own thinking was out of line with GHQ or Army policy – the inconvenient removal of a division from the XI Corps front, a reduction in the allocation of ammunition or a method of defence or attack that he would not have chosen – then his usual response was to act as required by his superiors without any particular debate. The interesting point is not simply that Haking was ready to conform, it was his method of conforming. His needless apology to Duchesne, his superior officer in Italy in 1917, for writing a report in English rather than French and his response to Horne when reprimanded for taking sick leave in May 1918 were unnecessarily obsequious. Not that Haking was incapable of disagreeing with the wishes of his superior – for example, he disagreed with Horne about large-scale trench raids in 1916 and, supporting Jeudwine, he changed the defence policy at Givenchy in April 1918 – but his natural reaction was to conform. In some respects, Haking's ready acceptance of authority was the mark of a "good soldier" – a willingness to accept unpalatable and inconvenient orders – and this feature of Haking's character must have been tested to the full when he was obliged to return to his XI Corps after his spell as First Army Commander in 1916. Overall, however, Haking's attitude to authority was subservient and was summed up in his comment at Monro's Army Conference in June 1916 that: "It depended on what the higher commanders desired."[15]

Among the personal characteristics that Haking brought to his role as a Corps Commander was a strong sense of duty. Despite Haking's obvious disappointment that he did not take part in any major battle; despite his failure to retain his temporary post as First Army Commander and despite his command being confined mainly to a waterlogged part of the front well-known for its poor operating conditions, Haking could always be relied upon to apply himself conscientiously to whatever task he was given. His words to the Portuguese at a Conference in September 1917: "All I care about is doing my duty",[16] were not empty rhetoric. They reflected an important aspect of Haking's character.

In addition to the nature of his personal characteristics – a complicated mix of strengths and weaknesses – there are two other factors critical to an understanding of Haking and his actions as a Corps Commander. The first is his relationship with Haig. The two men had met at Staff College as students, they had both served in South Africa and, before the war, they had been based at Aldershot where, among other social engagements, they had dined on several occasions with the King. Haking's 5 Brigade was part of Haig's I Corps during the retreat from Mons and on the Aisne, and, at Aubers, Haking's 1st Division was in Haig's First Army. It was as a result of his aggressive and successful actions following the crossing of the Aisne that Haking was Mentioned in Despatches and promoted in the field to Major General. Haig valued Haking as a "thruster" and it was because of Haig's backing that Haking, over a period of only nine months, became first a Divisional Commander and then a Corps Commander. Haking enjoyed Haig's patronage and their relationship was such that Haking went to extreme lengths to support Haig during the dispute over the reserves at

Loos. Haking played a further part in the dismissal of French when, on 23 October 1915, he, along with Gough, advised the King that French was unfit to lead the BEF. Haking's action on that occasion helped to pave the way for Haig's appointment as Commander in Chief and it reflected not only Haking's professional view of the situation, but also a marked self-interest.

There is a link between Haking's general readiness to accept authority and his specific relationship with Haig. To Haking, Haig was the supreme military figure, not just because he was the Commander in Chief, but also because of the personal support that he had received from Haig. The relationship was inevitably unequal. Any mention of Haking in Haig's diary was impersonal and contrasted vividly with Haking's somewhat reverential references to discussions with Haig during his period as First Army Commander. Haking held Haig in the highest esteem. The nature of this relationship between the two men is highly significant in understanding, for example, the 1st Division's continued assaults at Aubers in May 1915, Haking's handling of the 21st, 24th and 46th Divisions at Loos, and his revived enthusiasm for the attack at Fromelles in July 1916. It also helps to explain the otherwise bizarre conduct of Haking in berating Montagu-Stuart-Wortley over the supposed correspondence with the King. In all these cases the critical motivation for Haking was the belief that Haig, the ultimate figure of authority, wished the actions to take place. As Haking had said in May 1916: "The first essential is obedience of orders",[17] and orders emanating from Haig would have had a particular importance and urgency. Haking retained Haig's support and confidence throughout the war and it is significant that, in April 1918, Haig was quite prepared to appoint Haking as commander of the British troops in Italy when it was suggested that Cavan should return to France.[18] It was Haig who selected Haking as the British representative on the Armistice Commission in November 1918.[19]

The second factor key to an understanding of Haking as a Corps Commander is his absolute acceptance of the prevailing military thinking of his day. In his books and lectures Haking emphasized the importance of the offensive, the necessity for continued aggression to maintain a high level of morale among the troops and the importance of "determination of character" on the part of the commander. All of these points were well-established principles in pre-war military circles and they were in no way unique to Haking. There was also the acceptance by Haking and the great majority of his colleagues that the offensive would inevitably result in heavy casualties. In a lecture given by Haking in 1905 he commented: "Modern arms and modern fortifications have so greatly increased the resisting power of a fortress, that a successful siege must always be a very lengthy and a very costly under-taking." Haking went on to say that such a "costly undertaking" would be necessary "before the enemy's field army can be defeated".[20] Haking was present at a General Staff Officers' Conference in 1909 when esti-mated casualty figures following an attack of 25 to 30 per cent were discussed and accepted without question.

Haking's commitment to the doctrine of the offensive was therefore in line with mainstream military thinking of the time and conformed fully with the *Field Service Regulations* of 1905 and 1909. However, what is striking is Haking's consistent and determined application of that philosophy. His unwavering and wholehearted adherence to a policy of aggression was evident in his frequent policy statements, lectures and harangues as XI Corps Commander. Even when discussing matters of defence, Haking emphasized his belief in the "offensive-defence". In August 1916 he stated that: "The best defence is offence . . . if the enemy attacks and captures part of our line, I will not stop until we have got it back again . . . whatever the cost I am quite deter-mined to regain any trenches lost."[21] Haking's views as to the conduct of warfare had not been arrived at without considerable thought and discussion with his military colleagues. They were for Haking the rationale for his actions at Aubers, Fromelles, la Becque and his aggres-sive tactics during the years of trench warfare.

Haking's predominant characteristics were, therefore, a strong intel-lect, organizing ability, a sense of duty, ambition and drive, staying power, an instinctive aggression, a determination to carry out any task allocated to him and a strong constitution. These not inconsiderable strengths were, on occasions, diminished by a pedantic and mechanistic turn of mind, misplaced over- optimism, an exaggerated regard for authority, a lack of empathy with his subordinates on occasions of failure, and a marked element of self-interest. Humour was not a noticeable characteristic, though Haking was, from time to time, referred to as "jolly" and "cheery" and he wrote in May 1916 that it was the duty of all officers "to be always cheery and optimistic".[22] There is no evidence that Haking was particularly charismatic or inclined to form a close relationship with his immediate colleagues. He was a private man and his focus centred on the task in hand. It was these various and sometimes conflicting personal characteristics that Haking brought to his role as XI Corps Commander

A key factor influencing Haking's interpretation of his duties was the system of command in the BEF. The experience of XI Corps from its formation in 1915 was that the BEF command system was predomi-nantly top-down. GHQ formulated broad policy and even specific orders and these were communicated via the Army HQ to the Corps and then to the Divisions. That this was intended to be the official procedure was made clear in the War Office pamphlet SS 135 of December 1916:

> The Divisional Commander, having been allotted his task by the Corps . . . forms his own plan, which will include the task to be carried out by each body of infantry . . . As soon as this plan has been approved by the Corps Commander, it is issued immediately in the form of instructions to subordinate commanders.[23]

This study has pointed out many examples of directives that were originated at GHQ and passed through Army HQ to Corps HQ and down the line. The wording of these directives was frequently unchanged or only slightly amended as they were communicated downwards. The policy statements relating to BEF activities during the winter months of 1915–16, for example, are typical of the managerial system experienced by Haking and XI Corps. French, the then Commander in Chief, laid down the policy that was communicated to the Army Commanders. Haig, who was in command of the First Army, confirmed the details of this policy in his *Instructions for Divisional Training* and Haking in his turn, repeated the instructions of both French and Haig to his Divisional Commanders in his memorandum *Winter Campaign 1915–16*. In 1916 the "Secret Raids" operation that was so enthusiastically followed by Haking was both initiated and terminated by GHQ. Also in 1916, the series of minor operations associated with the Somme offensive, which included the Fromelles attack, was part of a total GHQ programme. The role of Haking was to ensure that these operations took place in accordance with the timetable required by GHQ and Army HQ.

In 1917, after the success at Vimy, the focus of British attention was Flanders and the First Army was required to carry out a supporting role in the sector south of Armentières. Here again, as far as XI Corps was concerned, a top-down system of command was evident. Horne, the First Army Commander, required his Corps Commanders to submit their proposals for limited offensive operations "so that the three Corps may be co-ordinated".[24] In his May XI Corps policy document Haking referred directly to Horne's instructions. In June the process was repeated and Corps Commanders were again required to put forward proposals for minor operations which were to reach Army HQ by, specifically, 12 June. In July Horne read to his Corps Commanders an instruction from GHQ to simulate, without delay, "preparations for an offensive against Lille" and Haking duly passed on these orders to his Divisions.[25] Not only were Corps operations initiated by GHQ and

Army HQ, they were often accompanied by a checking procedure. In January 1917 Haig notified his Army Commanders that their proposed schemes would be "returned with any remarks which may be necessary regarding the scope, object and execution of each operation" and that revised schemes would then have to be prepared.[26] Even in the second half of 1918 when Haking notified his battalion and company commanders that they should not wait for orders, but act on their own initiative, he was repeating the policies and words of both Haig and Birdwood. As far as XI Corps was concerned, the initiative for action invariably came from above.

In all the instances quoted, and there are many other examples in this study, Haking recognized that his role as a Corps Commander was essentially to communicate instructions from above to his Divisions. His position was that of a staging post and his main task was to ensure that the orders he received were transmitted to and carried out by his subordinates. The comments of Travers on the issue of Command and Control, as noted in the Introduction to this study, that "a vacuum opened up between Haig and his GHQ and between Haig and his Army Commanders" and that Army Commanders were "left largely alone" are only partly true.[27] The geographical position of the First Army was such that it was not involved in the major offensives and it was therefore not surprising that Haig, whose attention was elsewhere, was rarely seen. Monro, Horne and Birdwood, however, all attended Haig's conferences and they certainly received constant policy instructions and memoranda from GHQ. The preparations for Fromelles, for example, were very much under the scrutiny of GHQ in the person of Butler. The function of conferences at the various levels of command was primarily to reinforce the top-down system, but they were also an opportunity for communication and discussion. Monro and Haking were able to make their arguments to Butler before Fromelles and in August 1917 Horne discussed GHQ memoranda on offensive tactics with his Corps Commanders. Nevertheless, Haking would have had no doubt as to where XI Corps policy and instructions originated. During his brief period in command of the First Army Haking conferred directly with Haig and was keen to inform his subordinates that he had done so.

Travers' assertion that the "isolated" relationship between GHQ and Army HQ was mirrored at Army and Corps level and also at Division and Brigade levels was also largely inaccurate in respect of the First Army and XI Corps. Army and Corps Conferences were frequent and the emphasis placed on this form of communication by the Official Historian, also noted in the Introduction, was valid. Haking's contact with the Portuguese was characterized by a series of conferences and meetings as was his time in Italy. Travers' comment that Corps

Commanders did not normally visit the front clearly did not apply to Haking as shown particularly in his tours of the Portuguese trenches and his visits to the front in both Italy and France. The evidence from this study of XI Corps is that a clearer picture of the command and control system at Army, Corps and Division levels in the BEF would emerge from an examination of these units on an individual basis rather than from a general overview.

The same point can be made in relation to Andy Simpson's thesis that the Corps developed from being essentially an administrative function – a post-box – to become by 1917 a key part of the operational and planning process. The increased importance of the Corps resulting from its control of artillery through the GOCRA together with the addition of an RFC Wing had coincided with the appointment of Haking as a Corps Commander in August 1915. Through 1916 and 1917 Haking could be seen exercising control over both the artillery and the aircraft in his Corps and he was also involved heavily in the planning process. Even so, transmitting instructions from GHQ and Army HQ to his Divisions was central to Haking's role in XI Corps and to that extent the Corps retained its function as a post-box.

The experience of Haking and XI Corps indicates that the character of the individual Corps Commander and his particular relationships with his superiors were important factors in the nature of the command system in the BEF. Haking's high regard for authority, especially when Haig and GHQ were involved; his ease with paperwork and detail; and his devotion to the immediate task, made it possible for him to accept his largely administrative role in XI Corps without question – it was the result of both his training and his natural inclination. It is revealing that when Haking addressed his Staff in Italy in January 1918 he began by saying:

> It is . . . our first duty to make certain that our own Staff is working in perfect harmony according to the policy laid down by me, which *of course*[28] I receive from the Commander-in-Chief, and that further we must at all times "play up" to the higher Staff.[29]

This sentence provides a clear indication of how Haking saw his role as XI Corps Commander.

Haking had six direct superiors during his time as a Corps Commander. In France XI Corps was part of Haig's First Army from its formation in August 1915 and, when Haig was appointed Commander in Chief in December 1915, he was succeeded for a short period by Rawlinson. Although Rawlinson was Haig's preferred successor Kitchener refused to confirm the appointment and Monro replaced Rawlinson as First Army Commander in February 1916. When Monro departed for India in August 1916 Haking himself held temporary command of the First Army – a situation unacceptable to the War Office and Horne was therefore appointed at the end of September. From December 1917, XI Corps was in Italy and there Haking reported to the French General Duchesne. Haking returned to Horne's First Army in France in March 1918. In July 1918 Haking and XI Corps transferred to the reconstituted Fifth Army under the command of Birdwood and remained there for the rest of the war.

Haking's complicated relationship with Haig has already been discussed. His relationship with his other five superior officers was far more shadowy. Rawlinson was the Commandant of the Staff College when Haking was teaching there and it was Rawlinson who had supported Haking's promotion to Colonel with a glowing testimonial. The two men shared the same view about the need for aggression and the importance of trench raids and it is likely that Haking regretted Rawlinson's quick departure from the First Army.

The relationship between Haking and Monro was businesslike and cordial. There were some disagreements such as in May 1916 when Haking disputed Monro's instruction to construct dummy trenches, but when Monro insisted that his order should be carried out, Haking immediately conformed. Monro praised Haking on a number of occasions for his dedication to trench aggression and in August 1916 recommended him as his successor to command the First Army.[30] A similar relationship existed between Haking and both Duchesne and Birdwood. Haking was quite content to accept their authority and his natural high regard for his superiors avoided any problems and resulted in reasonable rapport.

Haking's relationship with Horne was quite different. Both men were Haig protégés and both were considered, at least by Haig, as possible successors to Monro. They were, within months, the same age and, while Haking was an infantryman and had attended Sandhurst and the Staff College, Horne had joined the Artillery and attended Woolwich. Until Horne's elevation to the First Army, they had matched one another in terms of promotion. Both were made Major Generals towards the end of 1914 "for Distinguished Service in the Field" and in August 1915 Haig had recommended them both as future Corps and Army Commanders. Horne was far from pleased when Haking was the first of the two to receive the KCB and complained to his wife that: "We do not get what we deserve" – a comment accompanied by several scurrilous remarks about Haking. There was therefore a strong element of rivalry in their relationship and, added to this, Horne made it clear, particularly in his letters home, that he had a low personal opinion of

Haking. To Horne, Haking was dull and unimaginative and a writer "of a very specious report".[31] During their time together in the First Army the relationship between the two men was, to say the least, cool. Despite this, Horne, noted for replacing incompetent commanders, made no effort to remove Haking. [32]

Haking had extremely varied relationships with his subordinates. Mention has already been made of Haking's unfortunate lack of empathy with his troops on occasions of failure such as Loos and Fromelles. This trait was also evident following the successful German raids on the positions of the 1st Royal Irish Rifles in August 1916. It could be argued that criticism of the Irish Rifles was justified but, as at Loos and Fromelles, Haking was just too ready to assign responsibility for failure to his subordinates. There was no sign on those occasions that Haking was prepared to take his share of any criticism or give moral support to his troops. On the other hand, Haking interceded successfully in March 1917 on behalf of his troops who were spread so thinly along the XI Corps front that they were only able to have limited rest periods. Horne responded personally to Haking and increased the number of divisions from two to three. In Italy Haking went to some lengths to ensure the welfare of his British and French soldiers by providing food, water, fuel and bathing facilities.

Haking also had mixed relationships with his officers. He had little time for Montagu-Stuart-Wortley and Game, both of the 46th Division, and they had little time for him. His dealings with some of the Portuguese officers, particularly General Machado and others of the Portuguese 1st Division, were less than cordial. Again, however, there were examples of positive relationships with, for example, Ker and his staff of the British Mission to the Portuguese and indeed with the Portuguese Commander, Tamagnini. The 35th Division was part of XI Corps during the first half of 1917 and their GOC, Pinney, received particular consideration from Haking even to the extent of playing "spillikin billiards" together.[33] There is little information available to give an indication of Haking's relationship with his senior Staff Officers – Generals H. M. de Montgomery, H. W. Studd, J. Brind, W. H. Anderson, and C. A. Ker. What there is, for example Haking's discussions with his new Staff in Italy, suggests that they worked together effectively and in reasonable harmony.

It has been noted in previous chapters that Haking's efforts to implement the orders received from his superiors faced a major obstacle – the ever-changing composition of his Corps as divisions came and went. XI Corps was made up of fourteen different divisions in 1916 and ten during the eleven months of 1917 when the Corps was in France. During those two years the length of stay of a division in XI Corps varied between two and five months. It is not surprising, therefore, that Haking's efforts to motivate his divisional commanders and create a Corps loyalty were severely constrained.

Haking dealt with the difficult task of leading his Corps in a number of ways. Despite the frequent changes in the composition of his command Haking took every opportunity to develop a sense of Corps identity. He published numerous Corps policy statements and memoranda, held frequent Corps conferences, visited his Divisional commanders and carried out troop inspections. Haking was particularly concerned to promote his Corps as having a reputation for aggressive action. His *Winter Campaign* document of November 1915 began: "The Corps has been distinguished since its formation for the constant offensive action it has been called upon to carry out",[34] and in March 1916 Haking spoke of "the offensive spirit that we have created and nourished during the last few months of the Corps".[35] In August 1917 he wrote that: "Every man should . . . understand that his Brigade, Division or Corps is the one that is really going to win the battle."[36] He fostered aggression among his divisions by dire warnings of the consequences of inaction – "if we do not raid the Germans, they will raid us";[37] by organizing a trench raids competition; by stressing the necessity to avoid "quiet times" in the trenches;[38] by comparing the Corps offensive operations with the "supine attitude" adopted by the enemy;[39] and by praising "the fine offensive spirit apparent in all units".[40] Haking supported these efforts to improve morale and encourage aggression by the frequent use of key words and phrases common across the BEF. "Offensive spirit", "moral superiority", "harassing", and "wearing out" the enemy, were all phrases constantly employed by Haking in his efforts to develop a unity of purpose within XI Corps.

Exhortation was a significant and necessary feature of Haking's style of command. In order to implement the instructions from GHQ and Army HQ, the main part of his job, he relied heavily on his personal efforts to persuade, cajole and motivate his subordinates. Haking's comments to Horne in March 1917 provide a rare insight into his perception of his role:

My Divisional Commanders bring their troubles to me, and I can encourage and cheer them and their troops to exceptional exertions, so long as I can tell them that we are helping in a great battle . . . If, however, I am unable to tell them this, or if I cannot produce sufficient arguments to carry much conviction the situation is not satisfactory.[41]

The continual attempts to foster an aggressive policy within XI Corps were appreciated by both GHQ and Army HQ and Haking would have been particularly encouraged by the note from GHQ in February 1916 commending the morale of XI Corps and "Gen. R. Haking's . . . policy of cumulative aggression."[42] However, there is evidence to suggest that Haking's subordinates in the divisions were less enthusiastic about the relentless pressure to take part in trench raids and other similar operations. An extreme, negative view of raids came from Private W. A. Tucker who served with the XI Corps Cyclists near Bethune: "raids were examples of murderous lunacy devised by short-moustached, over-medalled morons, who had never been nearer the trenches than distant Amiens and had assaulted nothing harder than French tarts."[43]

Trench raids and other minor attacks along the XI Corps front became known as Haking's "little shows". Major Christie-Miller, a Regimental officer in the 61st Division, noted in his diary that when the 2/5th Glosters were selected to carry out a raid in June 1916: "They had only done one tour and had hardly been in front of the parapet. They certainly had not that confidence in themselves and that feeling of 'ownership' of no-man's land, which is most necessary to embark on a raid with full assurance." Christie-Miller also noted that at the end of June: "The 11th and 12th Royal Sussex had been sent over in one of Haking's 'little shows' of which he was so proud."[44] Both raids resulted in heavy casualties and no territorial gain.

The 19th Division, which was with XI Corps from November 1915 until April 1916 showed little enthusiasm for "shows" and five of the twelve battalions in the Division did not plan or initiate a trench raid during that period. Just over 100 troops had taken part in the raids that were carried out and they collectively spent under one hour in the enemy's trenches.[45] It may well have been this lack of the offensive spirit that prompted Haking's comment to Monro that:

> The 19th Division, which by this time ought to be in first class condition, has not responded to treatment in the manner in which I expected. The whole truth is that it got into bad ways when it first came out and it has been extremely difficult to get it out of them.[46]

The 19th Division's unwillingness to take part in outright aggression was reflected in the statistics relating to trench raiding in both the First Army and XI Corps. The average frequency of trench raids over the whole of the First Army front during 1916–17 was only 1.5 raids per division per month. In the same period XI Corps carried out an average of 2.0 raids per division per month with I Corps having a frequency of

1.8. Since a division was made up of twelve battalions this means that, on average, a battalion in XI Corps performed a trench raid once every six months and that average included the flurry of raids around the time of the Somme offensive. Despite Haking's harangues and exhortations to encourage an offensive spirit these frequencies cannot be said to demonstrate a high commitment to the offensive on behalf of his troops. On this basis, Ashworth's description of the "live and let live" system seems to be relevant in the sectors covered by XI Corps. It can only be inferred that without Haking's constant calls for aggression, a major feature of his role as a Corps Commander, the frequency of raids would have been even lower.

There is a link between Haking's determination to develop an offensive spirit in his Corps and the role he acquired, officially or otherwise, as a trainer of "green" troops. His experience and inclination fitted him for this task. In addition, the front covered by XI Corps was unsuitable for large-scale operations by either side for a considerable period of the year. The combination of these two factors made the line Armentières-Givenchy highly suitable as a "nursery" for new troops. Certainly, Haking had in 1916 a far higher proportion of inexperienced divisions under his command than any other Corps in the First Army and when the Portuguese troops arrived in France in February 1917 they were immediately assigned to XI Corps. It was Haking's view that "green" soldiers would become battle-hardened and effective in a major operation only if they had already taken part in a series of minor attacks. Major Millward of the 35th Division noted that Haking "considered no Division a fighting unit in this present day warfare until they have accomplished a successful raid".[47] The corollary of this approach was that inexperienced divisions suffered casualties as part of the learning process. Haking's brutal comments following the heavy losses of the Royal Sussex battalions at the Boars Head and of the 61st Division and the Australian 5th Division at Fromelles should be read in that context. In both cases Haking stated that the combat experience, despite the high casualty figures, would improve the fighting qualities of the Divisions concerned. This was a view that he repeated when he wrote to Horne in June 1917: "This division [the 66th] has not been long in France and it would greatly improve its fighting value if it can successfully carry out the task I have given it."[48] That Haking was considered to be successful in carrying out his training role was acknowledged by Haig in his diary note of 23 June 1916: "Haking has done well in training new divisions and putting spirit into them."[49]

A further aspect of Haking's role as a trainer was his support of Schools. His commitment to formal learning was evident during his time at Staff College and in his books on *Staff Rides* and *Company*

Training. At the 1908 Senior Staff Officers' Conference Haking had advanced the then novel idea of "War Schools" specializing in tactics and administration for Regimental officers.[50] During the war, Army and Corps Schools were established in both France and Italy. Haking championed these Schools and encouraged his subordinates to attend. In Italy, Schools were set up for training in musketry, signalling, artillery and bayonet fighting and these were supported by Haking through visits and inspections. In France, during August 1918, XI Corps officers took part in a "Training for Open Warfare" programme and Haking, his Divisional Commanders and their Staffs attended a lecture by General Maxse, the Inspector of Training. Haking was particularly interested in sniping and, in 1916, encouraged Major Hesketh-Prichard to establish a School of Sniping, Observation and Scouting in France. As Hesketh-Prichard later wrote: "The chief reason, I think, for the success of the School was the great personal interest taken in it by the Corps Commander."[51] Haking, supported by Plumer and Cavan, was successful in developing a similar Sniping School in Italy.

Closely related to Haking's interest in training was a concern, which he shared with Monro, to promote the best men available. In March 1916 he instructed his Divisional Commanders to compile a list of young officers, NCOs and private soldiers who might be considered for promotion. The officers selected for promotion "should never be taken according to their rank but always according to their merit, without for a moment taking into consideration the feelings of any other officer who may be passed over." Haking added: "Rapid promotion is a great stimulant to efficiency and all vacancies which occur in future must be filled on the lines indicated above."[52] Of equal concern to Haking was the removal of ineffective officers. In April 1916 he considered that several of the senior officers in the 39th Division were inadequate and wrote to Monro: "I am recommending the immediate removal of all three Infantry Brigadiers. I think with young, active men in their places that the brigades will be reliable."[53]

The concept of a BEF "learning curve" was discussed in the Introduction. Given Haking's Staff College background and his general interest in training, it might be expected that the "learning curve" would show itself with great clarity in the activities of XI Corps. However, as far as XI Corps was concerned, it is difficult to see any particular "curve" or any point from which tactical and technological developments suddenly took on a character of continued progression leading to the successes of 1918. There was no date from which, as Paddy Griffith put it, a "changing of gear" was apparent.[54] In that sense, 1 July 1916 and the experience of the Somme, seen by proponents of the "learning curve" as the beginnings of the process, were not relevant to Haking and XI Corps. The absence of any marked movement by XI Corps towards the "full stature"[55] of the BEF during the Hundred Days is not surprising. In both 1916 and 1917 the role of XI Corps was essentially to hold the line and carry out minor operations in support of major offensives elsewhere. There was little scope to introduce any significant tactical initiative. In May 1917 Haking put forward the idea of holding outposts in parts of the enemy line, but this was hardly a move along a "learning curve".

What is noticeable, however, is a continuity of military thinking that was adapted to take into account technological developments. Long before 1916 Haking had shown an awareness of the importance of all-arms co-ordination. In a lecture delivered in January 1905 he advocated for garrison troops what amounted to all-arms training: "Four thousand modern rifles, eighteen quick-firing guns and six hundred mounted riflemen might easily be mistaken for a much larger force."[56] At the Conference of General Staff Officers in 1911 Haking stressed the need for "artillery and infantry to work together making the best of accurate firing and use of ground by infantry".[57] The 1914 *Field Service Regulations* stated (in bold type) that: "The full power of an army can be exerted only when all its parts act in close combination."[58] When French outlined his policy for the winter months of 1915–16 he emphasized the importance of local attacks using smoke, gas, mining, bombing from the air and the co-ordination of artillery and infantry including the "development of telephonic communication".[59] Haking repeated this policy in his XI Corps 1915–16 *Winter Campaign* document. At Fromelles, Haking employed all the arms available to him – artillery, aircraft and engineers as well as infantry. The plan for the March 1918 attack on the Piave by 15 Brigade of XI Corps was a model of a combined arms operation.

As artillery techniques gradually improved during the war – the creeping barrage, counter-battery work, flash spotting, sound ranging, and the 106-model fuse – they were automatically incorporated into operating practice. Hence, a First Army report referring to artillery operations in autumn 1915 – a year before the Somme experience – discussed counter-battery work, the importance of air observation and the role of the Topographical Section in "intersecting the exact position of batteries, observing stations, aiming points and conspicuous points in the enemy's line."[60] The importance of the creeping barrage with the infantry "rushing forward to the assault under the protection of walls of fire" was publicized throughout the BEF in June 1915.[61]

The development of the machine gun took place largely before the war. The Vickers gun was already in use in 1914 and the Lewis gun, prototypes of which were available in 1913, was issued to battalions in late–1915. A list of General Staff publications, issued in December 1915, included twenty-four development reports on Military Engineering and Trench Warfare, eighteen on Artillery, ten on Tactics, seven on Machine Guns and six on Aeronautics.[62] Learning was taking place all the time. A First Army document of November 1915 was headed "Some Artillery Lessons to be Learnt".[63] Nick Lloyd has written that the battle of Loos in the autumn of 1915 "undoubtedly had a considerable effect on British operational methods and marked an important milestone in the BEF's "learning curve".[64] It is difficult, therefore, to identify a particular period, such as July 1916, as the start of a "learning curve". The process was more of a continuum which extended back even before the war began.

Moreover, as Travers has pointed out, the successes of the BEF during the Hundred Days were much to do with the reduced circumstances of the enemy. In the spring offensives of 1918 the Germans had lost a million of their best troops. In particular, they had abandoned the heavily fortified frontline that had served them so well over the previous three years and, by August 1918, were holding more hastily contrived trenches along a significantly increased front. It was mainly for these reasons, not because of a "learning curve", that the task of Haking and XI Corps was quite different and significantly easier at la Becque than it had been at Fromelles.

Haking was open-minded, even eager, in accepting new developments. In April 1916 Haking pressed Monro for more trench mortars: "and I have already asked you to help me by getting 50 of the new Bellairs mortars, which, I understand, . . . can be constructed very rapidly".[65] Gas and mining operations were used extensively on the XI Corps front in 1916 and 1917. When, in March 1917, Haking was planning minor operations to support the Vimy attack, he asked Horne for the use of a tank: "the news of its arrival might be spread to the enemy and we could also test it in this muddy ground with a view to future operations".[66] In June 1917 Haking went out of his way to take General Tamagnini of the Portuguese Corps to a tank display. Haking made extensive use of aircraft as the RFC increased in size and technical ability. They were used in July 1916 at Fromelles and in March 1918, on the Piave, the RFC were given the important task of "driving back the enemy's fighter planes."[67] Even the organizational change that established the post of GOCRA at Corps level was associated with the improved availability of artillery pieces. Robertson noted the connection between the new appointment and "the increase in the number of heavy guns and howitzers with the Army and in the Field" in his memorandum of 23 October 1915.[68] The BEF took advantage of improvements in supplies and in technology as they became available.

As trench raiding techniques evolved XI Corps used trench models and pre-raid training sessions by way of preparation – a development that, in June 1916, earned Haking praise from Monro. A significant disagreement between Haking and his superiors on a matter of tactics came in January 1916 when Haking disputed the new policy of defence in depth. On that occasion, Haking quickly conformed with Monro's instructions, but clearly remained unconvinced of the merits of that policy. Haking insisted on manning the front line heavily at Givenchy in April 1918 and, as events showed, it was as well that he did. The GHQ policy of having a three-tier defence system was poorly understood and poorly applied and Haking was an example of those generals who would "have no truck" with it.

Overall, it is difficult to link Haking's activities in France or in Italy with any "learning curve" dating from mid-1916 and culminating in the autumn of 1918. Haking was open to new technical developments as they became available, but there is little sign of any tactical revolution dating from 1916 in XI Corps operations. Haking's September 1915 orders to the officers of 2 Guards Brigade at Loos to "always push on boldly whenever an opportunity offered" [69] echoed those of Haig: "I expect the greatest initiative from subordinate leaders. There must be no hesitating for orders to attack."[70] Both sets of instructions have a marked similarity to the XI Corps policy of August 1918 which stated that advances should take place "with the greatest vigour" and that "Battalion and Company Commanders . . . will not wait for orders but will act on their own initiative."[71] All these commands assumed an element of mobile warfare. In 1915 the assumption was invalid and the attack failed. In 1918 "initiative" and "vigour" resulted in success. The difference between the two occasions was the prevailing battle circumstances, not the tactical intention. As far as Haking and XI Corps were concerned, the years 1915–1918 saw an evolutionary progress along a continuum which had its origins well before the war and which incorporated the opportunities presented by British technical developments and German weaknesses.

The main aim of this study has been to analyze and assess Haking as a Corps Commander. The picture that emerges from the previous chapters is far from clear-cut. Haking's personal characteristics and the main factors that determined his attitudes and actions are a mixture of positive and negative features which showed themselves as strengths and weaknesses during his thirty-eight months as XI Corps Commander. His performance at Loos was poor and can only be excused partially by his inexperience as a Corps Commander and the bizarre circumstances surrounding the role of XI Corps as GHQ Reserves. Caught between

French and Haig he made no effort to resolve the command issue and his blatant support of Haig may have contained an element of candid professional judgement, but it was also a prime example of self-interest. His lack of personal identity with his troops was reprehensible.

Haking can take far more credit from his actions during the period of trench warfare. He accepted the instructions from his superiors and did his utmost to ensure that they were implemented. He endeavoured to create a Corps identity and was tireless in fostering an aggressive spirit among his divisions. His constant promotion of trench raids and other minor enterprises may have been unappreciated by many of his subordinates and they often resulted in significant casualty lists. Nevertheless, they served the necessary purpose of making troops "battle-hardened" and better fitted to carry out future actions. The British 61st Division and the Australian 5th Division may have been severely mauled at Fromelles, but they both acquitted themselves well in the later stages of the war.[72] As General Brudenell White wrote to Bean when the Australian Official History was being compiled: "War is not a soft hand business, nor can killing be avoided. If troops are kept long inactive opposite an enemy the risk of deterioration of moral[e] is great . . . I think in the majority of cases raids did more harm to the enemy than to us."[73] Bean noted on White's letter: "As exercises – A I. As stunts – wooden-headed." Some of Haking's raids may have been considered as stunts, but Haking himself would have regarded them as necessary exercises in aggression. Despite his commitment to the offensive, Haking's record as regards the frequency of trench raids and casualties was not significantly different from that of other Corps Commanders in the First Army.

Haking's largest attack was Fromelles and it was a tactical disaster. The inexperienced artillery had failed to destroy the German strongpoints, particularly the Sugar Loaf, and the inexperienced assault troops had little chance of success. Before the attack Haking had shown misplaced over-optimism. After it, as at Loos, he displayed his regrettable tendency to make inappropriate derogatory remarks about his troops. The main flaw in the plan was that the attack took place not only at the junction of two divisions, but at the junction of two Armies and immediately in front of the Sugar Loaf. Haking must share the responsibility for selecting that point of attack with both Monro and Plumer. Because of the strong Bavarian defensive system the attack never had more than a slim chance of success. Whatever chance it did have, however, was severely compromised by the dithering at GHQ and Army levels which reduced the preparation time, and by the last minute replacement of seasoned I ANZAC troops by the inexperienced 5th Division of II ANZAC. These two factors were disastrous both for the attacking troops and for Haking as the commander. The operation could have been called off and it should have been. That decision, however, rested with Monro, not with Haking. The size of the casualty list and the lack of success have provoked extensive critical comment, particularly from Australia, but what has rarely been taken into account is the evidence that suggests that Fromelles achieved its strategic objective. German troops opposite the XI Corps front were not moved down to the Somme for at least five weeks following the 19 July action – a significant period in relation to the Pozières attack on the Somme.

Haking's role as a trainer of "green" British divisions was carried out conscientiously and was acknowledged as a useful contribution to the development of the BEF. His efforts to bring the Portuguese troops to an acceptable standard, however, proved fruitless. The circumstances of political protocol and poor Portuguese command made the task hopeless. Haking nevertheless did all that he could and his support of the British Military Mission and his work with Tamagnini were appreciated and brought him credit. Also to Haking's credit was the part he played, anticipating the collapse of the Portuguese in April 1918, in establishing a strong support line and this was especially true at Givenchy.

During 1918 Haking carried out his duties with his customary commitment and energy. The twelve weeks that XI Corps were in Italy were undramatic, but they were constructive and Haking played his part in stabilizing the front, in training the Italians and in preparing the attack across the Piave. His contribution was valued to the extent that he was considered for the post of Commander in Chief in Italy. In France, while XI Corps was pushed back by the Germans in April 1918, the line did not break and the southern sector, around Givenchy, remained in place. The la Becque attack was well planned and executed and formed the base for the continued advance of XI Corps during the Hundred Days. Haking never did take part in the "glorious battle" that was clearly his ambition. XI Corps was always in a support role – for the Somme, for Arras, for Vimy, for Passchendaele. Even during the Hundred Days, the role of XI Corps, although positive, was relatively low-key. Despite this disappointment Haking soldiered on intent on doing his duty as he saw it.

The conclusion from the above discussion is that Haking did posses serious weaknesses and he made mistakes, but a balance sheet of his career as a Corps Commander would show that, overall, Haking made a worthwhile contribution to the British conduct of the war. The poor reputation that he has acquired, especially in Australia, has been the result of an uncontested barrage of negative criticism focused on

Haking's frailties and mistakes. This criticism has often been based on accepted wisdom rather than on objective assessment and positive aspects have been conveniently ignored. Haking's character may have been flawed and he was certainly a "thruster", but, given the circumstances of the war and the prevailing military thinking of the time, the epithets "butcher", "bungler" and "donkey" are inappropriate.

* * * *

It is not in the scope of this study to examine Haking's career after the war. It is relevant, however, to point out that he was held in sufficiently high esteem to be appointed to a series of important posts carrying out what Edmonds described as "tasks of great delicacy".[74] Haking became Chief of the British Armistice Commission (November 1918-August 1919); Head of the Mission to Russia and the Baltic (August 1919-January 1920); GOC the Plebiscite Area of East Prussia and Danzig (January 1920-November 1920); High Commissioner at the League of Nations (December 1920-January 1923); and GOC the British Army in Egypt (March 1923-1927). From 1924 until 1944 Haking was the Colonel of the Hampshire Regiment. He was promoted to full General in May 1925 and retired in 1927. He was Mentioned in Despatches on ten occasions.

It was the custom during the post-war period for newly-commissioned officers to meet the King. In 1931 Lieutenant L.C.R. Balding was one such officer and he recorded the occasion: "We were escorted by the Colonel-in-Chief of the Hampshire Regiment, Gen Sir Richard Haking, resplendent in scarlet and covered with orders and medals, the sign of a country's gratitude for his services in high command in the Great War."[75] The "gratitude" noted by Balding has generally been ignored by historians. It is now time to re-appraise Haking's contribution as a Corps Commander giving due credit where it is deserved – something that has rarely happened in the past.

Notes
1. Royal Military Academy, Sandhurst, *Gentlemen Cadet Registers*.
2. *DNB*.
3. Haking's Personal Papers, MOD, Glasgow.
4. TNA, WO 95/1228, Undated text of lecture probably early May 1915.
5. TNA, WO95/882, SS 1230.
6. TNA, WO 95/3066, SS 1206, 10 July 1916.
7. TNA, WO 95/885, 17 February 1916.
8. TNA, WO 95/885, RHS 1115/4.,12 June 1916.
9. Dunn, *The War the Infantry Knew*, p. 185.
10. TNA, WO 95/166, Conference Report, 9 September 1916.
11. TNA, WO 95/168, SS 1226/16, 18 March 1917.

12. National Army Museum, Millward Papers, 6510–143–5, Vols. III & IV, 22 June 1916.
13. Fielding, *War Letters to a Wife*, p.19.
14. IWM, 97/10/1, Lowther Papers, January 1915.
15. TNA, WO 95/164, June 1916.
16. TNA, WO 95/882, 21 September 1917.
17. TNA, WO 95/885. At a Conference held 29.5.16.
18. Sheffield and Bourne, *Haig Diaries and Letters*, p.398.
19. Blake, ed., *Private Papers of Douglas Haig,* p.343.
20. Lecture given at the Staff College during a Senior Staff Officers' Course, January 1905.
21. TNA, WO 95/162, First Army Conference, 15 August 1916.
22. TNA, WO 95/885.
23. SS 135, issued by the General Staff, December 1916, pp.6–7.
24. TNA, WO 95/170, GS 561.
25. TNA, WO 95/172, 10 July 1917.
26. TNA, WO 95/168 OAD 258, 2 January 1917.
27. Travers, "A Particular Style of Command: Haig and GHQ 1916–1918", p 368.
28. Author's italics.
29. TNA, WO 95/4211, 9 January 1918.
30. However, in the only biography of Monro there is no mention of Haking. See Gen Sir George Barrow, *The Life of General Sir Charles Monro*.
31. IWM, Letters of Gen Lord Horne to his wife, 5 February 1917.
32. See Robbins, "Henry Horne", in Beckett and Corvi, eds., *Haig's Generals*, pp.97–221.
33. Haking seems to have had some interest, if little skill, in billiards. Major Millward of 105 Brigade, records that on 25 February 1916, he and Haking "had a very pleasant dinner and played billiards of sorts." National Army Museum, Millward Papers, 6510–143–5, Vols. III and IV.
34. TNA, WO 95/160, RHS./298, 4 November 1915.
35. TNA, WO 95/881, 19 March 1916.
36. TNA, WO 95/173, S.G. 1236, 8 August 1917.
37. TNA, WO 95/168 RHS 837/16, 12 January 1917.
38. TNA, WO 95/160 RHS/298, 4 November 1915.
39. TNA, WO 95/881 RHS 726, 13 January 1916.
40. TNA, WO 95/160, RHS 298, 4 November.19 15.
41. TNA, WO 95/168, SS 1226/16, 18 March 1917.
42. TNA, WO 95/881, 13 Feb 1916.
43. IWM, 67/96/1, Papers of Pte W. A. Tucker, Undated.
44. Christie-Miller, *Second Bucks Battalion 1914–18: An Unofficial Record*, II, p.168.
45. James Roberts, "Making the Butterflies Kill", *Stand To!* 68, 2003, pp.38–44.
46. TNA, WO 95/161, RHS 856, 23 February 1916.
47. Millward Papers, National Army Museum, 6510–143–5, Vols. III and IV.
48. TNA, WO 95/171, SS 1230/4, 6 June 1917.
49. TNA, WO 256/11, 23 June 1917.

50. TNA, WO 279/18, p.37.
51. Maj. H. Hesketh-Prichard, *Sniping in France*, p.67.
52. TNA, WO 95/162, 25 March 1916.
53. Ibid., 2 April 1916.
54. Paddy Griffith, *Battle Tactics of the Western Front*, p.17.
55. Ibid., p.200.
56. Lecture delivered at the Staff College by Lt Col R. C. B. Haking during the Senior Staff Officers' Course, January 1905, p.34.
57. TNA, WO95/42, Report of Conference of General Staff Officers at the Staff College, 9–12 January 1911, p.69.
58. IWM, *Field Service Regulations*, Pt I. 1909 (1914 Reprint).
59. TNA, WO 95/159, OAM 97, 28 October 1915.
60. TNA, WO 95/160, 7 November 1915.
61. IWM, SS 24, *Object and Conditions of Combined Offensive Action* (Translated from French).
62. IWM, CDS 58, December 1915.
63. TNA, WO 95/160, 7 November 1915.
64. Nick Lloyd, *Loos 1915*, p.219.
65. TNA, WO 95/162, G.S. 331, 2 April 1916.
66. TNA, WO 95/168, SS 1226/14, 17 March 1917.
67. TNA, WO 95/4211, SS 11/45, 2 March 1918.
68. TNA, WO 95/757, OB/446, 23 October 1915.
69. TNA, WO 95/1220, 15 September 1915.
70. TNA, WO 95/158, First Army Conference, 6 September 1915.
71. TNA, WO 95/884, 3 August 1918.
72. For example, the 61st Division at St Julien and the 5th Division at Polygon Wood, both in 1918.
73. AWM, Bean Papers, 3 DRL 7953/4 Pt. 2, White to Bean, 11 February 1927.
74. AWM, 3 DRL 7953/34, Pt. I, Edmonds to Bean, 3 November 1927.
75. IWM, 96/7/1, Capt. L. C. R. Balding, Papers, headed "One of Seven".

Richard Cyril Byrne Haking

Date	Rank	Event	Notes	Ref.
24 Jan 1862		Born at 24 Lister Rd, King Cross, Halifax.	No Birth Certificate.	WO95/515
20 April 1862		Baptized at St Paul's Church, King Cross, Halifax, by his Father who was a curate at that Church.	Family name HACKING. Father also Richard. Mother's name Mary Elizabeth. Two daughters – Mary and Ethel.	Parish Records WDP 72/1
Sept/Nov 1862		Family move to Rodbourne Cheney in Wilts, where father installed as Vicar	Family name changed to HAKING.	Crockford's Directory 1870.
1865		A third daughter, Hilda, born.		
1873		Family moves to Easton Grey, Malmesbury, Wilts, where Father becomes the Rector.		Crockford's Directory 1880
1880		R.C.B. Haking at Sandhurst.		WO95/516
22 Jan 1881	2/Lt, 67th Foot			Personal Papers at MOD Glasgow.
22 Jan– 9 May 1881		Home Service		WO95/516
1 July 1881	Lt, the Hampshire Regt.			Personal Papers, Glasgow
1882		Father becomes Rector of Congham, Norfolk.		Crockford's Directory 1890
10 May 1881– 15 Nov 1885	Lt	Service in India.		WO95/516
16 Nov 1885– 13 Nov 1887		Burmese Expedition	MiD 22 June 1886	London Gazette WO95/516
14 Apr 1887– 7 Feb 1888		India		WO95/516

Date	Rank	Event	Notes	Ref.
31 Jul 1886–11 Jun 1891		Adjutant 2nd Bn Hampshires		WO95/516
April 1888	Captain			Glasgow
8 Feb 1888–15 Sep 1896		Home service with Regt, Chatham and Ireland		WO95/516
28 Sep 1891		Marries Rachel Violette Burford-Hancock	Rachel daughter of Sir Henry Burford-Hancock.	WO95/516
1894		Father dies in Norfolk		BMD search, Swaffam.
1896–98		Attends Staff College		WO95/516
24 Mar 1899	Major			Glasgow
1 Mar 1898–15 Sep 1899	DAAG	Cork District		
16 Sep 1899–15 Jan 1901	DAAG	South Africa	Queen's Medal and 3 Clasps. MiD	Glasgow
16 Jan 1901	Lt Col (Br)			Glasgow
Jan 1901–Feb 1904		Professor at Staff College		Army List 1914
26 Sep 1903	Lt Col			
3 Feb 1904–15 Jan 1906		DAAG Staff College		Army List 1914
19 June 1905	Col (Br)			
20 Feb 1906–23 Jun 1908	Col	AAG 4 Div. GSO I, 4 Div. GSO I, 3 Div.		
24 Jun 1908–22 Sep 1911	Brig Gen (Temp.)	GSO I, Southern Command		Army List 1914
23 Sep 1911–4 Aug 1914	Brig Gen	GOC 5 Brigade at Aldershot.		
5 Aug 1914–20 Dec 1914		With 5 Brigade in BEF.	MiD 19 Oct14	
21 Dec 1914–3 Sep 1915	Maj Gen	GOC 1st Div BEF	MiD 16 Feb15	
4 Sep 1915–6 Aug 1916	Lt Gen (T)	GOC XI Corps	MiD 1 Jan16	
7 Aug 1916–29 Sep 1916		Temporarily GOC First Army		

Date	Rank	Event	Notes	Ref.
30 Sep 1916– 14 Nov 1918		GOC XI Corps	Nov 1917-Mar 1918	
			MiD	
			4 Jan17	
			11 Dec 17	
			30 May 18	
15 Nov 1918– 21 Aug 1919	Lt Gen	Chief of British Armistice Commission	MiD	
			20 Dec 18	
			5 May 19	
22 Aug 1919– 23 Jan 1920		Head of Mission Russia and Baltic		
24 Jan 1920– 29 Nov 1920		GOC Plebiscite Area East Prussia and Danzig		
17 Dec 1920– 23 Jan 1923		League of Nations High Commissioner – Danzig		
16 Mar 1923–1927		GOC Army in Egypt		
30 June 1924 –1944		Col of the Hampshire Regiment		
25 May 1925	General			
1927		Retires to Mill Cottage, Bulford, Wilts.		
1939		Wife Rachel dies.		
9 Jun 1945		Gen RCB Haking dies at Bulford.	Haking's sisters had pre-deceased him. All were unmarried. The beneficiary of his will was his niece, Rachel Burford-Ford.	

Honours

1910   Companion of the Order of the Bath (CB).
1916   Order of St Vladimir IV Class with Swords. Russia
        Knight Commander Order of the Bath (KCB).
1917   *Croix de Commandeur*. Legion of Honour. France.
1918   Grand Officer. Order of the Crown. Italy.
        Knight Commander of the Order of St Michael and St George.
        2nd Class (KCMG).
        Order of Avis. 1st Class. Portugal.
        Croix de Guerre. France.
1921   Commander of the Order of St Maurice and St Lazarus. Italy.
        Knight Grand Cross of the Order of the British Empire. (GBE).
1942   Deputy Lieutenant, Wiltshire. (DL).

A Common BEF Vocabulary

The Offensive Spirit

"Foster and enhance the offensive spirit of our own troops".
French, 26 Oct 15 WO95/159

"Special attention should be paid . . . to the development of the offensive spirit."
Haig, 15 Nov 15 WO95/160

". . . all portions of the front must be imbued with the offensive spirit."
Haig, 15 Nov 15 WO95/160

". . . every effort should be made to foster this [offensive] spirit."
Haking, 4 Nov 15 WO95/881

"You must use every endeavour to inculcate the offensive spirit in all subordinates."
Haking, 13 Feb 16 WO95/881

". . . maintain the offensive spirit we have created . . . in the Corps."
Haking, 19 Mar 16 WO95/881

"I go about a lot among the Divisions and the Brigades, and I find everywhere a fine offensive spirit and a desire to attack."
Haking, 18 Sep 16 WO95/166

"Minor enterprises encourage the offensive spirit."
Monro, 29 Feb 15

"Special attention should be paid to . . . the development of the offensive spirit."
Butler, 10 Nov 15 WO95/160

". . . to obtain complete control of No man's land . . . is of special importance . . . for cultivating an offensive spirit."
                    SS135, Training and Employment of Divisions. *Jan 1918*

"Keep up your energy and that of your men, and maintain the offensive spirit most carefully."
                    IWM, SS145. Duties of an Officer *(undated)*

"Special attention should be paid to . . . the execution of an attack and the development of the offensive spirit."
                    WO95/160, Syllabus for First Army Training School.
                    (Intro.) Nov 1915

"The offensive spirit must be kept up by frequent raids on enemy trenches."
                    Major Christie-Miller, April 1916. IWM, 80/32/2

Moral(e)

"At no period in the war has moral superiority been more essential . . . "
                    French, 26 Oct 15 WO95/159

"Such enterprises lowers the enemy's moral[e] and raises the moral[e] . . . of the Division and Corps."
                    Kiggell, 27 Jan 16 WO95/161

"Success in war depends more on moral than on physical qualities."
                    IWM, Field Service Regs.*, 1914*

"Success in war depends more on moral than on physical qualities."
                    Haig, 15 Nov 15 WO95/160

"Minor enterprises lower the enemy's moral[e]."
                    Haig, 27 Jan16 WO95/160

"Good scouting at night causes perpetual uneasiness in the minds of the enemy and greatly improves the moral[e] of our own troops."
                    Haking, 4 Nov 15 WO95/881

"Lowering the enemy's moral[e] and raising that of our own troops is the object to be kept in mind."

Haking, 13 Feb 16 WO95/881

"These raids do a great deal of good in increasing the moral[e] of our own men and lowering the moral[e] of the enemy."

Rawlinson, 4 Jan 16 WO95/161

"Constant activity . . . achieves the double purpose of raising the moral[e] of our troops whilst lowering that of the enemy."

Notes for infantry Officers on Trench Warfare, *IWM, 40/WO/3476 Nov 1916, May 1917.*

"Moral[e] must be heightened by every possible means".

IWM, SS143. Actions for the Training of Platoons, 1917

"Too great a stress cannot be laid on the necessity of developing the moral[e] and soldierly spirit of all ranks."

WO95/160. Syllabus for First Army Training School (Intro.), Nov 1915

"The moral[e] of the opposing forces after our continuous success last year and this, may be taken as at least 3 to2 (British to German)."

Haking, 11 May 17 WO95/882

Harass

"The constant harassing of the enemy by minor enterprises . . ."

French, 26 Oct 10 WO95/159

"Artillery bombardments should be carried out to harass the enemy."

Haig, 25 Nov 15 WO95/160

"Rifle, machine gun fire and shelling carried out to harass the enemy . . . and generally lower the enemy's moral[e]."

Haking, Dec 1915 WO95/160

"Constant activity in harassing the enemy might lead to reprisals at first."

Notes for Infantry Officers on Trench Warfare, *IWM, 40/WO/3476 Nov 1916, May 1917*

"With a view to harassing the enemy . . . instructions have been issued to Corps and Divisional Commanders to arrange small carefully thought out artillery bombardments."

Haig, 23 Nov 15 WO95/160

"To harass the enemy . . . with the object of damaging depots of material, causing loss to reliefs, ration and work parties and generally lowering the enemy's moral[e]."

Haking, 25 Dec 15 WO95 /160

Raids, Patrols and Casualties

This Appendix examines various statistics to determine whether Haking's commitment to the offensive resulted in relatively more trench raids and more casualties in XI Corps than in other Corps in the First Army in 1916–17. In other words, it attempts to answer the question: does Haking deserve to be singled out as being particularly aggressive and wasteful of his soldiers' lives?

Tables 1, 2 and 3 record the number of trench raids carried out by the Corps in the First Army in 1916 and 1917 respectively. Table 4 shows the number of casualties in the First Army also in 1916 and 1917. The sources used for both trench raids and casualties are the various Corps Reports in the First Army Weekly Operations Reports (TNA WO95/161–173). Information on the varying number of Corps and Divisions in the First Army has been taken from several sources: TNA WO95/161 (Paper attached to First Army Conference 4 January 1916); WO394/1 (Statistical Abstract of Information Regarding Armies at Home and Abroad, 24 September 1916); WO394/2 (Statistical Abstract, etc., February 1917); WO95/29 (Divisions in Corps 1916). Table 5 is concerned with the terminology of trench raids and the sources are listed. All the statistics need careful interpretation and are discussed below.

1: Manpower.

The composition of Armies and Corps was fluid. Corps were regularly transferred between Armies, and Divisions were even more frequently transferred between Corps. Consequently, the number of Corps in the First Army and the number of Divisions in each Corps varied considerably during 1916 and 1917 (see Tables 1 and 2). To compound the difficulty, the number of men in the battalions that made up the divisions was also subject to variation. Despite these complications, however, the infantry numbers in a Corps and in a Division in the First Army generally held reasonably steady, at least in 1916 and early 1917,

274   *Lieutenant General Sir Richard Haking*

at around 60,000 and 12,500 respectively. Nevertheless, it can be seen that any effort to make like for like manpower comparisons between Corps is likely to be far from straightforward.

2: Terminology of Trench Raids.

In the Corps' Operations Reports a number of overlapping terms are used to describe the various incursions into no man's land. This habit of using the same word in several different ways was applied to many aspects of trench life and the practice was recognized as confusing. In December 1916, this concern was aired by a participant at one of the Commanding Officers' Conferences at the First Army Central School: "A vocabulary of military and current war terms would assist many officers and men (e.g. camouflet, camouflage, Russian sap, defilade). There is much more ignorance of these terms when read in orders and Intelligence than is realized by those who use them. There are also those words that have come into general use and need fixing so as to prevent their being used with different meanings (dugout, sniper, dud, etc.)."[1] The Conference participant might well have listed "raids" and "patrols" among the confusing terms since they were used in First Army and Corps reports with a variety of meanings and with little consistency.

Commentators on the First World War have generally considered that a raid was aimed at entering the enemy's trench; killing or capturing Germans; damaging his defences; and gaining information such as the identity of the opposing troops. The objective of a patrol, on the other hand, was to check the enemy's frontline defences and his working parties and generally be involved in the activities of no man's land. In other words, there has been an acceptance that the two activities served quite different purposes. The *Dictionary of Military Terms* gives the following definitions:

> Raid – An operation usually small scale, involving a swift penetration of hostile territory to secure information, seize hostages, confuse the enemy, destroy his installations, or carry out some other specific task. It ends with a planned withdrawal upon completion of the assigned mission.

> Patrol – A detachment to gather information or carry out destructive, harassing, mopping up, surveillance, or security missions.[2]

These definitions imply that a raid is a far more aggressive activity than a patrol. In terms of territorial scope, John Ellis wrote: "Going

over the top usually meant a patrol into no man's land to secure information about the enemy's dispositions and level of preparedness . . .
another technique was . . . the trench raid, a much bigger enterprise
than the patrol and with the avowed intent of actually entering the
enemy lines."[3] Richard Holmes describes the difference between the
two activities as: "Small patrols, perhaps an officer and one or two
men, crept out after dark to check the position of the enemy wire or
trenches . . . Larger raids were mounted to capture prisoners so that
German units could be identified."[4] Andy Simpson distinguishes
between raids and patrols as follows:

> Whereas raids were one-off operations, patrols were standing
> features of day-to-day operations. The former were generally
> intended to enter the German lines, both to cause alarm and inflict
> casualties, with the acquisition of prisoners as the ultimate prize.
> Patrols on the other hand, did not necessarily set out to make
> contact with the enemy (although 'offensive patrols' sometimes
> included disruption of their working parties) but to investigate
> features in No-Man's-Land in order to see whether likely outposts
> were garrisoned and German working parties active.[5]

Implied in Paddy Griffith's discussion of patrols and raids are these
same distinctions.[6]

Tony Ashworth has given an extensive analysis of the development
of raids. Initially ad hoc forays carried out mainly by elite units, raids
evolved through 1915 and, by 1916, had become highly planned, multi-
arm attacks controlled not at battalion but at Army and Corps levels.
However, Ashworth distinguishes between a patrol (sometimes referring to "fighting patrols") and a raid in much the same way as the
historians already quoted. He describes patrols as concerned essentially
with no man's land, while raids were acts of aggression into the enemy
trenches:

> The success of a raid, which was the most skilled form of small
> assault in trench war, depended in part upon control of no-man's-
> land by patrols in the period preceding the raid . . . Fighting
> patrols established ascendancy and gained intelligence of German
> defences and ground over which raiders would assault.[7]

It is worth noting that Ashworth's comments echo a War Office
pamphlet of March 1916, which states that raids can be carried out
successfully only if "superiority in patrol work between the lines has
been established".[8]

Mark Connelly, analyzing the raids carried out by the Buffs battalions (East Kent Regiment) on the Western Front, writes: "Some raids were planned and expected to cause local destruction and disruption to the enemy, whereas others were more overtly concerned with the acquisition of intelligence and information." Connelly does not touch on the purpose of the patrols undertaken by the Buffs.[9] However, Malcolm Brown describes patrols as: "forays out beyond the wire to spy on the enemy, assess his fighting potential, and generally assert pre-eminence in the space between the trenches". To define a raid, Brown quotes from the Official History: "a local attack on a small scale to gain ground, take any advantage of any tactical or numerical inferiority on the part of the enemy and capture prisoners for identification purposes i.e. to determine which units were on a particular front".[10]

It is probable that the volume of the Official History covering the winter period 1914–15, compiled in 1927 by Edmonds and Wynne and quoted by Brown, was probably the source of the definition of a raid as used by the historians cited above. Edmonds and Wynne suggest that the first "raid" was carried out on the night of 3/4 February 1915 by men of the 1st Worcesters.[11] They also include, as a note in the official history, the memorandum of 5 February 1915 from Sir John French giving official authority for "raids":

> Such enterprises are highly valuable and should receive every encouragement, since they relieve the monotony of our troops, while they have a corresponding detrimental effect on the moral[e] of the enemy's troops and tend in a variety of ways to their exhaustion and general disquiet.[12]

When Haig became Commander in Chief in December 1915, he not only endorsed French's policy on raids – he made raiding and aggression in no man's land a key part of his general strategy of attrition.[13]

Any clear-cut distinctions between patrols and raids, such as those covered in the above discussion, however, are difficult to sustain. An examination of First Army Corps' Operations Reports for the years 1916 and 1917 show a bewildering number of terms that refer to raids and patrols. These terms are rarely defined and lead to a degree of confusion on the part of the reader. An attempt has been made in Table 5 to list the various terms used in the Operations Reports, provide a meaning, and give an example of the use of each term.

Two main conclusions arise from the information in Table 5. First, different terminology is used to describe essentially the same sort of action. Dummy raids, feint attacks and Chinese attacks are indistinguishable. The same is true for stealth raids and silent raids; for bombing raids and bombing attacks; and for fighting patrols and strong fighting patrols. Second, and more pertinently, it is frequently difficult to distinguish between various forms of patrols and raids. A raid always aimed at entering the enemy trenches, but many patrols had the same objective. Item 10 in Table 5 gives five examples of patrols that had the clear intention of attacking the German lines and causing mayhem. Ashworth suggests that:"by the end of 1915, the raid was clearly distinguished from other forms of minor assault, such as the fighting patrol".[14] The formal raid had certainly developed into a highly sophisticated operation often involving preparation in simulated trench systems, the use of specialist troops and weapons and support by other arms such as artillery, smoke and gas. Nevertheless, it is apparent that in 1916 and 1917 raids and patrols overlapped both in terminology and in practice. There is even some evidence that the words "patrol" and "raid" were frequently used to mean the same thing and only the context explained what actually happened. For example, the XI Corps' Operations Report for 6-14 July 1916 recorded: "Patrol to raid enemy listening post at Fauquisart. No casualties."[15] The July 1917 Report had the following entry: "At noon on 15.7.17 seven fighting patrols of 4/5 Loyal North Lancs Regt raided the enemy trenches in the Fleurbaix section."[16] Again, on 20 July 1917: "Seven fighting patrols raided enemy lines." To confuse matters even further, an entry in the Operations Report of the Canadian Corps (29 July-2 August 1917) read: "There have been no active operations to report. Considerable patrol activity has, however, taken place."[17]

Terminology relating to patrols and raids is, therefore, somewhat confusing. To think of a patrol simply as an incursion into no man's land and a raid as the only form of aggression into enemy trenches is inaccurate. However, there is evidence to suggest that those serving at the Front were able to make distinctions, at least to their own satisfaction, between the two activities. The writer of the XI Corps Report for the week 15-22 June 1917 noted that there was "one raid and two fighting patrols", and in the following week there were "two raids and one fighting patrol".[18] Captain J. C. Dunn, of 2nd Battalion Royal Welsh Fusiliers, recorded that through the winter of 1915–16: "the CO had kept alive the fighting spirit of the Battalion by means of patrols whose duty was, in official terms, 'to deny no man's land to the enemy'."[19] Dunn later wrote: "The immemorial notion of a raid is to enter the enemy's lines by stealth or surprise, to kill or capture, plunder or destroy, and get away with no fighting or little."[20] Frank Richards noted in his memoirs: "Buffalo Bill [the Company Commander] decided to send a patrol out, consisting of a Corporal and two men . . . Corporal Pardoe, Private Miles and I went out on that patrol; our orders were simply to proceed as far as we could up the willow ditch and to discover what we could."[21] Edmonds, the editor of the British Official History, apparently had a clear idea of a "raid". In his discussion on trench warfare during the period July–November 1916 (i.e. at the time of the Somme), he recorded that the First Army had carried out 166 raids;[22] the Second Army 104; and the Third Army 40.[23] However, the official historian also wrote: "On the night of 31 October [1916] a patrol of the XIII Corps entered the German front line south-east of Hebuterne and found it unoccupied for a distance of fifty yards. Two patrols of the V Corps broke in opposite Serre on the following night and penetrated the German support line."[24] Both of these patrol activities would have fallen quite neatly into Edmonds' own official history definition of a raid, as would the comment in the 1916 War Office pamphlet on *Minor Enterprises*: "The German trenches have been entered by patrols of from 2 to 8 men."[25]

An examination of First Army Operations Reports for 1916 and 1917 shows that a wide variety of terminology was used to describe the different types of patrols and raids. It also shows that certain actions referred to as patrols were indistinguishable from raids. It can be argued, at least from the point of view of those who served at the front and especially those who took part in the often perilous patrols or raids, that clear-cut definitions and rigorous adherence to terminology, are unrealistic. The main concern for those who had to plan and carry out patrols or raids of whatever nature must have been the achievement of the task at the least possible cost to those involved. Recording the details of an event in an operations report may have been important, but the niceties of precise language were not. At least, that is what the evidence from war diaries and memoirs seems to indicate.

However, historians have generally adopted an easy distinction between patrols and raids without due attention to either the terminology used in the war diaries or to the actual action described. Any simplistic definition between the two activities is inappropriate. This, of course, presents a problem when, as in the case of this Appendix, a comparison is made of the incidence of raids among the Corps in the First Army. In an effort to reach some consistency, the raids recorded in Tables 1 and 2 have been recorded only when the word "raid" or "attack" has been used in the Corps' Operations Reports. In this sense, comparisons between Corps have been made on a like-for-like basis and despite the problems of terminology it is the most appropriate comparison possible. Raids were always raids on enemy trenches; some patrols were attacks on enemy trenches, but most were not. Haking, in an address to his Corps Commanders when he was temporarily in command of First Army, distinguished very clearly between a patrol and a raid: "Patrolling engenders an offensive spirit amongst all ranks and it gives us possession of the ground between our trenches and the enemy's, quite wrongly called no man's land, but which ought to be called British land." As regards raids: "we must at all costs do our utmost to wear down the enemy, reduce his moral[e] and at the same time improve the moral[e] of our troops, and prove to them, by their own action, that they can get into the German trenches whenever they are called upon to do so. This can only be done by raids."[26]

Even taking account of the above problems of terminology, the information used in this Appendix on raid frequency is considered sufficiently consistent (even if not mathematically precise) to make inter-Corps comparisons worthwhile.

3: Casualty Statistics.

The casualty figures in the Corps' Operations Reports follow the usual practice of including the dead, the missing (presumed dead), the wounded (except for the lightly wounded who might be expected to return to their units within a matter of days), and prisoners. However the casualties in Table 4 arose from a number of reasons, some of which were outside the control of a Corps Commander, regardless of the extent to which he promoted the offensive.

One of these factors was simply the corrosive effect of day-to-day life in the trenches – the result of sniping, bursts of machine-gun fire, mining and artillery fire as well as the occasional raid. The detonation of mines was particularly prevalent. On the First Army front in April 1916, the British exploded thirty-one mines and the Germans thirty-six, and each explosion was accompanied by frantic efforts by the opposing forces to gain control of the resulting crater.

Trench life had many "quiet" days, but the following extract from the XI Corps Operations Report for the week 8-15 June 1916 illustrates the underlying level of hostile activity that existed between the two forces.

8 June: In the Auchy section the enemy were prevented by our Artillery and trench Mortar fire from consolidating the lip of the new crater. In the Cuinchy section enemy patrols were active, but were driven off by our bombers. In the Neuve Chapelle section a successful raid was carried out by 14th Gloucester Rgt. Against the enemy trenches. The enemy's wire was cut and our raiding party entered the hostile trenches . . . German dug-outs were

bombed and at least 30 of the enemy were killed . . . The enemy retaliated heavily with only slight damage.

9 June: A train at Salome was set on fire by our artillery. In the Auchy Section we exploded a mine. We occupied the near lip of the crater; considerable damage was done to the enemy's trenches. In the Ferme du Bois section our trench mortars bombarded the enemy's trenches.

10 June: In the Cuinchy section the enemy blew a mine. No casualties or damage of consequence to us. In the Givenchy section the enemy blew a mine. We are pushing out a sap to this crater. Slight damage was done to one of our galleries. In the Ferme du Bois section, after a artillery preparation, a small raiding party reached the enemy's wire. The enemy was on the alert, so our party withdrew after throwing bombs into the enemy's trenches.

11 June: In the Cuinchy section we fired a defensive mine. The enemy had previously been heard working nearby. It was thought that damage was done to their gallery. In the Neuve Chapelle section the enemy attempted a small bombing raid. They were detected by a covering party and driven back.

12 June: In the Cuinchy section a small party of the enemy tried to bomb our sap-head during the night. We opened rapid fire and the hostile party withdrew.

13 June: In the Auchy section we dispersed an enemy working party and carried out a small organized trench mortar bombardment of their crater. In the Cuinchy section we shelled the enemy's communication trenches as a Relief was suspected. In the Neuve Chapelle section a hostile patrol was driven back by one of our Patrols.

14–15 June: In the Auchy section the enemy exploded a mine. No damage was done to our parapet and the crater is covered by fire from our mortars and machine guns. In the Cuinchy section we bombarded the German Brickstacks and trenches with trench mortars and 18 pdrs. Hostile retaliation was slight.[27]

The style of this report is interesting. There is a blasé air about it and the writer (Haking) clearly wishes to give the recipient (the First Army Commander, General Sir Charles Monro) the impression that everything is under control and that nothing out of the ordinary has occurred. Enemy activity was characterized as being largely ineffective. Nevertheless, the XI Corps casualty figures for that week were forty-nine killed, 233 wounded and five missing. The figures for the previous week were: 112 killed; 507 wounded; and twelve missing. In two weeks, the casualties had amounted to the equivalent of an entire battalion. Losses of this magnitude were endemic on the First Army front.

Some parts of the front were accepted as being more dangerous than others. I Corps, for example, held the line around Loos – a sector that in First Army terms was considered active and where casualties could be expected to be relatively high. It was considered worth noting, in the First Army Operations Report for the last week of August 1916, that: "The decrease in the casualties on the I Corps front from the average number generally incurred in the Loos Salient is striking." By contrast, most of the XI Corps front was regarded as relatively quiet, at least during the first half of 1916. Hence, in May 1916, it was thought appropriate for the unseasoned 61st Division, new to France, to be positioned near Laventie for a gradual initiation into trench life. An advanced party from that Division had noted a prevailing "live and let live" attitude among the troops already in that sector.[28] The decision as to where a Corps should be placed, however, was in the hands of the Army Commander or even GHQ. A Corps Commander was told where he and his Corps should go.

The second and most important cause of casualties was the major set-piece offensive.[29]

A graph of the monthly First Army casualty figures (from Table 4) is shown overleaf.

The highest casualty figures appear in July 1916 (Fromelles) and the two months of April/May 1917 (Vimy Ridge). During the period covered by Table 4 (thirteen months), the casualties in the three months July 1916 and April/May 1917 account for 56 per cent of all First Army casualties; 43 per cent of XI Corps casualties in the period occurred at the time of Fromelles while 70 per cent of the Canadian Corps casualties were associated with Vimy. Again, the important point is that, although planned and implemented at Army and Corps level, the operations at both Fromelles and Vimy were initiated not by Army or Corps commanders, but by GHQ.

❊ ❊ ❊ ❊

Despite all the above caveats and problems of interpretation and terminology it is nevertheless suggested that some general conclusions can be reached relating Haking's XI Corps' frequency of raids and casualties to those of other First Army Corps. As regards raids, Table 1 shows

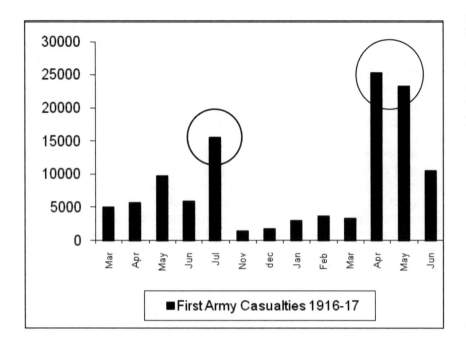

that a total of 206 raids were made in 1916. These raids were spread over forty Corps/months i.e. an average of 5.1 raids per Corps per month. Since the number of divisions in each of I, IV, and XI Corps is known, it is possible to calculate that, in those Corps, there was an average of 5.4 raids per Corps/month and an average 1.5 raids per division /month. Over the whole First Army front – some twenty miles – an average of four raids took place per week in 1916. Even during the summer months of June-October (which included the start of the Somme offensive) the average increased to only seven per week. These numbers hardly lead to the conclusion that raids were sustained or necessarily significant acts of aggression. Haking and his fellow Generals may have gone to great lengths to promote and encourage raids, but, in terms of frequency, they were so few and far between that they cannot be regarded as a major manifestation of the offensive spirit.

However, since Haking was a well-known "thruster" and took every possible opportunity to promote aggressive action, it might be expected that the incidence of trench raids in XI Corps would be significantly greater than in other Corps. Certainly, XI Corps (85 raids) carried out more raids than either I Corps or IV Corps (72 and 27), but when looked at in terms of raids per division/month, the difference between I Corps (1.6) and XI Corps (2.0) is minimal and the overall infrequency of raids makes any comparison inconclusive. Indeed, it would be more pertinent to enquire why the frequency of raids in IV Corps was so low.

The figures in Tables 1 and 2 (1916 and 1917) show that the number of Raids per Division Month ranged from 0.4 to 2.1 with an average of 1.5 across the First Army. These figures are in line with the number of raids carried out 1916–18 by 6th, 12th and 24th Divisions, which were 1.5, 1.1 and 1.0 respectively.[30]

The conclusions reached for 1917 are broadly the same as those reached for 1916: the First Army incidence of raids at just over four per week was at a modest level, and XI Corps was not particularly militant at just over two raids per division per month. The historians of the 5th Division have noted that: "Higher authorities" had ordered "at least two raids in each Division every week" during the winter months of 1916–17.[31] On that basis, the frequency of XI Corps raids was modest indeed. In 1917, XI Corps carried out relatively fewer raids than I Corps. It should also be noted that although the Canadian Corps carried out fewer raids than XI Corps, it bore the brunt of the major attacks in the Vimy area April-June 1917.

Table 3 summarizes the information in Tables 1 and 2 in terms of the number of raids per week for 1916 and1917. During those years, XI Corps was covering an eight-mile stretch of the front with some 60,000 men. In that context, an average of 1.5 raids per week, traumatic though they might have been for those involved, cannot be regarded as being excessively aggressive. This frequency of raids by XI Corps is confirmed by a note dated 12 January 1917: "Our last raid was carried out some four months ago . . . Before that time, the XI Corps carried out an average of 6 raids per month."[32]

* * * *

The First Army weekly operations reports generally, but not consistently, contained casualty figures. Table 4 shows the consolidated monthly figures for seven months of 1916 and also the first six months of 1917. These figures show that in 1916, XI Corps sustained a higher casualty rate (average 725 per Division per month) than either I Corps (average 687) or IV Corps (average 395) – the difference between I Corps and Haking's XI Corps being mainly due to the July Fromelles operation. During the first six months of 1917, XI Corps had the lowest casualty rate (ave. 303 per Division per month) and the Canadians the highest (ave. 1341). It should be noted that in April and May 1917, the Canadian Corps took the leading role in the attack on Vimy Ridge and related operations and suffered accordingly. During the entire period

March 1916–June 1917, the average Corps casualty rates in the First Army were:

Canadians	1,057 per Division per month
I Corps	741
IV Corps	395
XI Corps	554

A further source can be used to develop a view as to relative casualty rates. The Medical History of the War[33] shows that the average Ration Strength of the BEF in 1916 was 1,287,000 and that the number of battle casualties was 651,662. The casualty:strength ratio was therefore 1:2. Taking the XI Corps casualty figures in Table 4 – a total of some 26,000 in a period of just over one year – and assuming an average Corps strength of 60,000, the casualty ratio was 1:2.3. Statistically, therefore, a soldier in Haking's XI Corps had a marginally better chance of avoiding death or injury than the average soldier on the Western Front.[34] Compared to other parts of the First Army and to the BEF in general, XI Corps casualty rates were far from exceptional

* * * *

The information in this Appendix leads to the conclusion that any comparison of statistics relating to raids and casualties, because of the problems of interpretation and terminology, should be treated with great caution and cannot be expected to be precise. However, what can be reasonably concluded from the discussion is that there is little evidence to support the view that Haking's XI Corps, in terms of raids or casualties, was particularly more aggressive or casualty-prone than other Corps in the First Army.

Notes

1. TNA, WO 95/167, Report on Fourth Commanding Officers Conference, 10–17 December 1916. The Official History also touches on the problems of "a fresh vocabulary" See *BOH, 1915*, Vol. I, p.152.
2. N. Dupuy, G. P. Hayes, and C. Johnson, *Dictionary of Military Terms*, pp.169, 181.
3. Ellis, *Eye Deep in Hell*, pp.73, 76.
4. Richard Holmes, *Tommy*. p.311.
5. Andy Simpson, *Hot Blood and Cold Steel*, p.64.
6. Griffith, *Battle Tactics on the Western Front*, pp.40, 60–62, 74.
7. Tony Ashworth, *Trench Warfare 1914–1918*, pp.70–73, 89–98.
8. War Office, SS 10, *Notes on Minor Enterprises* (March 1916).
9. Mark Connelly, *Steady the Buffs, A Regiment, a Region and the Great War*. p.81.

10. Malcolm Brown, *The Imperial War Museum Book of the Western Front*, pp.105–06.
11. It has also been claimed that the first raid occurred on 4 October 1914, when a platoon of 1st Coldstream Guards attacked an enemy sap at Troyon Factory Road. See Stephen Bull, *World War I Trench Warfare (2)*. p.13. There is evidence from I Corps War Diary (TNA, WO 95/590) that a raid was carried out prior to the 1st Worcester attack of Feb 1915, viz. "a small bomb raid" by the 1st Irish Guards on 2 January 1915.
12. *BOH 1915*, Vol. I, pp.32–33.
13. See J. H. Boraston, *Sir Douglas Haig's Despatches*. pp.3–4.
14. Ibid., p.73.
15. TNA, WO 95/163.
16. TNA, WO 95/172.
17. Ibid.
18. TNA, WO 95/171.
19. Capt J. C. Dunn, *The War the Infantry Knew 1914–1919*, p.120.
20. Ibid, p.192.
21. Frank Richards, *Old Soldiers Never Die*, p.39.
22. Table 1 shows a total of 141 raids during that same period. Edmonds' total of 166 could not, therefore, have included patrols.
23. *BOH 1916*, Vol. II, p.544, Footnote 1.
24. Ibid., p.466.
25. War Office, SS107, March 1916.
26. TNA, WO 95/166, First Army Conference, 15 August 1916
27. TNA, WO 95/163, R.H.S. 691/23.
28. IWM, 80/32/2, Christie-Miller *Papers*.
29. However, John Terraine in an address, "Understanding", reproduced in *Stand To!* 34, Spring 1992, pp.7–12, examined casualties in a battalion that had spent the entire war on the Western Front and concluded that: "it was not the famous battles, Loos, the Somme, Arras, Passchendaele, that filled the cemeteries, but 1564 days of unceasing war". A glance at a bar chart showing casualties for each of the thirty-six months of 1915–17 and relating casualty levels to "famous battles" makes such a conclusion difficult to accept.
30. Connelly, *Steady the Buffs*, pp.246–50.
31. A. H. Hussey and D. S. Inman, *The Fifth Division in the Great War*, p.142. 5th Division was part of XI Corps during this period.
32. TNA, WO 95/168, RHS 837/16.
33. *Official History of the War: Medical Services: Casualties and Medical Statistics*, pp.148–9.
34. It should also be noted that the BEF numbers included a proportion of non-combat troops, whereas XI Corps was a front-line infantry formation and therefore more likely to incur casualties.

Table 1. Number Of First Army Raids In 1916

Corps Month	— I —		— III —		— IV —		— XI —		— XVII —		— Can —		Tot Rds
	Rds	Divs	Rds	Divs	Rds	Divs	Rds	Divs	Rds	Divs	Rds	Divs	
Jan	0	3	2	3	2	4	3	3					7
Feb	1	3	0	3	2	4	1	3					4
Mar	1	4			0	3	5	6					6
Apr	4	4			0	3	9	5					13
May	3	4			3	3	5	5					11
Jun	3	4			6	3	9	4					18
Jul	10	4			7	3	15	3					32
Aug	13	4			3	3	7	3					23
Sep	18	4			3	3	13	2	7	N/A			41
Oct	17	4			1	3	7	3	6				31
Nov	2	3					8	2			4	N/A	14
Dec	0	3					3	3			3		6
Total	72	44	2	6	27	32	85	42	13		7		206
Rd/D/M	1.6				0.8		2.0						1.5

NB: The number of Raids per Division Month (RDS/D/M) is calculated by dividing the number of raids by the total number of Division Months.

Table 2 Number Of Raids In The First Army 1917

Corpus Month	— I — Rds	Divs	— XI — Rds	Divs	Canadian Rds	Divs	— XIII — Rds	Divs	— V — Rds	Divs	Total Raids
Jan	9	2	2	3	9	4					20
Feb	5	4	13	2	13	4					31
Mar	4	3	4	4	13	4					21
Apr	3	2	1	3	2	4		4			6
May	5	2	11	4	2	4		4			18
Jun	11	2	13	3	8	4	4	3			36
Jul	9	2	6	2	6	4	4	5			25
Aug	4	2	7	2	4	4	0	5			15
Sep	3	3	0	3	2	4	2	5			7
Oct	1	3	1	2	0	4	2	3	0	N/A	4
Total	54	25	58	28	59	40	12	29	0	N/A	183
Rds/D/M	2.1		2.1		1.4		0.4		N/A		1.5

NB: The number of Raids per Division Month (RDS/D/M) is calculated by dividing the number of raids by the total number of Division Months. The total number of Division/Months is the sum of the months spent by each Division in the Corps.

The number of weeks recorded in 1917 is 42. Since the total number of raids carried out by the First Army was 183, the frequency per week was 4.35.

The information in Table 1 and Table 2 shows that the First Army frequency of raids per week over the two years 1916 and 1917 was 4.1.

Table 3. First Army Raids Per Week

Year/Corps	I	IV	XI	XIII	Canadian	First Army
1916	1.38	0.62	1.63	N/A	N/A	3.96
1917	1.28	N/A	1.38	0.42	1.40	4.35
Average	1.34	0.62	1.51	0.42	1.40	4.1

NB: The First Army numbers include III, XVII and the Canadian Corps in 1916, all of whom spent less than two months in the First Army. The number of raids per week has been arrived at by dividing the total number of raids in each year by the number of weeks recorded which were 52 in 1916 and 42 in 1917. The information in Tables 1 and 2 shows that, for example, the number of First Army raids in 1916 and 1917 totalled 389 which when divided by the total number of weeks (94) gives an average of 4.1 raids per week.

Table 4 First Army Casualties By Corps 1916 And 1917

1916			Corps										Tot Army Cas
Month	— I —			— IV —			— XI —			Canadians			
	Cas	Divs	% of Army Total	Cas	Divs	% of Army Total	Cas	Divs	% of Army Total	Cas	Divs	% of Army Total	
Mar	2746	4	55	586	4	12	1245	6	25				4990
Apr	3412	4	59	853	3	15	1456	5	26				5721
May	4452	4	46	3203	3	33	2103	5	21				9758
Jun	2638	4	44	885	3	15	2433	4	41				5956
July	3450	4	22	789	3	5	11348	3	73				15587
Nov	593	3	39				342	2	23	561	4	38	1496
Dec	574	3	26				375	3	21	805	4	46	1754
Total	17866	26		6316	16		20302	28		1366	8		45262
Av/Div/Mth	687			395			725				171		
1917													
Jan	909	2	30				724	3	24	1404	4	46	3037
Feb	812	4	22				768	2	21	2125	4	57	3705
Mar	1150	3	34				613	4	18	1570	4	47	3349
Apr	3999	2	16				778	3	3	16809	5	66	25328
May	2715	2	12				1063	4	5	7857	4	34	23261
Jun	2933	2	29				1805	3	17	3750	4	35	10538
Total	12518	15	18				5751	19	8	33515	25	49	69218
Av/Div/Mth	834						303			1341			
A/D/All Mth	741			395			554			1057			

NOTE: Other Corps served with the First Army during this time for short periods. In 1916, III Corps served one month (March) with 413 casualties. In 1917, II Corps served for three months (March-May) with 750 casualties; XIII Corps for four months (March-June) with 15,994 casualties; the Portuguese for three months (April-June) with 589 casualties and the Cavalry Division for two months (May-June) with 101 casualties. These casualty figures have been included in the Army Totals and therefore have been taken into account when calculating the casualty percentage figures for the other Corps.

The March 1916 figures cover three weeks. The fourth week is missing for all Corps.

Similarly, the casualty figures for the week 15-21 July 1916 are missing for all Corps. This was the week of the attack at Fromelles. Because of the high casualty figures incurred by XI Corps and the Australian 5th Division attached to it on that occasion (7,080 according to the British Official History 1916 vol. 2 p.133) that number of casualties has been added into the XI Corps figures for July 1916.

Table 5 – Terminology Of Raids And Patrols

1 RAID

MEANING: A generic term covering aggressive action on a German trench system. May be accompanied by artillery, trench mortars, smoke, machine-gun fire. Generally aimed at entering the enemy trench, killing Germans, capturing prisoners, gaining information and causing damage. Raids were carried out by variously sized groups from several men to a battalion or more.

EXAMPLE: 8–14 May 1916. IV Corps WO95/163: *1 Officer and 10 OR carried out a raid on German sap. Officer and 4 OR wounded.*

6 Dec 1916. Cdn Corps WO95/167: *A party of 2 officers and 44 other ranks successfully raided the enemy's front line trenches . . . occupied dugouts were bombed and 5 German dead were observed in the trench.*

12–19 Jan 1917. Cdn Corps WO95 /168: *Two raids were most effectively supported by artillery and machine-gun fire.*

2 MINOR RAID

MEANING: A raid by a small number of men.

EXAMPLE: 1–7 Dec 1916. Cdn Corps WO95/167: *At 8.30 am on 5 Dec, in the la Folie Section, a minor raid was carried out by the PPCLI resulting in the capture of a wounded German.*

3 ATTEMPTED RAID

MEANING: A raid that was aborted.

EXAMPLE: 28 July–4 Aug 1916. XI Corps WO95/165: *The raiders* [14 Hampshires] *attempted to penetrate through uncut wire, but were finally held up by high wire next to the enemy's parapet and were compelled to withdraw.*

4 DUMMY RAID and FEINT and CHINESE ATTACKS

MEANING: No raid takes place, but activity carried out (e.g. artillery bombardment) to cause the enemy to man their trenches in anticipation of a raid.

EXAMPLE: 1–8 March 1916. Cdn Corps WO95/168: *A dummy raid was carried out by the 10 Canadian Infantry Bn assisted by artillery . . . Trench Mortars also bombarded enemy front trench. The operation was successful and it disclosed the German signal for SOS. (Red flares repeated from trenches in rear until their Artillery opened up).*

8–14 Sept 1916. IV Corps WO95 /162: *Feint attack in Calonne section . . . Aim to kill Germans.*

28 July–4 Aug 1916. I Corps WO95/163: *Chinese attack by 48 Infantry Brigade. Manned parapet and cheered. Induced enemy to do likewise and they opened rifle fire whereupon our artillery opened fire with shrapnel.*

5 STEALTH RAID and SILENT RAID

MEANING: A raiding party operating without artillery or other gunfire.

EXAMPLE: 16–23 March 1916. Cdn Corps WO95/168: *A party carried out a stealth raid . . . enemy trench was bombed for 100 yards and five dug-outs destroyed.*

18–25 May 1916. XI Corps WO95/170: *A Silent raid by 1 officer and 16 ORs.*

6 BOMBING RAID and BOMB ATTACK

MEANING: A raid with specific intention to use bombs.

EXAMPLE: 15–21 March 1916. XI Corps WO95/162: *Bombing raid by 19 Div on Bird Cage Salient involving 100 men. 1 killed, 10 wounded.*

7–14 Jan 1916. XI Corps WO95/161: *Bomb attack by 7 KOR Lancasters on Boar's Head. 3 ORs wounded.*

7   RAIDING PARTY

MEANING: A raid by variously sized groups

EXAMPLE: 15–21 April 1916. 1 Corps WO95/162: *Raiding Party from 2 Bn R. Sussex of 1 officer and 15 ORs.*

8   PATROL

MEANING: Generally aimed at information gathering in no man's land, but also used for more aggressive purposes including entering enemy trenches.

EXAMPLE: 15–21 Oct 1915. III Corps WO95/159: *Patrols of 20 Div claim to have killed 15 Germans, whom they surprised working on their wire under cover of fog.*

15–21 Oct 1915. III Corps WO95/159: *Patrols of 20 Div claim to have killed 15 Germans, whom they surprised working on their wire under cover of fog.*

10–17 Dec 1916. XI Corps WO95/167: *Our patrols did extremely good work examining the enemy wire at numerous points and also directed Lewis Gun fire on any hostile working parties to be found.*

17–24 Aug 1917. I Corps WO95/172: *29 patrols sent out to examine, locate any posts possible and ascertain the enemy's method of holding the line.*

29 Dec–4 Jan 1917. XI Corps WO95/168: *Opposite the Fauquissart section our patrols have entered the enemy lines on six nights out of seven.*

9   OFFICER'S PATROL

MEANING: A patrol led by an officer. NCOs also led patrols.

EXAMPLE: 15–21 Oct 1915. III Corps WO95/159: *An officer's patrol raided a German listening post opposite the centre of 20 Div and killed two men of 17 Bavarian Reserve Regiment.*

12–19 July 1917. I Corps WO95/172: *An officer patrol entered the enemy's front line and bombed a dugout – no enemy encountered.*

10   FIGHTING PATROL and STRONG FIGHTING PATROL

MEANING: Patrols of various sizes with an aggressive objective.

EXAMPLE: 10–17 Dec 1916. XI Corps WO95/167: *On 10 Dec a fighting patrol left our lines with the object of entering and damaging the enemy's trenches.*

12–19 July 1917. I Corps WO95/172: *Four fighting patrols of the 8 Bedfords entered the enemy trenches in order to secure identification. One prisoner brought back.*

3–10 Aug 1917. I Corps WO95/172: *Another patrol entered the enemy's front line. Six of the enemy were shot and our party withdrew without casualties on the approach of enemy reinforcements.*

9/10 Aug 1917. Cdn Corps WO95/172: *Strong patrols of 11 Canadian Infantry Brigade pushed forward and occupied a portion of Alpaca trench.*

5/6 Sept 1917. XI Corps WO95/173: *A strong fighting patrol of 2/8 (King's) Liverpool Regt penetrated as far as the enemy's line in the Cordonnerie section.On the return journey they encountered a post in the enemy's front line and succeeded in taking prisoner 2 men of 101 RIR thus obtaining a most valuable identification.*

11   BOMBING PATROL

MEANING: A patrol armed specifically with bombs.

EXAMPLE: 19–26 May 1916. XI Corps WO95/163: *A bombing patrol sent against a German Working Party.*

12   MINOR OPERATIONS

MEANING: A term used to cover various aggressive actions from a raid to a major attack.

EXAMPLE: 3–10 Oct 1917. XIII Corps WO95/173: *Minor Operations have been as follows: a small raid was attempted on enemy lines . . . : over 500 drums of gas were successfully projected on Fresnoy Park . . . artillery, trench mortars and machine guns co-operating with creeping barrage over gassed area.*

Analysis of Divisions in I, IV and XI Corps (First Army) 1916.

I Corps (Jan-Dec)

	Total Div./Months	%
Experienced Divs.		
1,2,3,6,8,12,16,15,21,24,32,33.	33	75
Inexperienced Divs.		
16,40.	11	25

IV Corps (Jan-Sep)

Experienced Divs.		
1,2,6,9,15,24,37,47,63.	26	90
Inexperienced Divs.		
23	3	10

XI Corps (Jan-Dec)

Experienced Divs.		
Guards, 5,8,30,33,37.	17	40
Inexperienced Divs.		
19,35,38,39,61.	25	60

Sources: TNA WO95/29 (QMG Branch, GHQ): Martin Middlebrook, *Your Country Needs You*: Chris McCarthy, *The Somme. The Day by Day Account*: Captain E. A. James, *A Record of the Battles and Engagements of the British Armies in France and Flanders, 1914–1918*: Ray Westlake, *Kitchener's Army*.

Bibliography

Unpublished Primary Sources

Army Personnel Centre, Glasgow
General Sir Richard Haking Papers
Arquivo Historico Militar, Lisbon
General Fernando Tamagnini Papers
Australian War Memorial, Canberra
Captain C. E. W. Bean Papers
S. K. Donnan Papers
Brigadier General H. E. Elliott Papers
A. J. Winter Diary
A252 Series (War Diaries)
Bayerisches Hauptstaatarchiv, Abt. IV, Munich
6th Reserve Division, Bund 8
Centre For Buckinghamshire Studies
Lieutenant Colonel G. Christie-Miller Typescript
Captain I. Stewart-Liberty Papers
The Lee Magazine
Imperial War Museum
Captain L. C. R. Balding Papers
Lieutenant Colonel G. Christie-Miller Papers
Captain R. C. G. Dartford Diary
Sir Philip Game Papers
General Lord Horne Papers
Sapper Hollwey Diary
Sergeant Major S. W. D. Lockwood Memoirs
Major General Sir Cecil Lowther Papers
General Sir Ivor Maxse Papers
Major General G. R. J. Pinney Diaries
Field Marshal Sir Henry Wilson Papers
Private W. A. Tucker Notebook
Landesarchiv Baden Wurttemberg, Stuttgart
M113, 114,411 Series
Liddell Hart Centre for Military Archives, King's College London
Field Marshal Viscount Allenby Papers
Major General Sir Thompson Capper Papers
Brigadier General Sir James Edmonds Papers

292

Sir Basil Liddell Hart Papers
Field Marshal Sir William Robertson Papers
The National Library of Scotland
Lord Haldane Papers
National Army Museum
Millward Papers
The National Archives, Kew.
Cabinet. CAB 23, 44, 45, 103 Series
War Office. WO95, 106, 154, 157, 158, 256, 279, 394 Series
The Royal Archives, Windsor
HM King George V Diaries
The Royal Hampshire Regiment Museum, Winchester
Regimental Chronicle
Royal Military Academy, Sandhurst
Gentlemen Cadet Registers
H. C. Potter Notebooks

Published Primary Sources

General Staff, *Field Service Regulations* 1905, 1909, 1914 edns.
—— SS Publications 10, 24, 107, 109, 135, 158, 210.
—— Notes for Infantry Officers on Trench Warfare, 1916, 1917.
The Army List.
Barton, Peter, *Report on Fromelles* (For Australian Army Unit, 2007).
Bean, C. E. W. *Official History of Australia in the War of 1914–1918*, Vol. III, The AIF in France, 1916 (Angus and Robertson, Sydney, 1929).
Blake, Robert (ed.), *The Private Papers of Douglas Haig, 1914–1918* (Eyre & Spottiswoode, London, 1952).
Boraston, Lt Col J.H. (ed.), Sir *Douglas Haig's Despatches (1915–1919)* (Dent, London, 1919).
British Infantry Tactics and the Attack Formation Explained by an Adjutant of Militia (Mitchel & Co., Charing Cross, 1880).
Crockford's Directory of Clergy.
Dunne, Capt J.C., *The War the Infantry Knew* (Jane's, London, 1987).
Edmonds, Sir James, *History of the Great War, Military Operations France and Belgium 1914–1918*, XIV Vols (IWM and The Battery Press, Nashville, 1995 edn.).
French, Sir John, *The Complete Despatches of Lord French 1914–1916* (Chapman and Hill Ltd., London, 1917).
Haking, Col R. C. B., *Four Lectures Delivered at the Staff College during the Senior Staff Officers' Course* (HMSO, London, 1905).

Haking, Brig Gen R. C. B., *Staff Rides and Regimental Tours* (Hugh Rees Ltd., London, 1908).

Haking, Brig Gen R. C. B., *Company Training* (Hugh Rees Ltd., London, 1913).

James, Capt E. A., *A Record of the Battles and Engagements of the British Armies in France and Flanders, 1914–1918* (Naval and Military Press, Aldershot, 1924).

Kirke Committee, *Report on Lessons of the Great War* (War Office, London, 1932).

The London Gazette.

The Melbourne Argus.

Official History of the War: Medical Services; Casualties and Medical Statistics (HMSO, London, 1931).

Oxford Dictionary of National Biography.

Scott, David, *Douglas Haig; Diaries and Letters 1861–1914* (Pen and Sword, Barnsley, 2006).

Sheffield, G. and Bourne, J. (eds), *Douglas Haig Diaries and Letters 1914–1918* (Weidenfeld & Nicolson, London, 2005).

Sollender, Dr Fridolin, *Vier Jahre Westfront: Geschichte des Regiment List. RIR 16* (Verlag Max Schick, Munchen, 1932).

Sydney Morning Herald.

Thomas, J., *The Attack for Company, Battalion and Brigade* (1889, Chester).

The Times.

Two Hundred and Fifty One Divisions of the German Army which Participated in the War (1914–1918) (Government Printing Office, Washington, 1920).

Der Weltkrieg 1914–1918. XII Vols. (Reichskriegministerium, Berlin, 1936).

Who's Who? 1918 (A.C. Black, London, 1918).

Wilson, Maj B.T., *A Study of German Defences Near Lille* (1919, Charham).

Published Secondary Sources

MEMOIRS AND BIOGRAPHIES

Barrow, Gen Sir Charles, *The Life of Gen Sir Charles Monro* (Hutchison, London, 1931).

Carrington, Charles, *Soldier From the Wars Returning* (Hutchinson, London, 1965).

Carton de Wiart, Adrian, *Happy Odyssey* (Jonathan Cape, London, 1950).

Charteris, Brig Gen John, *Field Marshal Earl Haig* (Cassell & Co. London, 1929).

Churchill, Winston, *World Crisis 1911–1918*, III Vols. (Thornton Butterworth, London, 1927).

Crozier, Brig Gen F. P., *The Men I Killed* (Michael Joseph, London, 1937).

Coppard, George, *With a Machine Gun to Cambrai* (Papermac, London, 1986).

Downing W. H., *To The Last Ridge* (Grub Street, London, 2002).

Duff Cooper, *Haig*, II Vols. (Faber and Faber, London, 1935).

Falls, Cyril, *Marshal Foch* (Blackie & Son, London, 1939).

Graves, Robert, *Goodbye To All That* (Penguin Books, Harmondsworth, 1957 edn).

Fielding, Rowland, *War Letters to a Wife*, ed J. Walker, (Spellmount, Staplehurst, 2000).

Gladden, Norman, *Across the Piave* (IWM/HMSO, London, 1971).

Hamilton, Ian, *A Staff Officer's Scrapbook*. II Vols. (Edward Arnold, London,1907).

Hesketh-Prichard, *Sniping in France* (Hutchinson, London, Undated).

Hindenburg FM von, *The Great War*, ed. Charles Messenger (Greenhill Books, London, 2006).

Lee, John, *A Soldier's Life* (Pan Books, London, 2000).

Lloyd George, David, *War Memoirs*, II Vols. (Odhams Press, London, 1936).

Ludendorff, Erich, *My War Memoirs* (Hutchinson, London, 1919).

Joffre, Marshal, *Memoirs* (Geoffrey Bles, London, 1932).

Rees, Maj R. T., *A Schoolmaster at War* (Haycock Press, London, undated).

Richards, Frank, *Old Soldiers Never Die* (Faber and Faber, London, 1964).

MONOGRAPHS

Altham, A. E., *Principles of War Historically Illustrated* (London:1914).

Ashworth, Tony, *Trench Warfare 1914–1918. The Live and Let Live System* (Pan Books, London, 2000).

Atkinson, C. T., *The Regimental History of the Royal Hampshire Regiment*, II Vols., (Robert Maclehose & Co. Ltd., Glasgow, 1950).

Barnes, A. F., *The Story of the 2/5 Gloucester Regiment 1914–1918* (The Crypt House Press Ltd., Gloucester, 1930).

Beckett, Ian, *The Great War 1914–1918* (Longman, Harlow, 2001).

Bernhardi, Gen F. von, *On War Today* II Vols. (London: 1912).

Bewsher, Maj F. W., *The History of the 51st (Highland) Division 1914–1918* (W.M. Blackwell & Son, Edinburgh and London, 1921).

Blaxland, Gregory, *Amiens 1918* (W.H.Allen & Co. Ltd., London, 1981).

Bond, Brian, *The Victorian Army and the Staff College 1854–1914* (Eyre & Methuen, London, 1972).

Bosworth, Richard, *Italy and the Approach of the First World War* (Palgrave, Basingstoke, 1983).

Bristow, Adrian, *A Serious Disappointment* (Leo Cooper, London, 1995).

Brown, Malcolm, *Tommy Goes To War* (J.M. Dent & Son Ltd., Stroud, 1999).

Brown, Malcolm, *The IWM Book of the Western Front* (Pan Books, London, 2001).

Bull, Stephen, *World War I Trench Warfare* (2) (Osprey Publishing Ltd., London, 2002).

Carlyon, Les, *The Great War* (MacMillan, Sydney, 2000).

Carlyon, Les, *Gallipoli* (Doubleday, New York, 2002).

Clark, Alan, *The Donkeys* (Pimlico edn., London, 1993).

Connelly, Mark, *Steady The Buffs!* (OUP, Oxford, 2006).

Cruttwell, C. R. M. F., *A History of the Great War* (Clarendon Press, Oxford, 1934).

Dupuy, N., Hayes, G.P. and Johnson, C., *Dictionary of Military Terms* (H. H. Wilson Company, New York, 1986).

Cobb, Paul, *Fromelles 1916* (Tempus Publishing Limited, Stroud, 2007).

Corfield, Robin, *Don't Forget Me Cobber* (Corfield and Company, Rosanna, 2000).

Downing, W. H., *To the Last Ridge* (Grub Street, London, 2002).

Dudley-Wood, C. A., *The History of the Welsh Guards* (John Murray, London, 1925).

Dudley-Ward, Maj H. C., *The Fifty-Sixth Division 1914–1918* (Naval and Military Press, London, Undated).

Duffy, Christopher, *Through German Eyes: the British on the Somme 1916* (Weidenfeld & Nicolson, London, 2006).

Ellis, Capt A. D., *The Story of the Fifth Division* (Hodder & Stroughton, London, Undated).

Ellis, John, *Eye Deep in Hell, The Western Front 1914–18* (Croom Helm, London, 1976).

Farrar-Hockley, A. H., *The Somme* (Pan Books Ltd., London, 1966).

French, David, *The Strategy of the Lloyd George Coalition, 1914–18* (Clarendon Press, Oxford, 1995).

Gilbert, Martin, *First World War* (Weidenfeld & Nicolson, London, 1994).

Griffith, Paddy, *Battle Tactics of the Western Front. The British Army's Art of Attack 1916–1918* (Yale University Press, New Haven, 1994).

Griffith, Paddy, *Forward into Battle* (Anthony Bird Publications, Chichester, 1981).

Gwynne, G. S., *If Germany Attacks. The Battle in Depth in the West* (Tom Donovan Editions, Brighton, 2008).

Gwynne, S., *The Anvil of War: Letters Between F.S. Oliver and his Brother 1914–1918* (MacMillan, London, 1936).

Harris, J. P. and Barr, Niall, *Amiens to Armistice. The BEF in the Hundred Days' Campaign* (Brasseys, London, 1998).

Hart, Liddell, *History of the First World War* (Viking, London,1991).

Headlam, Lt Col C., *The Guards Division in the Great War*, II vols. (John Murray, London, 1924).

Henderson, Col G. F. R., *The Science of War* (Green & Co., London, 1908).

Holmes, Richard, *Tommy* (Harper Collins, London, 2004).

Hussey, A. H. and Inman, D. S., *The Fifth Division in the Great War* (Nesbittt & Co., London, 1921).

Hutchinson, Garrie, *Pilgrimages. A Travellers Guide to Australian Battlefields* (Black Inc., Victoria, 2006).

James, Lt Col L., *The History of the King Edward's Horse* (Sifton, Praed & Co. Ltd., London, 1921).

Johnson, H. C., *Breakthrough* (Presidio Press, Novato CA, 1994).

Kipling, Rudyard, *The Irish Guards in the Great War* (John Murray, London, 1925).

Kitchen, Martin, *The German Offensives of 1918* (Tempus, Stroud, 2001).

Kleet, van der W., *The Lessons of War* (The History Press, Stroud, 2008).

Laffin, John, *British Butchers and Bunglers of World War One* (Alan Sutton, Stroud, 1992).

Lindsay, Patrick, *Fromelles* (Hardie Grant Books, Prahan, Victoria, 2007).

Lloyd, Nick, *Loos 1915* (Tempus Publishing Ltd., Stroud, 2006).

Macdonald, Lyn, *Somme* (Papermac, London, 1985).

Maude, F. N., *The Evolution of Infantry Tactics* (London, 1905).

McCarthy, Chris, *The Somme. The Day by Day Account* (Greenwich Editions, London, 1996).

McLachlan, Matt, *Walking with the Anzacs* (Hachette, Australia, 2000).

de Meneses, R., *Portugal 1914–1926. From the First World War to Military Dictatorship* (Dept of Hispanic, Portuguese and Latin American Studies, University of Bristol, 2004).

Middlebrook, Martin, *Your Country Needs You* (Pen and Sword Books Limited, Barnsley, 2000).

Moran, Lord, *The Anatomy of Courage* (Constable & Co. Ltd, London, 1945).

Morselli, Mario, *Caporetto, 1917: Victory or Defeat?* (Frank Cass, London, 2001).

Neillands, Robin, *The Great War Generals on the Western Front 1914–1918* (Robinson Publishing Ltd., London,1991).

Nicolson, Harold, *King George V* (Constable & Co. Ltd., London, 1953).

Pallazzo, Albert, *Seeking Victory on the Western Front* (University of Nebraska Press, Lincoln, 2000).

Pederson, Peter, *Fromelles* (Pen and Sword, Barnsley, 2004).

Powell, Geoffrey, *Plumer: The Soldiers' General* (Pen and Sword Military Classics, Barnsley, 2004).

Prior, Robin, and Wilson, Trevor, *Command on the Western Front, The Military Career of Sir Henry Rawlinson 1914–1918* (Pen and Sword Military Classics, Barnsley, 2004).

Prior, Robin and Wilson, Trevor, *Passchendaele, The Untold Story* (Yale University Press, New Haven, 1996).

Prior, Robin, and Wilson, Trevor, *The Somme* (Yale Univ. Press, New Haven/London,2005).

Renzi, William A., *The Shadow of the Sword: Italy's Neutrality and Entrance into the Great War, 1914–15* (Peter Lang, New York,1987).

Riddelll, Brig Gen E. and McClayton, Col M. C., *The Cambridgeshires 1914–1919* (Bowes and Bowes, Cambridge, 1934).

Robbins, Simon, *British Generalship on the Western Front 1914–18* (Routledge, London, 2005).

Senior, Michael, *No Finer Courage: A Village in the Great War* (Sutton Publishing, Stroud, 2004).

Sheffield, Gary, *The Forgotten Victory The First World War: Myths and Realities,* (Headline Book Publishing, London, 2001).

Silkin, John, (ed), *The Penguin Book of First World War Poetry* (Penguin Books, Harmondsworth, 1981).

Simpson, Andy, *Directing Operations: British Corps Command on the Western Front 1914–1918* (Spellmount Ltd, Stroud, 2006).

Simpson, Andy, *Hot Blood and Cold Steel. Life and Death in the*

Trenches of the First World War (Tom Donovan Publishing Ltd, London, 1993).

Spiers, Edward, *The Late Victorian Army 1868–1902* (Manchester University Press, Sandpiper Books edn., Manchester, 1999).

Staniforth-Smith, Lt the Hon., *The Australian Campaigns in the Great War* (MacMillan & Co., Melbourne, 1919).

Terraine, John, *To Win a War, 1918, The Year of Victory* (Papermac, London, 1986).

Thayer, John, *Italy and the Great War* (University of Wisconsin Press, Madison, WI, 1964).

Travers, Tim, *The Killing Ground. The British Army, The Western Front and the Emergence of Modern War* (Pen and Sword Military Classics, Barnsley, 2003).

Travers, Tim, *How The War Was Won* (Routledge, London, 1992).

Warner, Philip, *The Battle of Loos* (Wordsworth Editions, London, 2000).

Warner, Philip, *Field Marshal Haig* (Cassell & Co., London, 1991).

Wauchope, Maj Gen A. G., *A History of the Black Watch (Royal Highlanders) in the Great War 1914–1918*, III Vols. (The Medici Society Limited, London, 1926).

Westlake, Ray, *Kitchener's Army* (Spellmount, Staplehurst, 1998).

Wilks, John and Eileen, *The British Army on Italy 1917–1918* (Leo Cooper, Barnsley, 1998).

Williams, H. R., *The Gallant Company; An Australian Soldier's Story of 1915–1918* (Angus and Robertson, Sydney,1933).

Williams, John F., *Anzacs; The Media and the Great War* (University of New South Wales, Sydney, 1999).

Wilson, Trevor, *The Myriad Faces of War* (Polity Press, Cambridge, 1986).

Wray, Christopher, *Sir James Whiteside McCay: A Turbulent Life* (OUP, Sydney, 2002).

Young, G. D. F., *A Short History of the 5th Brigade* (The Forces Press, Aldershot, 1965).

ARTICLES

Beckett, Ian, "Gough, Malcolm and Command on the Western Front" in Brian Bond (ed), *Look to Your Front!* (Spellmount, Staplehurst, 1999).

Beckett, Ian, "King George V and His Generals", in Hughes, Matthew and Seligman, Matthew (eds), *Leadership and Conflict 1914–1918* (Pen and Sword Books, Barnsley, 2000).

Danchev, Alex, "Bunking and Debunking. The Controversies of the 1960s", in Brian Bond (ed), *The First World War and British Military History* (Clarendon Press, Oxford, 1991).

Howard, Michael, "Men Against Fire: The Doctrine of the Offensive in 1914", in Peter Paret, *Makers of Modern Strategy* (Clarendon Press, Oxford, 1986).

Hughes, Matthew, "Personalities in Conflict, Lloyd George, the Generals and the Italian Campaign in 1917–18", in Hughes and Seligman eds., *Leadership in Conflict 1914–1918* (Pen and Sword Books, Barnsley, 2000).

Robbins, Simon, "Henry Horne", in Beckett and Corvi eds, *Haig's Generals* (Pen and Sword Military, Barnsley, 2006).

Simkins, Peter, "Haig and the Army Commanders", in Brian Bond and Nigel Cave eds, *Haig; A Reappraisal 80 Years On* (Pen and Sword, Barnsley, 2009 edn).

Simpson, Andy, "British Corps Command on the Western Front 1914–1918", in Garry Sheffield and Dan Todman, eds., *Command and Control on the Western Front. The British Army's Experience 1914–18* (Spellmount Ltd., Staplehurst, 2004).

Wilcox, Vanda, "Generalship and Mass Surrender during the Italian Defeat at Caporetto" in Ian Beckett (ed.), *1917: Beyond the Western Front* (Brill, Leiden, 2009).

Williams Rhodri, "Lord Kitchener and the Battle of Loos. French Politics and British Strategy in the Summer of 1915", in Laurence Freedman, Paul Hayes, and Robert O'Neill (eds), *Strategy and International Politics* (OUP, Oxford, 1992).

Wilson, Trevor, "The British Army on the Somme: July–November 1916", in Michael Howard (ed.), *A Part of History; Aspects of the British Experience of the First World War* (Continuum, London, 2008).

JOURNALS

Bryan, Peter, "The Re-Call Of Sir John French", *Stand To!*, 22–24, 1988, The Western Front Association.

French, David, "The Meaning of Attrition, 1914–1916", *English Historical Review*, 103, 1988.

Johnston, Maj G. R., "The Portuguese Army in the Great War", in *The Army Quarterly*, XXXV, Oct., 1937.

McMullin, Ross, "Pompey Elliott and the Butcher of Fromelles", in *The Australian Magazine*, July, 1996.

Pederson, Peter, "Bringing the Past to Life", in *Battlefields Review*, 25, 2003.

Robbins, Simon, "The Right Way to Play the Game – The Ethos of the British High Command in the First World War", *IWM Review*, 6, Undated.

Roberts, James, "Making the Butterflies Kill." in *Stand To!*, No. 68, 2003, The Western Front Association

Simpson, Keith R., "Capper and the Offensive Spirit", in the *Journal of the Royal United Services Institute*, 118, 1973).

Terraine, John, "Understanding", in *Stand To!*, No. 34, 1992, The Western Front Association.

Travers, Tim, "A Particular Style of Command. Haig and GHQ 1916–18", in *The Journal of Strategic Studies*, Vol. 10, 1987.

Travers, Tim, "Technology, Tactics and Morale. Jean Bloch, the Boer War and British Military Theory, 1900–1914", in the *Journal of Modern History*, 51, 1979.

Williams, J. F., "Words on 'A Lively Skirmish'", *Journal of the Australian War Memorial*, Oct., 1939.

Index

Military Formations/Units

ALLIES

British, C'wlth & Imp:
GHQ , 4– 6, 12, 43, 45–8, 51–2,
99,104,114–16, 119–20, 126–8,
130, 133, 146, 153, 232–3, 244,
247–50, 253–4, 259–60, 281

Armies:
First, 1, 7, 10, 36, 42–3, 45–53, 57, 60,
62–3, 65, 68, 74–8, 80–2, 84–5,
87–93, 95–9, 102–4, 114–17, 119,
130–1, 133, 143–4, 147–8, 151–3,
155, 157–8, 160–2, 179, 181,
185–6, 191, 193, 197–9, 209,
219, 221–2, 224–5, 233, 242,
245–6, 248–52, 254–5, 257–8,
260, 273–4, 276, 278–84, 286–8,
291
Second, 114–16, 127, 152–3, 156, 166,
207, 221–2, 233, 278
Third, 82, 144, 278
Fourth, 82, 87, 217, 229, 237
Fifth (also Reserve),11, 152, 207,
224–5, 228–9, 231–2, 237

Corps:
I, 4, 6, 34, 42, 44, 46, 49–50, 56–7, 62,
82, 84, 94, 103, 117, 154, 160–1,
245, 254, 281–4, 291
II, 4, 288
III, 212, 232, 288
IV, 44, 46, 49, 53, 56–7, 60–2, 103,
116, 282–4, 291
V, 278
XI, 1, 4, 7–13, 38, 42–3, 45–50, 52–4,
57, 59–68, 74–90, 92, 94–6,
98–104, 114–17, 119–21, 133–5,
143–8, 152–3, 157–62, 165, 167,
170–81, 185, 187–8, 191–4,
198–200, 202–4, 206, 208,
210–13, 218–22, 224–33, 236–8,
243–5, 247–59, 261, 273, 277,
279, 281–3, 288, 291
XIII, 224–5, 278, 288,
XIV, 167, 179, 243
XV, 90, 200, 206, 211, 222–4
XVII, 92, 243
XVIII, 212
I Aus, 126
Cdn, 94, 143, 148, 161, 208, 277, 281,
283
Indian, 35, 46, 74

Divisions:
Cavalry, 46, 49, 59,
Guards, 42, 48, 52, 59, 61–2, 65–6, 79,
102, 243
1st, 35–6, 66, 208, 231, 242, 245
2nd, 34
4th, 36
5th, 167–70, 173, 177, 179, 218, 222,
224, 233, 235, 255, 283
8th, 41
9th, 62, 92
12th, 60–1
15th, 62, 66
19th, 9, 79, 103, 225, 230–1, 254
20th, 243
21st, 42, 45, 48, 50, 54, 58–9, 62–4,
67, 146
23rd, 42, 167,
24th, 45, 49, 53–4, 58–9, 62–4, 67–8,
93, 148, 167
25th, 198
29th, 222–3
30th, 92
31st, 223–4
32nd, 92
33rd, 75, 82
34th, 144
35th, 101, 252, 255
37th, 144
38th, 198, 243
39th, 84, 89, 104, 256
40th, 202, 206

302